United States Penetration of Brazil

United States

Penetration

of

Brazil

JAN KNIPPERS BLACK

University of Pennsylvania Press/1977

Library of Congress Cataloging in Publication Data

Black, Jan Knippers, 1940-
   United States penetration of Brazil.

   Bibliography: p.
   Includes index.
   1. United States--Foreign relations--Brazil.
2. Brazil--Foreign relations--United States. 3. Brazil
--History--Revolution, 1964. 4. Armed Forces--Brazil--
Political activity. 5. Economic assistance, American--
Brazil. I. Title.
E183.8.B7B47   301.29'73'081   76-53192
ISBN 0-8122-7720-1

Printed in the United States of America

To my beloved late husband, John D. Black, whose unwavering commitment to the cause of the poor and oppressed everywhere was, and is, a constant source of inspiration.

We should then see the multitude oppressed by domestic tyrants in consequence of those very precautions taken by them to guard against foreign masters. . . . We should see the rights of citizens and the liberties of nations extinguished by slow degrees, and the groans and protestations and appeals of the weak treated as seditious murmurings.

Rousseau, *Discourse on the Origins of Inequality*, 1750

Contents

Foreword

After this book had been submitted to the publisher, some documents at the Lyndon B. Johnson Library in Austin, Texas, dealing with the 1964 coup d'etat in Brazil, were declassified. These documents confirmed the allegation contained in this book that the United States was prepared to intervene with naval and airborne units if necessary in support of the military conspirators who toppled the civilian government of João Goulart.

Among the documents is a message from the Air Force Chief of Staff directing the commander of the Military Air Transport Service (MATS) to appoint Major General George S. Brown mission commander for "project Brother Sam" and directing the Tactical Air Command to designate a subordinate mission commander to be responsible for fighter and tanker escort operations in support of "Brother Sam." In accordance with a contingency plan proposed by U.S. Ambassador Lincoln Gordon, the Air Force was ordered on 31 March 1964 to send six C-135 transports to pick up 110 tons of small arms and ammunition assembled at McGuire Air Force Base in New Jersey for reshipment. Additional arms and fuel were to be assembled in Puerto Rico. A "fast" Carrier Task Group, composed of an aircraft carrier, a helicopter support group, destroyers, and oil tankers, was ordered to take positions off the Brazilian coast near Santos and await orders from Gordon. "Replenishment forces" were to be sent to the area as required. Deployment messages, classified Top Secret, were distributed to the White House, the Department of State, the CIA, and several sections of the Department of Defense.

The success of the coup was assured on 1 April, when the formerly recalcitrant commander of Brazil's Second Army declared support for the conspirators. On 2 April, "Brother Sam" was canceled and the Carrier Task Group was ordered to carry out its cover operation, "Quick Kick." A message issued by USCINCSO (U.S. Southern Command in Panama) on 3 April 1964 recommended that TAC, SAC, and MATS in support of Brother Sam be released, and that only that part of the "POL movement" which the Ambassador considered essential be continued.

It recommended, however, that the arms and ammunition be held at McGuire pending Gordon's determination of "whether Brazilian military forces or state police forces will require early U.S. support," and that the Carrier Task Group continue toward the South Atlantic "until Ambassador states that port calls or other U.S. demonstration of naval power are definitely not wanted." A dispatch from Ambassador Gordon on 2 April had indicated that the military conspirators, referred to throughout the communications as the "democratic forces," might still need fuel.

Meanwhile, on 1 April an inter-agency economic task force had begun work on plans for emergency and long-term assistance to the new government.

Preface

More than a dozen years have passed since a "revolution" reversed the course of development in Brazil. Seven years elapsed between the conception of the basic outline of this book and its publication, and we Americans, North and South, are an older and sadder, and perhaps wiser, people.

As a Peace Corps Volunteer in Chile in the early 1960s, I had taken seriously the claim that the Alliance for Progress was designed to promote a redistribution of wealth and to bolster democratic processes. When my Chilean friends suggested that the 1964 coup d'état in Brazil was supported by the CIA, I accused them of being paranoid, but many of us have learned since then that the fact that one is paranoid does not necessarily mean he is not being followed.

In light of the facts that redistribution of wealth in Latin America, in the wake of the Alliance, tended to be from the bottom up, and that democratic processes in most countries had been obliterated rather than bolstered, most of the early post-mortem reports on the Alliance amounted to hand-wringing admissions of the impotence of the United States to impose its will upon its southern neighbors. It was rarely suggested by U.S. scholars that this turn of events might be indicative, in part, of the efficacy of U.S. influence rather than the lack of it.

It was that seeming gap in the literature, as well as the virtual absence of considerations of ideological content in the not-so-great debate on the consequences of U.S. military assistance, that inspired this study. The study was undertaken, in particular, to shed more light on the relationship between the security issue, as conceived by the United States, and the political role of the military in Latin America. The choice of Brazil as the focus for this work grew out of my curiosity, in the late 1960s, as to why so many U.S. scholars, writing about the 1964 coup d'état there and its aftermath, ignored what so many Latin American scholars took for granted (but failed to document): U.S. complicity.

My own research has confirmed my darkest suspicions—that evidence of the sort that might be convincing to those who have come to view the United States as the "good neighbor," more benevolent somehow than all previous great powers, is hard to come by. As C. Wright Mills pointed out in *The Power Elite,* "We must expect fumbles when, without authority or official aid, we set out to investigate something which is in part organized for the purpose of causing fumbles among those who would understand it plainly."[1]

Not in spite of the elasticity of the concept, but because of it, "security" has been chosen as the issue area from which to approach the phenomenon of U.S. influence in Brazil. It would be counterproductive to attempt to define security at this point, as the arbitrariness of its usage is in large measure the subject of this study. Likewise, U.S. security policy, for any given era, is not viewed here as a particular set of commonly understood guidelines for action, directives contained in a single piece of legislation or statement of executive intent, but rather as a myriad of often self-serving interpretations of the national interest, employed by a vast array of individuals and agencies with sometimes common and sometimes divergent interests.

The processes which have been the focus of this study are those by which the United States has attempted to modify or perpetuate the internal balance of political forces in Brazil. The dimensions of U.S. policy and influence having a direct or indirect bearing on the outcome of domestic political competition in Brazil during the period under consideration encompass all three of the "linkage processes" identified by James N. Rosenau: the reactive, the emulative, and the penetrative.[2] However, as the reactive process might be seen as an aspect of traditional government-to-government diplomacy, and as emulation still means what it always has, I will elaborate here only on what has been termed the penetrative process.

Penetration, in contemporary global politics, is almost as difficult to define as it is to ignore. A penetrative process occurs, according to Rosenau, when members of one polity serve as participants in the political processes of another. Similarly, Andrew M. Scott sees informal (as opposed to formal—government-to-government) penetration

1. C. Wright Mills, *The Power Elite* (New York: Oxford University Press, 1956), p. 363.

2. James N. Rosenau, "Pre-theories and Theories of Foreign Policy," in R. Barry Farrell, ed., *Approaches to Comparative and International Politics* (Evanston, Ill.: Northwestern University Press, 1966). Also, James N. Rosenau, ed., *Linkage Politics: Essays on the Convergence of National and International Systems* (New York: The Free Press, 1969).

as existing when one country's agents or instruments come into contact with the people or processes of another country in an effort to achieve certain objectives.[3] Further explanations of the concept, however, have tended to make it even more broad and vague, even less precise.

Rosenau, for example, says that the participation of nonmembers is accepted by the target country's officialdom as well as by its citizenry, so that the decisions to which nonmembers contribute are no less authoritative and legitimate than are those in which they do not participate. And he adds that the nonmembers to whom he refers may include any category of actors from occupying armies to foreign aid personnel to subversive cadres. I am inclined to doubt that the decisions of occupying armies are accepted as "legitimate" by the citizenry or that the decisions of subversive cadres are accepted as "authoritative" by the officialdom. At any rate, it appears to me that the means and objectives of the penetrating power are the crucial elements for identifying the process and that such concepts as legitimacy and authoritativeness constitute excess baggage.

The examples of penetration offered by Scott also include military occupation, together with cultural exchange programs aimed toward no more ambitious objective than cultural exchange. Subsequent definitions or descriptions of penetration have tended to be even more all-encompassing. Wolfram F. Hanreider, for example, would include among penetrative phenomena external events and trends that take place without the direct and authoritative participation of nonmembers of the affected society.[4] And the areas of penetration mentioned by Rosenau—the allocation of the society's values and the mobilization of support on behalf of its goals—have been modified, and expanded by Clair Karl Blong to include the selection of goals, the allocation of costs, the mobilization of resources, and the integration of the polity.[5]

While viewing national and international politics as a seamless web and recognizing that the competition for power and material gain often appears to render the globe a stateless polity, I think it would be useful for the development of case and comparative studies to draw in the

3. Andrew M. Scott, *The Revolution in Statecraft: Informal Penetration* (New York: Random House, 1965).

4. Wolfram F. Hanreider, "Compatibility and Consensus: A Proposal for the Conceptual Linkage of External and Internal Dimensions of Foreign Policy," *The American Political Science Review* 61 (December 1967): 971–82.

5. Clair Karl Blong, "External Penetration and Foreign Policy Behavior" Ph.D. diss. draft (University of Maryland, 1975). Blong's study incorporates a very useful model for assessing the degree to which a political system has been penetrated.

reins on the runaway concept of penetration. I would suggest, for example, that while external events and trends and attempts to influence policy through government-to-government interactions may facilitate penetration, they fall beyond the bounds of the penetrative process itself. And I suggest that military intervention and occupation indicate a breakdown in the penetrative process. Cultural and informational exchange may or may not be of a penetrative nature. The determining factor might be whether those exchanges constitute facets of an attempt by the government of one country to modify or perpetuate the internal balance of political forces in another country. Although penetration could conceivably involve or result in the mobilization of resources for domestic purposes or the integration of the polity, I believe it is more likely to involve or result in the denationalization of resources and the disintegration of the polity.

A time-tested means of manipulating the balance of political forces in a target country has been the cultivation of "linkage groups," defined by Karl Deutsch as groups in the domestic polity which have particular ties with the international environment.[6] Johan Galtung has pointed out that the elite (center) of a hegemonic power characteristically links itself with the elites of the nations within its sphere of influence in order to contain or control the masses of those nations:

> There is a vertical division of labor within as well as between nations. And these two levels of organization are intimately linked to each other . . . in the sense that the center in the periphery interaction structure is also that group with which the Center Nation has its harmony of interests, the group used as a bridgehead. Thus, the combined operation of the two mechanisms at the two levels builds into the structure a subtle grid of protective measures against the major potential source of "trouble," the periphery in the Periphery.[7]

Scott sees penetration, with certain isolated historical exceptions, as a post-World War I phenomenon, arising in large part from the tactics employed by the communists and the reaction of the West, particularly the United States, to those tactics. I suggest that penetration is an essentially timeless phenomenon, and that the massive expansion of its use and diversification of its vehicles—in this case by the United States in the Western Hemisphere in the post-World War II period—is a response, on the one hand, to the inflation of U.S. "security" interests and, on the other, to the acceleration of the structural differentiation of

6. Karl Deutsch, "External Influences on the Internal Behavior of States," in Farrell, ed., *Approaches to Comparative and International Politics.*

7. Johan Galtung, "A Structural Theory of Imperialism," *Journal of Peace Research* (Oslo) 8, no. 2 (1971): 81–117.

the political systems in the Latin American states. In other words, in order for the U.S. elite to protect or promote its interests in Brazil, it became necessary for this elite, through the U.S. government, to expand contacts and influence in tandem with the expansion of the politically articulate or participatory sectors of the Brazilian population. The proliferation of U.S. agencies injected into the fray, however, has increased the problem of coordination (not to mention, from the viewpoint of the scholar, the problem of analysis). While coordination has on some occasions been explicit, it has probably more often been intuitive, and at times it has disintegrated completely into confusion or conflict.

It has not been possible, in the course of this study, to probe very deeply into the activities of agencies that operate covertly or to determine the extent to which activities carried out under the auspices of AID or the Department of Defense, for example, have actually been guided by the CIA. The admission (leaked to the press in late 1974) by CIA Director William E. Colby before a congressional oversight committee that the CIA had pursued a policy of destabilizing the constitutional government of Salvador Allende in Chile has aroused curiosity about the activities of that and other intelligence agencies. It is to be hoped, however, that this long overdue focus on the most conspicuously gnarled trees will not obscure the forest. It probably makes little difference to the victims of U.S. penetration in Latin America whether the architect of the scheme which was their undoing was the CIA or the Department of the Treasury.

I have attempted here to examine a patch of the trees and, through the fog, to sketch a dim outline, in theoretical terms, of the forest. The introduction places in historical context the U.S. approach to the security issue in the Western Hemisphere in the 1960s. The first section presents, in abbreviated form, the background of the Brazilian crisis of the 1960s and notes some of the features of the Brazilian political system that made it vulnerable to penetration by a hegemonic power. It also discusses some aspects of relations, both formal and informal, between the U.S. and Brazil, leading up to and following the 1964 coup. The second section traces the strengthening or undermining of several of the politically articulate sectors of the civilian polity in Brazil by U.S. agencies. The third section deals with the interaction of U.S. and Brazilian military elites and describes the common attitudes and interests that might be expected to reinforce authoritarian tendencies. The final section addresses the question of whose interests have actually been served by the activities and influence of the United States in Brazil.

I make no pretense of having exhausted the sources for a study of such scope. The sources, in fact, have exhausted me. While concrete evidence of U.S. intent to modify or control the domestic balance of political forces in Brazil appears to be scarce, leads are everywhere; and I believe it would be impossible to determine how much of the relevant information exists only in the heads of certain closed-mouthed individuals, how much is documented but classified, and how much is actually on the public record—somewhere. I believe, for example, that many of the consequential interactions, such as mutual understandings among military elites, have been not only informal and undocumented, but inexplicitly articulated as well. And the available statistics on the training and equipping of the military and the police and on the very selective allocation of economic assistance do not necessarily "speak for themselves" as to intent or consequences.

Furthermore, even if all the "facts" of U.S. involvement in the internal affairs of its neighbors were made public, it would be impossible to establish with certainty the relative weight of U.S. influence on a particular outcome. Simulation possibilities notwithstanding, we mortals cannot "control" the referent political system in order to arrive at a quantitative measurement of the potency of variables. A full understanding of the workings of the penetrative process in this case would call for tracing consequences back to actions, actions to intents, and intents ultimately to attitudes—a useful exercise in speculation, but far beyond the reach of empirical testing. Nevertheless, I feel that difficulties in research and analysis are no excuse for shying away from the important questions.

Rather than focusing my attention on a particular kind of source material for this study, I have focused it upon particular questions and have sought the answers wherever they might be found. My sources have included books, articles, newspapers, and newsletters originating in the United States and Brazil as well as in Hispanic America and Europe. I have made extensive use of U.S. Congressional hearings and reports and of materials published by various departments, agencies, and grantees of the executive branch. I have also made use of publications by or for elements of the international business community.

Major sources, particularly for the third section of this study, have been U.S. and Brazilian military journals and training materials. Books, articles, and speeches by architects of U.S. and Brazilian policies and by participants in bilateral programs have also been included. The most enjoyable aspect of my research has been interviewing U.S. and Brazilian officials and private citizens with widely varying experience and interest in relations between the two countries.

Some of what I perceived several years ago as the gaps in the literature have in fact been filled in while my work was in progress. Thus, on several topics, this study expands upon, draws together, or summarizes the original findings of others. My intent has been not only to generate new data, but, more importantly, to combine and analyze readily available data in such a way as to draw a pattern from seemingly isolated incidents or unrelated programs.

I have not been able in every case to unearth several unlike sources of the same information, and I would not presume to vouch for the veracity or authenticity of every allegation or document drawn on for this study. In this era of enlightened disillusionment, I doubt that there is any widely accepted standard by which to judge the reliability of a particular source. I have attempted, however, to portray a pattern of interaction between the agents of a hegemonic power and allies and adversaries of those agents in a client state the dynamics of which are recognizable, even if some of the interactions might be explicable without reference to the pattern. For a clearer understanding of the pattern I strongly recommend to my readers the hearings and reports of the U.S. House and Senate select committees that investigated U.S. intelligence operations in 1975–1976, and particularly the Senate committee's reports on *Alleged Assassination Plots Involving Foreign Leaders* and *Covert Action in Chile, 1963–1973*.

As a matter of personal taste, I feel that a theoretical framework should serve more or less the same function as a girdle—to give shape to otherwise amorphous material—and that it need not be the most conspicuous element of the final product. Therefore, I have used "linkage politics" primarily as a tool for organizing data and my own thoughts and have intentionally refrained from what I consider the unnecessary use of jargon.

The object of this study has been to describe what is and has been rather than what should be. I have not tried to address myself to the question of how a bull might go about making itself useful in a china shop. Nevertheless, I have made no attempt to conceal my values, as I feel that such an attempt would be self-defeating for the writer and deceptive to the reader.

One of my objectives in writing this book, that of contributing in some small way to saving the people of Uruguay and Chile from a fate similar to that of the people of Brazil, has been overtaken by events. And if President Richard Nixon had not been foolish enough to tape-record his own indiscretions, and if a few members of the U.S. Congress had not been courageous enough to ventilate the issue of the outrages committed by U.S. intelligence agencies at home and abroad, the warning for the United States implicit in this book might have been overtaken by events as well. While I refrain from prescription, I suggest that it is not enough for the people of the United States simply to wring their hands and concede that the role of the U.S. government in Latin America is predestined by geopolitics to be an exploitative and repressive one. It is, after all, our government, and for us there are only two logical choices. We must assume responsibility for what has been done in our name with our tax dollars, or we must face the fact that we, too, have been victimized by the same apparatuses of exploitation, propaganda, intimidation, and repression, that the attitudes that underlie so much of our foreign policy threaten our freedom, too, and that if we fail to use what is left of our celebrated "popular sovereignty," it too will be lost.

The individuals who have offered me their advice, opinions, observations, and access to documents are far too numerous to name. I am indebted particularly to the members of my dissertation committee at American University, Brady Tyson, chairman, Harold E. Davis, John Finan, and Theodore Couloumbis, and to my colleague and friend, and now my husband, Martin C. Needler.

Introduction:

The Shadow of the Colossus

In the late 1960s, a U.S. journalist, asked if he had been under pressure from J. Edgar Hoover, responded, "Hoover does not have to exert pressure, he *is* pressure." From the viewpoint of Latin Americans, much the same might be said of the United States. The shadow of the colossus, falling long and dark over the hemisphere, constitutes a permanent and pervasive sort of pressure that most Latin Americans understand all too well. The thrust of that pressure, however, has been the subject of much confusion and obfuscation among North Americans.

If this book does not serve to alleviate the confusion, it should at least make intentional obfuscation more difficult. As a case study, it deals primarily with the nature and consequences of U.S. influence in Brazil in the 1960s. In a larger sense, however, it outlines the avenues and vehicles of penetration employed by the United States elsewhere in Latin America and perhaps, with variations, by the United States and other hegemonic powers in other parts of the world.[1] The approach assumes that as power and political articulation become differentiated or dispersed in a client state, the hegemonic power will expand and diversify its own operations in order to maintain links with each politically relevant group. These links will be used to reinforce natural allies, sway the uncommitted, co-opt the co-optable, and eliminate from the political arena the authentic leaders or spokesmen of groups whose pursuits are seen as inimical to the interests of the hegemonic power. The hegemonic power thus maintains a varying degree of control over the foreign and domestic policies of its client states not only directly, through government-to-government pressures, but also indirectly, through tilting the distribution of power within their political systems.

1. See Preface for discussion of penetration theory.

1

Although no exact measure of the degree or impact of U.S. penetration in Brazil is undertaken, we do attempt to indicate something of the scope and content of the penetrative process—the attitudes and objectives underlying and propelling it, the access points it encounters, the vehicles it employs and the systemic transformations to which it contributes. We examine both the subversive penetration, or "destabilization," undertaken to undermine the government of João Goulart in the period culminating with the coup d'état of 1964 and the supportive penetration designed to bulwark the military regime thereafter.

This study focuses in particular on the actions undertaken by agents of the U.S. government, in concert with agents of U.S. private interests, in the name of "security," actions that contributed to the expansion of the political role of the military in Brazil and the creation of a new military elite in that country. It is shown that such actions included attempts to undermine movements springing from or appealing to the aspirations of the lower classes, as well as attempts to strengthen the military and other groups favorably disposed toward U.S. capital.

Although it cannot be done with any precision, an effort is made to distinguish between the long-term trend of United States co-optation and denationalization of elites and conspiracy in an immediate sense and to indicate how the former encourages and facilitates the latter. We also seek to distinguish between what was attempted, within the collage of particular interests that constituted United States policy toward Brazil in the 1960s, and what was accomplished.

It is not suggested that United States influence has been the only factor, or necessarily the overriding factor, contributing to the collapse of a constitutional system and the establishment and institutionalization of an authoritarian military regime in Brazil. It is proposed, however, that the participation of the United States has been a significant contributing factor.

Paranoids Have Enemies, Too

The suspicion among Brazilians that U.S. government and business exercise a veto, not only over specific policies, but over who is allowed to govern, is not a recent phenomenon. When Getúlio Vargas committed suicide in 1954 rather than submit again to being ousted from the presidency by the military, the note he left accused "reactionary foreign and national interests" of blocking his policy of national independence and social justice. Similarly, President Jânio Quadros declared, upon submitting his resignation in 1961,

> I was overcome by the forces of reaction . . . I wanted Brazil for Brazilians and I confronted in that battle corruption, lies, and cowardice which subordinated general interests to the appetites and the ambitions of groups of individuals, including some from abroad.[2]

In an address on 30 March 1964, President João Goulart alerted the sergeants to what he believed to be an externally financed conspiracy against his government:

> If the sergeants ask me—these are my last words—where so many resources come from for a campaign so powerful, for a mobilization so violent against the government, I would simply say, Brazilian sergeants, that all these come from the money of the businessmen who received the illicit remission of profits that I recently regulated by means of a law. It is the money provided by the enormous international petroleum interests and [Brazilian] companies which are against the law I also signed giving a monopoly on the importation of oil to Petrobras. . . . Finally workers, finally military men, finally Brazilians, it is the money of the large foreign medical firms, of firms that will have to follow the law or will have to be subordinated to the law.[3]

James R. Kurth has noted that in hegemonic systems, "Often, there is a general expectation among elites and counter-elites in the [client] states . . . that there are certain diplomatic and political limits to a small state's behavior, the transgressing of which will provoke the great power to undertake intervention within the offending state."[4]

This relationship has been further explained by Richard R. Fagen and Wayne A. Cornelius, Jr.:

> To such diverse elements as moderate leftists contemplating land reform, militaries plotting a coup, planners intent on expanding secondary education, guerrillas organizing armed struggle, industrialists calculating investment opportunities, or diplomats considering an expansion of contacts with Eastern Europe, the anticipated reaction of the relevant United States policy elites or interest groups is never far from the focus of attention. The political process in Latin America is thus affected by the United States not only through direct and indirect economic, political, and military intervention, but also through a complicated web of mutual perception and expectations.[5]

2. Eduardo Galeano, "The Ambivalence of Jango Goulart," in Richard R. Fagen and Wayne A. Cornelius, Jr., eds., *Political Power in Latin America: Seven Confrontations* (Englewood Cliffs, N.J.: Prentice-Hall, 1970.), pp. 201–5.

3. João Goulart, "Address to the Sergeants, March 30, 1964," in Fagen and Cornelius, eds., *Political Power in Latin America*, pp. 182–86.

4. James R. Kurth, "United States Foreign Policy and Latin American Military Rule," *Military Rule in Latin America: Function, Consequences and Perspectives*, ed. Philippe C. Schmitter (Beverly Hills, Calif.: Sage Publications, 1973), pp. 244–322.

5. Fagen and Cornelius, eds., *Political Power in Latin America*.

Testifying in hearings on military assistance training before the House Foreign Affairs Committee in 1970, Alfred Stepan made this observation about "sphere of influence" perceptions in Latin America:

> When I came to Latin America, the thing that immediately struck me was that policies we found completely acceptable when pursued by Africans we somehow find a bit less acceptable in Latin America. For instance—and I am really talking about a very basic cast of mind—when De Gaulle was going to make his trip through Latin America, many of the Latin Americans interviewed said that they were under very real pressure by various American groups not to be very warm toward De Gaulle, because we considered Latin America within the United States area of influence.[6]

At the same hearings, G. Warren Nutter, Assistant Secretary of Defense for International Security Affairs, reminded by committee members that part of Latin America is farther from the United States than Moscow, maintained nevertheless that all of Latin America is vital to the security of the United States because "I see Latin America as our backyard."[7]

Awareness among Latin Americans of being considered interloping homesteaders in the U.S. backyard has generated a bitter resentment that has on occasion been a powerful stimulus to revolutionary movements. Porfirio Díaz, whose *entreguista*[8] regime succumbed to the Mexican Revolution in 1910, is said to have lamented, "Poor Mexico, so far from God and so close to the United States."[9]

At the level of national political competition and leadership in Latin America, however, the more pervasive consequences of the relationship have been the more subtle ones. Popularly elevated nationalistic presidents or parties have failed to take the steps necessary to consolidate political power for fear of provoking intervention or in hopes of forestalling it. Opposition groups have refused to come to terms with such leadership in the expectation that with external assistance they could turn the tables. And authoritarian regimes have not felt con-

6. U.S., Congress, House, Committee on Foreign Affairs, Subcommittee on National Security Policy and Scientific Developments, *Military Assistance Training*, Hearings, 91st Cong., 2d sess., 6, 7, 8 October 1970, 8 and 15 December 1970, p. 120.

7. Ibid., p. 145.

8. A much-used epithet in Latin America for one who "sells out" the national patrimony or interests for the benefit of foreigners.

9. Porfirio Díaz, cited in George Blanksten, "Foreign Policy of Mexico," *Foreign Policy in World Politics*, ed. Roy C. Macridis, 2d ed. (Englewood Cliffs, N.J.: Prentice-Hall, 1962), pp. 311–34.

strained to respond to popular demands, as they have assumed that in a crunch they could count on the United States to come to their defense.

An even more insidious aspect of this divisiveness has been poignantly portrayed by Bolivian writer Sergio Almaraz Paz. Paz observed that after "the assumption of power by the North Americans . . . Bolivians began to feel uncomfortable with each other. . . . Local functionaries don't know how to deal with their colleagues from another office because they don't know the latter's relationship with the foreigner. . . . Citizens are left segregated, incommunicado, and suspicious."[10] Such suspicions are no doubt exaggerated at times, but they are not inexplicable. Bolivian Minister of the Interior Antonio Argüedas, who had masterminded a large-scale crackdown on labor, students, and other leftist groups, publicly admitted in August 1968 that he had been a CIA agent and that the agency had penetrated all levels of the Bolivian government.[11]

Reflections on the "who lost China" debate of the McCarthy years should call attention to the policy implications of the preposterous assumption that China was "ours" to lose. And if the United States could have harbored such notions regarding an ancient nation of more than half a billion people, it is easy to see how U.S. policy-makers might consider the Latin American countries "ours" to control. This proprietary attitude was exemplified by White House National Security Adviser Henry Kissinger in a secret meeting of the "40 Committee" in June 1970 to consider developments in Chile. Kissinger reportedly said, "I don't see why we need to stand by and watch a country go communist due to the irresponsibility of its own people.[12]

A high-ranking official who testified in 1975 before a special U.S. Senate committee investigating the U.S. "destabilization" of the government of Salvador Allende spoke of Chile's position in a worldwide strategic chess game in 1970.[13] To those strategists who play

10. Sergio Almaraz Paz, cited in Cole Blasier, "The United States and the Revolution," *Beyond the Revolution: Bolivia Since 1952*, ed. James M. Malloy and Richard S. Thorn (Pittsburgh, Pa.: University of Pittsburgh Press, 1971), p. 92.

11. Charles D. Corbett, *The Latin American Military as a Socio-Political Force: Case Studies of Bolivia and Argentina* (Coral Gables, Fla.: University of Miami Press, 1972), pp. 53–54.

12. Seymour Hersh, "Censored Matter on Book on CIA," *New York Times*, 11 September 1974.

13. U.S., Congress, Senate, Select Committee to Study Governmental Operations with Respect to Intelligence Activities (hereafter cited as Senate Intelligence Committee), *Covert Action*, Hearings, 94th Cong., 1st Sess., 4 and 7 December 1975, vol. 7.

chess with the lives of whole nationalities, Brazil, Latin America's largest and most populous state, has long loomed as a very significant pawn. And to those paternalists who consider Brazil as in some sense a ward of the United States, it is not surprising that the apparent decline in U.S. control over the distribution of wealth and power in the Brazilian system in the early 1960s was viewed as a "security threat."

Likewise, whatever the verifiable actions or intentions of agents of U.S. government and business, the belief on the part of Brazilian elites and counter-elites that the United States will not permit a large-scale redistribution of wealth and power in their country might be expected to demoralize those on the left who would like to believe that a revolution in liberty is possible and to reinforce those on the right in their opposition to majority rule.

The Elasticity of the Security Issue

Whether expressed in the scientific jargon of the law of oligopoly or in the terminology of folk wisdom, it is frequently noted that such attributes as wealth, power, and status tend to accrue to those who already have them. Relatively speaking, neither wealth nor any other attribute for which individuals or social aggregates compete trickles down. Trickle-up—or concentration—seems to be the general rule of the post-industrial period.[14] Reversal or mitigation of that process—redistribution—is a political act. Furthermore, it is a political act that is by nature conflictual.

Those who have can usually be counted upon to seek to prevent or minimize redistribution. The term which they have often employed to describe these efforts is "security." Security, in its least extravagant denotation—physical survival—is, of course, a common concern of rich and poor. The usefulness of the concept, however, is to be found in its elasticity; the delimitation of what must be secured expands to accomodate what a nation, class, institution, or other social entity has, or thinks it has, or thinks it should have. It follows, then, that it is often the nations, groups, or individuals whose wealth and power would appear to make them most secure who are, in fact, most paranoid, and

14. For arguments that traditional economic theories assuming a natural trickle-down process are inapplicable to contemporary economic problems, see John Kenneth Galbraith, *Economics and the Public Purpose* (London: Andre Deutsch, 1974) and Paul M. Sweezy, "Demand under Conditions of Oligopoly," Earl J. Hamilton, Albert Rees, and Harry G. Johnson, eds., *Landmarks in Political Economy* (Chicago: University of Chicago Press, 1962), ch. 12.

who, by their frenetic attempts to ensure their security, bring on their own destruction.

National systems have characteristically sought to ensure their sovereignty or to enhance their capacity for goal attainment through the formation of alliances or security systems. Likewise, individuals within national societies have aligned themselves in various ways (political parties, associational and institutional interest groups, etc.) in order to protect or promote their particular concerns. However, just as the stakes of domestic political competition do not necessarily coincide with the interests of territorially defined constituencies, the stakes of world politics cannot be adequately analyzed in terms of national interests.

The overlap between the intergroup struggle for dominance at the national level and the simultaneous competition for the expansion or preservation of hegemonic spheres at the international level generates the phenomenon which James N. Rosenau has designated "penetration."[15] In simple terms, this means that hegemonic powers share in the domestic political decisions of "who gets what when where and how" of the nations within their spheres of influence. (To a lesser extent, the reverse is also true: interest groups of client states attempt to influence policy and power distribution within the paramount state.) Political forces in the weaker states rely on foreign support to disestablish, destroy, or disenfranchise their opponents. Stronger states encourage such dependence in order to solidify their hegemonic positions. Furthermore, groups native to the stronger states, with economic or institutional interests of global scope, cultivate such relationships in order to enhance their wealth or to strengthen their own positions within their national polities.

Thus the security of individuals and groups within a national system is affected unevenly by the nature of the international system and the interactions of its national, transnational, and supranational actors. When nations become linked in a security system, the firmest link is formed by a single institutional interest group, the military establishment.

In a security system such as that of the Western Hemisphere, composed, as the late President Allende of Chile pointed out, of "one cat and twenty mice,"[16] it stands to reason that the security considerations

15. Rosenau, ed., *Linkage Politics.*

16. Salvador Allende, cited by Felipe Herrera, retiring president of the Inter-American Development Bank, in an address at American University, Washington, D.C., 9 November 1970.

(including the interpretation of what constitutes security) of the dominant national actor will generally prevail. The carrots and sticks available to it make it possible to play off not only one client state against another, but also one group or faction within a client state against another. Furthermore, because the military establishments within each national system form the dominant linkage group for the security system, it is inevitable that the institutional interests of the military will weigh heavily on the interpretation of what constitutes security.

Furthermore, the interaction pattern generated by the security issue appears to be self-perpetuating. The clumsy manner in which U.S. hegemony is often asserted (i.e., the 1965 invasion of the Dominican Republic) generates anti-Yankee sentiment. That sentiment is often expressed in economic nationalism and a desire for nonalignment, which in turn is interpreted by U.S. policy-makers as threatening to security and leads to additional clumsy assertions of U.S. hegemony.

It is not suggested that U.S. influence in the hemisphere has been unidimensional. The overarching hemispheric policy of the United States, however, has been relatively consistent since the issuance of the Monroe Doctrine: the protection of the American states (with or without their approval) from political or military intervention (broadly defined) from any other part of the world.[17] As nationalism in a dependent or client state virtually by definition takes the form of resentment against the paramount or hegemonic power, nationalism itself has often been viewed by U.S. decision-makers as a manifestation of foreign influence, or as essentially anti-American.[18]

Variation in U.S. policy over the long term has had more to do with style and capability than with basic orientation. This variation might be seen within the context of two trends, one cyclical and the other linear. The cyclical trend is a function of changing perceptions of the degree or immediacy of the "security threat." Escalating manifestations

---

17. Interpretation of what constitutes such intervention has been quite arbitrary. In 1954 the importation by Guatemala of small arms from Czechoslovakia was cited by the United States as justification for the CIA involvement it denied in the overthrow of Arbenz. In the late 1960s Uruguay was importing large quantities of small arms from Czechoslovakia for use by the Uruguayan police and their U.S. advisors in combatting the Tupamaros, a national revolutionary group with a philosophy more akin to that of the U.S. "new left" than to orthodox Marxism.

18. For elaboration on this tendency, see David Green, *The Containment of Latin America: A History of the Myths and Realities of the Good Neighbor Policy* (Chicago: Triangle Books, 1971).

of social unrest in Latin America, especially in conjunction with wars, hot or cold, have generally resulted in an intensification of U.S. official interest in the area. This has been reflected in a posture of paternalistic activism, characterized by the extension of both carrot and stick. As the perception of threat subsides, U.S. policy returns to a posture of "mature partnership," or what some might call "malign neglect"; that is, relatively speaking, the carrot is withdrawn.

The linear trend is one of ever expanding stakes—of U.S. investment and presence—and the concomitant inflation of "security interests." The territorial self-image of the United States was enhanced by the country's rise to the status of regional, then world, power. Given the hemispheric cooperation that developed during World War II and the decline of the Western European powers, the U.S. strategic "soft underbelly" concept that had been more or less confined to the Central American and Caribbean region was extended to Tierra del Fuego. Links between the U.S. and Latin American military establishments have been enhanced by the increasing militarization of the U.S. foreign policy decision-making apparatus. And "strategic" economic interests have been expanded by the increase in U.S. investment in Latin America from about U.S. $3.5 billion in 1913 to $9.2 billion in 1960, $14.7 billion in 1970, and $16.6 billion in 1972.[19] Expanding military and economic interests have in turn generated increasing involvement by various U.S. public and private entities in the affairs of the area.

It is not suggested that these trends have been sustained through a well-defined "grand design," carefully coordinated among all entities, public and private, based in the United States and passed down intact from one administration to the next. Rather, they are seen as products of a decision-making process that, to twist the jargon a bit, might be termed "disjointed incremental greed"[20]—that is, a symbiosis of the profit motive and the institutional imperative.

In the early 1960s the United States was undergoing a transition in its global Cold War military strategy from an emphasis on massive retaliation to an emphasis on counterinsurgency. This change in em-

19. U.S., Congress, Senate Committee on Foreign Relations, Subcommittee on Multinational Corporations, *The Multinational Corporations in Brazil and Mexico: Structural Sources of Economic and Non-Economic Power*, 94th Cong., 1st sess., August 1975, p. 34.

20. David Braybrooke and Charles E. Lindblom discuss "disjointed incrementalism" as the most common approach to foreign policy decision-making in "Types of Decision-making," James N. Rosenau, ed., *International Politics and Foreign Policy: A Reader in Research and Theory* (New York: The Free Press, 1969), ch. 20.

phasis, especially as it related to Latin America, had been set in relief by the Cuban Revolution. As a consequence of that revolution and the adherence of the Castro government to Marxist-Leninism, social unrest elsewhere in the hemisphere was seen as constituting a security threat of such magnitude as to require a posture of paternalistic activism. This posture was labeled the Alliance for Progress.

The goals ostensibly embodied in the Alliance for Progress represented the boldest undertaking by the United States in the history of inter-American relations. In addition to the professed extension of economic incentives for far-reaching socioeconomic reform, the Alliance purported to promote and reinforce democratic processes actively. As Karl Deutsch has pointed out, the same degree of power used negatively as a veto or as a power of denial against some highly specific outcome produces far less impressive results when applied to promoting an outcome which is fairly improbable in the first place.[21] Even if such an outcome had ever been seriously intended and backed by consistent and coordinated policy, it would have been one thing, for example, to eliminate a Trujillo, and quite another to bring about among the traditionally repressed Dominicans a political culture conducive to stable democracy.

Furthermore, not even the most innovative U.S. policy could have been introduced in 1961 into a vacuum. There was long-standing and justifiable skepticism toward U.S. policies on the part of many Latin American nationalists oriented toward basic reform and popular participation in government. There was a pattern of conditioned reflex in the United States, reflected in Congress and in most entities of the executive branch, that equated socialistic slogans and anti-American sentiment with the "communist menace." There were also institutional and personal vested interests based on earlier security and economic policies and traditional elite relationships.

U.S. policy has often contained contradictory elements. The uncritical acceptance by the architects of the Alliance for Progress of the dubious propositions that reform is an antidote to revolution and that "stability" (viewed as the absence of popular pressure for fundamental change) is a prerequisite for economic development (as distinguished from economic growth and modernization) brought these contradictions into particularly sharp focus. The Departments of State and Defense have often appeared to be marching to different drummers. And it has not been uncommon for the Peace Corps to find itself

21. Karl W. Deutsch, *The Analysis of International Relations* (Englewood Cliffs, N.J.: Prentice-Hall, 1968), pp. 26–27.

working at cross-purposes with the other members of a country team. Generally speaking, if the Peace Corps has had any significant effect at all it has been that of mobilizing lower class groups.[22] (It came as no surprise that the Committee of Returned Volunteers received more coverage in J. Edgar Hoover's 1969 report to Congress on subversive organizations than the Mafia.) However, the U.S. concept of security has been so all-encompassing, involving economic and political hegemony as well as strictly military considerations, that it has tended to nullify some of the United States' unprogrammed influences and to undermine those of its own policies that might have encouraged democratic or redistributive tendencies.

President Kennedy and the New Frontiersmen of his administration recognized both the potential for social upheaval which accompanied efforts to redistribute wealth and status, even on a minor scale, and the probability that unleashed populist movements would take the direction of demands for freedom from U.S. hegemony. Thus, in addition to the pre-existing obstacles to the fruition of professed Alliance goals, countervailing forces were programmed into the package deal which was to comprise the Alliance. Aid to Latin American police forces, initiated in 1954, was stepped up, and a new role for the armed forces, "civic action," was added to the many activities grouped under the umbrella concept of "counterinsurgency."

It was reasoned that U.S. law enforcement personnel would train their Latin American counterparts in more "humane" and yet more efficient methods of maintaining internal security. It was also claimed that the intensified linkage itself between the U.S. military and its counterparts, through more extensive training programs and through U.S. Military Assistance Groups working in the Latin American countries, would engender "democratic attitudes" on the part of Latin American military establishments. Furthermore, it was assumed that the military civic action projects would improve the image of the military while allowing it to keep tabs on potentially subversive groups in out-of-the-way places. It was also suggested that keeping the military establishments busy in this way might mean that they would have less time and inclination to conspire against constitutional regimes.[23] But the insurgents or potential insurgents they were being

22. The writer served the Peace Corps as a Volunteer in Chile from 1962 through 1964 and as a staff member in the United States for the first six months of 1965.

23. Willard F. Barber and C. Neale Ronning, *Internal Security and Military Power: Counterinsurgency and Civic Action in Latin America* (Columbus: Ohio State University Press, 1966).

trained to deal with as the enemy were their own compatriots. And "civic action" was soon transformed into "nation-building." A recognition policy designed to discourage coups d'état was introduced, but it was not consistently followed. After Kennedy's assassination, it was abandoned altogether.[24]

On 16 March 1964, the third anniversary of the Alliance for Progress, speaking at the Pan American Union, President Johnson pledged that "the full power of the United States is ready to assist any country where freedom is threatened by forces dictated from beyond the shores of this continent."[25] Two days later, at a meeting of U.S. ambassadors to Latin America, Assistant Secretary of State for Latin American Affairs Thomas Mann reportedly suggested a less passionate commitment to political freedom and social justice and urged that greater attention be paid to immediate national security interests, such as protection of U.S. investments and resistance to communism.[26] By the end of the month, Brazil's constitutional government had fallen victim to a military coup d'état.[27]

Most U.S. policy-makers, and many scholars as well, have argued that the recent spate of coups d'état and the prevalence of military dictatorships in Latin America are consequences of the political, social, and economic histories of those countries rather than of U.S. influence, as if it were an either/or proposition—as if living under the shadow of the Colossus of the North were not an inextricable aspect of those histories. Furthermore, many scholars who have addressed themselves to the question of correlation between military assistance and military coups have concluded that military assistance cannot be viewed as the single causal factor, and from there they have made a quantum leap in logic to the conclusion or implication that such assistance is not causal at all.[28]

24. Kenneth A. Bode discusses this recognition policy and the inconsistency in its implementation in "An Aspect of United States Policy in Latin America: The Latin American Diplomats' View," *Political Science Quarterly* 85 (September 1970): 471–91.

25. Lyndon B. Johnson, cited in Edwin Lieuwen, *Generals Versus Presidents: Neo-Militarism in Latin America* (New York: Praeger, 1964), pp. 142–43.

26. Thomas Mann, cited in ibid.

27. Charles Bartlett, a political columnist reputed to have excellent contacts in Washington, confided to his readers in *The Boston Globe* (23 March 1964) that this change of policy was meant to urge the Brazilian military to move against Goulart. Cited in Joseph A. Page, *The Revolution That Never Was: Northeast Brazil 1955–1964* (New York: Grossman, 1972), p. 189.

28. Among the articles tending to dismiss U.S. influence as a factor in contemporary Latin American militarism are the following: John M. Baines,

Samuel Huntington, for example, noting that many countries that have received such assistance have not experienced coups, said that military assistance is in itself politically sterile.[29] That, in this writer's opinion, is somewhat akin to asserting that pneumonia is not fatal. Certainly it is not always fatal; the outcome depends, for example, on the degree of contamination and the general condition of the organism.

The United States, of course, is not responsible for the traditional position of the military in Latin American national societies. The preponderant political role of the military in most of these countries grew out of the struggle for independence. However, some of the countries now under military rule (Chile, Uruguay, and Brazil, for example) had enjoyed sustained constitutional and more or less democratic rule throughout most of the twentieth century. Furthermore, in most of these countries, countervailing political forces such as organized labor and mass-based parties had arisen to challenge the power of the military and the oligarchy.

The United States has not always succeeded in imposing its anti-redistributive standards of security upon its neighbors (Cuba being the most agonizing failure). But to the extent that it has succeeded, it has done so by co-opting, dividing, discrediting, or otherwise weakening popular movements, rendering the bourgeoisie dependent upon foreign capital, and reinforcing and modernizing the role of the military as a political force in Latin America.

The sweeping generalization of John J. Johnson, that without the military every government in the Latin American orbit would be further to the left than it is now, would be hard to substantiate.[30] (Unless, of course, one states the obvious—that in any society the existence

---

"U.S. Military Assistance to Latin America: An Assessment," *Journal of Interamerican Studies and World Affairs* 14 (November 1972): 469–87; Elizabeth H. Hyman, "Soldiers in Politics: New Insights on Latin American Armed Forces," *Political Science Quarterly* 87 (September 1972): 401–18; James D. Cochrane, "U.S. Policy Towards Recognition of Governments and Promotion of Democracy in Latin America Since 1963," *Journal of Latin American Studies* [London] 4 (November 1972): 275–91.

29. Samuel P. Huntington, *Political Order in Changing Societies* (New Haven: Yale University Press, 1968), p. 193. Even if military assistance could, in theory, be politically sterile (which this author doubts) its donor was hardly politically neutral. According to the Senate Intelligence Committee's report on *Alleged Assassination Plots Involving Foreign Leaders* (Report no. 94–465, 94th Cong., 1st sess., 20 November 1975), the CIA's Chilean Task Force complained in 1970 that it was frustrated in its attempts to provoke a coup by "the apolitical, constitutional-oriented inertia of the Chilean military" (p. 240).

30. John J. Johnson, *The Military and Society in Latin America* (Stanford, Calif.: Stanford University Press, 1964), pp. 143–44.

of some organized force is necessary on occasion to keep the "have-nots" from going after what the "haves" have.) Any such hypothesis would have to take into account military backing for the quasi-populist regimes of Vargas of Brazil, Peron of Argentina, and Ibañez of Chile, for example, and the more recent developments in Peru and Panama. Military establishments nurtured and strengthened by the United States have not in all cases adhered to domestic and foreign policies favored by the United States once in power; but those that have chosen, or have found it necessary, to repress popular movements severely in order to assume or maintain power have generally received the generous support of the United States for that effort and, in turn, have found it possible to express their "nationalism" in ways inoffensive to their benefactor.

Although the military establishment in Brazil has by no means been a monolithic body, its influence and intervention since World War II have been exerted on balance in support of the upper and middle classes. Brazilian scholar Helio Jaguaribe said of the coup of April 1964:

> It was a counterrevolution fully aware of the implications involved in such a term, and since it could not reconcile itself to this limitation, it felt the need to compensate by styling itself a "revolution."[31]

President Lyndon B. Johnson's response to that "revolution," telegraphed within a few hours after the military's assumption of power, expressed "warmest good wishes" and approval that the matter had been settled "within the framework of constitutional democracy."[32]

31. Helio Jaguaribe, *Economic and Political Development: A Theoretical Approach and a Brazilian Case Study* (Cambridge: Harvard University Press, 1968), p. 187.

32. Thomas E. Skidmore, *Politics in Brazil, 1930–1964: An Experiment in Democracy* (New York: Oxford University Press, 1967), p. 330.

Part I:

United States
Security and the
Brazilian "Revolution"

Introduction

From the early part of the twentieth century until the early 1960s, Brazilian policy-makers had for the most part accepted U.S. concepts of what constituted security and threats to security in the Western Hemisphere. Public opinion on foreign policy was under any circumstances a scarce commodity, and on occasions, when journalists or other opinion-makers criticized U.S. policies, government spokesmen countered by coming to the defense of the U.S. position. While most of the leaders of Hispanic America were protesting the dollar and gunboat diplomacy in the Caribbean (a policy practiced in accordance with the Roosevelt corollary to the Monroe doctrine), Brazil's foreign minister applauded it. And while some South American states vacillated or remained aloof, Brazil cooperated fully with the United States in both World Wars. But by the early 1960s increasing urbanization and industrialization had generated the beginnings of political mobilization among Brazil's lower classes, and foreign policy had become an issue open to public debate.

Nowhere was the test of the Alliance for Progress considered to be more crucial than in Brazil. The Brazilian economy was undergoing a structural crisis. Demand for staple, nondurable consumer goods was seriously outstripping supply. In order for inflation to be brought under control, either the nature of the country's productive capacity would have to be transformed or demand on the part of the lower classes would have to be curtailed. Most of the economists at the service of the government of João Goulart (1961–1964) felt that a change in the country's productive capacity would require a greater measure of national control over the economy. The attempt to increase national control set the government on a collision course with U.S. private investors, and thus with the U.S. government.[1]

1. Celso Furtado, interview, 18 December 1972, Washington, D.C.

To equip itself for such a confrontation, the Brazilian government needed a broad popular base. One of the means employed to cultivate such a base was the adoption of what its formulators regarded as an "independent" foreign policy. This policy, conceived as a defensive one, was generally seen by U.S. policy-makers as indicative of aggressive anti-Americanism. They saw their leverage being chipped away by the countervailing force of the actual or potential popular base of the Brazilian government, and they professed fears that Brazil was moving toward the communist camp.

The following chapters will examine the historical context of the Brazilian crisis of the 1960s, its foreign policy implications, and the response of the United States. It will be noted that while the roots of that crisis were predominantly domestic, the dependence of the country's economy and the fragility of its civilian political institutions made Brazil particularly vulnerable to penetration by a hegemonic power.

[1]

Brazil: The Crisis of the Sixties

Martin Needler noted in 1966 that over the past three decades military intervention in domestic politics in Latin America had increasingly tended to take the following forms: (1) veto coups, designed to preserve the status quo; (2) coups toppling constitutional regimes; (3) coups forestalling the election or inauguration of reformers; and (4) coups showing an increase in popular resistance. Needler also noted that coups occurred with greater frequency during periods of economic decline.[1]

In *Political Order in Changing Societies,* Samuel Huntington has theorized that "in the world of oligarchy, the soldier is a radical; in the middle-class world he is a participant and arbiter; as the mass society looms on the horizon, he becomes the conservative guardian of the existing order."[2] And "Espartaco," in "The 'Latin American Crisis' and its External Framework," maintained that the only kind of government that can effectively assert economic nationalism is one with a strong, well-organized popular base.[3]

Ascribing a measure of validity to these observations and theories, we will address ourselves to Brazil's vulnerability in 1964 to a coup

---

1. Martin C. Needler, "Political Development and Military Intervention in Latin America," *The American Political Science Review* 60 (September 1966): 616–26.

2. Huntington, *Political Order in Changing Societies.*

3. Espartaco, "The 'Latin American Crisis' and its External Framework," *Latin American International Politics: Ambitions, Capabilities, and the National Interest of Mexico, Brazil, and Argentina,* ed. Carlos Alberto Astiz with Mary F. McCarthy (Notre Dame, Ind.: University of Notre Dame Press, 1969), pp. 18–58.

d'état, to the particular kind of coup it experienced, and to the establishment of what Helio Jaguaribe has termed a "colonial-fascist"
system. Jaguaribe defines this system as one in which authoritarian
control and oligarchical privilege cannot be maintained without
external assistance, assistance bought at the price of massive denationalization of resources.[4]

Patrimonialism and Corporatism:
The Vulnerability of Civil Institutions

It should be considerably less difficult to note what was missing in
the Brazilian political system as it entered the decade of the sixties
than to describe what was present. Philippe Schmitter characterized
the system, in Interest Conflict and Political Change in Brazil, as a corporatist one in which the modus operandi, and even, in some cases, the
very existence, of interest or pressure groups as such was dependent
upon the allocative framework established and maintained by the
central government.[5] In "Power, Politics, and Patronage: A Model of
National Integration," Sydney Greenfield depicted it as a patrimonial
system based on patronage networks incorporating pyramids of dyadic
contracts.[6] But these are not necessarily contradictory. As Schmitter
pointed out, political development in Brazil had proceeded by sedi-
mentation rather than metamorphosis, generating, by the early 1960s,
what Charles Anderson has termed a "political museum."[7]

Until the 1930s, political power rested on a very narrow base. The
president and the heads of the most important state machines made the
major policy decisions, while at the local level, under a system known
as coronelismo, the political boss (coronel), generally the head or
representative of the dominant patriarchal landholding family, delivered the vote that maintained the state machines in power.

Greenfield noted that the patron-dependent relationship of the
plantation-based society gradually evolved during the nineteenth

4. Helio Jaguaribe, "Political Strategies of National Development in Brazil,"
Latin America," The American Political Science Review 60 (September 1966):
Movements, ed. Irving L. Horowitz, Josué de Castro, and John Gerassi (New
York: Random House, 1969), pp. 390–439.

5. Philippe C. Schmitter, Interest Conflict and Political Change in Brazil
(Stanford, Calif.: Stanford University Press, 1971).

6. Sydney Greenfield, "Power, Politics and Patronage: A Model of National
Integration" unpublished manuscript (University of Wisconsin, 1971).

7. Charles W. Anderson, "The Latin American Political System," The Dynamics of Change in Latin American Politics, ed. John D. Martz, 2d ed. (Englewood Cliffs, N.J.: Prentice-Hall, 1971), pp. 289–304.

century into a patron-client relationship. By the end of the Republican era in 1930, the power of the *coroneis* was based not only on the plantation system, but also on the control of goods and services available through government and the liberal professions. During the Vargas era, however, the urban-rural relationship ceased to be symbiotic, as a schism developed between the power bases of rural and urban politics. The patrimonial system of the rural areas was not dismantled or transformed; it was simply ignored.

The necessity of import substitution, as a consequence first of the depression of the thirties and later of World War II, gave a big push to industrialization. But largely as a result of rural sector stagnation and imported capital-intensive industry, urbanization outpaced industrial employment. The bureaucracy swelled to absorb the unemployed, thereby creating a middle class abnormally large for the level of structural differentiation of the economy. The middle class was thus dependent and insecure, and the magnitude of the foreign presence in the economy inhibited the development of a "self-confident" national bourgeoisie.[8]

Urban development represented not merely a shift in the base of power, but a considerable expansion in the power of the central government. Although the *coroneis* system persisted, the leverage contained in the brokerage role of the *coroneis* was encroached upon by an overlay of interventors under the *Estado Novo*, which made the government itself a semi-autonomous source of negotiable goods and services. The regional base of power also began to spread, as the power monopoly of the two wealthiest and most populous states, São Paulo and Minas Gerais, was broken.

Interest groups proliferated in response to the bureaucratic buildup. Most pre-existing elite groups were absorbed and accommodated and emerging groups were co-opted and manipulated. The expanded organization of urban labor, for example, was stimulated by President Getulio Vargas himself and carried out under the auspices of the labor ministry in an attempt to offset the pressures of the oligarchy and foreign interests without alienating them. The power of recognition under the corporatist system made all formal groups dependent, although among the upper classes private associations continued to exercise influence through "connections."

8. For a discussion of foreign penetration of the economy in the early twentieth century, see Richard Graham, *Britain and the Onset of Modernization in Brazil, 1850–1914* (Cambridge: Cambridge University Press, 1968), and T. Lynn Smith and Alexander Marchant, *Brazil: Portrait of Half a Continent* (Westport, Conn.: Greenwood Press, 1951).

The party and electoral systems that developed after the fall of Vargas in 1945 contributed to a partial integration of the patrimonial and corporatist elements of "O Sistema" (The System).[9] The patron-client relationship was institutionalized as the vote became the major negotiable commodity of lower-class literates; *cabos electorais*, or political middlemen, proliferated between local and national systems. Individuals had some options among patrons, and local factions (consisting generally of a leader and his followers rather than of collectivities recognizing common interests) shifted among parties.[10]

Popular participation was expanding. Voter turnout, for example, increased from 6.2 million in the 1945 presidential election to 14.7 million in the 1962 congressional and gubernatorial elections.[11] But all the important organizations functioning as mediators between the State and the individual were really entities connected with the State itself, rather than effectively autonomous organizations.[12]

The economic system established by Vargas persisted into the 1950s. Brazilian scholar Caio Prado Jr. described this system as "bureaucratic capitalism," a privatized version of state capitalism, characterized by the socialization of losses and the division of spoils.[13] The political manifestation of this system was a process of continuous accommodation whereby previous power holders, as long as their perquisites remained intact, could be pressured into making concessions to new power contenders. The system could be maintained as long as economic growth provided for an "expanding-sum game"; that is, while the quantity of goods and services available for distribution was expanding, a favor to one pressure group was not necessarily at the expense of another. But by the early 1960s inflation had become rampant and the economy had entered a downward spiral. The economic crisis, generated in part by production geared for the few and increasing demand by the many, was deepened by a credit freeze imposed by Western financial institutions.[14]

9. For elaboration on the workings of "O Sistema," see James W. Rowe, "The 'Revolution' and the 'System': Notes on Brazilian Politics, Part II: The 'System'—Full Flower and Crisis," American Universities Field Staff Reports, *East Coast South America Series*, vol. 12, no. 4 (1966).

10. Greenfield, "Power, Politics and Patronage."

11. Alfred Stepan, *The Military in Politics: Changing Patterns in Brazil* (Princeton: Princeton University Press, 1971), p. 138.

12. Francisco C. Weffort, "State and Mass in Brazil," *Masses in Latin America*, ed. Irving L. Horowitz (New York: Oxford University Press, 1970), ch. 11, p. 393.

13. Cited in Schmitter, *Interest Conflict and Political Change*, p. 376.

14. Furtado interview.

Thus the system took on the characteristics of a "zero-sum game": with a shrinking economic pie, the upper and middle classes, and particularly the military, squared off against labor, assuming that its gains could only be at their expense.[15] Octavio Ianni wrote that sectors of the military had been openly complaining about the progressive lowering of their standard of living.[16] He also noted that inflation and the narrowing gap between wages and salaries had led the middle class in general to feel that it was being proletarianized. Some officers saw in these developments a plunge toward communism. A confidential document delivered by the Armed Forces Chief of Staff to the president on 31 March 1964, asserted that "Lenin declared monetary inflation to be a precious ally of communism in capitalist countries."[17]

Meanwhile, some elements had begun to break with Brazil's corporatist pattern. Ação Popular (Popular Action) and other groups that had engaged in rural literacy compaigns under the auspices of the Church now clashed with the hierarchy. Strikes and demonstrations began to go beyond the Labor Ministry's control, and rural unionization became a free-for-all among the peasant leagues, radical Catholics, moderate Catholics, and communists. And finally, noncommissioned officers began to mutiny against the brass. The *jeito* (a distinctively Brazilian form of political sleight of hand), which had previously proved so useful in resolving competing claims within classes, was a tool useless in confronting this incipient class conflict.[18] The development of political consciousness and independent organization on the part of the have-nots, however, had proceeded only far enough to alarm the haves (and their external allies); the masses remained overwhelmingly passive, unorganized, and dependent. Gilberto Amado summed up the dysfunctionalism in the Brazilian democratic system this way: "Before 1930, elections were false but representation was real; after 1930 elec-

15. Kenneth Paul Erickson, "Corporatism and Labor in Development," *Contemporary Brazil: Issues in Economic and Political Development*, ed. H. Jon Rosenbaum and William G. Tyler (New York: Praeger, 1972), pp. 145–53.

16. There was a glimmer of *déjà vu* in the crisis of 1964. A decade earlier, on 22 February 1954, Goulart had resigned from the post of Minister of Labor in Vargas' cabinet under pressure from the military, as his proposed wage bill would have raised the pay of some manual laborers above that of a junior officer. See Ross K. Baker, *A Study of Military Status and Status Deprivation in Three Latin American Armies*, report prepared for American University, Center for Research in Social Systems (Washington: Government Printing Office, October 1967), p. 27.

17. Octavio Ianni, *Crisis in Brazil*, trans. Phyllis B. Eveleth (New York: Columbia University Press, 1970), pp. 131–39.

18. Several scholars have discussed this change in political competition as one from distributive to redistributive stakes.

tions were real, but representation was false."[19] In a similar vein, João de Scantimburgo, in a 1969 study, maintained that the military did not actually "seize" power; rather, the civilian political "class," never having succeeded in institutionalizing its form of government, disintegrated.[20]

But let us backtrack now and trace in greater detail the domestic developments culminating in the "revolution" of 1964 and the entrenchment of a regime as rigidly authoritarian as any the Western Hemisphere had yet sustained. We examine, in particular, the changing role of the military in these developments.

The Traditional Military Role and the Counterrevolutionary "Revolution"

While the armed forces of most of the Spanish American countries had risen through the independence movement to a preponderant role in national politics, the peaceful transition to independent status provided no such opportunity to the Brazilian military. It was not until the War of the Triple Alliance (1864–1870) enhanced its numerical strength and prestige that the military assumed a political role in Brazil, ultimately deposing Emperor Dom Pedro II in 1889. The military maintained control of the government (directly or indirectly) until 1894, despite the promulgation of a new constitution in 1891.[21] It was not until 1964 that the military again assumed full control over the institutions of government, but its role of defending the constitution during the intervening years was interpreted with great latitude.

The activities of the *tenentes,* a group of young lower middle-class officers who staged a dramatic rebellion in the 1920s in the name of national renovation and social justice, had provided something of the social undercurrent and the leadership of the coup that placed Vargas in power in 1930. The military again assisted Vargas in 1937 in instituting the *Estado Novo,* but after elections had been scheduled in 1945

19. Cited in Genival Rabelo, *O Capital Estrangeiro na Imprensa Brasileira* (Rio de Janeiro: Editôra Civilizaçao Brasileira, 1966), p. 4.

20. João de Scantimburgo, *A Crise de republica presidencial do Marechal Deodoro ao Marechal Castelo Branco* (São Paulo: Livraria Pioneira Editôra, 1969).

21. June E. Hahner, *Civil-Military Relations in Brazil, 1889–1898* (Columbia: University of South Carolina Press, 1969). For further discussion of the role of the military since the late nineteenth century, see Frederick M. Nunn, "Military Professionalism and Professional Militarism in Brazil, 1870–1970: Historical Perspective and Political Implications," *Journal of Latin American Studies* 4 (May 1972): 29–54.

and it appeared that Vargas was shifting his power base to the left, the military deposed him.

The party system that prevailed from 1945 to 1965 was a legacy of the Vargas era. The Social Democratic Party (Partido Social Democrático—PSD), dominated largely by landowners and industrialists, and the Brazilian Workers' Party (Partido Brasileiro dos Trabalhadores—PTB), led by elites but representing organized labor and other lower income groups, were formed by supporters of Vargas. The government, during most of that period, rested on a tenuous coalition between the two parties. The National Democratic Union (União Democrático Nacional—UDN), similar in social composition to the PSD but aggregating anti-Vargas forces, was the strongest opponent of the coalition. By the early 1960s there were also a number of minor parties, most of which were explicitly ideological and programmatic or personalistic.

The PSD was the largest party and during most of the period of democratic rule the UDN ranked second, but both parties steadily lost ground to the PTB. Meanwhile, a nationwide network of university student organizations and an outspoken body of worker-priests, inspired by the Christian social principles expounded in papal encyclicals, joined organized labor and sectors of the government bureaucracy in calling for basic socioeconomic reforms. By 1964, the political system was largely polarized as the increasingly militant leftist nationalist movement confronted traditional and newly emerging economic interest groups.[22]

As a result of regional loyalties and ideological differences among the predominantly middle class officers, as well as rivalry among the three services, the motives and consequences of military intervention during the 1945–1964 period were not entirely consistent. Using the PTB and PSD as his vehicles, Vargas returned to power in 1950 as a popularly elected president, but his populism and his economic nationalism alienated conservative elements in the congress and in the military. An attempt by the military to depose him in 1954 led to his suicide. In 1955, when a conservative faction of the military (mainly the navy, in alliance with civilian conspirators) threatened to prevent liberal President-elect Juscelino Kubitschek of the PSD from taking office, a counter-coup assured his inauguration. Jânio Quadros, elected president in 1960 on the UDN ticket, soon deadlocked with Congress

22. For more in-depth coverage of the period from the rise of Vargas to the "revolution" of 1964, see Skidmore, *Politics in Brazil, 1930–1964*; E. Bradford Burns, *Nationalism in Brazil: A Historical Survey* (New York: Praeger, 1968); and Jordan M. Young, *The Brazilian Revolution of 1930 and the Aftermath* (New Brunswick, N.J.: Rutgers University Press, 1967).

over his attempts to expand the power of the executive, and he alienated conservatives with his insistence on an independent foreign
policy. When Quadros resigned abruptly in 1961, the more conservative elements of the military moved to prevent Vice-President João
Goulart from replacing him, but the Third Army (from Goulart's home
state, Rio Grande do Sul) threatened civil war if he were not allowed to
take office. A compromise among the military antagonists allowed
Goulart to take office, but under a parliamentary rather than a
presidential system.

Following the fall 1962 congressional and gubernatorial elections
that reflected a gradual trend leftward, Goulart appealed for the restoration of his full powers. Congress finally agreed to a plebiscite on a
constitutional change, which pronounced five to one in favor of the
presidential system on 6 January 1963. Congress then voted almost
unanimously to restore it. With the restoration of the presidential
system, Goulart promised strong executive leadership. The government lacked a consistent economic policy, however, and inflationary
pressures continued unabated. Furthermore, the still basically conservative Congress was frequently unwilling to muster a quorum to
take up the business of the day—much less a majority to pass important
legislation. In the face of this stalemate, Goulart, on 5 October 1963,
requested that the congress declare a state of siege. Protests from both
right and left, however, caused him to withdraw the request two days
later.[23]

Goulart then decided to appeal directly to the people to pressure
Congress into enacting his program. His policy proposals included a
limited agrarian reform program, abolition of the literacy requirement
for voting, legalization of the Communist Party, tax and banking
reform, and antitrust legislation. He attempted to use the tactic, successfully employed by Vargas, of encouraging pressure against his own
government as a means of maintaining contact with popular movements.

Leonel Brizola, Goulart's brother-in-law, a member of the Chamber of
Deputies and former governor of Rio Grande do Sul, and Miguel Arraes, governor of Pernambuco, organized a populist movement known
as the Popular Mobilization Front (Frente de Mobilização Popular—
FMP) to mobilize mass support for Goulart's proposed reforms. The
FMP became so militant in staging strikes and demonstrations,
however, that it tended to undermine the president's ability to compromise and conciliate in the face of contradictory pressures. By late

23. Stepan, *The Military in Politics*, p. 70.

March of 1964, the complex power struggle had raised political tension to a new high.[24]

The military elite had long feared Goulart's cooperation with communists, his increasingly neutralist position in the Cold War, and his reform-mongering; furthermore, having removed him from Vargas' cabinet in 1954 and forced him to accept a parliamentary system in 1961, they feared his vengeance. Interservice rivalries had restrained them during the first two years of his administration, but by 1963 the conviction that the president was trying to build up a following among noncommissioned officers had served to unite the commissioned officers in opposition to him. When three thousand sailors and marines, calling for basic social reforms, rebelled against their anti-Goulart officers on 25 March, the president indicated that they would receive an amnesty. After a nationally televised speech on 30 March, in which Goulart attacked the emphasis of the military hierarchy on discipline and order, the officers moved on 31 March to depose him.

The coup d'état of 31 March–2 April 1964, was carried out swiftly and almost without bloodshed. The moves of the armed forces to seize the machinery of government were supported by several state governors and most of the country's powerful economic groups. The president, unable or unwilling to mobilize any important sector of the nation in defense of the constitutional government, fled to Uruguay.[25]

The phenomenon of military intervention prompted by a deadlock between a left-leaning president and a right-leaning Congress was by no means new in twentieth-century Brazil, but the outcome of that intervention was. Contrary to tradition and to the expectations of the civilian opponents of Goulart who cooperated in the takeover, the military officers who assumed control in 1964 did not abdicate power in favor of the civilian politicians. The president of the Chamber of Deputies, Ranieri Mazzili (next in line of succession according to the Constitution) assumed the title of Acting President, but the military's

24. The writer was in Brazil in March 1964. Everyone from taxi drivers and hotel clerks to one of Goulart's special assistants calmly informed me that in a matter of weeks or days there would be a coup d'état or a civil war.

25. General Vernon A. Walters told this author on 21 May 1976 that he had heard General Assis Brasil, who had been chief of Goulart's Military Household, recount Goulart's words as the coup got under way: "O seu dispositivo [military loyalists] e uma merda." For more detailed accounts of events surrounding the coup, see Abelardo Jurema, *Sexta-Feira, 13: as últimos dias do govêrno João Goulart,* 3d ed. (Rio de Janeiro: Edições o Cruzeiro, October 1964); Alberto Dines et al., *Os Idos de março e a queda em abril* (Rio de Janeiro: José Alvaro, Editor, 1964); and Ianni, *Crisis in Brazil.*

Supreme Revolutionary Command, comprising the commanders-in-chief of the three armed services, actually ruled.

The Command set out immediately to eliminate from the political scene elements of alleged subversion and corruption, and within a week of the coup they had arrested more than seven thousand persons. The first of a series of sweeping decrees, designated Institutional Acts, was issued by the Command on 9 April. Among other items, the Act asserted the right of the Command to suspend constitutional guarantees; to cancel the mandates of elected federal, state, and local officials; to remove political appointees and civil servants; and to deprive individuals of the rights of voting and holding office for ten years. The constitutional requirement of direct election for the presidency was set aside and, on 11 April, the decimated Congress, in response to the demands of the heads of the three armed services, elected Marshal Humberto Castello Branco, chief of the Army General Staff, to fill Goulart's unexpired term.

Castello Branco proceeded with what he termed the moral rehabilitation of Brazil, and within seven months his government had removed from office some 9,000 pro-Goulart civil servants and military officers and about 112 holders of elective office, including seven state governors, one senator, 46 federal deputies and 20 alternates. Three hundred seventy-eight of the country's most influential political and intellectual leaders were deprived of their political rights (most, but not all, of these were left-of-center); among them were former presidents Goulart, Quadros, and Kubitschek, Communist Party leader Luis Carlos Prestes, Peasant League leader Francisco Julião, economist Celso Furtado, architect Oscar Niemeyer, Pernambuco Governor Arraes, Deputy Brizola, and Justice Minister Abelardo Jurema. The campaign against alleged subversives particularly decimated the labor and education ministries and the universities, and it brought the surviving labor and student organizations under tight military control.[26]

In addition to the campaign for "moral rehabilitation," the Castello Branco government placed top priority on the control of inflation, changes in the electoral system, and the promotion of economic growth through the provision of incentives to foreign investors. The rate of inflation was reduced and economic growth slightly outdistanced population growth during Castello Branco's term, but these gains did not bring the government popularity with the general public because wage

26. Charles Daugherty, James Rowe, and Ronald Schneider, eds., *Brazil: Election Factbook No. 2* (Washington, D.C.: Institute for the Comparative Study of Political Systems, September 1965), p. 12.

freezes formed the basis of the austerity program, making the inequity in the distribution of income even more pronounced. Furthermore, the concessions to foreign enterprises ran counter to the wave of economic nationalism that had been building since the early 1950s.

The presidential election scheduled for October 1965 was postponed for a year, but the president, ignoring pressures from the so-called hard-line *(linha dura)* military officers, decided to proceed during that month with the election of governors and vice-governors of eleven of the twenty-two states. The government maintained a veto over candidacies, but otherwise pledged nonintervention in the elections. The results were a stunning setback to the armed forces. The winners in more than half of the states, including Guanabara and Minas Gerais, were opposition candidates, supported by the PSD, the PTB, the Social Progressive Party (Partido Social Progressista—PSP), or some combination of the three. Moreover, on the day following the election, former President Kubitschek returned to the country after sixteen months in exile and was greeted with great public enthusiasm.[27]

While asserting that the outcome of such elections was largely determined by local considerations, the government turned to even stronger measures to insulate itself against real or potential opponents. The newly elected governors were allowed to assume office, but on 27 October the government issued a second Institutional Act which asserted the president's power to suspend Congress and rule by decree, assume greater control over government expenditures, and ban all political activity on the part of individuals deprived of their political rights. The Act increased the membership of the Supreme Court and the Federal Appeals Court, outnumbering the Kubitschek and Goulart appointees who had formed a majority in the judiciary, and extended the authority of the military courts to include the trial of civilians accused of subversion.

More importantly, the second Institutional Act provided for both the indirect election of the president and vice-president by the National Congress and the dissolution of the existing political parties. In the place of the old parties, an official government party, the National Renovating Alliance (Aliança Renovadora Nacional—ARENA) and an official opposition party, the Brazilian Democratic Movement (Movimento Democrático Brasileiro—MDB) were created.

A third Institutional Act, promulgated on 6 February 1966, replaced

27. Ronald Schneider, ed., *Brazil Election Factbook No. 2, Supplement* (Washington, D.C.: Institute for the Comparative Study of Political Systems, November 1966).

the direct election of governors with indirect elections by state assemblies and eliminated the election of mayors of capital cities, substituting presidential appointees. The following months witnessed the issuance of a series of decrees, designated "complementary acts," further limiting the authority of elected officials at all levels. They also witnessed the defection of a number of important supporters, both military and civilian, of the Castello Branco government. The most important of these was former governor of Guanabara, Carlos Lacerda, who proposed the formation of a broad opposition front including Kubitschek and his supporters. Meanwhile, clashes between the security forces and the National Union of Students (União Nacional dos Estudantes—UNE) and between the military authorities and the Northeast bishops, who issued a manifesto in support of rural workers, contributed to an atmosphere of crisis.

The MDB was nominally allowed to participate in the gubernatorial elections in twelve more states on 3 September 1966, but the election of ARENA candidates, most of whom had been selected by Castello Branco himself, was assured as the government maintained its veto over candidacies, canceled the mandates of a sufficient number of MDB legislators in each state assembly to ensure an ARENA majority, and forbade ARENA legislators to vote for MDB candidates. It also established the revocation of political rights as the penalty for resigning in protest.

The futility of opposition thus established, the MDB decided not to run a candidate for the presidency; the unopposed ARENA candidate, Marshal Artur da Costa e Silva, was elected by Congress on 3 October 1966 without incident. The dismissal of six federal deputies on 12 October, however, precipitated a new crisis, because the congressional leadership of both parties refused to recognize the cancellation of mandates. Castello Branco responded by recessing Congress until after the congressional elections scheduled for 15 November and proceeded with a new wave of cancellations of mandates.

In January 1967 a Congress comprising 276 ARENA members (as opposed to 131 members of the MDB) in the Chamber of Deputies and 42 ARENA members and 23 MDB members in the Senate approved a new constitution which enhanced the powers of the presidency at the expense of Congress and further centralized public administration. It also passed a new law placing tight controls on the communications media.

The inauguration of Costa e Silva as president on 15 March 1967 temporarily led to a somewhat lower profile for the military; half of his twenty-two cabinet members were civilians, and his references to "re-democratization" and the "humanizing" of economic policies gave encouragement to some who had opposed his predecessor. The death of Castello Branco in an air accident in July temporarily increased Costa e Silva's maneuverability and, for more than a year, he permitted a wider latitude of political activity. The hardliners among the president's advisors, however, had not capitulated. On 13 December 1968, after Congress refused to allow the government to try one of its members, Marcio Moreira Alves, for criticizing the armed forces, Costa e Silva, through the Fifth Institutional Act, ordered Congress recessed indefinitely. The same Institutional Act asserted additional rights of intervention in states and municipalities, tightened press censorship, and suspended the guarantee of habeas corpus for those accused of political crimes. Another wave of arrests, exiles, job dismissals, and cancellations of mandates followed the promulgation of this act. Two hundred ninety-four more citizens, including Supreme Court justices, senators, deputies, mayors, military officers, and journalists, were deprived of their political rights and the principal leaders of the MDB were placed under house arrest. Hundreds of students and professors were removed from the universities.[28]

Since the inception of the so-called revolution in 1964, the military had effectively defused the potential opposition of civilian party politicians. By allowing some to participate, while disqualifying others and allowing those who cooperated to profit from the demise of those who did not, it had kept the opposition disorganized and disoriented. Until late 1968, the most consistent and vocal oppositon to the government came from student organizations and the progressive members of the Catholic clergy. But when virtually all traditional forms of political competition and expression of dissent had been delegitimized, the focus of opposition devolved upon urban guerrilla movements, made up largely of university students.

The boldest of the clandestine groups were the National Liberation Action (Ação Libertadora Nacional—ALN), reportedly headed by Carlos Marighella, a former Communist deputy who had split with the Moscow-oriented party, and the Revolutionary Movement of 8 October (Movimento Revolucionario de 8 de Octubro—MR–8), which derived its name from the date of the execution of Che Guevara by Bolivian authorities in 1967. Their bank robberies and other activities designed to harass and humiliate the government and to acquire arms were

---

28. "Prices Down, Arrests Up: News You Won't Find in Brazil's Newspapers," *The New Republic,* 2 August 1969, pp. 11–12.

paralleled on the right by vigilante actions such as machine-gunning universities and Church-related institutions.[29]

The government announced in August of 1969 that during the first week in September Costa e Silva would decree amendments to the Constitution of 1967 and reconvene Congress, but on 1 September a triumvirate comprising the ministers of the army, navy, and air force assumed the powers of the presidency, announcing that Costa e Silva had suffered a "circulatory crisis with neurological manifestations." The three military commanders (General Aurelio de Lyra Tavares of the army, Admiral Augusto Rademaker of the navy, and Air Marshal Marcio de Souza e Mello) issued another institutional act giving themselves complete control over national security and related matters, and they began routine business "in the name of the chief of government," thus bypassing the civilian vice-president, Pedro Aleixo. The reconvening of Congress was postponed indefinitely.[30]

Three days after the triumvirate assumed control of the government, the United States Ambassador, C. Burke Elbrick, was kidnapped by members of the ALN and the MR–8. The abductors issued a manifesto stating that the Ambassador would be executed unless fifteen political prisoners were released within 48 hours. After some delay and confusion the government bowed to the demands of the guerrillas, and on 7 September the prisoners were flown to asylum in Mexico. Elbrick was released unharmed that evening.

Immediately after Elbrick's release, the triumvirate declared the country to be in a state of "internal revolutionary war." More than two thousand persons were arrested in Rio de Janeiro alone, and guarantees which had appeared in every constitution since 1891 against banishment, life imprisonment, and capital punishment were cast aside by decree. Former President Kubitschek was placed under house arrest, although he was later allowed to travel to New York for medical care.[31]

During the last two weeks of September 1969 and the first week of October, meetings took place almost daily among the upper echelons of the three branches of the armed forces in preparation for the selection of a successor to Costa e Silva. Using this procedure, the military es-

29. *Brazil Herald* (Rio de Janeiro), 9 September 1969, p. 3. A prominent Brazilian journalist, who had been a student leader in the late 1960s, told the author that the state police of São Paulo had worked openly with one vigilante group in assaulting and harassing students.

30. *Washington Post*, 27 August 1969 and 1 September 1969; *New York Times*, 2 September 1969; *Evening Star* (Washington), 2 September 1969.

31. *Latin America* (London), 16 September 1969, p. 1; *New York Times*, 14 September 1969, p. 22; *Washington Post*, 5, 6, 8, 10, and 11 September 1969.

tablishment functioned somewhat in the manner of a highly fac-
tionalized ruling party in a single-party system. No civilian was
considered eligible for the presidency or vice-presidency or even for a
role in the selection process.

It was decided initially that only four-star generals would be eligible
for the presidency, but eligibility was later extended to lower-ranking
generals and to the highest air force and naval officers. The preferences
of the 118 generals, 60 admirals, and 61 air force brigadiers were can-
vassed, but since the army was by far the strongest branch it was
recognized that the opinions of the generals, and particularly of the ten
generals of the Army High Command, would weigh heavily in the final
decision.[32]

On 7 October 1969, the Armed Forces High Command announced
the selection of presidential candidate General Emilio Garastazú
Médici, commander of the Third Army and former head of the National
Intelligence Service. Médici, who was to govern for five years, had
served forty-two years in the army but was little known by civilians.[33]
After the promulgation of the new Constitution of 1969, which le-
gitimized increased authoritarian rule, the National Congress was
reconvened from its ten-month forced recess to validate the selection of
Médici.

Meanwhile, by late 1969, accounts of gruesome torture practiced on
political prisoners, without discrimination in respect to age, sex, or occupation, were appearing with increasing frequency in the world press.
The December 1969 *Review of the International Commission of Jurists*
(the commission serves the United Nations in an advisory capacity)
made reference to "allegations from informed sources that torture is being systematically used against political prisoners."[34] For some while,
the Brazilian government categorically denied all such charges, but it
refused to allow any international organization, including the Inter-
American Commission on Human Rights, to investigate. In December
1970 the Brazilian Minister of Education acknowledged that there was
torture of political prisoners in Brazilian jails but denied that it was
"systematic."[35]

32. *O Estado de São Paulo,* 18 September 1969; *Brazil Herald,* 18 and 20
September 1969.

33. *Business Latin America* (New York), 9 October 1969, p. 328; *Latin
America* (London), 28 September 1969 and 6 October 1969; *Brazil Herald,* 3
October 1969; *New York Times,* 8 October 1969, p. C–16.

34. *Review of the International Commission of Jurists,* no. 4 ed. Sean Mac-
Bride, (December 1969), pp. 15–18.

35. "Tortures Exist, Brazilian Admits," *Washington Post,* 3 December 1970.

An inquiry conducted in 1969 through State Department channels (the results of which are highly classified) substantiated the reports of systematic use of torture. A Pentagon inquiry conducted at the same time refuted those reports. The military attaché responsible for the report claimed that he questioned fifty high-ranking Brazilian officers and all disclaimed any knowledge of torture.[36]

Some of President Médici's ambitions for his term in office were contained in a master plan entitled "Project Brazil: Great Power." In particular he sought—and in large measure achieved—dramatic increases in economic growth, expansion in the provision of technical training and of "moral and civic" education, expansion in governmental capabilities in the areas of intelligence and communications, and progress toward the physical integration of the country through the construction of the Transamazon and peripheral highway systems. Upon assuming office, Médici had pledged to leave democracy firmly installed by the end of his term. In early 1970, however, he explained that the pledge had been an expression of hope rather than a commitment, and that in the meantime the president would retain extraordinary emergency powers.

Meanwhile, in late 1969 and in 1970, conflict between Church and State over the issue of torture had escalated. The use of torture on political prisoners and the kidnapping of diplomats by guerrilla groups who wished to free political prisoners appeared to reinforce each other. The arrests of some four thousand persons in November 1970, the month when congressional elections were held, was condemned by the National Conference of Bishops. In the following month, the Swiss Ambassador was kidnapped and ransomed for the release of seventy political prisoners.[37]

Although censorship had spared the public from many categories of information, the media had not ceased to be an important vehicle for political communication. The government made extensive use of radio and television to identify the military leaders with the Brazilian soccer team's victory in the 1970 World Cup competition, to disseminate patriotic oratory and symbolism in connection with the celebrations of the 1972 sesquicentennial of national independence, and in general to provide the public with a sense of vicarious participation in the na-

36. Interview with Vernard Lanphier, State Department, Intelligence and Research Division, 16 November 1970, Washington, D.C.

37. Ronald Schneider, *The Political System of Brazil* (New York: Columbia University Press, 1973), pp. 312–39.

tional prosperity, modernization, and progress toward great power status that had come about since 1964.[38]

There was a strictly enforced ban on any mention of the issue of the selection of a presidential successor until 18 June 1973, when Médici announced that General Ernesto Geisel would be the candidate of the government party. Geisel had been chief of the military household in the government of Castello Branco and had served more recently as president of PETROBRAS, the state petroleum monopoly. Geisel's only public statement between the announcement of his candidacy and his election by the electoral college on 15 January 1974 was an assertion that he would "follow along the same tracks" as Médici. The electoral college gave him 400 of the 476 votes cast.[39]

The MDB charged that the electoral college was a farce, as thousands of dissenters had been banned from any participation in politics. Twenty-one of the party's would-be electors refused to vote at all, maintaining that voting would signify that they acceded to the farce. The remaining seventy-six, however, agreed to participate in exchange for the right to express themselves more or less openly in an "anti-campaign." Speaking to the electoral college, MDB party leader and presidential "anti-candidate," Ulysses Guimarães, urged the government to do away with "unemployment, arbitrary arrests and persecution, police terrorism, torture, and violence."[40]

In a brief televised address to the nation following his election, President Geisel pledged "stability" and progress toward Brazil's "destiny as a great nation." He also warned that "any subversive tendencies or acts of corruption" would be stopped "in an exemplary manner and fast." He was inaugurated on 15 March 1974.[41]

Geisel's efforts, immediately after assuming office, to open a dialogue with the Church had generated some speculation that his administration might tolerate a degree of political liberalization. The Rio de Janeiro newspaper *O Jornal,* for example, editorialized in March that "political stagnation, deemed necessary until now, must be followed by some no less necessary democratic activity." Such speculation was dampened before the end of Geisel's first month as

38. Rosenbaum and Tyler, eds., *Contemporary Brazil,* pp. 3–27.

39. *Washington Post,* 16 January 1974; *Quarterly Economic Review: Brazil* (London) no. 1 (1972): 2.

40. *Washington Post,* 16 January 1974; *Foreign Broadcast Information Service,* 12 February 1974.

41. *Washington Post,* 16 January 1974; *Christian Science Monitor,* 13 March 1974; *Foreign Broadcast Information Service,* 21 January 1974.

president, however, by the arrests in São Paulo of about sixty clergymen, professors, students, and labor leaders, as well as by the closing of *O Jornal* and two radio stations.[42]

Although the ten-year suspension of political rights ran out in April for about one hundred of the more than twelve hundred persons affected, Minister of Justice Armando Falcão made it clear that "challenges and contradictions" would not be allowed and the government would "use the legal instruments, ordinary and extraordinary, available to it to continue guaranteeing maximum order, peace, and stability. . . ." He added that under no circumstances would those responsible for "the situation which threatened to lead the country to chaos" be allowed to return. On another occasion, Falcão commented that "our struggle is hard and difficult against common crime, subversion, and communism," and he stressed the urgency of rationalization and modernization of the entire police structure, using all the latest technological advances.[43]

President Geisel also made it known that he would tolerate no assertiveness on the part of members of Congress or the government party, or even of the industrialists who had strongly supported the military government. MDB Deputy Francisco Pinto was being prosecuted for characterizing Chilean President Augusto Pinochet in derogatory terms; twenty other members of his party were risking prosecution along with him by expressing agreement with his characterization of Pinochet. And despite the urging of São Paulo industrialists, who were also ARENA party leaders, Geisel vetoed the candidacy of former Finance Minister Delfim Neto for the governorship of that state.[44]

Those who had anticipated a measure of economic relief for the most deprived were also disappointed. On 1 May 1974, the Federal Accounting Court published an opinion accusing the Médici government of making "inexplicable mistakes" in financial policy and of "resuscitating inflation." The new finance minister, Mario Henrique Simonsen, blamed the increasing rate of inflation on "excessive price controls" during the last months of the Médici government. He stated that, under the new government, prices of food and other basic necessities were reaching realistic free-market levels, and that consumers would simply have to pay more.[45]

42. *Foreign Broadcast Information Service*, 8, 17, and 25 April 1974; *Latin America* (London), 5 and 26 April 1974; *Washington Post*, 1 April 1974; *Brazil Herald*, 29 March and 23 April 1974.

43. Ibid.

44. Ibid.

45. *Washington Post*, 2 May 1974.

[2]

Diplomatic and Undiplomatic Relations

As Brazil's political and economic nucleus was shifting in the early twentieth century from the sugar-producing states of the Northeast to the coffee-producing South-Central states, relations with the United States, the best customer of the coffee producers, assumed greater importance than relations with the country's previous patron, Great Britain. José Mariá da Silva Paranhos, better known as the Baron of Rio Branco, foreign minister from 1902 until his death in 1912, saw the interests of Brazil and of the United States as complementary. The foreign policy principles and positions established by Rio Branco were followed in broad outline until 1961.

The beginnings of a policy which its supporters labeled "independent" can be traced, however, to the last Vargas administration (1951–1954). It differed from earlier policy primarily in its opposition to the unrestrained penetration of foreign capital and in its opposition to the U.S. position in the Cold War. A 1952 decree, for example, placed restrictions on foreign investment and on the repatriation of profits, and the PETROBRAS bill of 1953 established a government monopoly over the exploitation of petroleum. Sensitivity to domination by foreign capital was encouraged by Vargas himself, and Brazil refused to participate in the U.S.-instigated United Nations "police actions" in the 1950s in Korea and Lebanon.

The election in 1955 of Kubitschek, an avowed admirer of Vargas, as president and of Goulart as vice-president caused alarm at the U.S. Embassy in Brazil and, according to a U.S. foreign service officer who was

37

in the embassy at that time, the embassy looked favorably upon the conspirators whose plan to prevent the inauguration of Kubitschek aborted.[1] Kubitschek proceeded to sign a trade agreement with the Soviet Union, but he also presided over a great influx of foreign— mainly U.S.— investment.

In a public opinion poll taken before President Quadros assumed office in 1961, 63 percent of those questioned expressed a preference for neutrality in the Cold War. A poll of legislators conducted at about the same time indicated that 80 percent favored the establishment of diplomatic relations with the Soviet Union, 83 percent favored increased trade with the Soviets, and 74 percent favored diplomatic relations with the People's Republic of China. Persons of upper- and middle-class status, however, were consistently more favorable toward the United States and more hostile toward communist countries.[2]

Under Presidents Quadros and Goulart, the country's position vis-à-vis the United States, the communist countries, and the so-called "third world" of developing and largely nonaligned countries was substantially altered. Both presidents expressed the conviction that the Cold War was obsolete. Goulart, in fact, hedged his bets by adorning one of the walls of his oblong private office in Brasilia's presidential palace with a life-sized photograph of himself with Kennedy and the other with a life-sized photograph of himself with Khrushchev.[3]

Representatives of the U.S. government and business community,

1. Source not for attribution. Of this abortive coup, Chilean journalist Robinson Rojas reported in Estados Unidos en Brazil (Santiago: Prensa Latinoamericana, 1965), pp. 62–66, that Standard Oil and U.S. Steel, seeking more generous terms for U.S. investors in the aftermath of Vargas' suicide "gathered together Lacerda, Jânio Quadros (then governor of São Paulo), Café Filho, Pena Boto, and Carlos Luz, in order to stage a coup d'état. On 11 November 1955 Mariscal Humberto Teixeira Lott did what years later Goulart would not do: he headed off the coup and mobilized troops before the conspirators could. Jânio Quadros had in mind a scheme now familiar: the conspirators Lacerda, Luz, Cafe Filho, and Boto would take refuge in São Paulo and there they would form a rebel government, which would receive immediate aid and recognition from the United States, in accordance with an agreement with the United States Ambassador. But the conspirators lost their nerve and the plot was aborted."

2. Keith Larry Storrs, "Brazil's Independent Foreign Policy, 1961–1964: Background, Tenets, Linkage to Domestic Politics, and Aftermath," Cornell University Latin American Studies Program Dissertation Series, no. 44 (Ithaca, N.Y., January 1973), pp. 248–49.

3. The writer observed this for herself in March 1964.

however, had established close ties with like-minded Brazilians, who found the Cold War to be still conveniently flourishing.[4]

The Independent Policy and Deteriorating Relations

The stated objectives of the "independent" foreign policy of Quadros and Goulart were two: economic independence and development through domestic control of the national economy; and the control of external factors so as to make possible a reconciliation of representative democracy with social reforms. Implicit in this was the curtailment of the power of U.S. and other foreign investors through the mobilization of countervailing domestic forces. Specific measures included the resumption of diplomatic and commercial ties with other communist countries, opposition to the isolation of Cuba, the adoption of an anti-colonial position in the United Nations, the establishment of closer ties with the nonaligned countries, and use of the United Nations to balance the influence of the United States in the Organization of American States. The emerging concept of economic nationalism was expressed in the 1962 law limiting annual profit remittance abroad to ten percent of registered capital investment and in the announcement of government plans for eventual nationalization of all foreign public utility companies.

Relations between the United States and the Quadros government got off to a bad start with the visit of Adolf Berle, a special envoy from President Kennedy, a few weeks after Quadros' inauguration in 1961. Berle was seeking backing for the Bay of Pigs invasion, then scheduled for early April, and, according to Ambassador John Moors Cabot's account (as reported by Peter Bell), Berle offered, in effect, a "bribe" of $300 million in foreign assistance for Brazilian cooperation. Quadros rejected the offer with visible irritation; no Brazilian official accompanied Berle to the airport the following day.

Ambassador Cabot felt that "Quadros spent his time plucking the Eagle's feathers," and he recommended that Quadros be kept on a "short leash." He expressed the view that "we shouldn't go all out for Quadros requirements without getting some muffling of Quadros in return." On 21 May 1961, the United States offered $100 million in new credits, the first such loan in two years, but Quadros continued to refuse to see any high-ranking U.S. official, including the Ambassador,

4. For comprehensive historical treatment of U.S. influence in and economic exploitation of Brazil, see Moniz Bandeira, *Presença dos Estados Unidos no Brasil* (Rio de Janeiro: Editôra Civilizaça Brasileira, 1973).

from the visit of Berle until the visit of Adlai Stevenson in July, a few weeks before Quadros resigned.

The U.S. Embassy had been disturbed by the election of Goulart to the vice-presidency in 1960, and even before the inauguration of Quadros the Embassy had initiated "a broad and deep appraisal of the implications of Goulart."[5] Lt. Colonel Edward King, Military Secretary representing the Joint Chiefs of Staff on the Inter-American Defense Board and the Joint Brazil-U.S. Defense Commission from 1966 to 1969, described the mood more bluntly. He said that as early as 1960 there had been an undercurrent of concern running through the assessments of the CIA and the Defense Intelligence Agency that Quadros was vulnerable to communist influence. When Goulart took over, concern at the State Department and the Pentagon turned to panic.[6]

Niles Bond, U.S. chargé d'affaires in Brazil at the time of the crisis over Quadros' succession, told this author that Goulart's opponents in the military and their supporters in the American business community attempted to enlist embassy support for a movement to deny the presidency to Goulart, but he maintains that the United States did not take a position.[7] Other sources indicate, however, that Washington supported a curb on Goulart's power at that time.[8]

Goulart apparently attempted for a time to accommodate U.S. officialdom. He even reportedly consulted Ambassador Lincoln Gordon, who assumed the post in October 1961, as to the "acceptability" of high-ranking Brazilian officials. Nevertheless, Gordon testified in March 1963 before the House Foreign Affairs Committee that he was concerned about communist infiltration in the labor movement, student organizations, and the government itself. And President Kennedy dispatched his brother Robert to Brasilia to inform Goulart that further aid would depend on evidence that Brazil was putting "its own house in order."[9] The list of U.S. demands presented by Kennedy at that time was so similar to those being circulated by Goulart's domestic

5. Peter D. Bell, "Brazilian-American Relations," *Brazil in the Sixties*, ed. Riordan Roett (Nashville, Tenn.: Vanderbilt University Press, 1972), ch. 3.

6. Lt. Colonel Edward L. King, interview, 10 January, 1973, Washington, D.C.

7. Niles Bond, interview, 17 May, 1976, Washington, D.C.

8. Stephen S. Kaplan, "U.S. Military Aid to Brazil and the Dominican Republic: Its Nature, Objectives, and Impact," U.S. Department of State Foreign Area Research Series, no. 16217 (September 1972), p. 42.

9. Bell, "Brazilian-American Relations."

opponents that Goulart, according to Celso Furtado, exclaimed, "How can it be that you are in contact with my enemies?"[10]

Goulart paid an official visit to Washington in April 1962, and as late as April 1963 agreement was reached on a loan from AID of $398.5 million.[11] However, the momentum of political mobilization in Brazil was such that Goulart had to choose between attempting to placate the United States and attempting to maintain his domestic base of support. He opted for the latter.[12] Nationalist opposition, for example, caused Goulart to postpone indefinitely the agreement that had been reached in April for the Brazilian purchase of the ten overpriced subsidiaries of the American and Foreign Power Company.

By June 1963 the deterioration of U.S.-Brazilian relations had become precipitous. Except for the PL 480 surplus wheat agreements (from which the Embassy derived large amounts of local currency for its own usage) and projects nominally in cooperation with the Superintendency for the Development of the Northeast (SUDENE) (but actually, as we shall see, undermining it), aid to the federal government was suspended, although the U.S. continued to subsidize certain state governments and private entities in Brazil. During the presidencies of Quadros and Goulart, USAID had approved loans to Brazil amounting to $600 million, but the disbursement of more than three-fourths of that amount was withheld until after the 1964 coup.[13]

Consultation with Conspirators

Celso Furtado recalls that all U.S. functionaries in Brazil in the 1962–1964 period had panicked for fear that they were losing control of the situation. By the time of the coup, he says, it was widely believed by Americans and Brazilians alike that Goulart and his supporters would rally part of the army, along with contingents of workers and peasants, and fight to defend the government.[14]

10. Furtado interview.

11. Bell, "Brazilian-American Relations."

12. Unlike Argentina's Frondizi, who had faced a somewhat similar dilemma in 1961.

13. James F. Petras and Morris H. Morley, "U.S.-Chilean Relations and the Overthrow of the Allende Government: A Study of U.S. Relations with Chile, Brazil, and Peru," manuscript (Department of Sociology, State University of New York at Binghamton, August 1974), p. 40.

14. Furtado interview.

Gordon acknowledged, in an interview with the author in March 1975, that tension had been mounting in the Embassy for some two years before the coup. He said that shortly after he arrived in the country, Admiral Silvio Heck, one of the three military ministers who had signed the manifesto designed to prevent Goulart from assuming office, asked for an appointment with him. Heck told him that Goulart was a communist and that there was a plan, supported by most of the military and many civilians as well, to overthrow the president. Heck said he hoped that when the time came the United States would not take a dim view of the move. Gordon maintains that he was noncommittal, but that he checked out the story and concluded that the plotters did not have nearly as much support as Heck had reported.[15]

Gordon said that Goulart had made it clear from the beginning of his term that he did not plan to play the Queen Elizabeth role in the parliamentary government, and that U.S. relations with his government began to deteriorate in May 1962, when his speeches, in Mexico and elsewhere, veered off toward populism. The U.S. Embassy was approached from time to time during the second half of 1962 by groups plotting against Goulart. Gordon maintains that all such overtures were met with the response that the resolution of the matter was a Brazilian affair. But he adds that he did not disguise the embassy's alarm about the tendencies of the Goulart government.

Gordon did not believe that Goulart himself was a communist. He saw him as an opportunist who tended to vacillate, but he felt that at times Goulart was mesmerized by Brizola. Gordon was particularly concerned about Brizola's "grupos do once" (literally, groups of eleven, allegedly organized to establish or defend a leftist government) and the strength of the communist unions supporting Goulart. He was also convinced that funds were being siphoned off from PETROBRAS into a political slush fund for Goulart. By late 1963, Gordon confirms, he had begun to express to Brazilian leaders his fears that Goulart was engaged in "superversion"—that is, plotting a Vargas-styled coup from the top.[16]

Assistant Secretary of State Thomas Mann, in congressional testimony in May 1964, said, "We were aware in January by the time I got there—I do not know how much earlier—that the erosion toward Communism in Brazil was very rapid."[17] In his exposé, *Inside the Company: CIA Diary*, published in London in 1975, former CIA agent Philip

15. Lincoln Gordon, interview, 12 March 1975, Washington, D.C.

16. Gordon Interview.

17. Stepan, *The Military in Politics*, p. 125.

Agee, confirmed that events in Brazil at that time were viewed as critical. Agee's diary entry for 10 February 1964 reads as follows:

> I spent a night out at Jim Noland's house. . . . After return to head-quarters Noland was assigned as Chief of the Brazil Branch in WH Division— a key job, with Brazil's continuing slide to the left under Goulart. Noland made several trips to Brazil last year and from what he says Brazil is the most serious problem for us in Latin America— more serious in fact than Cuba since the missile crisis.[18]

Most of the U.S. officials (in Brazil or involved with the making or implementation of policy toward Brazil at the time of the coup) with whom this author spoke expressed vague fears of a communist takeover in Brazil but conceded ultimately that they were speaking of long-term developments. They admitted that Goulart was not a communist and that the Communist Party was not in itself a threat, but they generally compared the position of Goulart to that of Czechoslovakia's Eduard Beneš or the U.S.S.R's Kerensky. Defense Attaché Vernon A. Walters (at that time a colonel, later promoted to brigadier general, and from 1972 to 1976 deputy director of the CIA), for example, admitted that Goulart was not a communist, but he claimed that Goulart was "inept" and hostile to the United States. And he agreed with Gordon's assessment that Goulart was plotting "superversion."[19] Niles Bond spoke initially of his fears of a communist takeover; he concluded, however, that it was not the Communist Party he feared, but rather "the people around Goulart." Of Goulart, he said it was common knowledge in Brazil that "I didn't like the sonuvabitch."[20]

Colonel Walters, who had been in Brazil since 1961, had served as liaison officer with the Brazilian Expeditionary Force in Italy during World War II. As such, Walters had developed a close friendship with Marshal Castello Branco and others among the conspirators, as well as among Goulart's own military *dispositivo*. He reportedly wired full details of the organization of the coup to Washington a week before it took place.[21]

Walters confirmed to this author that he had been well informed on the plans for the coup. He said that his job was to find out what was going on and to report it to Ambassador Gordon. He was under no obligation, he said, to inform the Goulart government of plots against it.

18. Philip Agee, *Inside the Company: CIA Diary* (London: Penguin Books, 1975), p. 321.

19. General Vernon A. Walters, interview, 21 May 1976, Washington.

20. Bond interview.

21. Burns, *Nationalism in Brazil*, pp. 115–116.

Walters said that Goulart had felt that the United States was working against him and had asked Roberto Campos whether Walters was plotting to overthrow him. Campos responded that Walters was keeping informed but that he did not believe Walters had "authorization" to plot.[22]

Walters says that his information on the conspiracy came mostly from a group of brigadier generals in Rio de Janeiro, one of whom, in January 1964, told him, with great relief, that Castello Branco had joined the plotters. Walters and Castello Branco dined together frequently both before and after the coup, and in addition to their own friendship, which dated back to the Italian campaign, Walters' mother and Castello Branco's wife had become very close. Walters was at Castello Branco's home about three or four days after the coup when Lacerda broadcast the news that Castello Branco was to be the candidate for the presidency under the new regime. Walters was the first person to lunch with Castello Branco after his inauguration, and as the time approached for him to leave office, Castello Branco told Walters that it was only appropriate that he should share his "last supper" as well. Walters confirmed what several other principals in the events of 1964 in Brazil had suggested—that he was probably Castello Branco's best friend. Nevertheless, Walters maintains that Castello Branco never so much as hinted to him before the coup that he was involved in the plotting against Goulart.

Walters denied, of course, that he was involved in the plotting. It is apparent, however, even from the anecdotes he told this author, that there were some who saw him as a central figure in the conspiracy. Walters related, for example, that the old leftist general who was heading PETROBRAS approached him shortly before the coup, when it was clear which way the wind was blowing, and denounced the leftists in the government in an attempt to identify himself with what it appeared would be the winning side.[23]

Thomas E. Skidmore noted that a series of documentary articles published in *O Estado de São Paulo* after the coup included descriptions of three contacts between military conspirators and the Embassy before 31 March 1964. The last of these contacts is described as follows:

> A high [Brazilian] official was asked about the possibility of meeting with one of the members of the military section of the Embassy of the United States. He agreed to hold a conversation at the office of the latter.

22. Walters interview.
23. Walters interview.

The meeting took place, and on that occasion he received, couched in diplomatic language, an offer of war materials in case of necessity.[24]

The Brazilian officer, according to the article, responded that he did not expect to need additional arms, but that he might need fuel.

U.S. Army Lieutenant Colonel Robert Schuler, who was sent to Brazil immediately after the coup on a "secret" mission, told this author that the United States did not promise assistance but conceded that "if they had run into trouble, we probably would have stepped in." He further volunteered that there was a contingency plan for intervention "in case the Russians moved." Schuler maintained that the Soviets were in fact directly supporting the communist takeover that was in the offing. He implied that Soviet submarines were on hand, and he compared the situation faced by the United States to the challenges to the Monroe Doctrine in Venezuela at the turn of the century.[25]

Contingency planning, according to standard operating procedures and to several of the principals in the events, was the province of the U.S. Southern Command (SOUTHCOM) in Panama. According to Chilean journalist Robinson Rojas, this contingency planning was quite elaborate. He reported that General Andrew O'Meara, Commander of SOUTHCOM, flew to Rio de Janeiro a week before the coup to consult with Castello Branco. The assistance offered by O'Meara, which proved to be unnecessary, was said to have included dropping paratroopers from the Canal Zone in the area where Goulart attempted to hold out against the insurgents.[26]

Walters told this author that he did not recall O'Meara's having been

24. Thomas E. Skidmore, *Politics in Brazil, 1930–1964;* pp. 329–30. In its report on *Alleged Assassination Plots Involving Foreign Leaders*, the Senate Intelligence Committee noted that in 1970 the U.S. Ambassador to Chile was authorized to inform military conspirators that if a coup attempt should result in civil disorder, the U.S. would be prepared "promptly to deliver support and material that might be immediately required" (p. 232).

25. Interviews with Lieutenant Colonel Robert Schuler (U.S. Army Attaché in Brazil, April 1964–1967), 30 November 1970 and 4 October 1972, Washington, D.C. Schuler expressed the opinion that the civilian political leaders were hopelessly corrupt and obviously could not handle the business of governing, but he felt that the military men were not adequately prepared to take over the government. He recalled that shortly after he arrived in Brazil, he had met with Castello Branco's son to interpret for him U.S. laws and regulations governing the Federal Communications Commission and the Department of Defense and to determine how they might be adapted to suit the needs of their counterpart entities in Brazil.

26. Rojas, *Estados Unidos en Brazil,* pp. 72–73.

in Rio de Janeiro a week before the coup, but that he did remember that O'Meara was in the city about six months before it. Walters said that O'Meara, like most U.S. officials in Brazil, anticipated civil war. At one point in the conversation, Walters told this author that things had been "touch and go" and that as late as a week before the coup there was fear that it might not succeed, but he said that he had reassured O'Meara that "things would fall into place pretty quickly."[27]

Gordon said that he became convinced after Goulart's speech of 13 March that radical change was inevitable, the only question being, "What kind of radical change?" And he saw civil war as a real possibility. Three days after that provocative speech, Gordon departed for Washington, where he conferred with Secretary of State Dean Rusk and Assistant Secretary Thomas Mann about the situation in Brazil. He returned to Brazil on Palm Sunday, and the following day, 23 March, he assembled his ranking staff members from posts throughout the country to discuss the matter. Gordon maintained that Walters had a copy of the manifesto that was being circulated by Marshal Castello Branco, and that the 23 March meeting was the first time the importance of Castello Branco to the movement against Goulart was brought to his attention.

Gordon said that on Tuesday of the following week he, Gordon Mein, his deputy chief of mission, Walters, and the CIA station chief were assembled in his office when they received word that "the balloon was up" in Minas Gerais. The four U.S. officials remained there throughout the day to follow the progress of the rebellion. That evening, Gordon said, he paid a visit to Kubitschek in order to encourage him to prevail upon members of congress to assert themselves in the formation of a new government.

As the rebellion spread to Rio de Janeiro, Gordon recalled, there was great anxiety at the Embassy, because a couple of student demonstrations in support of the government had been planned in the vicinity. (In fact, students had approached the steps of the Ministry of War; two had been killed and several wounded.) Records were moved to the top floor of the Embassy and the air conditioner was turned off, because if a fire had been started, the air conditioner would have caused it to spread quickly. There was a great sense of relief in the Embassy when the U.S. personnel received word that the army was in control of the city. Gordon says that when they all looked to him for some profound comment, his famous first instructions were to turn the air conditioner on.[28]

27. Walters interview.
28. Gordon interview.

A *Washington Post* report that American naval units were on hand at the time of the coup "to evacuate U.S. citizens" has been confirmed in substance by several other sources. Admiral Eugene LaRocque, former Assistant Chief of Naval Operations for Strategic Plans and Director of the Inter-American Defense College, recalled that there was a carrier task group on "maneuvers" in the South Atlantic near Brazil at the time of the coup. He saw this as no coincidence, but as being in accord with the standard operating procedure of having U.S. forces on hand in areas where they might be needed, as in the cases of Guatemala in 1954, Lebanon in 1958, and the Dominican Republic on several occasions.[29]

A former CIA agent who was on assignment in Latin America at the time of the coup (and who preferred not to be named) informed this author in 1972 that the CIA had an important role in supporting the conspirators. Philip Agee's 1975 publication failed to fill in the details of the 1964 operation, but it confirmed the thrust of the "company's" efforts. Agee's diary entry for 1 April 1964 observed that "U.S. recognition of the new military government is practically immediate, not very discreet but indicative, I suppose, of the euphoria in Washington now that two and a half years of operations to prevent Brazil's slide to the left under Goulart have suddenly bloomed." Agee added, "Goulart's fall is without doubt largely due to the careful planning and consistent propaganda campaigns dating at least back to the 1962 election operation."[30]

A letter on official FBI stationery, photocopied and published in a Chilean newspaper in 1964, reads as follows:

Washington 25, D.C.
April 15, 1964

PERSONAL

Dear Mr. Brady,

I want to take this means to express my personal appreciation to each agent stationed in Brazil for the services rendered in the accomplishment of "Overhaul."

Admiration for the dynamic and efficient manner in which this large scale operation was carried out in a foreign land and under difficult conditions, has prompted me to express my gratitude. The CIA people did their part well and accomplished a great deal; however, the efforts of our agents were especially valuable. I am particularly pleased that our participation in the affair was kept secret and that the Administration did not have to make any public denials. We can all be proud of the vital part

29. Admiral Eugene LaRocque, interview, 5 April 1973, Washington, D.C.

30. Agee, *Inside the Company*, p. 362.

the FBI is playing in protecting the security of the Nation, even beyond its borders.

I am quite aware that our agents often make personal sacrifices while fulfilling their duties. Living conditions in Brazil may not be of the best but it is indeed encouraging to know that because of loyalty and a realization that you are contributing a vital if not always glamorous service to your country you stick to the job. It is this spirit which today is enabling our Bureau to successfully discharge its very grave responsibilities.

Sincerely yours,

(signed: J. E. Hoover)[31]

In his CIA diary, Agee reported from Montevideo on 5 April:

Headquarters has begun to generate hemisphere-wide propaganda in support of the new Brazilian government and to discredit Goulart. For example, Arturo Jauregui, Secretary-General of ORIT, has sent a telegram pledging ORIT support.

And on 18 April, he wrote:

Holman returned [to Montevideo] from a Chiefs of Stations conference with the grudging acknowledgement that we'll have to devote more attention to the Brazilian exiles. The decision was made, apparently by President Johnson himself, that an all-out effort must be made not only to prevent a counter-coup and insurgency in the short-run in Brazil, but also

31. The author has been unable to verify the authenticity of this letter, published in *Ultima Hora* (Santiago), 24 July 1964, p. 1. However, Agee confirmed that the FBI had an office (cryptonym ODENVY) in the Embassy in Rio de Janeiro, under Legal Attaché cover, in 1964 (*Inside the Company*, p. 356). The FBI is not authorized by law to engage in overseas operations, but its activities in connection with the narcotics smuggling business, with offering advice for public safety programs, and with apprehending fugitives from U.S. justice have given it a useful cover for gathering intelligence and other activities in foreign countries. According to Agee, Mexico is the only Latin American country in which the FBI continued regular operations against the local left when the CIA took over in 1947. Nevertheless, the Bureau has an External Affairs Division in addition to the Intelligence Division which embraces legal attachés (Ibid., p. 527). It was reported by Rowland Evans and Robert Novak (in "Hoover's Empire Abroad," *Washington Post*, 21 January 1973) that the overseas network of FBI agents had gradually been expanded to some twenty countries and that plans were being made to open FBI offices in five or six additional cities. On 17 February 1975, the *Washington Post* reported that the Bureau had sent Joseph A. Burton, a former salaried employee, to Canada to infiltrate and disrupt Communist groups in that country. An FBI spokesman, James Murphy, confirmed that the Bureau has sent Americans abroad to collect intelligence information. But he emphasized that "the FBI is not operational outside the U.S." because it sends informants abroad rather than its own agents.

to build up their security forces as fast and as effectively as possible for the long run. Never again can Brazil be permitted to slide off to the left where the communists and others become a threat to take things over or at least become a strong influence on them.[32]

Senator Frank Church, Chairman of the American Republics Subcommittee of the Senate Foreign Relations Committee, noted in 1971 that "it is not coincidental" that American aid to Brazil "was used in such a way as to support the new [post-coup] government and that [Brazil's] restrictions on foreign investment were then swept away."[33]

Brazil Declares Its Dependence

The coup d' état of 1964 resulted in a reversal of the trend toward economic nationalism and in a particularly strong repudiation of the "independent" foreign policy. One of the first acts of the new government was the revocation of the law limiting the remittance of profits by foreign firms. That act, with the opening of various areas of the national economy to foreign investments and the signing of a bilateral investment guarantee treaty, resulted in a sharply increased flow of private United States capital to Brazil. The Castello Branco government agreed to institute austerity measures for the control of inflation that had been recommended by the United States and the International Monetary Fund (IMF), and the United States, in turn, increased its economic and military aid. In fact, a $50 million loan from AID's emergency contingency fund was extended within hours after the military had taken over.[34]

The Inter-American Development Bank (IADB) and the World Bank (IBRD), both heavily influenced by their major national creditor, also dramatically increased their loans. The IADB contribution increased from an average of U.S. $22 million in FY 1962–1964, to an average of $97.7 million in the next three years.[35] And the World Bank, which had extended no loans at all to Brazil in FY 1962–1964, loaned an average

32. Agee, *Inside the Company*, pp. 363–65. Jauregui was among those listed by Agee as CIA agents.

33. Dan Griffin, "Senator Church Assails U.S. Aid to Brazil Police," *Washington Post*, 25 July 1971, p. A–2.

34. U.S., Congress, Senate, Committee on Appropriations, *Foreign Assistance and Related Appropriations for 1965*, Hearings on H.R. 11812, 88th Cong., 2d sess., 1964, pp. 26–27, 379–96.

35. Stephen S. Kaplan and Norman C. Bonsor, "Did United States Aid Really Help Brazilian Development? A Perspective of a Quarter-Century," *Inter-American Economic Affairs* 27 (Winter 1973): 25–46.

of $75.5 million in FY 1965–1967. Just a few days after the coup, the IADB approved a number of loans that the U.S. director of the bank had reportedly been prepared to veto or delay. And the IMF, which had denied loans to Brazil since 1959, came through with two $125 million "standby" credits before the end of the year. In December 1964 a program was drawn up whereby $1 billion was to be loaned to the Brazilian government for its economic development activities in 1965. USAID had agreed to contribute $375 million. About $450 million of the remainder was to be provided by the IMF, the World Bank, the U.S. Export-Import Bank, private banks, and private Brazilian creditors in the United States and Europe.[36] (See appendix, Table 1.)

Speaking on 31 July 1964 to the graduating class of the Instituto Rio Branco, the foreign service school, President Castello Branco told the young diplomats that under his government the country was to be firmly aligned with the United States and its allies of the "free world" in the struggle to protect values threatened by the Soviet sphere.

The first of President Castello Branco's foreign ministers, Vasco Leitão da Cunha, stated on a national radio and television network on 6 July 1964 that the objectives of the external policy were

> . . . to defend the traditional policy of the good neighbor in America and the security of the continent against aggression and subversion, whether external or internal; to strengthen all the ties with the United States, our great neighbor and friend of the North; to broaden our relations with Western Europe and the Western community of nations.[37]

And Leitão da Cunha's successor, retired General Juracy de Montenegro Magalhães, in a major foreign policy speech on 21 November 1966, hailed the United States as the "unquestionable leader of the Free World" and the "principal guardian of the fundamental values of our civilization."[38]

Colonel Ferdinando de Carvalho, director of the post-coup official military investigation of "communism and corruption" in the Goulart administration, charged that the "communists" (by definition, all who opposed the coup) had attempted to demoralize foreign investors, discredit the Alliance for Progress, and isolate the United States. He asserted that previous Brazilian policy that claimed to be independent was actually "superdependent because, besides creating new unnecessary dependencies, it put our country in an ambiguous position

36. Petras and Morley, "U.S.-Chilean Relations," pp. 40–50; also Jerome Levinson, interview, 13 March 1975, Washington, D.C.

37. E. Bradford Burns, "Tradition and Variation in Brazilian Foreign Policy," *Journal Of Inter-American Studies* 9 (April 1967): 195–212.

38. Ibid.

vis-à-vis the Free World, whose distrust increased to the detriment of our interests."[39]

The Brazilian role in Western Hemisphere politics in the early 1960s had been one of leadership in asserting the independence of the Latin American countries from United States influence. In the OAS, Brazil had acted as spokesman for Latin America on such issues as nonintervention and the sovereign equality of member states. This role was sharply reversed following the coup d'état of 1964; the military government under Castello Branco served as a spokesman for United States policies in the hemisphere. Foreign Minister Magalhães regarded the Western Hemisphere as the natural international stage of action for Brazil, and as the new government was particularly concerned with the maintenance of collective security against subversion in the hemisphere, its policies were in concert with those of the United States. In fact, the policies of the two countries became so closely identified that Latin diplomats and intellectuals began to speak of the "Washington-Rio Axis."[40]

Brazil's relations with Cuba were severed in May 1964, and the following June, at the ninth Inter-American Meeting of Foreign Ministers of the OAS, Brazil urged the adoption of an inter-American diplomatic and economic quarantine of the Castro government. Brazil also supported the intervention of the United States in the Dominican Republic in April 1965 and provided the commanding officer and most of the twenty-five hundred Latin American troops that were subsequently employed in the OAS "peacekeeping" operation. A colonel involved in the operation explained Brazil's participation in the following terms:

> The armed forces brilliantly stopped communism from taking over Brazil. Another brilliant example is their participation in the Dominican Republic in the operation initiated by the American marines where they also stopped communism from taking over that country.[41]

39. Colonel Ferdinando de Carvalho, "Revolutionary War in Brazil," in Fagen and Cornelius, eds., *Political Power in Latin America*, pp. 196–200. The *White Book of the Change of Government in Chile* released by the Chilean junta in an attempt to justify the coup of 1973 was so similar to the document released by the Brazilian government after the coup of 1964 that this author wondered at first glance if it had been translated in part from the Portuguese. It now appears that both may have been translations from English. The Senate Select Committee on Intelligence noted in its *Covert Action* report that two CIA collaborators had assisted the Chilian junta in the preparation of the *White Book* (p. 187).

40. Barry Sklar, "The Foreign Policy of Brazil, 1964–1969," unpublished research paper (American University, January 1970), p. 9.

41. Burns, "Tradition and Variation in Brazilian Foreign Policy," p. 208.

Magalhães subsequently visited seven South American capitals to urge support for the creation of a permanent inter-American peacekeeping force on the order of the temporary one that had been dispatched to the Dominican Republic.

President Castello Branco expressed his government's solidarity with the United States position in Vietnam. The medical team and supplies provided by his government were the only contributions by a Latin American government to the United States war effort there. In August 1964 Foreign Minister Leitão da Cunha declared that Brazil's preoccupation with the conflict in Southeast Asia was equal to that of the United States, and that Brazil would enter that war should it be transformed into a world conflict.[42] Castello Branco, furthermore, increased the purchase of United States arms from a value of U.S. $2.5 million in 1965 to U.S. $12 million in 1966.[43]

Brazil's relations with neighboring countries came to be increasingly conditioned by geopolitical considerations. Castello Branco's government became obsessed with the threat of attack from its neighbors. This led to a strategy for populating the border areas and the Amazon Basin. Geopolitical works that became popular among the military spoke ominously of the "advance of platine imperialism" from Argentina and the continuing instability in Uruguay, and frequent reference was made to the unviability of some neighboring states.[44]

A de-emphasis on relations with Africa and Asia was accompanied by an emphasis on relations with the West. The abandonment of informal recognition of a divided Germany and of support for African nationalism resulted in improved relations with West Germany and Portugal.

The 1964 coup had taken place while the United Nation Conference on Trade and Development (UNCTAD) was underway in Geneva. Whereas Brazil had entered the Conference as a leader of the Latin American states most committed to radical change, the new delegation named in mid-stream urged moderation. Although Brazil's voting record on the forty-five disputed resolutions finally passed by the conference placed the country far from the extreme opposition demonstrated by the United States, Brazil's voting more nearly approximated that of the United States than did the record of any other

42. Vladimir Reisky de Dubnic, "Trends in Brazil's Foreign Policy," *New Perspectives of Brazil*, ed. Eric N. Baklanoff (Nashville, Tenn.: Vanderbilt University Press, 1966), pp. 78–100.

43. Burns, *Nationalism in Brazil* p. 116.

44. Caio Lossio Botelho, *Brasil: A Europa dos Tropicos* (Rio de Janeiro: Gráfica Record Editôra, 1967), p. 130.

Latin American country.[45] One observer maintained that Brazil had played a key role in pulling the Latin Americans out of the bloc of underdeveloped countries, thus allowing the Western powers to get their way.[46]

Following the 1964 coup, United Nations votes on such ideologically charged issues as the seating of Communist China and the status of Portugal's African colonies were reversed.[47] However, while the military rulers viewed the workings of the international system as a struggle between East and West, they did not sever relations with the Soviet Union and its East European allies; in fact, they significantly increased trade with the area. Ironically, they reasoned that unlike their civilian predecessors, they could not be suspected by the United States or by conservative domestic groups of being "soft" on communism, and that as long as their internal security measures minimized the circulation of Marxist literature and ideas, they need not allow ideological conflict to jeopardize the development of a profitable economic relationship.[48]

The United States Extols Dictatorship

Writing in the mid-1960s, journalist Edmundo Moniz, sociologist Nelson Werneck Sodre, political scientist Helio Jaguaribe, and economist Celso Furtado viewed the U.S. economic objectives in their native Brazil and in the rest of Latin America as leading inevitably to authoritarian rule. Moniz said:

> In reality, the movement of April was not against communism or even those who defended consequentially or inconsequentially the nationalist cause. . . . The objective was to keep Brazil from escaping the status of a semi-colony.[49]

Sodre suggested that the "U.S. imperialists" recognized what the Brazilian radical left did not—that democratic reforms were steps toward socialism and thus were threatening to the interests of foreign capitalists. He maintained that events in Brazil did not indicate that "imperialism" had grown stronger—only more frantic. It is natural, Sodre said, that when persuasion no longer suffices to repress

45. Storrs, "Brazil's Independent Foreign Policy," pp. 410–11.

46. The comment was contained in a letter from Hamza Alavi to Andre Gunder Frank, according to a letter of 6 March 1973 from Frank to the author.

47. Interviews with William Kelly, Bureau of Intelligence and Research, State Department, 28 October 1969, Washington, D.C., and Affonso Celso de Ouro-Preto, Political Officer, Brazilian Embassy, 7 November 1969, Washington, D.C.

48. José Oswaldo de Meira Penna, "Brazilian Relations with Eastern Europe," *Studies on the Soviet Union* [Munich, Germany] 3 (1968): 81–90.

49. Edmundo Moniz, *O Golpe de Abril* (Rio de Janeiro: Editôra Civilização Brasileira, 1965), p. 49.

resistance, the ultimate and only recourse is military violence. He compared it to an orchestra reduced to a single instrument.[50]

Jaguaribe characterized the Castello Branco government as having "an intrinsic propensity for becoming a colonial fascist regime." He explained that a regime lacking support at home must seek it abroad:

> Given the present conditions prevailing in Latin America, the simple truth is that right-wing nationalism cannot hope to win a clear victory over colonial fascist tendencies. Since it emphasizes the preservation of the existing social order as much as does colonial fascism, it would require external aid, for both economic and political reasons, and could not remain nationalist without losing support both at home and abroad.[51]

Celso Furtado linked repression in Brazil to U.S. economic policies:

> The U.S. government's program for development in Latin America, based as it is on the activities of the great American business corporations and on preventive control of 'subversion' is not viable, except as a means of freezing the social status quo. . . . State action would therefore have to be essentially repressive in character.[52]

Finally, Moniz said:

> It would be nice to know, after all that has happened, what is the present condition of Brazil— if the American government continues to have permission to intervene in internal Brazilian politics, in order to change the regime or those who govern.[53]

Ambassador Gordon told this author in 1975 that he had hoped, in 1964, for the reestablishment of civilian rule in Brazil and had been surprised and dismayed by the issuance of the institutional acts that served as the vehicles of increasingly authoritarian rule. At the time, however, for U.S. as well as Brazilian audiences, Gordon and other spokesmen of the executive branch expressed only unqualified praise of the new regime.

Testifying before the House Foreign Affairs Committee in hearings on the Foreign Assistance Act of 1965, General O'Meara said of the 1964 coup d'état, "The nation needed it in order to free itself of a corrupt government which was about to sell us [sic] out to international communism."[54]

In anticipation of the first anniversary of the "revolution" in 1965,

50. Nelson Werneck Sôdre, *Introdução a revolução brasileira*, 3d ed. (Rio de Janeiro: Editôa, Civilização Brasileira, 1967), pp. 254–55.

51. Jaguaribe, *Economic and Political Development* p. 190.

52. Celso Furtado, "U.S. Hegemony and the Future of Latin America," in *Latin American Radicalism*, ed. Horowitz, Castro, and Gerassi, pp. 73–74.

53. Moniz, *O Golpe de Abril*, p. 33.

54. U.S., Congress, House, Committee on Foreign Affairs, *Foreign Assistance Act of 1965*, Hearings, 89th Cong., 1st sess., 16–19 March 1965, p. 783.

Secretary of State Dean Rusk spoke glowingly of how, under Castello Branco, "the situation has changed dramatically for the better. Political stability has been restored. The climate which helped the Communists and other extremists infiltrate and exercise disproportionate influence has given way to one which inhibits violence and extreme actions." As Ambassador, and later as Assistant Secretary of State for Inter-American Affairs (1966–1967), Gordon lavished praise on the government of Castello Branco, describing it as "totally democratic" and "the best government Brazil has ever had," and referring to the "revolution" as "the single most decisive victory for freedom in the mid-twentieth century."[55] In a speech to Brazil's Superior War College (ESG) on 5 May 1964, Gordon heralded the "revolution" as an event which "may well take its place alongside the initiation of the Marshall Plan, the ending of the Berlin Blockade, the defeat of Communist aggression in Korea, and the solution of the Cuban missile-base crisis as one of the critical points of inflection in mid-twentieth century world history."[56]

In 1969, having departed from government service, Gordon expressed second thoughts about the ongoing "revolution." At that time he joined some three-hundred scholars in sending cablegrams to the Brazilian government protesting the arbitrary "retirement" of scholars in that country. By the time of the official visit of President Médici to the United States in December 1971, a large number of U.S. legislators, scholars, clergymen, and other citizens had publicly expressed bitter criticism of the systematic repression in Brazil and of U.S. support for such a government, but the official position of the United States remained one of strong support and unadulterated praise. On the occasion of that visit, President Nixon said of General Médici that "in the brief time that he has been president of Brazil there has been more progress than in any comparable time in the whole history of that country." Nixon added, "We know that as Brazil goes, so will go the rest of that Latin American continent."[57] And Treasury Secretary John Connally was quoted by *Jornal do Brasil* in early 1972 as having said that "the United States could well look to the Brazilian example to put its own economy in order."[58]

55. Sklar, "Foreign Policy of Brazil, 1964–1969," p. 9, and E. Bradford Burns, "Brazil: The Imitative Society," *The Nation*, 10 July 1972, pp. 17–20.

56. Lincoln Gordon, "Letter to the Editors," *Commonweal*, August 1970, reprinted in Committee of Returned Volunteers, *Brazil: Who Pulls the Strings, or Alliance for Repression.* (Chicago, n.d.).

57. "Visit of President Médici of the Federative Republic of Brazil," *Weekly Compilation of Presidential Documents*, vol. 7, no. 50, 13 December 1971, pp. 1625–26. See also *O Estado de São Paulo*, 30 January 1972.

58. *Jornal do Brasil*, 4 February 1972.

A decade after the coup, however, U.S. spokesmen were still going out of their way to deny U.S. complicity. In late 1973, Jack Kubisch, Assistant Secretary of State for Inter-American Affairs, addressing the Inter-American Council of Washington, D.C., was asked if the United States had been involved in any way in the overthrow of the government of Salvador Allende in Chile. Kubisch responded that the United States had had nothing whatsoever to do with that coup. And he added, gratuitously, that the United States had had nothing to do with the 1964 coup in Brazil either.

We have seen that for a number of reasons Brazil, in 1964, was particularly vulnerable to a coup d'état. Structural dysfunctions in the economy, some induced by domestic causes, some externally imposed, had generated an atmosphere of crisis. The military, as a predominantly middle-class institution, saw in the increasing demands of the masses a threat to its material well-being and social status. But the mobilization of the lower classes had proceeded only far enough to frighten the upper and middle classes. Strong and autonomous grass roots organization was virtually nonexistent. The "independent" foreign policy, designed in part to contribute to the building of a popular base, proved too dangerous for a government that did not already have a well-organized popular base. The outcome, then, of the crisis of the early 1960s was a veto coup, toppling a constitutional regime and establishing in its place a regime with sufficient authoritarian control to favor the upper and middle classes and to repress with force effective demand on the part of the masses.

Although the full extent of U.S. complicity in the Brazilian "revolution" may never be generally known, it is clear to this author that the United States was prepared to go to great lengths to reverse the trends toward economic nationalism and popular mobilization that had been accelerating under the Goulart government. The United States generously supported the new military regime; the military regime, in turn, reversed most of the foreign policies that had been identified with the short-lived "independent" era, particularly those that had placed constraints on foreign capital. Under the military, Brazil also apparently assumed the role of cooperative subparamount to the United States in the South American continent.

Part II:

Linkage Groups and the
Denationalization
of Interests
and Values

Introduction

In light of many factors—the extent of concern or panic, freely admitted (then and since) by U.S. officials involved in making or implementing policy toward Brazil at the time of the 1964 coup; the verifiable extent of U.S. foreknowledge and encouragement of the coup; the circumstantial evidence of covert complicity; and the apparent willingness to resort to open armed intervention if opposition to the coup had gotten out of hand—the remarkable aspect of the outcome was that Ambassador Gordon was able to assert to a congressional committee in 1966 that "the Brazilian revolution of 1964 was a purely 100 percent Brazilian product, not a hidden U.S. product in any way, shape, or manner."[1] And the United States was able to avoid the kind of embarrassment and international condemnation it suffered in the wake of the intervention in the Dominican Republic a year later.

The explanation appears to lie in the fact that there were a sufficient number of important individuals and groups in Brazil who were willing or anxious to conspire with the United States to undermine and finally depose the elected government of their own country. This "internalization of external influence" is by no means new or unusual.[2] Such misalliances have been commonplace in Latin America (as elsewhere) since the conquest. But the processes and relationships involved are sadly understudied.

The individuals and groups of the dependent countries who tend to be drawn into such misalliances might be designated "stringers," "linkage groups," and "transnational subcultures." Stringers, a concept borrowed by Espartaco from the news business, are individuals

1. "Brazil's Independent Foreign Policy, 1961–1964."
2. Phrase coined by José Nun, *Latin America: The Hegemonic Crisis and the Military Coup* (Berkeley: University of California Press, 1969), pp. 53–54.

who serve as information conduits for and promote the interests of external actors for money or as a quid pro quo for the promotion or protection of their interests in their own societies.[3] The "linkage group" concept, as employed by Karl Deutsch, refers to groups within the domestic polity which have particular ties with the international environment.[4] A subculture, which may be subnational or transnational, has been defined by Abdul Said as "any group whose shared, mutually reinforcing sets of expectations have led to stereotyped behavior . . . [encompassing] some sense of distinctive group identification."[5] Individuals whose group allegiances are unstable (e.g., opportunistic politicians), or whose ties to external forces tend to be for short-term purposes, could be seen as stringers, and groups with well-established mind-sets or long-term interests that transcend national frontiers (groups such as the military or the managerial or technocratic functionaries of the multinational corporations) might be seen as components of transnational subcultures. For the sake of simplicity, however, the term "linkage group" will generally be used to incorporate all the above categories.

Such groups undergo a process of denationalization—of self-imposed existential or spiritual exile from the national community—to the extent that their values and attitudes cease to derive from the common experience of the common people, or even from the common experience of a national elite, and are ingested instead from an external reference group. This alienation of values will generally be found to have been preceded by, or to have evolved in conjunction with, an alienation of material or status interests. For example, when the material advancement of a linkage group is unaffected by or actually damaged by measures conducive to the material advancement of the majority of the national community, and when it is enhanced by collaboration with a foreign group, it may be said that the interests of that linkage group have been denationalized.

In "External Influences on the Internal Behavior of States," Karl Deutsch has theorized that there are several means by which external influences exerted through linkage groups may be diminished. These include: (1) breaking input links; (2) reducing linkage groups; (3) tying linkage groups to the domestic community or diminishing their in-

3. Espartaco, "The 'Latin American Crisis,' " pp. 31–34.

4. Karl Deutsch, "External Influences on the Internal Behavior of States," in Farrell, ed, *Approaches to Comparative and International Politics.*

5. Abdul A. Said, ed., *Protagonists of Change: Subcultures in Development and Revolution* (Englewood Cliffs N.J.: Prentice-Hall, 1971), p. 7.

fluence upon it; and (4) strengthening the domestic system through measures such as social, political, and economic integration and enhancement of "legitimacy."[6]

Reversing the model—that is, (1) expanding input links; (2) cultivating and strengthening linkage groups; (3) alienating hypertrophied linkage groups from the national community; and (4) contributing to the disintegration of the domestic system through the generation of fear and economic chaos, for example—sets the mechanics of subversive penetration into motion.

Former CIA Deputy Director Richard Bissell has described the penetrative process as consciously employed by his agency:

> Covert intervention is usually designed to operate on the internal power balance, often with fairly short-term objectives in view. . . . The essence of such intervention in the internal power balance is the identification of allies who can be rendered more effective, more powerful and perhaps wiser through covert assistance. Typically these local allies know the source of the assistance but neither they nor the United States could afford to admit to its existence. Agents for fairly minor and low sensitivity interventions, for instance, some covert propaganda and certain economic activities, can be recruited simply with money. But for the larger and more sensitive interventions, the allies must have their own motivation.[7]

In the larger picture of penetration and the development of dependence relationships, the short-term, unequivocally subversive activities of the CIA probably pale to insignificance beside the long-term infusion of U.S. assistance and investment in Latin America, an infusion that has caused the motivations of many well-positioned foreign nationals to coincide or dovetail with those of agents of U.S. government and business.

The formal program of U.S. bilateral economic assistance to Brazil was begun in 1942, with a wartime focus on minerals exploration. From 1946 through 1961, economic and military assistance, predominantly in the form of loans, amounted to more than $1.6 billion. More than $400 million more was authorized (though not expended) in 1962 and 1963. The total for the period from 1964 through 1970 was about $2 billion, constituting the third largest program of U.S. "assistance" in the world (following U.S. aid to Vietnam and India).

---

6. Most of these methods were to some extent consciously employed by and to some extent forced upon the Soviet Union, the People's Republic of China, and Cuba following their revolutions.

7. Miles Wolpin, *Military Aid and Counterrevolution in the Third World* (Lexington, Mass.: D. C. Heath & Co., 1972), p. 106.

Meanwhile, U.S. private investment in the country had increased from about U.S. $1 billion in 1961 to U.S. $1.6 billion in 1969, amounting to about 14 percent of U.S. private investment in Latin America. (See Appendix, Tables 2 and 3.) Annual bilateral trade, by the end of the 1960s, exceeded $1.4 billion, representing 30 percent of Brazil's imports and 26 percent of its exports.[8]

Senator Allen J. Ellender was shocked and dismayed on his 1966 visit to Brazil to find that, aside from the Embassy staff itself and Peace Corps Volunteers, the total complement of U.S. personnel in the country had almost tripled in less than a decade—from 542 in fiscal 1958 to 1,357 in 1967. Including the 96–member Embassy staff, 565 Peace Corps Volunteers, and "quite a list of agency attachés," official U.S. representation amounted to more than 2,100, and the U.S. payroll included about an equal number of local employees.[9]

Ambassador John W. Tuthill, who assumed the post in 1966, was also appalled at the size of the U.S. contingent in Brazil and, over the vehement opposition of the departments and agencies involved (particularly the military), Tuthill initiated Operation Topsy, a gradual weeding-out process whereby U.S. representation was cut back to 1,104 by 1969 and 898 by 1971. Nevertheless, after the 1971 Senate hearings on U.S. Policies and Programs in Brazil, Senator Church observed that, without counting the Peace Corps, the U.S. still had twice as many officials in Brazil in proportion to the host country population as the British had had in India "when they were providing the government for that entire country."[10] Furthermore, while official representation was shrinking in the late 1960s, the local U.S. business community continued to grow. By 1972 the Brazilian-American Chamber of Commerce had 1,650 members in São Paulo alone.[11]

8. U.S. Congress, Senate Committee on Foreign Relations, Subcommittee on Western Hemisphere Affairs, *United States Policies and Programs in Brazil* Hearings, 92d Cong., 1st sess., 4, 5, and 11 May 1971 (hereafter cited as Church Hearings), pp. 164–257. See also Agency for International Development, *U.S. Foreign Aid and the Alliance for Progress: Proposed Fiscal Year 1971 Program* (Washington: Government Printing Office, 1970); and Ronald A. Krieger, *Brazil* (New York: First National City Bank, March 1971), p. 59.

9. U.S., Congress, Senate, Senator Allen J. Ellender, Report to the Committee on Appropriations, *Review of United States Government Operations in Latin America* (hereafter cited as Ellender Report), Senate Document no. 18, 90th Cong., 1st sess. 1966, pp. 332–400.

10. Church Hearings, p. 275; and Dan Griffin, "Sen. Church Assails U.S. Aid to Brazil Police," *Washington Post*, 25 July 1971.

11. *Brazilian Information Bulletin*, no. 8 (October 1972), p. 9, reprinted from *Miami Herald*, 27 August 1972.

U.S. economic assistance to Brazil from FY 1946 through FY 1973 amounted to $4.3 billion in loans and $655 million in grants.[12] Bilateral development assistance extended through AID was decreasing in the early 1970s, but overall foreign aid to Brazil was increasing as a consequence of increases in military assistance and in loans from the U.S. Export-Import Bank and international leading institutions. Brazil had become the best customer of the Export-Import Bank and the largest single recipient of loans from the IBRD. And, as we shall see in subsequent chapters, both U.S. military assistance and U.S. private investment were increasing dramatically.

The chapters that follow trace some of the means through which the expansion of input links, through the infusion of U.S. dollars and the burgeoning U.S. presence, contributed to the proliferation and strengthening of linkage groups, the alienation of those groups from the national community, and their complicity in the dissolution of a pluralistic political system. We shall also see how such groups were used, and in some cases subsequently abused, in the process of the institutionalization of the military dictatorship.

12. U.S., Central Intelligence Agency, *National Intelligence Handbook* (Washington, D.C.: Government Printing Office, January, 1976), p. 23.

[3]

Electoral Economics: Co-optation of the Political Elites

Celso Furtado has asserted that for the United States to protect its investments and its military presence in Brazil, it must avoid having a government there that it cannot control.[1] One of the means by which the United States has attempted to maintain control has been the exercise of a veto over groups to which a government (or power contender) might appeal, or from which it might "accept" support.

Testifying on 18 February 1963 before the Subcommittee on Inter-American Affairs of the House Committee on Foreign Affairs, Edwin M. Martin, then Assistant Secretary of State for Inter-American Affairs, explained:

> There certainly have been occasions in which presidential candidates have sought Communist support. . . . It is one of the things we are concerned about, and rather regularly talk to presidential candidates and their immediate associates to try to assure they are aware that this camel's nose under the tent cannot always be gotten out easily. It is a matter of concern. We don't like candidates who seek this kind of support.[2]

Other means of exercising control have included weakening a regime's supporters, strengthening its adversaries, and using carrot-and-stick leverage to sway the uncommitted. This chapter will deal with some of the means employed by the United States to co-opt political elites and to influence the outcome of elections in such a way as to weaken the Goulart government and to strengthen its adversaries.

1. Furtado interview.
2. Andre Gunder Frank, "Brazil and Pakistan: A Comparison of American Aid," manuscript provided to the author by A. G. Frank, 6 March 1973 (Santiago: University of Chile, n.d.).

"Islands of Sanity" and Centers of Revolt

The strategy adopted in mid-1963 in lieu of the traditional government-to-government aid became known as the "islands of sanity" policy. As then-Assistant Secretary of State for Inter-American Affairs Thomas Mann later testified, the policy meant that instead of providing balance of payments support, budgetary support, or any other kind of assistance that benefited the federal government directly, the Agency for International Development gave support to "states which were headed by good governors we think strengthened democracy."[3]

Ambassador Gordon, originator of the phrase "islands of sanity," insisted that his own objective for the policy was to keep Alliance for Progress projects going in Brazil, but he conceded to this author in 1975 that others such as Thomas Mann, who were less committed to Alliance goals, apparently saw it primarily in political terms. Gordon acknowledged that there was no legislative authority for direct aid to state governments or private entities, but he maintained that the aid agreements were cleared by Brazil's federal government.[4]

A General Accounting Office report issued in 1968 strongly criticized AID for deficiencies in both planning and implementation of eleven major capital projects involving more than $100 million in U.S. funds authorized between 1963 and 1965 (ten "just prior to," and one after, the "revolution").[5] AID's defense for its mismanagement of these projects was summed up by the GAO as follows.

> AID considered that it was impossible to support a coherent economic and social program by the Brazilian government, and given the increasingly extremist political trends of the administration then ruling, AID adopted a strategy of cooperation with individual Brazilian State governments, autonomous public agencies, and the private sector to the extent that this was possible.
>
> An AID official informed us that the accelerating rate of inflation had made the planning of projects virtually impossible. He further stated that overriding United States political and diplomatic interests had required the continuation of some financial assistance; this was a key part of United States policy toward Brazil at that time. AID believed that, to implement that policy, it was essential to do a limited amount of lending to those state institutions with which it was possible to work out effective projects. AID considered that political and economic conditions during 1964, 1965 and 1966 had improved measurably.

3. Bell, "Brazilian-American Relations," p. 89.

4. Gordon interview.

5. Comptroller General of the United States, *Review of Administration of United States Assistance for Capital Development Projects in Brazil*, Report to the Congress, no. B–133283, 16 May 1968.

In the 1971 Senate hearings on U.S. Policies and Programs in Brazil, William A. Ellis, U.S. AID Director in Brazil, testified that the projects criticized by the GAO had been part of "a deliberate strategy, to support state governors or regional institutions which were ready to cooperate with the United States in the development of these states or institutions under the Alliance for Progress." Further testimony on the matter was deleted from the public record.[6]

The "islands of sanity" policy apparently served as a catchall categorization for most aspects of the political use of U.S. assistance in the period of a year or two preceding the coup, and its full scope remains a matter of speculation. Among the governors most frequently cited by scholars and journalists as beneficiaries of U.S. largesse in that period have been Carlos Lacerda of Guanabara, José de Magalhães Pinto of Minas Gerais, Adhemar de Barros of São Paulo, Cid Sampaio of Pernambuco, and Aluisio Alves of Rio Grande do Norte.[7] About half of the money involved in the eleven projects criticized by the GAO was earmarked for the Northeast. Most of the remainder of the expenditures authorized before the coup was destined for the states of Guanabara and Minas Gerais.[8]

On the negative side, Miguel Arraes apparently enjoyed top priority among intended victims of this immediately and specifically political use of economic assistance. By 1962, Arraes, Mayor of Recife, had come to be considered the most effective advocate of radical change in the Northeast. He insisted that this change could be achieved within the framework of the constitution and without violence, but his critics labeled him a communist and a dangerous subversive. His most controversial program was a literacy campaign in Recife: it utilized a primer that contained such inflammatory phrases as "Democracy is a government of the people, by the people, and for the people."[9]

Arraes was nominated by the Brazilian Labor Party for the governorship of Pernambuco. Elections were to be held in October and the incumbent governor, Cid Sampaio, was prohibited by law from running for reelection. Sampaio was Arraes' brother-in-law, but he was a member of the UDN, and he drew support from the economic elite of Pernambuco. Furthermore, Sampaio harbored hopes of running for na-

6. Church Hearings, p. 250.

7. Interviews with Marcio Moreira Alves, 10 March 1972, Washington, D.C., and Pat Holt, 2 February 1973, Washington, D.C.; also Stepan, *The Military in Politcs*, p. 125; Bell, "Brazilian-American Relations"; and Rojas, *Estados Unidos en Brazil*, pp. 83–84.

8. Comptroller General's *Report*, no. B–133283, p. 10.

9. Joseph A. Page, *The Revolution That Never Was*, p. 111.

tional office in 1965, and he considered it essential that his party's candidate, João Cleofas, succeed him. He assigned another brother-in-law to serve as liaison between IBAD, which had established an office in Recife early in the campaign, and the local Cleofas forces.

Circumventing the Superintendency for the Development of the Northeast (SUDENE), on 6 June 1962, just as the Recife mission was beginning to function, U.S. AID signed a $1 million accord with Governor Sampaio for a crash program of school construction. It was funded apart from the $131 million encompassed in the U.S.-Brazilian Northeast Agreement, and, according to Joseph Page, it amounted to "a desperate and unsuccessful attempt on the part of U.S. AID to help defeat Miguel Arraes."

The North Americans in Recife had supported Cleofas quite openly, and CIA agents had confidently predicted an easy win for him, "in part because their imperfect grasp of Portuguese forced [the North Americans] to rely heavily on information from the relatively few Northeasterners (mostly upper class) who could speak English." The electoral victory of Arraes convinced the American colony that the communists were about to take over the state.

Page maintains that there was never a hint of a state policy of harassment against Americans, but Arraes made no secret of his resentment of U.S. policies and attitudes. At one point he said, "You talk of us as if we were an international menace, and what we are is a poor region full of suffering and human problems."[10]

Arraes was informed shortly after he took office that U.S. AID was prepared to work with him on the agreement that had been signed by his predecessor. But Arraes did not see these accords as an unmixed blessing. He noted that "by parcelling out its aid among various projects in Pernambuco, each of which it finances only in relatively small part, the USAID Mission was demanding and getting control over the entire state financial and administrative apparatus concerned with these projects." Particularly disturbed by the fact that the U.S. government was thereby dictating Pernambuco state educational policy, Arraes appointed a study group to reexamine the accords.[11] The group found them to be in violation both of the Brazilian constitution, which reserves official relations with foreign governments to the federal government, and of the Northeast Agreement, which by the Brazilian interpretation would have required the participation of SUDENE. Arraes, following the recommendation of his study group, abrogated the accords.

10. Ibid., pp. 74–141.
11. Frank, "Brazil and Pakistan."

Apart from Pernambuco and Rio Grande do Norte, the "islands of sanity" most highly favored by the United States were Guanabara, governed by Carlos Lacerda; Minas Gerais, governed by José de Magalhães Pinto; and São Paulo, governed by Adhemar de Barros. Defending itself against GAO criticisms of a loan (authorized on 17 September 1962) of $4 million to the Industrial Development Bank (COPEG) of Guanabara, U.S. AID noted that "the governor of the state of Guanabara was then Carlos Lacerda, who had an active development plan for the state, was an able administrator and was favorably disposed to the U.S." AID maintained that the loan was made in the expectation that the federal government would provide an exchange risk guaranty for the project (a claim which the GAO found dubious). No federal guaranty was obtained until after the "revolution," but AID explained that "given the developing political situation in Brazil and the key role played in it by Governor Lacerda, it was deemed inadvisable to deobligate the loan."[12]

Lacerda had long been a harsh critic of (some would say conspirator against) Goulart and Goulart's political mentor, Vargas, and, when it suited his purposes, had been a "friend" of the United States. Initially one of Quadros' strongest supporters, Lacerda had broken with him and publicly criticized his foreign policies by August 1961. Robinson Rojas maintained that the U.S. ambassador had promised Lacerda the lion's share of Alliance for Progress funds so that he could construct demonstration projects that would serve as a "trampoline to get to the presidency of Brazil." Rojas observed that from the end of 1961 until 1963, the state of Guanabara, with four million inhabitants and the highest standard of living in the twenty-two states of Brazil, received from the U.S. $71 million, which was spent on works bearing the enormous sign: "Works of the Government of Carlos Lacerda." By way of comparison, Rojas noted that the Northeast, with a population of twenty million and a standard of living among the lowest in the world, received in the same period only $13 million in U.S. assistance.[13]

Jean Marc von der Weid, who later became president of the National Student Union (UNE) and suffered imprisonment and torture in the hands of the "revolutionary" government, told this author that in 1964, as a teenager, he had been recruited to serve with one of a number of armed groups organized by the management of American Light and Power to support Lacerda. He was stationed at Lacerda's palace on the night the coup got under way. His group had submachine guns, but

---

12. Comptroller General's *Report*, no. B–133283, Appendix II, p. 8.
13. Rojas, *Estados Unidos en Brazil*, pp. 62–66.

they were without ammunition until a long black limousine arrived. The back seat had been removed and in its place were containers that looked like caskets, full of ammunition. The man who got out and began distributing the ammunition was speaking in English.[14]

In 1966 Lacerda reported that Ambassador Gordon had told him that he was grateful that the Brazilian military had overthrown Goulart so that it was not necessary for the U.S. military to do so. The U.S. Embassy, of course, denied that the statement had been made.[15]

Former Foreign Affairs and Finance Minister San Thiago Dantas reportedly informed Goulart before the coup that the United States had promised the Brazilian conspirators that it would support a "free government" established in São Paulo if Goulart managed to hold Rio de Janeiro.[16] Reputable Brazilian journalists also reported having learned from the governors of São Paulo and Minas Gerais that prior to the coup the U.S. had offered them substantial military assistance in case of civil conflict. They reported that they were told that if they declared a state of belligerency against the Goulart government, they could depend on an infusion of helicopters, machine guns, rifles, and other military equipment.[17] Robinson Rojas reported that on 17 March 1964, Ambassador Gordon, had suggested to Castello Branco that the state of Minas Gerais would be a good place to initiate the rebellion, and that President Johnson had pledged immediate recognition "to any rebel government that proclaims itself in Brazilian territory and asks military assistance, in the name of democracy, to fight against international communism and President Goulart."[18]

General Vernon Walters told this author that there had been several groups plotting a coup more or less separately, though each knew of the others' existence. The major ones were the Sorbonne group, headed by Castello Branco; Lacerda's group; a group centering around Adhemar de Barros, which included General Oswaldo Cordeiro de Farias (of BEF and ESG prominence), General Nelson de Melo, who had formerly commanded the Second Army in São Paulo, and General Olympio Mourão Filho, commander of the Fourth Army but headquartered in Minas Gerais; and a younger group of officers led by

14. Jean Marc von der Weid, interview, 23 February 1973, Washington, D.C.

15. Storrs, "Brazil's Independent Foreign Policy," p. 392.

16. Jerome Levinson and Juan de Onis, The Alliance that Lost its Way: A Critical Report on the Alliance for Progress (Chicago: Quadrangle Books, 1970), p. 89.

17. Sidney Lens, "Brazil's Police State," The Progressive 30 (December 1966): 31–35.

18. Rojas, Estados Unidos en Brazil, p. 112.

General José Pinheiro de Ulhoa Cintra and apparently, to some extent, by Costa e Silva. Walters reported that Mourão Filho had drawn Magalhães Pinto into the plotting.[19]

The major obstacle to a successful coup appeared to be General Amaury Kruel, commander of the Second Army. Niles Bond said that the CIA was in contact with colonels in the Second Army who were involved in the plotting and that Kruel's brother was attached to Lacerda's plotters, but that Kruel seemed inclined to remain loyal to Goulart.[20] John W. F. Dulles reported that Ambassador Gordon told him that when an American resident of São Paulo asked on 31 March what could be done to support the movement against Goulart, Gordon said that Kruel should be persuaded to join it.[21]

On 31 March, in the state of Minas Gerais, Governor Magalhães Pinto and General Mourão Filho announced on the radio that the revolution to save Brazil from communism had begun, and a contingent of the Fourth Army began its march toward Rio de Janeiro. General Luiz Tavares da Cunha Mello, attempting to defend the government, led a contingent of the First Army against the troops of Mourão Filho, but most of his units defected and Cunha Mello was soon captured. The War Ministry changed hands several times on 31 March, but by the time Cunha Mello was brought in General Costa e Silva was in charge and he was accompanied by General Vernon Walters.[22]

Meanwhile, in São Paulo, U.S. Consul General Niles Bond paid a visit to Governor Adhemar de Barros at five o'clock on the afternoon of 31 March. Bond told the author that the governor was a personal friend of his and had briefed him some months earlier on the plans for the coup, but he maintained that his appointment that day was in relation to a matter of cultural exchange. Bond said that de Barros was in a state of anxiety, and that the governor spoke with Magalhães Pinto on the telephone several times while Bond was in the office. The launching of the revolution in Minas Gerais had been premature; the anticipated next step had been for São Paulo to join in the rebellion, but General Kruel was still holding out. General Nelson de Melo "happened to stop by" the governor's office, however, in time to have a chat with Bond and Bond said that de Melo was less worried than de Barros about the indecision of Kruel.

Bond said his "guess" was that if Kruel had announced that he was

19. Walters interview.

20. Bond interview.

21. John W. F. Dulles, *Unrest in Brazil: Political Military Crises 1955–1964* (Austin: University of Texas Press, 1970), pp. 324–25.

22. Walters interview.

remaining loyal to Goulart, he would have been arrested by Nelson de Melo and his loyalists, and de Melo would have taken control of the Second Army.[23] General Walters said that in fact Nelson de Melo went down to arrest Kruel and replace him, but Kruel's brother ultimately "bridged the gap."[24] Just after midnight on April 1, Kruel announced on the radio his adherence to the revolution.

In Pernambuco, Cid Sampaio and his colleagues kept U.S. consular officials informed of the conspirators' plan from the very beginning. The Fourth Army, headquartered in Pernambuco, had early cast its lot with the opponents of Goulart. As the rebellion spread to the Northeast, Governor Arraes, hoping to avoid conflict, had ordered the state police to stay in their barracks. A crowd of university students, however, attempting to reach the governor's palace to demonstrate their support for him, faced off with troops of the Fourth Army. The troops fired into the crowd and two students were killed. The palace was surrounded by troops and Arraes was informed that he had been removed from office. Arraes, refusing to "consent to be deposed," was placed under arrest and later imprisoned in a military installation on the island of Fernando de Noronha. The Supreme Court ordered his release in April 1965, but the military in Pernambuco kept arresting him, so in May he took asylum in the Algerian Embassy and flew to Algiers, where he took up permenent residence.[25]

Much has been written about the tendency for revolutions to consume their own children. The case of Brazil suggests that the same may be true of counterrevolutions. Cid Sampaio, feeling that he was in line for a major appointment, had cast a covetous eye on the directorship of SUDENE, but his ambitions clashed with those of an old adversary, General Cordeiro de Farias. The latter not only vetoed any appointment for Sampaio, but also threatened to prosecute him or to deprive him of his political rights.[26]

General Walters said that the U.S. Embassy had expected Carlos Lacerda to succeed Castello Branco in the presidency, but that Lacerda had retarded the return of civilian government by "behaving strangely."[27] Only a year after the coup, Lacerda decried the new "politics of technocrats, clasping a neo-colonialist concept of Brazil."[28] In 1967 he

23. Bond interview.

24. Walters interview.

25. Page, *The Revolution That Never Was*, pp. 142–224.

26. Ibid., pp. 199–211.

27. Walters interview.

28. Carlos Lacerda, *Brasil entre a verdade e a mentira* (Rio de Janeiro: Bloch Editôres, 1965).

noted a growing current of anti-Americanism in Brazil because the United States had been "indiscreet in interfering in Brazilian political affairs and unwise in business and aid relationships." Indicting the U.S. Embassy and the CIA, he added, "I am convinced that the U.S. helped with the 1964 revolution."[29]

By the end of the decade, Lacerda, Aluisio Alves, and Adhemar de Barros had been deprived of their political rights. Magalhães Pinto fared better than most of his civilian co-conspirators: he became the third foreign affairs minister of the "revolutionary" government. By 1973, however, he too was publicly bemoaning the loss of liberty. In a speech before the Senate on the thirtieth anniversary of the Manifesto dos Mineiros of 1943, he read those parts of the manifesto which demanded the return of constitutional guarantees; he asserted that the manifesto was relevant to the present situation, and that in making the speech he was symbolically signing it again.[30]

The Brazilian Institute of Democratic Action

Converging in support of some of the same individuals served by the "islands of sanity" policy, but operating on a much broader scale, was an organization (or organizational complex) known as the Brazilian Institute of Democratic Action (Instituto Brasileiro de Ação Democrática—IBAD). This organization, founded in 1959 with the alleged objective of "defending democracy," penetrated, or established links with, virtually all of the groups having an obvious input into the political process—among them, holders or aspirant holders of elective or appointive office, the communications media, the military, and student and labor groups.[31] IBAD itself apparently had little active member participation; it served largely as a conduit of funds to ideologically compatible associations and individuals. It was alleged that the Institute of Research and Social Studies (Instituto de Pesquisas e Estudos Sociais—IPES), for example, was among its beneficiaries.

By 1962, the Brazilian Institute of Democratic Action had spawned two subsidiaries with greater functional specificity. While IBAD itself continued to serve as the conduit of massive funds and the fount of ideological guidance, Democratic Popular Action (Ação Democrática Popular—ADEP) handled electoral campaigns, and Sales Promotion, Inc. (S.A. Incrementadora de Venda Promotion, better known simply as

29. *Washington Star*, 17 April 1967.

30. *Brazilian Information Bulletin*, no. 12 (Winter 1974), p. 3.

31. Eloy Dutra, *IBAD, Sigla da Corrupção* (Rio de Janeiro: Editôra Civilização Brasileira, 1963), pp. 5, 13.

Promotion) served as the publicity agent for political ideas and candidates. IBAD and ADEP shared offices and administrative personnel.[32] Nevertheless, Ivan Hasslocher, who by his own admission served as director-president of both IBAD and Promotion and was the most important member of the national board of ADEP, staunchly maintained that there was no connection among the three organizations.

ADEP, along with its parent IBAD, achieved notoriety during the electoral campaign of 1962 when it recruited and funded the campaigns of about 250 candidates for federal deputy, 15 for the federal Senate, and 600 for state deputy, and contributed to the support of 8 candidates for governorships and an indefinite number of candidates for municipal offices.[33] The criteria for selection as a beneficiary of IBAD's largesse were not partisan, but ideological. Candidates were reportedly required a sign a "compromisso ideologico," which pledged them to place their loyalty to IBAD above loyalty to party, to fight communism, and to defend foreign investment. The unprecedented amounts of money being expended by IBAD and its subsidiaries (more than 5 billion cruzeiros, or about U.S. $12,500,000, in the 1962 campaign alone) aroused widespread suspicion concerning the national origin of that money.

In 1963 a congressional commission of inquiry (Comissão Parlamentar de Inquérito—CPI) was established to investigate the modus operandi and the source of funding of both IBAD and IPES. The commission was handicapped from the beginning, in that a majority of its members had been beneficiaries of IBAD. Nevertheless, the investigation clearly established that IBAD and its subsidiaries had been responsible for "a terrible and unprecedented process of electoral corruption." (The fact that many of the messages passing among operatives were in code and were accompanied by instructions to tear up and burn struck some commission members as circumstantial evidence of illegal operations.)[34] The commission was dissolved before the funding could be traced to its ultimate sources, but circumstantial evidence that the sources were external was strong.

Hasslocher initially maintained that his operations were funded by seventy industrial and commercial firms of Rio de Janeiro and São

32. Schmitter, *Interest Conflict and Political Change*, p. 218.

33. Dutra, IBAD, pp. 13–14. According to Schmitter, ADEP publicly claimed an even greater number of beneficiaries (*Interest Conflict and Political Change*, p. 219). The figures cited by Dutra were confirmed in Agee's CIA diary.

34. Dutra, *IBAD*, pp. 17–43. I will resist the overwhelming temptation to compare the modus operandi of this organization to that of Richard Nixon's Committee for the Re-election of the President (CREEP).

Paulo, but he refused to name them and no national firm or businessman's association would admit to having contributed. He later revised his story and asserted that the money had been contributed by 126 individuals, mainly Paulistas, but he still refused to name any of them. He also maintained that a considerable amount of the money arrived in the form of "anonymous contributions through the mail." Several persons intimately associated with the country's wealthy families and the national business community testified that it was highly unlikely that such sums could have been raised from national sources alone. Castilho Cabral, who was offered the directorship of the entity that became ADEP, testified that he turned down the offer because he would be expected to "defend foreign capital." Cabral also pointed out that he had been given an initial offer of one billion cruzeiros (about U.S. $2,500,000) for the job (the offer was later confirmed by Hasslocher), and he noted that Hasslocher had no traceable background in Brazilian politics, business, finance, or any of the national professions—a circumstance which led Cabral to believe that foreign interests were behind the operation. Hasslocher's principal deputy, Frutuoso Osorio Filho, a former employee of a foreign oil company, testified to the congressional commission that no one in IBAD knew the actual source of the funds—that "Ivan scarcely knows himself." He admitted, however, that 339 million cruzeiros had been allocated to the Northeast alone, and that in Pernambuco, the state where the most money had been spent, expenditures were in accordance with the directives of Governor Cid Sampaio.[35]

Both the former secretary-general and the former treasurer of ADEP testified that in the hundred-fifty days preceding the 1962 elections, ADEP alone spent more than one billion cruzeiros. All IBAD, ADEP, and Promotion money was drawn from the Brazilian branches of three foreign banks: the Bank of Boston; the First National City Bank of New York; and the Royal Bank of Canada.[36] (Only Hasslocher himself was authorized to withdraw funds from the three banks.) The banks refused to respond to congressional subpoenas for information concerning those who deposited funds into the account of IBAD, ADEP, and Promotion. The commission was able to determine, however, from records on the movement of those funds, that transactions were never recorded in round figures, as might be expected from the volume of the currency

35. Ibid., pp. 13–69.

36. The participation of a Canadian bank might be explained by the fact that Brazilian Traction, 75 percent Canadian owned and 25 percent U.S. owned, had investments amounting to $573 million in Brazil in 1959, and fourteen companies providing telephone and electrical services in Rio and São Paulo.

involved; rather, transactions were recorded in exact figures, down to centavos. This reinforced the hypothesis that the cruzeiro sums so precisely recorded had been exchanged for foreign currency.[37]

On the basis of the extant evidence of illegal activities, the president by decree closed the offices of IBAD and ADEP in October 1963. (Article 145 of the Electoral Code declared anonymous campaign contributions illegal; there was also evidence of outright purchase of votes, forging of documents, etc.) The presidential delegitimization of these organizations however, did not result in their dissolution. Claiming that the president's action had demoralized Congress, the majority of IBAD beneficiaries on the congressional commission suspended the inquiry in November, on the eve of the scheduled testimony of Hasslocher. At the initiative of party leaders, a new congressional commission was formed shortly thereafter, and it was composed of persons untainted by favors from IBAD. But time was running out, and the "revolution" of April 1964 put an end to the investigation.

The inquiry had failed to prove conclusively that IPES had been clandestinely funded by IBAD.[38] It was conclusively demonstrated, however, that two labor organizations, the Democratic Trade Union Movement (Movimento Sindical Democrático—MSD) of São Paulo and the Democratic Resistance of Free Workers (Resisténcia Democrática dos Trabalhadores Livres—REDETRAL) of Rio had come under the control of IBAD and that IBAD's agents had infiltrated various other labor groups, including the CGT.[39] It was also shown that IBAD, operating through the Democratic Student Movement (Movimento Estudantil Democrática—MED), had pumped funds into university elections.

Members of the Superior Council of the Producing Classes (CONCLAP) were prominent participants in IBAD's activities, and it was alleged that the headquarters of the National Commercial Confederation (CNC) were used as the locale for IBAD reunions.[40] A network of retired military officers was hired to influence active duty officers.[41] It was alleged that *ibadianos* had established important cells at the headquarters of the Fourth Army and at the ESG; and the attempts of IBAD

37. Dutra, *IBAD*, pp. 26–53; Agee lists all three banks as "CIA funding mechanisms" (*Inside the Company*, pp. 599–624).

38. Schmitter, *Interest Conflict and Political Change*, p. 446.

39. Rojas maintains that the infamous Operation Gaiola, the roundup of labor leaders on the night of 31 March 1964 (organized by General Mourão Filho) was financed by Standard Oil through the intermediary of IBAD (*Estados Unidos en Brazil*, p. 174).

40. Schmitter, *Interest Conflict and Political Change*, p. 446.

41. Stepan, *The Military in Politics*, p. 154.

to turn the 1962 elections at the Clube Militar against supporters of the government caused the Minister of War, General Jair Dantas, to join those who were calling for a congressional investigation.[42]

The congressional commission was dissolved before it could name the (presumably foreign) sponsors of IBAD, but even before the revelations by Agee various theories circulated and some individual investigators claimed to have that information. Philippe Schmitter noted that it was widely believed (and vigorously denied) that the money came from the cruzeiro surplus accumulated by U.S. PL 480 wheat sales to Brazil.[43] Robinson Rojas listed Standard Oil of New Jersey, U.S. Steel, Texas Oil, Gulf Oil, Hanna Corporation, Bethlehem Steel, General Motors, and Willys Overland among the depositors in the accounts of IBAD-ADEP-Promotion.[44] Jean Marc von der Weid maintained that more than one hundred foreign enterprises and some national ones were involved in financing the institute, and that the Rockefeller Group—IBEC—was one of the major benefactors.[45] Niles Bond, asked by this author if IBAD had been funded by the CIA, responded, "I don't know who else would have been funding them."[46]

In 1975, former CIA agent Philip Agee confirmed many of the findings and suspicions of the Brazilian congressional commission. The entry in his diary for 10 February 1964 includes this observation:

> Operations in Brazil haven't been helped by a Brazilian parliamentary investigation into the massive 1962 electoral operation, that began last May and is still continuing in the courts. The investigation revealed that one of the Rio Station's main political-action operations, the Brazilian Institute for Democratic Action (IBAD) and a related organization called Popular Democratic Action (ADEP), spent during the 1962 electoral campaign at least the equivalent of some 12 million dollars financing anti-communist candidates, and possibly as much as 20 million. . . .
>
> The parliamentary investigating commission was controlled somewhat—five of its nine members were themselves recipients of IBAD and ADEP funds—but only the refusal of the First National City Bank, the Bank of Boston, and the Royal Bank of Canada to reveal the foreign source of funds deposited for IBAD and ADEP kept the lid from blowing off.[47]

Beneficiaries of IBAD were prominent among the conspirators in the coup of 1 April and some, particularly military beneficiaries, were among those who gained power as a consequence of it. The purging of

42. Schmitter, *Interest Conflict and Political Change*, p. 449; Dutra, *IBAD* p. 13.

43. Schmitter, *Interest Conflict and Political Change*, p. 446.

44. Rojas, *Estados Unidos en Brazil*, p. 151.

45. Von der Weid interview.

46. Bond interview.

47. Agee, *Inside the Company*, p. 321.

the congress left the *ibadianos* with greater strength in that crippled body. The *Jornal do Brasil* stated on 6 September 1965 that eighty deputies had been subsidized by IBAD. It also identified the Minister of Aviation, Marshal Juarez Tavora, and the Minister of Industry and Commerce, Daniel Faraco, as IBAD beneficiaries.[48]

And what of those members of the congressional commission who had made a relentless effort to trace the IBAD money to its source? The head of that commission in the spring of 1964 was Rubems Beroydt Paiva. Paiva was among those who lost their legislative seats and their political rights in the first wave of cassations after the coup. Later that year he assumed the editorship of *Ultima Hora*. After the supercoup of December 1968 and the tightening of press censorship, he decided that attempts at journalism were useless, so he returned to the engineering business for which he had been trained. On 20 January 1971 he was arrested, along with his wife and sixteen-year-old daughter. His wife and daughter were subsequently released, but they have heard nothing since from him. Other prisoners, released later, reported having seen Paiva "in bad condition," apparently from beatings and torture. The army was still denying two months later that it had Paiva in custody, but it was reported in the *Washington Post* that the army had returned his clothing and personal effects to his wife.[49]

Doubtless the full scope of efforts on the part of the United States to win or strengthen allies and to defeat or undermine adversaries among the political elites in Brazil in the early 1960s extends beyond what has become public knowledge through such piecemeal revelations. And we remain obliged to deal with an assortment of "plausible" and implausible denials from U.S. officialdom. It seems clear, however, that AID project loans and CIA funds channeled through organizations such as IBAD were used for those purposes. Such efforts were not in themselves uniformly successful. If it had appeared to the foreign and domestic opponents of Goulart that the leftward trend of political development could be reversed merely through financing electoral campaigns and co-opting political elites, the use of violence probably would not have been found necessary. Nevertheless, the climate of distrust and crisis generated during the 1962 campaign and thereafter, and the adherence of several governors of states that had been designated "islands of sanity" to the move to depose Goulart were important factors in the disaggregation of the state that facilitated the military takeover.

48. Norman Blume, "Pressure Groups and Decision-Making in Brazil," *Studies in Comparative International Development* 3 (1967–1968): 205–23.

49. Frank Mankiewicz and Tom Braden, "Brazilian Blood on Our Hands," *Washington Post*, 23 March 1971.

[4]

Denationalizing Business Elites

The assertion of national control over basic natural resources, as well as a more general assertion of control over the productive capacity of the economy, had been seen by the Goulart government as a prerequisite to the redistribution of income. The advocacy of economic nationalization had also been seen as one of the most promising means of mobilizing mass support for the government. U.S. businesses, with the support of the U.S. government,had generally been able to fend off the proposed constraints of nationalistic but weak governments. If the mobilization of the masses had not appeared to be a threat or a possibility, it seems likely that the combined pressures of the multinational corporations and those elements of the Brazilian business community whose fortunes were linked to them would have been sufficient to intimidate the Brazilian government into backing down on its nationalistic designs. But regardless of the actual potential in 1964 for the mobilization of the masses, Goulart apparently believed that it was possible, and his enemies, foreign and domestic, apparently feared that he was right.

At a military and academic conference on Latin America at West Point in the fall of 1964, David Rockefeller of the Chase Manhattan Bank told a discussion group that it had been decided quite early that Goulart was not acceptable to the U.S. banking community, and that he would have to go.[1] The U.S.-based financial institutions and multinational corporations, with their own resources and the backing of the U.S. government, were not without leverage in dealing with or under-

1. Edwin Lieuwen, in conversation, 19 July 1976, Albuquerque, N.M. Lieuwen had been present when the remarks were made.

mining an antagonistic government. But their position was strongly reinforced by the adherence of an important sector of the business and professional community in Brazil. This chapter examines some of the activities of an organization of local businessmen whose values and interests had become identified with those of the U.S.-based corporations. It also traces the actions and fortunes of one U.S.-based corporation through the change of government and outlines the relative fortunes of domestic and foreign-based firms in the years following the coup.

Philippe Schmitter partly attributed the underdevelopment or ineffectiveness of associational interest groups composed of Brazilian industrialists and businessmen to the fact that the U.S.-based multinational corporations failed to work through such groups and generally applied pressure directly on the national decision-makers.[2] Diplomatic intervention on behalf of U.S.-based corporations was virtually automatic in the period immediately preceding the coup. Simon Hanson said that Robert Kennedy, as his brother's special envoy to Brazil in 1963, accompanied his advocacy on behalf of International Telephone and Telegraph with a threat of a cutoff of economic cooperation. This "caused the Brazilian regime to surrender abjectly and to give ITT so much money for its broken-down properties that had been nationalized that it became a joke on the floor of the Senate and among foreign-policy analysts, and even for the highest executives of the ITT, to discuss how much had been milked out of Brazil by the sheer invoking of Kennedy's willingness to intervene directly in Brazilian political life."[3] And Peter Bell maintained that it was Ambassador Gordon's threat to invoke the Hickenlooper Amendment that inspired Goulart to agree to a settlement of U.S. $8 million.[4]

The U.S. government's policy of intervention on behalf of private overseas interests, a stratagem camouflaged in development rhetoric in the early 1960s, was reiterated in unmasked form a decade later. President Nixon's Secretary of the Treasury, John Connally, asserted before a congressional committee in April 1972 that the United States should give greater support to American corporations threatened with

2. Philippe C. Schmitter, interview, 23 February 1973, Washington, D.C. Jim Rowe, on special assignment to the Senate Subcommittee on Multinational Corporations, maintained that U.S. corporations are now participating directly as members of the Brazilian business syndicates (Interview, 27 February 1974, Washington, D.C.).

3. Simon G. Hanson, "Kissinger on the Chilean Coup," *Inter-American Economic Affairs,* 27 (Winter 1973): 61–85, 77.

4. Bell, "Brazilian-American Relations."

expropriation in foreign countries. He advocated that the U.S. government warn other governments, "You don't negotiate with American business enterprise; you negotiate with the U.S. government."[5]

Nevertheless, neither U.S. businessmen nor the U.S. government was relying on diplomacy alone for the protection of economic interests in the early 1960s. In fact, U.S. businessmen, in concert with the U.S. government, were feverishly attempting to influence and mobilize the local business community and other groups active or potentially active in the political process. To say, however, that the U.S. businesses were working through the Brazilian business community would be to blur an important distinction within that community. By that time, a large proportion of the native entrepreneurial class, especially in the more dynamic, less traditional sectors, had become managers of predominantly foreign firms.

A recent study of multinational corporations by Louis Turner concluded that such corporations create, in the so-called underdeveloped countries, local elites whose tastes and standards of living are imitative of the status system of more highly industrialized countries and whose attention is distracted from the interests of their own people.[6] And James R. Kurth saw this co-optation leading to a new sort of "international," with its own ideology, centered in postindustrial America, but including businessmen, managers, and technocrats from all industrial nations.[7]

Celso Furtado noted that multinational corporations began to pour into Brazil after World War II and that Brazilian industrialists and technocrats linked with this multinational structure were receiving their training in management and technology from the Superior War College (ESG). The outlook they developed was quite different from the liberal or populist orientation of elite groups that had been able to come to power through elections. Like their military counterparts, these businessmen viewed discipline and hierarchy as the essential components of an industrial system. As members of an international bourgeoisie, they were concerned about growth, but not about national independence. Furtado maintains that it was this sector of the business

5. *Washington Post*, 6 June 1972.

6. Louis Turner, *Multinational Companies and the Third World* (New York: Hill & Wang, 1973).

7. James R. Kurth, "Multinational Corporations as New Actors in International Politics" Address prepared for delivery at the 1973 International Studies Association-Washington Conference (George Washington University, Washington, D.C., 16–17 November 1973), p. 17.

community that allied itself with the military and the U.S. government to topple Goulart.[8]

Likewise, Jean Marc von der Weid maintained that the coalition that conspired to overthrow Goulart was composed primarily of Brazilians linked to foreign investments, particularly to the U.S.-based multinational corporations. Von der Weid recalled that a meeting took place in his home in 1963 among various representatives of the communications media and the advertising industry, including the head of the second largest advertising company in Rio de Janeiro (McCann Erickson) and a manager of American Light and Power. The purpose of the meeting was to discuss means of participating in the IBAD-IPES campaign against Goulart and the labor-left. Von der Weid's uncle, who was chief legal counsel for American Light and Power, became involved in the campaign. A close friend of Niles Bond, cultural attaché in the U.S. Embassy at the time, the uncle had long maintained that the only hope for the salvation of the country was U.S. intervention.[9]

During the week before the coup, two huge anti-Goulart marches took place in São Paulo and Belo Horizonte, the capitals of the states in which the insurrection began. As the plan for the coup had been drawn up for some time before the marches took place, it appears that the marches were staged in order to provide legitimization and an auspicious climate for the impending military moves. General Vernon Walters told this author that until the marches took place there was fear that the movement to overthrow Goulart would not succeed.[10] Carlos Carmelo de Vasconcelos Mota, Cardinal Archbishop of São Paulo, prohibited his bishops from participating in the march, as he maintained that it was being organized by the U.S. advertising agency, McCann Erickson.[11] According to Levinson and de Onis, U.S. businessmen residing in Brazil, who were in close contact with the CIA representatives there, helped to organize and finance these demonstrations.[12]

8. Furtado interview.

9. Von der Weid interview.

10. Walters interview.

11. Rojas, *Estados Unidos en Brazil*, p. 198.

12. Levinson and de Onis, *The Alliance that Lost its Way*, p. 89. Richard Helms, former CIA director, reported to the Senate Foreign Relations Committee in February 1973 that he had a policy of going right to the top of American business firms in trying to get their cooperation in gathering intelligence overseas. Associated Press reported that some two hundred persons are operating as U.S. intelligence agents under the cover of businessmen. See "Helms Tells of Using Top U.S. Businessmen," *Washington Post*, 11 March 1974.

The principal overt sponsors of the demonstrations, the Women's Campaign for Democracy (Campanha da Mulher pela Democrácia—CAMDE) in Rio and the Women's Civic Union (União Cîvica Feminina) in São Paulo were among the groups receiving financial support and political guidance from the Institute of Research and Social Studies.[13] Philip Agee accounted for at least a part of the covert sponsorship in his CIA diary. He recorded that "the Rio station and its larger bases were financing the mass urban demonstrations against the Goulart government, proving the old themes of God, country, family, and liberty to be as effective as ever."[14]

The Institute of Research and Social Studies

The Institute of Research and Social Studies (Instituto de Pesquisas e Estudos Sociais—IPES) was formally established in 1961, largely through the efforts of Paulo Ayres Filho and Gilbert Huber, Jr. Ayers, president of a São Paulo pharmaceutical firm, had been strongly influenced in the early 1950s by the Foundation for Economic Education in Irvington-on-Hudson, New York, which had proselytized for limited government and free enterprise. Huber, a young businessman from Rio de Janeiro, published Brazil's telephone-directory yellow pages, the Listas Telefónicas Brasileiras.[15] His economic empire was linked to American Light and Power (Toronto-based, but 80 percent U.S.-owned).[16] The Guanabara group was affiliated with the Committee for Economic Development, a private research organization headquartered in the United States. At the time of the congressional investigation of 1963, IPES claimed five hundred members.[17]

The businessmen who founded IPES were alarmed by what they saw as the leftward drift of the government, by the mounting verbal attacks on the United States and on capitalism in general, and by strident demands for the nationalization of industry. Ayres, who (according to a

13. Blume, "Pressure Groups and Decision-Making," p. 217.

14. Agee, Inside the Company, pp. 361–62. The U.S. Senate Intelligence Committee noted in its report on Covert Action that similar demonstrations in Chile, the "marches of the empty pots," were indirectly funded by the CIA as part of a larger strategy for undermining the Allende government. The report also cites the funding of a research organization as a part of that strategy.

15. Philip Siekman, "When Executives Turned Revolutionaries, A Story Hitherto Untold: How São Paulo Businessmen Conspired to Overthrow Brazil's Communist-infested Government," Fortune 70 (September 1964): 147–49, 210–21.

16. Furtado interview.

17. Blume, "Pressure Groups and Decision-Making," p. 214.

sympathetic account in *Fortune* magazine) tended to apply the term "Communism" to a broad spectrum of political thought, contended that even under the presidency of Kubitschek, "Communists began showing up in student groups, labor unions, and even professional and managerial associations and chambers of commerce."[18]

Another sympathetic account of the activities of IPES and groups affiliated or aligned with it described the mission of members of these organizations as "to shake awake their tolerant, warm-hearted fellow citizens, whose easy-going political attitudes were too often summed up in the phrase, 'yes, he's a communist, but a nice fellow.' "[19]

The sources and extent of funding for IPES remain something of a mystery. Unlike IBAD, IPES had the open adherence of a number of Brazil's wealthiest businessmen and corporations. The effective national base of many of the corporations involved, however, was open to question. Rojas maintained that of the 398 firms in Rio and São Paulo listed by IPES as contributors, 297 were actually "North American firms with Brazilian names."[20] Norman Blume found that no manifestly American companies were "officially" members of the Guanabara branch of IPES, although a leader of that group, Glycon de Paiva, had informed him that American participation had been solicited. But a number of observers remained convinced that unofficial contributions of American companies to IPES had been substantial. One source (not for attribution) claimed that American Light and Power was among the contributors and that DELTEC had made contributions from its $7 million kitty in the Bahamas.

Niles Bond confirmed to this author that many of the IPES businessmen were associated with U.S. firms. He said that he was sure that U.S. funds were going into the IPES operation, although he maintained that they were not being channeled through his office. He suggested, for example, that Alberto Byington, a Harvard graduate employed by a U.S. aluminum company in Brazil, was "probably" receiving U.S. funds and passing them on to IPES.[21]

Blume notes that IPES led a double life financially. The largest item

18. Siekman, "When Executives Turned Revolutionaries," p. 148.

19. Clarence W. Hall, "The Country That Saved Itself," *Reader's Digest* 85 (November 1964): 133–58.

20. Rojas, *Estados Unidos en Brazil*, p. 71.

21. Bond interview. In speaking of "U.S. funds," Bond did not distinguish between public and private funding. It is likely that, as in the case of the campaign to depose the Allende government (see U.S. Senate reports on *Alleged Assassination Plots* and *Covert Action*), some private funds were passed directly to conspirators on the advice of the CIA.

listed in the budget for 1963, amounting to 64,965,465,80 cruzeiros, was subsidization of other groups, but the total expenditure of 219,166,236,50 cruzeiros in the formal budget reported to the public failed to account for considerable expenditure for publications. Initially the efforts of IPES were limited to various forms of proselytizing. The organization (with some acknowledged assistance from U.S. public and private sources) published booklets and pamphlets and distributed hundreds of articles to newspapers. And in 1963 alone it distributed 182,144 books throughout Brazil. It also underwrote lectures, financed students' trips to the United States, sponsored "leadership training" programs for some two thousand-six hundred businessmen, students, and workers, and subsidized organizations of women, students, and workers. To reach a wider public, it showed a series of films all over the country, and the São Paulo Group made extensive use of the electronic media.[22]

By late 1962, however, many IPES members had grown impatient with what they considered a defensive role. A São Paulo industrialist, cited by Siekman, organized vigilante cells to counter left-wing hecklers at anti-communist meetings with "intellectual methods—like a kick in the head." The vigilante groups later armed themselves with light weapons, establishing a clandestine hand-grenade factory, and drew up contingency plans for the civil war they considered inevitable.[23] Meanwhile, IPES, like IBAD, had hired a network of retired military officers to exert influence on those on active duty. Important links between IPES and the military had existed from the beginning (many of the key civilians at IPES had attended the Superior War College before IPES was founded[24]) and some of the founding staff members of the ESG, such as General Golbery do Couto e Silva, later joined IPES.[25] IPES members had made a point of inviting military officers to visit their factories and had used such occasions to express their fears.[26]

From 1962 to 1964, IPES, by its own estimate, spent between U.S. $200,000 and $300,000 on an intelligence gathering and distribution network composed of retired military officers. This network, headed by General Golbery, was designated the "Research Group." Its mission was to monitor "communist" influence on the government and to dis-

22. Ibid.; Siekman, "When Executives Turned Revolutionaries," p. 149.
23. Siekman, "When Executives Turned Revolutionaries," p. 149.
24. Blume, "Pressure Groups and Decision-Making," p. 215.
25. Stepan, "The Military in Politics," p. 186.
26. Siekman, "When Executives Turned Revolutionaries," p. 110.

tribute its findings clandestinely to key active duty officers throughout the country. It also produced literature for general distribution. Such literature, circulated without identification of source, included a chart that identified "communist" groups and their leaders.[27]

A prime mover in the military-IPES liaison from early 1963 was Lieutenant Colonel Rubens Resstel, then stationed in the São Paulo headquarters of the Second Army. He had seen action with the Brazilian Expeditionary Force (BEF), which fought as part of the U.S. Fifth Army in Italy in World War II. Resstel sought to make the BEF the moving force among the military conspirators.[28]

The movement, by mid-1963 aimed unequivocally at ousting Goulart, had been strengthened by the adherence of the Mesquita family, owners of the prestigious daily newspaper *O Estado de São Paulo*, and Adhemar de Barros, governor of the state of São Paulo, who commanded a well-trained and well-equipped militia of some forty thousand men. The "Mesquita group" alone had spent some U.S. $10,000 on weapons (U.S.-made, according to a journalist who claims to have seen some of them), and upper- and middle-class residential areas of São Paulo had been organized on a block-by-block basis.[29] Extra stores of gasoline were obtained and stashed in industrial lots around São Paulo, and a supply of U.S. Food for Peace "discovered" on the docks at Santos was stored. The conspirators calculated at this point that even in the event of civil war they could hold out for ninety days, but they assumed that after that they would need outside help.

A much-quoted article in *Fortune* magazine, sympathetic to the "revolution," recounted that the Mesquita group sent an emissary to Ambassador Gordon in the spring of 1964 to ascertain what the U.S. position would be if civil war broke out. The emissary reported back that Gordon was cautious and diplomatic, but that he had left the impression that if the Paulistas could hold out for forty-eight hours they would get U.S. recognition and help.[30]

Gordon told this author that some of the members of IPES had been friends of his since before he became ambassador and that he had been aware that they were engaged in an attempt to undermine the government, including putting pressure on Governor Adhemar de Barros and General Amaury Kruel, although Gordon said that he was not aware

27. Blume, "Pressure Groups and Decision-Making," p. 215; Stepan, *The Military in Politics*, p. 154.

28. Siekman, "When Executives Turned Revolutionaries," p. 210.

29. Rojas, *Estados Unidos en Brazil*, p. 72.

30. Siekman, "When Executives Turned Revolutionaries," pp. 214–216.

before the coup of all their activities. He claimed that he had made no promises to those who approached him seeking U.S. support. But he added that they had good reason to believe that the Embassy would be sympathetic, as he had told them that Goulart was mismanaging the economy and that he suspected Goulart of plotting a takeover.[31]

Many of the civilians recruited by the military government established after the coup were drawn from the ranks of IPES, and the ideological influence of IPES was apparent in the policies adopted by the new government. One of the companies that benefited most immediately from these policies was the Hanna Mining Company. Since the "revolution," the Guanabara branch of IPES has become highly dependent upon the financial contributions of companies of the Antunes group, which is engaged in large-scale joint ventures with the Hanna Mining Company and other foreign enterprises.[32]

The Hanna Mining Company in Brazil

Brazilians have long assumed, partially on faith, that their national territory was a cornucopia of mineral wealth. Not surprisingly, then, one of the earliest and most forcefully articulated issues of Brazilian nationalists was the assertion of control over mineral resources. The 1954 Mineral Code, which classified subsoil rights as public domain, was an outgrowth of this concern. In the mid-1950s, U.S. interests began to pressure the Brazilian government to allow the U.S. Air Force to renew its wartime aerial geodetic photographic mapping survey program in Brazil, but these efforts were successfully withstood through counterpressures from nationalists until the coup of 1964. And the Goulart government had stated its intention of establishing a national monopoly over the exploitation of minerals.

A conflict between Hanna Mining Company and the Brazilian government, one that had been escalating for several years, was being viewed as a test case in the period just before the coup. In 1956, Hanna had purchased majority interest in an English gold mining company whose landholding claim dated back to 1833. The claim, in Minas Gerais, included land later found to contain one of the richest iron ore deposits in Brazil. The most formidable opposition to Hanna's claim arose from the government-controlled iron ore company, Companhia Vale do Rio Doce. In response to the company's objections, the Brazilian Congress launched an investigation of the claim, and in 1961 Quadros initiated an executive-branch investigation of the legal ramifi-

31. Gordon interview.
32. Blume, "Pressure Groups and Decision-Making," pp. 214–17.

cations of the issue. In 1962 Goulart used the case developed by his predecessor's government as the basis for an expropriation decree. Even before Hanna itself protested, the U.S. government issued an official protest. Apparently unwittingly, the protest note listed as president of the company Lucas Lopes. Lopes' association with Hanna had not been generally known, and it was a matter of great interest to Brazilian nationalists, as Lopes had served in Kubitschek's cabinet at a time when Hanna had received generous concessions. Hanna, which by this time controlled seven other enterprises in Brazil, challenged the decree in the Brazilian courts. At the time of the 1964 coup, the case had reached the Federal Court of Appeals, which was expected to uphold the executive branch.[33]

Meanwhile, Hanna was not lacking in influential backers or forums for the expression of its views (on the merits of its case as well as of the general situation in Brazil). In 1963, for example, Hanna (along with a Walter C. Lawson) funded a conference on "The Political-Military Defense of Latin America" at Arizona State University's Bureau of Governmental Research. A participant in that conference, U.S. Army Lieutenant Colonel Theodore Wyckoff, warned that the communists all over Latin America were "getting ready to strike when the time is ripe" and that "an anti-Communist counter-offensive may provide a far better defense for free peoples and institutions than any passive measures."[34] Hanna's contributions to this "defense for free peoples" included the provision of trucks for the Minas Gerais troops that launched the "revolution."[35]

The third largest iron ore producer in the United States, Hanna was only a part of a much larger Cleveland-based industrial complex, which included National Steel, fifth largest U.S. steel producer; Consolidated Coal, the largest U.S. coal producer; and Chrysler, third largest automobile producer and fifth largest U.S. corporation. Furthermore, Hanna had interlocking directorates with some of the major financial, industrial, and commercial complexes with operations in Brazil, including the Rockefeller group, the Mellon complex (ALCOA, etc.), Morgan Guaranty Trust Company, and General Electric.

33. Rojas, *Estados Unidos en Brazil*, pp. 28, 80; Edie Black and Fred Goff, "The Hanna Industrial Complex" (New York: North American Congress on Latin America, 1969).

34. Lieutenant Colonel Theodore Wyckoff, U.S. Army, "Communist Military Capabilities in Latin America: The Spectrum of Violence," *The Political-Military Defense of Latin America*, ed. Bruce B. Mason (Tempe: Arizona State University, Bureau of Governmental Research, 1963), ch. 3, pp. 26–27.

35. Source preferred not to be named.

The complex of which Hanna was a part had long served as a major fundraiser for the Republican Party in the United States. George Humphrey, who, as a partner in the Hanna Mining Company in 1920, had carried out an aggressive policy of expansion, served as secretary of the treasury during the presidency of Eisenhower. While serving in that post, he dispatched his Cabinet cohort's son, John W. F. Dulles, to organize Hanna's operations in Brazil.

Herbert Hoover, Jr., son of the former U.S. president and a noted oil, mining, and electronics engineer, served the Brazilian government (among others) as an engineering consultant between 1942 and 1952. After completing a special assignment in Iran in 1953 and 1954, Hoover assumed the position of undersecretary of state. In 1960 he joined Hanna's board of directors. Another prominent Republican, John J. McCloy, former president of the World Bank and board chairman of the Chase Manhattan Bank, and a partner in the Rockefeller-associated law firm of Milbank, Tweed, Hadley and Mc-Cloy, had been retained as Hanna's counsel in 1964. After the coup, he reportedly escorted U.S. Ambassador Gordon to the office of President Castello Branco to suggest that the restoration of Hanna's concession might be one condition for receiving U.S. economic assistance.[36]

As it turned out, economist Roberto Campos (unaffectionately known in Brazil by the English translation of his name, Bobby Fields), who had previously served as a technical adviser to Hanna, was appointed finance minister under the Castello Branco government, and Hanna's problems were over. A presidential decree of 24 December 1964 endorsed the private development of Brazil's iron ore reserves, and on 15 June 1966 a reconstituted Federal Court of Appeals ruled in favor of Hanna's right to exploit the deposits.

The presidential decree of 24 December 1964 had also endorsed Hanna's plans to build loading facilities at Sepetiba Bay, an undeveloped deep-water harbor sixty miles south of Rio, and to construct a railway cutoff from the government-owned Central do Brasil railroad to the bay, The harbor development plan, which bestowed upon Hanna exclusive use of the port for thirty years, had actually been developed by Campos himself, in his former capacity as technical adviser, but had been rejected by the Goulart government.[37] Hanna's acquisition of the right to construct the railway cutoff was no doubt facilitated by the newly appointed director of the federal railway network, Oto de Araujo Lima; he, too, had served as a technical adviser to Hanna.

36. Black and Goff, "The Hanna Industrial Complex."

37. Eduardo Galeano, "The De-Nationalization of Brazilian Industry," *Monthly Review* 21 (December 1969): 11–30.

The development of the port was to be subsidized to some extent by Brazilian taxpayers. Even before the right to develop the harbor had been conceded to Hanna, an oceanographic vessel of the Brazilian navy was engaged full time in studies of the harbor area for Hanna's benefit. Rojas found this generosity on the part of the Brazilian navy unsurprising, as the navy was totally dependent upon the distribution system of Esso Brasil (Standard Oil of New Jersey) for its petroleum.[38]

Hanna's acquisition of the harbor generated a storm of public protest. *Comercio Exterior*, for example, commented: "This constitutes a privilege which will transform the Hanna Company into an absolute master of the internal mineral market of the country."[39] But the Castello Branco government did not waver. When a television interviewer suggested to Minister of Aviation Gino Juaréz Tavora that the concession might be subjected to a national plebiscite, Tavora became enraged, pounded the table, and said, "Such decisions are not for the public. The public doesn't know anything, and the government must solve problems in the manner it considers most convenient, without consulting the public, which is ignorant."[40]

The new position of Roberto Campos was also helpful to the American and Foreign Power Company. As Brazilian Ambassador to the United States he had signed, in April 1963, without his government's authorization, an agreement for Brazil to purchase the power company's ten subsidiaries in Brazil for about U.S. $70 million. Both the price and other aspects of the transaction had provoked protests from Brazilian nationalists, who considered them unduly favorable to the American company. Goulart, therefore, had repudiated the terms of the agreement and postponed settlement of the issue indefinitely. As minister of planning after the "revolution," Campos consummated the purchase for U.S. $135 million, plus $17.7 million compensation for the delay in fulfilling the 1963 agreement.[41]

In July 1964 the U.S. Air Force, under the auspices of the Inter-American Geodetic Survey, began its low-level photographic flights over areas that were believed to contain rich mineral deposits. The original contract between the Brazilian government and the U.S. Air Force specified that the photographs were to be processed in the United States and that the negatives were to be returned to Brazil and were not to be made public. In December 1966, however, Rio's *Jornal*

38. Rojas, *Estados Unides en Brazil*, pp. 118–19.

39. Andre Gunder Frank, *Latin America: Underdevelopment or Revolution* (New York: Monthly Review Press, 1969), p. 198.

40. Rojas, *Estados Unidos en Brazil*, pp. 129–30.

41. Frank, *Latin America* pp. 197–98.

do Brazil published statements by an Army colonel to the effect that North American corporations used the survey in getting mining concessions in Minas Gerais.[42]

Hanna, like other U.S.-based mining companies, has also profited from the largesse of the World Bank and other international financial institutions. The Companhia Mineira de Aluminio (ALCOMINAS), for example, controlled by ALCOA (50 percent) and Hanna (23.5 percent), could not operate without the Rio Grande hydroelectric system, constructed with loans from the World Bank. ALCOMINAS also received a direct loan of U.S. $22 million from the World Bank in FY 1968, and the Aguas Claras iron mine, in which Hanna has a 49 percent interest, received a loan of $96 million from the World Bank in FY 1972.[43]

World Bank loans have also enabled the Brazilian government to push ahead with its U.S. $500 million road-building project in the Amazon Basin. Various scholars and journalists have commented that the major beneficiaries of this "infrastructure" project will be large foreign corporations. The Transamazon Highway, for example, will pass remarkably close to the U.S. Steel concession at Serra do Carajas. The Serra do Carajas deposits, reported to exceed in quality even the Minas Gerais claims of Hanna, are being exploited jointly by U.S. Steel (49 percent) and the Companhia Vale do Rio Doce (51 percent).[44]

Business Latin America reported that Brazil would export some 45 million tons of iron ore in 1973. Most of the export business was to be handled by the government-controlled Cia. Vale do Rio Doce.[45] The only other major iron exporter, which accounts for some three million tons annually, is Mineraçãos Brasileiras Reunides (MBR). MBR is a joint venture of Brazilian millionaire Augusto Tranhano de Azevedo Antunes (51 percent) and Hanna (49 percent), but Antunes yielded control of the company's operations by signing a management contract with the North American firm.[46]

42. *The North American Congress on Latin America's Latin America and Empire Report*, vol. 7, no. 4 (April 1973), p.4. Pat Holt, General Counsel of the Senate Foreign Relations Committee, could not confirm unequivocally that the surveys were distributed to U.S. businessmen, but he affirmed that he believed that to be the case.

43. *Brazilian Information Bulletin*, no. 9 (January 1973).

44. Ibid., no. 1 (February 1971).

45. *Business Latin America* 24 October 1973.

46. Black and Goff, "The Hanna Industrial Complex," p. 4.

The "Economic Miracle"

The process of denationalization assumed a dizzying pace in the years after the coup. By 1966, according to E. Bradford Burns, foreign capital controlled some 50 percent of Brazilian private industry.[47] This was accomplished, however, with a lower level of direct new investment in the "key" years of denationalization—1965, 1966, and 1967— than had entered the country in 1961. A partial explanation of this development was to be found in Campos' "theory of constructive bankruptcy."[48] Locally owned firms, already at a disadvantage vis-à-vis the multinational corporations, were further disadvantaged by government policies.

Not surprisingly, the U.S. Chamber of Commerce in Rio de Janeiro greeted the new government with a resolution endorsing its repressive "First Institutional Act."[49] An investment guarantee pact afforded "extraterritoriality" to U.S. enterprises. This permitted the repatriation of their earnings, reduced their taxes, and extended to them extraordinary credit facilities. Along with other foreign firms, U.S. corporations enjoyed a special rate of exchange in case of devaluation, and they had access to foreign credit, which was denied to domestic firms. Thus, while domestic firms, under the credit squeeze prescribed by the IMF, paid up to 48 percent for credit obtained locally, the foreign firms obtained loans abroad at 7 or 8 percent. Furthermore, as almost half of the assets of the banks operating in Brazil belonged to foreign capital, foreign firms had access to internal credit denied to many domestic firms.

The higher tax and credit rates paid by domestic firms exacerbated the already overwhelming problems these firms faced in attempting to compete with the multinationals. Technological dependence, for example, is expensive. The use of trademarks, patents, or technical assistance had to be paid for in dollars and the costs were multiplied by periodic devaluations of the cruzeiro. When domestic firms ceased to be able to meet payments, foreign creditors converted unpaid debts into investments. Central Bank figures indicate that 20 percent of the new direct investments of foreign origin in the years 1965 through 1967 were conversions of loans.

47. Burns, "Brazil: The Imitative Society."

48. Paulo R. Schilling, "Brazil: The Rebellion of the Downtrodden," *Marcha* (Montevideo), 16 July 1971, reprinted in *Latin American Documentation Center* II, 9b, November 1971.

49. Schuler interview, 30 November 1970.

The credit squeeze also facilitated the old technique of strangulation of domestic industry by price-cutting. A locally owned adhesive-tape factory, Adesite, for example, was doing well in São Paulo until the Minnesota Mining and Manufacturing Company came in and began to sell its Scotch tape cheaper and cheaper on the Brazilian market. By the time its prices had been cut by 40 percent, Adesite was in bad trouble. Its sales had dropped drastically and it could not get credit. Union Carbide appeared on the scene just in time to buy out Adesite at a desperation price. Then Minnesota Mining and Union Carbide divided up the market and raised their prices by 50 percent.[50]

In a 1971 article entitled "Booming Brazil Finds a Key to Growth" Alfredo Marques Vianna, vice-president of Rio's Chamber of Commerce, was quoted as asserting that the country was moving toward "liquidation of national private enterprise and a conflict between state and foreign capital."[51] Although the state sector would later assert itself more forcefully, foreign capital appeared at that time to be winning. PETROBRAS, once the pride of nationalists, had been deprived of its monopoly of petrochemicals. The government-controlled National Motor Factory, created by the Vargas government, was denied the advantages extended to its foreign-owned competition and in 1968 it was sold to Alfa Romeo. Public opinion was not allowed to delay the process. At about the same time that this impending transaction was announced, it was announced that elections would be canceled in sixty-eight municipalities. One of these was Duque de Caxias, city of some 350,000, that was the home of the National Motor Factory.[52]

A congressional committee that was investigating the denationalization process at the time the Congress was dissolved in December 1968 had found that foreign capital controlled: 40 percent of the capital market; 62 percent of foreign trade; 82 percent of maritime transport; 77 percent of the overseas airlines; 100 percent of tire production; 80 percent of the pharmaceutical industry; 50 percent of the chemical industry; 59 percent of machine production; 62 percent of auto parts production; 48 percent of aluminum; and 90 percent of cement. About half of this foreign capital was of U.S. origin.[53]

It was reported that in the aftermath of the consolidating coup of December 1968, U.S. Ambassador John Tuthill, who had succeeded

50. Galeano, "De-Nationalization of Brazilian Industry."

51. *Business Week*, 13 March 1971, pp. 90–93.

52. "Brazil: Empiezan a fallar las instituciones," *The Economist para America Latina*, Edición Quincenal, 29 May 1968, pp. 11–12.

53. Galeano, "De-Nationalization of Brazilian Industry."

Gordon in 1967, wanted to issue an official note protesting the anti-democratic measures. When the issue was put to Secretary of State Dean Rusk, he reportedly asked only two questions: had the Costa e Silva regime murdered many people? and was there any danger to U.S. investment? The answer to both was no, and his decision was no note.[54]

U.S. enterprises, in collaboration with the ESG, with AID, and on their own, are preparing future generations of Brazilian managers and technocrats to enter into the multinational corporate structure. The Education Committee of the American Chamber of Commerce in Rio de Janeiro, for example, sponsors seminars to acquaint students with the "practical needs of the business world."[55] Meanwhile, the military-industrial complex had been multilateralized, as General Golbery do Couto e Silva, head of the Brazilian intelligence apparatus (Servicio Nacional de Informações) under the Castello Branco government, took over as local president of Dow Chemical (until he was recalled in 1974 to serve the government of President Geisel) and General Adhemar de Queiroz, Army minister under Castello Branco's government, became local president of ALCOA. At least eight other persons of cabinet rank in the Castello Branco government had assumed the local presidency or directorship of foreign enterprises.[56]

By the early 1970s, those former leaders of IPES who had not been totally at the service of foreign interests had come to see the cruel irony of their victory. Paulo Ayres declared in 1971, "The government is de-capitalizing us."[57] And Rui Mesquita, director of *O Estado de São Paulo*, wrote to the minister of justice expressing "profound humiliation and shame" concerning censorship. Mesquita compared the Brazilian regime to Hitler's Germany.[58]

We have seen that the values, the interests, and the fears of representatives of multinational corporations operating in Brazil were shared by important elements of the domestic business community, particularly by those who performed managerial or technical functions for the multinational corporations or who had joint ventures with them. It was this element of the domestic business community which,

54. "Prices Down, Arrests Up: News You Won't Find in Brazil's Newspapers," *New Republic*.

55. "American Chamber's Program in Brazil Both Preps Students and Closes a Gap," *Business Latin America*, 18 January 1973, p. 24.

56. *Brazilian Information Bulletin*, no. 5 (August-September 1971), p. 3.

57. *Business Week*, 13 March 1971, pp. 90–93.

58. *Brazilian Information Bulletin*, no. 11 (Fall 1973), p. 15.

through organizations such as IPES, cooperated with U.S. business and the U.S. government in preparing the way for the 1964 coup. In the aftermath of the coup these "denationalized" local elites assisted the military government in opening up the nation's resources for exploitation by U.S.-based firms such as the Hanna Mining Corporation, and supported government offers of lavish concessions to foreign investors. Among the groups most seriously disadvantaged by the reversal of economic policies following the coup was the genuinely national bourgeoisie—that sector of the domestic business community that was not at the service of foreign capital.

[5]

Manipulation of the Media

Brazilian journalist Genival Rabelo has characterized the dilemma facing his profession, even before the "revolution," in the following terms:

> This is the sad choice: to swim against the current, standing firm on a legacy of convictions . . . or to leave ourselves at the mercy of the current, fattening ourselves like pigs for—who knows?—the inexorable sacrifice of the great feast of the conquerors.[1]

U.S. government and business have acquired access to the media, thus to a means of molding public opinion, in various ways, including direct diplomatic pressure to silence or manipulate the content of local media output. One instance of direct diplomatic pressure is an incident that is said to have occurred in Pôrto Alegre in early August 1967. A radio commentator announced that foreigners had acquired vast tracts of land in the Amazon basin. The U.S. consulate in Pôrto Alegre then reportedly pressured local authorities to caution the station director against a repetition of such "pernicious" commentaries.[2]

Other means employed to acquire access have been: the overt and covert activities of the United States Information Service; covert saturation campaigns involving massive subsidies to particular journalists,

1. Rabelo, *O Capital Estrangeiro*, pp. 264–65.
2. Rabelo, *Ocupação da Amazonia* (Rio de Janeiro; Empresa Jornalística PN, 1968), p. 54.

publishers, and electronic media for short-range purposes;[3] control of the advertising industry; and the long-range trend of denationalization both of specific periodicals and radio and television stations and of the sources of information. The latter, of course, is the most effective of the several means. This chapter elaborates on the means employed for acquiring access to the media, the directions in which the United States has sought to mold public opinion, and the consequences for the Brazilian communication media and the Brazilian public.

The Varied Role of USIS

Overt activities of USIS in Brazil, as elsewhere, have included nationwide distribution of material for use by radio, television, and publications. USIS also makes available a daily news file and maintains binational centers equipped with libraries and documentary films. Voice of America broadcasts in Portuguese include news, features, and cultural programs. USIS has conducted a number of other activities, however, both overt and covert, that are less well known.

3. Agee explains that official propaganda is divided into three categories: white, gray, and black (*Inside the Company*, pp. 70–72.) White propaganda is acknowledged as coming from the U.S. government, often from USIA. Gray propaganda, which may be issued by USIA as well as the CIA, is attributed to people or organizations who do not acknowledge the U.S. government as their sponsor. Black propaganda, supposedly authorized only by the CIA, is unattributed, attributed to a nonexistent source or falsely attributed to a real source. It may take the form of books, magazines, radio, television, wall-painting, handbills, decals, religious sermons, and political speeches, as well as items in the daily press.

The U.S. Senate Select Committee on Intelligence noted in its final report that "until February 1976, when it announced a new policy toward U.S. media personnel, the CIA maintained covert relationships with about 50 American journalists or employees of U.S. media organizations. They are part of a network of several hundred foreign individuals around the world who provide intelligence for the CIA and at times attempt to influence foreign opinion through the use of covert propaganda. These individuals provide the CIA with direct access to a large number of foreign newspapers and periodicals, scores of press services and news agencies, radio and television stations, commercial book publishers, and other foreign media outlets."

The Committee expressed concern, in particular, over the domestic "fallout" of covert propaganda placed overseas. They noted that in 1970 the CIA had expressed satisfaction that its propaganda placements in Chile were being "replayed" throughout Latin America as well as in the United States (I: 191–201).

For comprehensive accounts of CIA propaganda campaigns in Chile from the presidential election of 1964 through the coup of 1973, see the Select Committee's report on *Covert Action* and Fred Landis, "Psychological Warfare and Media Operations in Chile, 1970–1973," Ph.d. diss. (University of Illinois at Urbana, October 1975).

Like other U.S. agencies in Brazil, USIS was in a state of panic in the early 1960s. One USIS official, concerned about the wandering minstrels of the Northeast that were publicizing the feats of the Peasant Leagues, proposed that a U.S. folk singer be sent to the Northeast to counter the minstrels—in English. That project was never executed. Nevertheless, after the coup, USIS did not hesitate to distribute the most incredible "documents" issued by the military regime to justify its repressive tactics.[4]

In a 1966 report to the Senate Appropriations Committee, Senator Allen J. Ellender expressed dismay at the expanse of the USIS operation in Brazil. The number of Americans on location had almost tripled, from 26 in 1958 to 67 in fiscal 1967, and the number of locals employed by the agency had increased in that period from 16 to 164. USIS maintained three libraries, a reading room, and nine binational centers in the country. Interestingly, while media operations were being expanded dramatically between 1962 and 1967, the number of persons involved in the exchanges of students, teachers, and researchers, programs also overseen by USIS (but less subject to content control by government), dropped steadily from 69 Americans and 104 Brazilians in 1962 to an estimated 34 Americans and 65 Brazilians in 1967. In addition to these activities, USIS Rio conducts a program for the translation of American books into Portuguese. According to USIS, these books cover "such subjects as American history, economics, science, communism, literature, etc." In the years 1965 through 1967, 442 books were published under this program. USIS also publishes a monthly periodical on labor, *O Trabalhador*, for distribution to all unions and other labor groups. The cost of this operation in 1967 was $14,647.[5]

The generally acknowledged mandate of USIS is to project a favorable image of the United States abroad, but in overt as well as covert operations, the scope of the content it projects is both broader and more goal-oriented. The agency's actual activities include projecting a favorable image of governments, political figures, and policies favored by the United States. William Rogers describes, for example, a tasteless commercial released by USIS in 1968, which utilized sex appeal to praise Brazil's industrial development.[6]

In 1972 the Senate Foreign Relations Committee probed into the

---

4. Page, *The Revolution That Never Was*, pp. 130, 217.

5. Ellender Report, pp. 333–35, 340–55. Rabelo maintained that a number of Brazilian publishers are on the USIS payroll (*O Capital Estrangeiro*, p. 69).

6. William Rogers, "The Agony of National Development in Brazil," manuscript (Ithaca, N.Y., October 1970).

content of unattributed information being distributed in Latin America by USIS (the practice itself had been classified as confidential). One such item was a pamphlet on the benefits of private oil exploration. Another was a cartoon booklet on urban terrorism entitled *El Desengaño (The Disillusionment)*. According to USIS officials, as reported in the *New York Times*, 148,000 copies of *El Desengaño* were distributed to agency posts in ten Latin American countries.[7]

Another USIS activity in Latin America in the early 1970s was obtaining surveys, under a contract arrangement, to determine the degree of exposure of populations to the various communications media and the relative effectiveness of each medium. The results of such surveys are classified, but they are sometimes released to foreign government agencies that indicate a need for them. The potential value of such information to a host government is obvious.[8]

Ethel Berger, a Brazilian national employed by the Voice of America for the last thirteen years, first in Brazil and later in Washington, writes special programs for Brazil on education in the United States. She told this author that she writes, in particular, of innovative means of diminishing student dissent, such as the "university without walls" concept for off-campus study.[9]

The Saturation Campaign

The covert CIA and/or U.S. business subsidization of media campaigns for short-range goals is of course harder to document, but the activities of IBAD and its subsidiary, S.A. Incrementadora de Vendas Promotion, during the elections of 1962 provide some examples. Promotion, though somewhat older than IBAD itself, was virtually unknown within the Brazilian advertising industry prior to 1960. Its annual budget up to that time had never been more than 10 million cruzeiros. The two largest associations representing the advertising industry, Associação Brasileira de Propaganda and Associação Brasileira das Agencias de Propaganda, testified before the congressional commission investigating the paternity of IBAD that neither Promotion nor any of its directors had ever been affiliated with their organizations. Nevertheless, the commission found that Promotion withdrew about 1.4 billion cruzeiros from the National City Bank of New York, the Bank

7. John W. Finney, "USIA Confirms Role in Unattributed Pamphlets," *New York Times*, 22 March 1972.

8. Information gained through conversations with several employees of USIA, 1971–1972.

9. Ethel Berger, interview, 25 April 1973, Copenhagen.

of Boston, and the Royal Bank of Canada during the electoral campaign of 1962.[10]

In addition to more than eighty weekly radio programs scattered throughout the country, Promotion, on the eve of the election, sponsored some three hundred additional hours of radio and television advertising and saturated the press with its materials. It also provided an unknown quantity of billboards, pamphlets, and the like in support of *ibadiano* candidates. Apart from the activities of Promotion, IBAD itself kept dozens of journalists on its payroll and edited a monthly magazine, *Ação Democrática*. The magazine, which used top-quality paper and was published in quantities of some 250 million copies, was distributed free and carried no advertising. IBAD also translated and distributed at least one book, *Assalto ão Parlamento*, in which the Czech author, Jan Kosak, described how the communists came to power in his country. But the project that aroused the greatest indignation among Brazilian journalists was IBAD's renting for ninety days the editorial pages of Rio's evening paper, *A Noite*.[11]

Other organizations of questionable parentage, such as IPES, sponsored hundreds of newspaper articles, as well as pamphlets and books, in the period preceding the coup of 1964, and a lesser volume in the period following it.[12] In an in-depth study of the Guanabara branch of IPES, Norman Blume found that the organization had sought and received assistance from the U.S. Embassy's book program. The Embassy assisted, for example, in the publication of Sonia Seganfredo's *UNE—Instrumento de Subversão (UNE—Instrument of Subversion)*, which was distributed to university students as part of an attempt by IPES to gain control of the student movement. Such publications were distributed free and without attribution.[13]

Other U.S. entities functioning in a semiprivate, or ostensibly private, capacity have contributed to the informational campaigns of IPES. One of the IPES-sponsored booklets, with a million-copy distribution in the early 1960s, was André Gama's "Nossos Males e Seus Remedios" ("Our Ills and their Remedies"). It was distributed primarily by manufacturers and merchants to their employees. Gama is the pseudonym of a U.S. citizen who was residing in Petropolis. IPES's Central de Bibliotécnica in Rio, which promotes the publication of children's books, has been assisted by the Franklin Book Company, a

10. Dutra, IBAD pp. 17–18.
11. Ibid., pp. 14, 17, 28, 68.
12. Hall, "The Country That Saved Itself," pp. 138–43.
13. Blume, "Pressure Groups and Decision-Making," p. 215.

clearing house for U.S. publishers who wish to have their books distributed abroad, and the organization's Study Group has entered into contract since the coup with the U.S. Committee for Economic Development for the publication of works on the Brazilian economy.[14]

Celso Furtado maintains that U.S. Embassy funds derived from PL 480 sales were being expended for the publication of books and other materials in Brazil during Goulart's presidency. The director of the Fundo de Cultura, which published books on economics denouncing socialism and espousing free enterprise, told Furtado that his operation was U.S.-funded.[15]

But the activities of USIS, acknowledged or secret, and the saturation campaign of limited duration and more or less limited objectives, pale to insignificance beside the general trend toward denationalization outlined by Brazilian journalist Genival Rabelo in *O Capital Estrangeiro na Imprensa Brasileira (Foreign Capital in the Brazilian Press)*. Rabelo noted that journalism is both a profession of the utmost significance in terms of popular and national sovereignty—the fourth estate—and a business enterprise; as such, it is in a position of double jeopardy, subject to political reprisals not only directly through the actions of governments, but also indirectly, through the clients and agencies of the advertising industry.

The Alienation of the National Media

The legislators who drafted and promulgated Brazil's Constitution of 1946 recognized both the importance of a communications media free of foreign control and the hazards facing such a national system. Article 160 of that constitution reserves to native-born Brazilians the rights of ownership, direction, and administration of the communications media.[16] Nevertheless, long before the "revolution" of 1964, the Brazilian market had been invaded by periodicals controlled by U.S. capital, but published in Portuguese in Brazil. With the superior resources at their command, they had entered the battle for the formation and conquest of Brazilian public opinion and were pushing national enterprises off the market with formidable speed and precision.

The invasion began in the 1940s, when *Seleções de Reader's Digest*,

14. Ibid, pp. 215–17.

15. Furtado interview.

16. Rabelo, *O Capital Estrangeiro*, p. 23. Alan Wells notes in *Picture Tube Imperialism? The Impact of Television on Latin America* (Maryknoll, N.Y.: Orbis Books, 1972) that the United States has similar laws governing radio and TV broadcasting (p. 95).

which had been imported and subject to customs duties, was granted the right to publish in Brazil in the São Paulo offices of Editôra Ipiranga on the pretext that its content was cultural and scientific only, devoid of political implications. With that the floodgates were open. *Seleções* was followed in 1950 by *Visão*, whose parent organization, Vision, Inc., with offices in New York,[17] went on to edit in Brazil *Dirigente Industrial, Dirigente Rural,* and *Dirigente Constructor.* In 1964 it also took over *Direção*, which had belonged to McGraw-Hill Publishers, Inc. The major group of suspected U.S. origin operating in Brazil, however, is Editôra Abril. Its local manager, Victor Civita, was born in Italy, launched his journalistic career with Time-Life, Inc., in New York, and transferred to Brazil in 1951. Within fifteen years, he was operating one of the largest publishing complexes in Latin America, with twenty-two periodicals having a combined monthly circulation of 4,500,000. The most popular magazine published by Editôra Abril is *Realidade*, with a circulation of some 200,000.[18] At the same time that Victor Civita emigrated to Brazil, his brother, Cezar, emigrated to Argentina and founded an Editôra Abril in Buenos Aires. Its flag magazine, *Panorama*, carries the name "Time-Life" on its masthead.[19]

One of the means employed by such periodicals, beginning with *Dirigente Industrial,* to capture select elements of the Brazilian market and mold Brazilian opinion was the device of controlled circulation or house organ—that is, free distribution to select readers. Another device which set such periodicals apart from European journals, like *Paris Match,* which paid customs duties and were clearly identified as to national origin, was the liberal usage of Brazilian national symbols. Rabelo noted that the weekly *Visão,* for example (a magazine with a circulation of some 80,000, which covers, among other things, local politics) fools a great part of its readership as to the interests represented in its editorial commentary because "se veste camuflada-mente de verde-amarelo"[20] ("It camouflages itself in green and yellow"—Brazil's national colors). In addition to such periodicals of allegedly disguised ownership and national origin, there were in circulation by the mid-1960s a number of specialized journals of obvious

17. E. Blum in "Time-Life Caper, Brazil's Yankee Network: Infiltration of Communications Media," *The Nation*, 29 May 1967, pp. 678–81, noted that in 1966, amidst the uproar over links between Time-Life and TV Globo, the corporate links between *Visão* and Vision, Inc., were ostensibly severed.

18. Rabelo, *O Capital Estrangeiro*, p. 24.

19. E. Blum, "Time-Life Caper."

20. Rabelo, *O Capital Estrangeiro*, p. 44.

U.S. ownership, such as *Propaganda,* controlled by J. Walter Thompson, and *Reporter Esso.*[21]

In 1963 pressures began to build for an official investigation into foreign encroachment on the communications media and, largely through the initiatives of federal deputy João Dória, a congressional investigating committee (Comissão Parlamentar de Inquérito—CPI) was established for this purpose. In addition to examining the infusion of foreign-owned periodicals and radio and television stations into the national market, the committee was empowered to investigate the practice of extortion by the major foreign advertising agencies against Brazilian-owned publications.

The original committee was dissolved after the "revolution" without having presented its findings, and, for his efforts on that committee (as well as the one investigating IBAD), Dória was stripped of his electoral mandate; he subsequently went into exile in Europe. In response to accusations by the authorities of Guanabara, a new congressional committee was established in October 1965 for the more limited purpose of investigating the links between O Globo (Organização Rádio, TV e Jornal O Globo) and Time-Life.[22] The pressure to squelch the investigation was so great that some of the deputies who had petitioned for the formation of the committee in the first place asked that their names be removed from the petition.[23] But the chorus of accusations was so strong that the committee was allowed to continue its work, and a presidential investigating panel was formed as well.

The immediate catalyst of the investigation was an inadvertent discovery by Carlos Lacerda. A Cuban employed by TV Globo, denounced to Lacerda's security police as a Castroite "agent," turned out to be a "refugee" and a Time-Life executive earning U.S. $20,000 a year. Under questioning, he "spilled the beans" to the Guanabara authorities about the "deal" between Time-Life and O Globo.[24]

A "technical assistance" and "joint participation" agreement of 1962, when TV Globo was still in the planning stage, labeled Time-Life's 30 percent interest in the enterprise a "foreign investment." And despite a constitutional provision that management of news media

21. Ibid., pp. 75, 100.

22. A foreign service officer who had served in Brazil in the 1950s told this author that the CIA had a policy of attempting to own or control at least one major newspaper in many countries. In Brazil, he said, it had owned or controlled O Globo. I have been unable, however, to confirm this.

23. Rabelo, O Capital Entrangeiro, pp. 78, 108–15.

24. Blum, "Time-Life Caper."

paigns is not designed to expound qualities of commercial products, but rather to sell the idea of 'free initiative' in the exploration of petroleum and to point out the disadvantages of state monopoly—through so-called institutional propaganda."[29]

U.S. advertising agencies had obtained an early foothold in Brazil. J. Walter Thompson was the first, entering the market in 1930. McCann Erickson followed in 1935. By 1966, according to Rabelo, eight U.S.-owned agencies accounted for 50 percent of all advertising in the country.[30] Rabelo remarked that a publication shunned by these agencies is a publication condemned, and another Brazilian journalist, E. C. Ribeiro, noted that the major clients of these agencies, also foreign for the most part, are in a position to dictate the rules which the Brazilian press must follow.[31]

This situation means, for one thing, that domestic periodicals in direct competition for general or specialized readership with those that are U.S.-owned are in jeopardy. *O Cruzeiro Internacional* succumbed, for example, in the early 1960s, because of the competition of *Life International*. When *Life* put its Spanish edition into the field, the U.S. corporations that had been the advertising backstay of *O Cruzeiro* dropped the latter and swung behind *Life*.[32] In the specialized sector of engineering and architecture, more than forty Brazilian journals, including the prestigious *Módulo*, founded and directed by Oscar Niemeyer, had gone under by 1966.

The implications of the predicament for media with considerable news content and political commentary were even more sinister. In the first place, such media are largely dependent on U.S. wire services, which are not necessarily forthcoming with all types of information. (An internal memorandum of UPI Brazil dated 29 July 1955, entitled "Instruction to All Editors," contained the following: "I recommend that no telegram pertaining to the profits of Standard Oil be translated and distributed. Please pass on to me any dispatch on this matter that arrives." It was signed by W. W. Copeland, general manager of UPI in Brazil.) Furthermore, the agencies and agency clients that control the flow of funds to the media are in a position to veto vertain types of arti-

29. Rabelo, *O Capital Estrangeiro*, pp. 115, 225.

30. Ibid., pp. 27, 182, 162. E. Blum noted that four of these handled about 37 percent of all agency billing in the country ("Time-Life Caper"); and Wells maintained that by 1970 all but two Latin American countries had more U.S.-owned than domestic ad agencies (*Picture Tube Imperialism?*, pp. 121-32).

31. Rabelo, *O Capital Estrangeiro*, pp. 165, 218.

32. Blum, "Time-Life Caper."

cles, to insist on the dismissal of certain journalists, or, if the periodicals or other media refuse to bow to such pressure, to withdraw all
financing and force the offenders to fold.

Manchete, for example, was subjected to the article veto when its director, Justino Martins, returning from the Soviet Union in 1962, began
what was billed as a series of articles on life in a socialist state. The first
article turned out also to be the last, as a group of important U.S advertisers threatened reprisals if the series were continued. *Ultima Hora*
was forced to dismiss its noted journalist Arapuã as a consequence of
such pressures. The departure of Luis Alberto Bahia from the editorial
staff of *Correio da Manhã* and the brief sojourn of Antonio Callado as
chief editor of that paper have similar explanations. The paper was
advised that only a 180-degree turn from its editorial bent would
forestall economic reprisals.

The list of periodicals, such as *Diário Carioca* and *Política e
Negócios* (which had the audacity to protest the denationalization of
the media), that had folded from such starvation tactics even before the
"revolution" of 1964 is probably very long; but we have no precise
record of their comings and goings because the specialized nationally
owned periodicals, such as *Anuario Brasileiro de Imprensa, Anuario
de Publicidade*, and *Serviço de Imprensa Inter*, that might at least have
provided the obituaries had themselves folded.[33]

Official data revealed that by the end of the decade of the 1960s, 99
percent of the country's advertising industry was controlled by foreign
capital.[34] Total advertising expenditure in Brazil in 1971 amounted to
U.S. $430 million—a 22 percent increase over the previous year—and
in 1972 it was estimated at more than one-half billion dollars. J. Walter
Thompson remained the largest agency, with more than 300 employees
in 1971 and reported billings of $24 million; and McCann Erickson
remained in second place. *Advertising Age* reported in 1973 that for
every U.S. agency already in Brazil there were at least two more struggling to get in. And the Brazilian agencies, having become accustomed
to exchanging shares for "know-how," apparently were not struggling
to keep them out. Many of the contemporary generation of Brazilian
agency executives boast of experience with J. Walter Thompson.
Geraldo Alonso, head of Norton Publicidade, the largest Brazilian
agency, and president of the Brazilian Association of Advertising

33. Rabelo, *O Capital Estrangeiro*, pp. 51–79, 151, 163, 249–50.

34. Schilling, "Brazil: The Rebellion of the Downtrodden." Figures cited
here were drawn from a *Visão* publication on the order of a Who's Who of Brazilian businesses, with official data supplied by two government agencies, the
National Department of Commerce and Central Bank of Brazil.

Agencies, said, "It is important to Norton to establish an international connection with an American agency. It is not reasonable for us to expect to keep our position without knowledge from the United States."[35]

Ironically, *Seleções de Reader's Digest*, the first of the foreign-owned periodicals to sidestep Article 160 of the Constitution by claiming that its content was devoid of political implications, published a 23-page feature article in November 1964 entitled "A Nacão que se salvou a si mesma" ("The Country That Saved Itself"). The cover page of the U.S. edition bore this notation: "The inspiring story of how an aroused Brazilian people stopped the communists from taking over their nation. Because it is a document of unusual significance, this feature has been especially bound so that it can be detached and mailed to other interested readers." For this article venerating the conspirators who overthrew Goulart, Clarence Hall, senior editor of *Reader's Digest*, was personally congratulated by Castello Branco. The new president asserted that "the publication of this article was among the major contributions of an organ of the press to the movement restoring democracy to Brazil. *Seleções de Reader's Digest* may be justifiably proud of having carried to millions of readers around the world the faithful account of the political events of 1964 in our country."[36]

By the mid-sixties the experience of the Brazilian media had aroused concern elsewhere. *El Comercio*, for example, dean of the Peruvian press, published an editorial concluding with this warning:

> The experience of Brazil must serve as an example for us. Journalism is not merely a business, it is fundamentally a daily platform for decency and morality. These are not values that can be assessed with the wallets of foreign merchants. When one confronts such a deformation of the journalistic profession, one is confronting a danger to democracy.[37]

A New Role for the Media

After 1968, when journalists found themselves under the heavy hand of official censorship and government repression, the dilemma that had faced the media in the early 1960s became, at least temporarily, a moot point. Many of the journalists and publishers who had been among the most enthusiastic supporters of the "revolution" had themselves be-

---

35. Ramona Bechtos, "Brazil's Marketing Scene Reflect's Nation's Growth," *Advertising Age*, 12 February 1973, pp. 3, 60; "Brazilian Agencies Growing Faster than U.S. Shops: Finances Strong," 19 February 1973, pp. 46 48–49; "Brazilian Agencies Big on Creativity: Many Execs Boast JWT Experience," 26 February 1973, pp. 160–61.

36. Rabelo, *O Capital Estrangeiro*, p. 243.

37. Ibid., p. 103.

come victims of governmental repression. The press, prohibited from publishing any news about the military's "coup within a coup" of 13 December 1968, responded with a touch of surrealism. Rio's *Correio da Manhã* carried the headline, "Rich Cat Dies of Heart Attack in Chicago." *Jornal do Brasil* featured a weather report: "Weather bleak. Temperature suffocating. The air is unbreathable. The country is being swept by a strong wind."[38]

Law No. 5.250 of 9 February 1967, had put "all the news that's fit to print" into the category of delegated (as opposed to residual) rights. A lecturer at the Superior War College noted, "The Press Law even enumerates those cases in which the exercise of liberty of thought is not abused. . . ."[39] The monitors of thought must have concluded, however, that they had left some loopholes. A directive distributed to the media by the Minister of Justice in June 1969 prohibited the publishing of news, commentaries, interviews, or statements about: anyone charged with or convicted of a political offense; any student group which the government had suspended; any demonstrations or strikes or conflicts between authorities and students; any criticism of official decrees or acts such as the press censorship order; any word of political imprisonment or any facts of a political nature, unless verified by a competent authority. The directive also prohibited criticism of the economy, the federal government, or Brazilian "customs." News concerning the political attitudes of clergymen was also prohibited, as was news of protests or rebellion in other countries. The section entitled "As to the Rockefeller Mission" explicitly prohibited publication of news or photographs of hostile acts against the "illustrious visitor" in any Latin American country or reference to postponements or cancellations of his visits.[40]

By the early 1970s each paper had a staff member who served as the resident censor and received the official word as to what might be published. Even so, the government occasionally got its own wires crossed. In one case in 1971, the papers were originally forbidden to

38. Burns, "Brazil: The Imitative Society," p. 19.

39. Presidência da República, Estado-Maior das Fôrças Armadas, Escola Superior de Guerra, Departamento de Estudos, T139–73, "Legislação Brasileira e Segurançã Nacional," Part 2 (Presentation by a panel consisting of Desembargador Antonio de Arruda, do Corpo Permanente; Ministro Carlos Coqueijo Forreão da Costa, do Corpo de Estagiários e dos Assessores de Ministério das Communicações; Dr. Vincente Greco Filho e Dr. Gaspar Luiz Grani Vianna, 18 July 1973), pp. 26–27.

40. Ministries in Higher Education, West Coast Region, "Press Censorship in Brazil Intensified in Connection with Rockefeller's Visit," mimeographed (n.d.).

print that a governor had been charged with corruption and forced to resign. Then the word came down that the story was to be run, as some explanation for the resignation appeared to be necessary. But when the weekly magazine *Veja* appeared with the account, all its issues were confiscated.[41] The ultimate absurdity in information control was a presidential decree issued in November 1971 in which President Médici authorized himself to make secret laws.[42] And the argument concerning censorship and civil rights took an ironic twist in 1976 when twenty-one government censors, faced with dismissal for failing a psychological screening test, appealed to the courts on the grounds that their civil rights had been infringed.[43]

The obliteration of unofficial news and free expression, however, has not necessarily meant a lesser role for the media. Television, in fact, has been exhaustively used to sell the government and its policies as well as to generate artificial demand for consumer products. Richard Barnet has noted that Brazil is perhaps "the world's first technocratic dictatorship" in that, unlike the fascist and communist systems that have utilized coerced mass participation, the Brazilian regime has sought to enhance its power through appealing to "the glazed eyes of millions of TV viewers, each sitting in isolation."[44]

Advertisers in Brazil spend proportionately more than their counterparts in the United States on television, as opposed to other forms of advertising. In 1968, television accounted for 45 percent of total expenditures, as opposed to 16 percent for radio and 39 percent for print. Wells noted that the presence of U.S. agencies, their U.S. clients, and U.S.-owned television corporations in Latin America "serves to emphasize that the structure of U.S. television operations in Latin America is geared to business, not developmental, imperatives. Their prime responsibility is a good yield for their stockholders, and expansion. The effect is to channel Latin American wealth into the American international corporations."[45]

41. Richard Barnet, "Letter from Rio: Fairly Cruel but Sensible Policies," *Harper's Magazine* 245 (September 1972): 16–22.

42. Burns, "Brazil: The Imitative Society."

43. Jonathan Kandell, "21 Brazil Censors, Long in Power, Fail Psychological Screening Test," *New York Times*, 3 April 1976.

44. Barnet, "Letter from Rio," p. 20. According to USIA's *Country Data: Brazil* (Washington, D.C., 1 November 1973), there were 7 or 8 million black and white receivers in the country and some 35,000 to 66,000 color receivers. São Paulo and Rio de Janeiro accounted for about two-thirds of these sets. The country's potential viewing audience was estimated at over 30 million, and the TV market was expanding in the early 1970s at the rate of 20 percent a year.

45. Wells, *Picture Tube Imperialism?*, pp. 131–32, 183.

Commenting upon the U.S. exportation of artificially induced consumer needs, a U.S. theologian noted in 1970 that in Recife, where most of the children who escape starvation are dressed in castoff rags, the smart shops were sporting a new U.S. visitor—"Barbie Doll," complete with a guidebook on the clothes Barbie will need to be well dressed for all occasions.[46]

We have seen that the U.S. government has sought to influence public opinion in Brazil both through the programs of USIS and through media saturation campaigns. Over the long run, U.S. publishing companies with interests in Brazil, U.S advertising agencies, and the U.S.-based corporate clients of advertising agencies have apparently contributed even more heavily to fashioning or controlling the output of the communications media.

In the early 1960s the U.S. government, in concert with U.S. business, made use of its access to the Brazilian media to spread scare propaganda about the communist threat posed by the Goulart government and its supporters and to promote certain political figures and organizations while denouncing others. After the 1964 coup, this access was used to promote the image and the programs of the new military regime.[47]

Even before the timid remains of political debate in the media were smothered by official censorship in 1968, open expression of views offensive to the U.S. government or U.S. business had proven risky, as it often provoked economic reprisals from the U.S. advertising agencies and their U.S. clients. Furthermore, a great many Brazilian journals and other channels of communication had been pushed off the market by illegal competition from U.S.-based publications. As the military regime moved toward ever harsher measures to repress free expression, the most significant form of U.S. influence transmitted through the media appeared to be the promotion of consumerism, and thus the glorification of materialism.

46. Harvey G. Cox, *Christianity and Crisis* 30 no. 7 (27 April 1970): 1.

47. The Senate Intelligence Committee noted that after the 1973 coup in Chile, "The goal of covert action immediately following the coup was to assist the junta in gaining a more positive image, both at home and abroad . . .(*Covert Action*, p. 187).

[6]

Leashing the Labor Movement

It has been noted that U.S. attempts to influence the internal balance of power in Brazil in the early 1960s included not only strengthening those groups that shared U.S. fears of communism and nationalization, but also co-opting and weakening those that did not. The Brazilian labor movement, on the whole, did not share those fears. In fact, it was, to a large extent, the immediate object of them. One of the instruments devised to deal with labor in Brazil and throughout Latin America was the American Institute for Free Labor Development (AIFLD). AIFLD's mission was to train a new breed of leaders who would cooperate with their U.S. counterparts and benefactors and would replace and restrain their more radical colleagues. This chapter traces the development of AIFLD and its activities and influence in Brazil.

The United States labor movement's attempts to acquire hegemony over its Latin American counterparts antedate the Cold War by a couple of decades. The American Federation of Labor proposed to the International Federation of Trade Unions in July 1929 that the AFL-backed Pan American Federation of Labor (PAFL), established 11 years earlier, be given the exclusive right to organize unions in Latin America.[1] Later, the Inter-American Regional Organization (ORIT) of the International Confederation of Free Trade Unions (ICFTU), which superseded the defunct PAFL in 1951,[2] became the channel through which the

1. Joseph John Palisi, "The Latin American Confederation of Christian Trade Unions (CLASC), 1954–1967" (American University, Washington, D.C., 1968).

2. On the sequence of labor federations, see Robert J. Alexander, "Latin America's Secular Labor Movement," *Government and Politics in Latin America: A Reader*, ed. Peter G. Snow (New York: Holt, Rinehart and Winston, 1967), Ch. 22.

AFL-CIO sought to combat the socialistic and nationalistic orientations of most Latin American unions and to expand on the toehold of United States labor's influence in Latin America.

In the early 1960s, however, given the threat that Castroism was believed to represent to United States interests and the opportunities that the Alliance for Progress offered to various groups interested in expanding their influence on foreign policy, it was decided that a more direct conduit for the exertion of United States influence on labor in Latin America was in order. In August 1961, the AFL-CIO chartered the American Institute for Free Labor Development (AIFLD) as a nonprofit corporation. George Meany, AFL-CIO president, became president of AIFLD also, and Joseph A. Beirne, president of the Communications Workers of America (CWA) became secretary-treasurer. The raison d'être of AIFLD was stated unequivocally when, in the wake of the Bay of Pigs fiasco, President John F. Kennedy endorsed the idea of a program "through which the talents and experience of the United States labor movement could be brought to bear on the danger that Castro . . . might undermine the Latin American labor movement."[3]

The financial contributions of United States corporations to AIFLD have been minimal, amounting to only $175,000 by 1967. Corporate representation, however, on AIFLD's board of trustees has been equal to that of labor. In addition to its chairman, J. Peter Grace, president of W. R. Grace and Company, AIFLD's board has included Charles Brinckerhoof, chairman of the board of the Anaconda Company; William M. Hickey, president of the United Corporation; Robert C. Hill, director, Merck and Company; Juan C. Trippe, chairman of the board of Pan American World Airways; and Henry S. Woodbridge, chairman of the board of the Tru-Temper Copper Corporation.[4] In addition, International Telephone and Telegraph and some fifty-five other corporations are listed as contributors.[5]

AIFLD became the principal instrument of the United States government for supplying technical assistance to Latin American trade unions, and its projects were highly favored by such multilateral sources of credit as the IADB. By 1967, the fiscal yearly budget for

3. Ronald Radosh, *American Labor and United States Foreign Policy: The Cold War in the Unions from Gompers to Lovestone* (New York: Random House, 1970). Citations here are drawn from chapter 13, "American Labor in Latin America: The AIFLD, the State Department, and the AFL-CIO."

4. Radosh, *American Labor and U.S. Foreign Policy; The AIFLD Report*, vol. 10, no. 6 (June 1972), p. 2.

5. Eugene H. Methvin, "Labor's New Weapon for Democracy," *Reader's Digest*, 45th year, October 1966, pp. 21–28.

AIFLD was over $6 million. Overt U.S. government funding of AIFLD increased from 62 percent of the total in 1962 to 92 percent in 1967. The contribution of AID amounted to $15.4 million for that period. The full amount of government funding is not to be found in the public record of AID, however; it was revealed in the spring of 1967 that AIFLD and a number of its constituent unions were among the organizations receiving funds from foundations that served as conduits for the CIA. This relationship was denied, of course, by AIFLD spokesmen.[6]

The U.S. Senate Select Committee on Intelligence reported in April 1976 that the CIA, during the 1950s and 1960s, had "turned increasingly to covert action in the area of student and labor matters, cultural affairs, and community development," and that CIA interest in these matters reached a peak in the mid-1960s. By fiscal year 1967, over $6 million had been budgeted for labor programs. Most of these funds, the Committee reported, were transmitted through "legitimate or 'devised' foundations—that is, fictitious entities established by the CIA."[7]

In his CIA diary, Agee explained that prior to the founding of AIFLD, the agency's labor operations had been carried out largely through the ICFTU, ORIT, and the international trade secretariats, but that there had occasionally been problems of coordination between the operations of the international and regional agencies and those of the CIA's country stations. Furthermore, there was controversy in the agency over the general effectiveness of ORIT, and there were "limits on the amount of money that can be channelled covertly through the stations and through international organizations like ORIT and the ICFTU."[8] AIFLD, then, was seen as a channel through which to improve coordination and to "accelerate expansion of labour-organizing activities in Latin America in order to deny workers to labour unions dominated by the extreme left and to reverse communist and Castroite penetration." Agee noted that a first priority of AIFLD would be the establishment of training institutes in each of the Latin American countries, headed where possible by salaried CIA agents "with operational control exercised by the stations." He added that "spotting and assessment of

6. Palisi, "CLASC: 1954–1967," p. 234; Radosh, *American Labor and U.S. Foreign Policy*. According to the *Washington Post* (10 January 1975, p. A–10), a former high-ranking intelligence agent reported that he had taken part in intercepting the mail of George Meany, Jay Lovestone, and other AFL-CIO officials in order to monitor their use of CIA funds destined for European unions.

7. U.S., Congress, Senate Intelligence Committee, Book I, *Foreign and Military Intelligence*, 94th Cong. 2d sess. 26 April 1976, pp 181–82.

8. Agee, *Inside the Company*, pp. 74–77, 243–45.

potential agents for labour operations will be a continuing function of the Agency-controlled staff members both in the training courses in Latin America and in the Washington courses."[9]

Serafino Romualdi, who resigned as the AFL-CIO's Inter-American Representative to become AIFLD's first executive director, was described by Agee as a long-time agent of the CIA's International Organizations Division and the principal agent for labor operations in Latin America. William Doherty, initially AIFLD's social projects director, who succeeded Romualdi as executive director, was also described as a CIA agent, as was Andrew McClellan, who replaced Romualdi as AFL-CIO Inter-American Representative. Meany, Grace, and Beirne are described as CIA collaborators. All AIFLD programs, according to Agee, were sooner or later to be run closely by the CIA country stations, but initial expansion was so fast that in many cases nonagents were sent out as country directors and control had to be exercised through Washington.[10]

United States labor leaders were not unanimously enthusiastic about this cozy bedfellow relationship among labor, management, and government.[11] But Grace and Meany saw eye to eye in terms of the mutual interests of labor and management in the preservation of the capitalistic system and the defense of United States investments abroad. In a speech on 2 April, 1965, Meany reassured the Council on Latin America that labor understood that "the investors of risk capital also must be rewarded." In a radio interview in December 1963, AIFLD Executive Director William C. Doherty, Jr., said that AIFLD welcomed the cooperation of management "not only financially but in terms of establishing our policies. . . . The cooperation between ourselves and the business community is getting warmer day by day."[12] On other occasions, Doherty has asserted that Latin American unionists also oppose nationalization and that labor-management cooperation on AIFLD's board should dispel the hostility of Latin American workers toward United States corporations.

Among the overt activities of AIFLD has been the operation of an extensive system of training schools for selected Latin American labor union leaders. The main school in this network is located at Front Royal, Maryland. By 1968 over five hundred students had completed its three-month program, and some thirty thousand to sixty thousand

9. Ibid.

10. Ibid., pp. 244, 307, 368.

11. Radosh, *American Labor and U.S. Foreign Policy.*

12. Suzanne Bodenheimer, "U.S. Labor's Conservative Role in Latin America," *The Progressive,* 31 (1967): 26–30.

more had received training through the fourteen Latin American field offices. Graduates of the Front Royal Institute returned to their native countries under a nine-month salaried internship program.[13]

The curriculum at Front Royal in 1968 included only five hours in collective bargaining and the problems of labor in rural areas. No instruction was offered in profit-sharing, workers' education, or labor legislation. Each student, however, was given an average of 18 hours' training in "democracy and totalitarianism."[14] A popular method used by the instructors, some of whom were Cuban exiles, in political training was role-playing. Eugene H. Methvin describes one such role-playing session he witnessed as follows:

> Another session rehearsed a meeting of auto workers wherein "Red infiltrators" were trying to divert matters to political ends. "You are a puppet of Yankee imperialists trained in Washington!" shouted planted hecklers at Juan, the Argentine chairman. "American workers are the highest paid in the world under the free enterprise system of class cooperation," Juan shot back. "And what did you Communists learn in Cuba? How to reduce living standards by 15 percent in five years? How to destroy free unions and replace them with government bosses and forced labor? Is that how you plan to 'emancipate' the working class? If that's the best you have to offer us, take your doctrines back to Moscow—or is it Peking you're taking orders from this week?"[15]

One of the points emphasized in the AIFLD training manuals was that "communist infiltrators" often camouflaged their actual affiliations and ideological convictions and that it would therefore be necessary to identify them through their words and deeds. (It was suggested, for example, that those who expressed admiration for the Cuban experiment should be carefully watched.)[16] In accordance with this subjective method of identifying communists, the enemies of the "free trade movement" were by no means limited to self-designated communist or Marxist unions. Several observers have commented that the main targets of AIFLD criticism have been noncommunist unions that reject AIFLD doctrine. Ronald Radosh maintains that "any opposition to United States economic penetration and informal control of Latin America is described in these [Castroite or communist] terms." The Latin American Confederation of Christian Trade Unions (CLASC) has

13. Ibid.; Radosh, *American Labor and U.S Foreign Policy.*

14. Radosh, *American Labor and U.S. Foreign Policy.*

15. Methvin, "Labor's New Weapon."

16. Prior to the revelations in the fall of 1967 concerning CIA funding of AIFLD, this writer had tentatively agreed to illustrate a voluminous AIFLD manual. After reading the manual, however, I reneged on the agreement as the manual appeared to constitute little more than a clumsy propaganda effort.

been particularly vilified by AIFLD spokesmen. Joe Beirne, for example, stated in a 1963 news conference, "[CLASC has] been infiltrated and I think captured by the Communists. . . ."[17]

The development of the labor movement in Brazil had been well contained within the co-optation policies of the patrimonial state. Vargas had granted benefits to labor before they were demanded and thereby had controlled the movement while nurturing it as a power base. The Communist Party returned to prominence in the movement while it enjoyed government recognition between 1945 and 1947, and the Brazilian Labor Party (PTB) gained a foothold during that period, but between 1947 and Vargas' return to the presidency in 1951, labor activities were severely curtailed.

During the presidencies of Vargas and of Kubitschek in the 1950s, union elections, collective bargaining, and affiliation with international labor organizations were permitted and minimum wage levels were raised. Under the presidency of Goulart, labor moved into the period of its greatest independence. As labor minister and PTB leader, Goulart had been able to pose as labor's advocate regardless of government policy, but as president he was confronted with countervailing pressures. Labor, therefore, became more militant. Although the formation of a central labor organization on a national scale was prohibited by law, the illegal General Workers Command (CGT) openly pressured the government, and the Communist Party again became highly influential in the labor movement.[18]

Several years before the founding of AIFLD, a number of United States labor leaders (of the AFL) had expressed alarm over the growing strength of the communists within the Brazilian labor movement and, in league with the State Department, had attempted to reverse that trend. In 1956, for example, Serafino Romualdi, then the AFL-CIO's inter-American representative, made arrangements through Labor Attaché Irving Salert and Ambassador James C. Dunn for a number of Brazilian labor leaders to visit the United States. The purpose of the visit, as Romualdi explained it, was to develop "a corps of labor leaders who . . . could turn back Communist attempts to capture the Brazilian labor movement."[19] Although Jay Lovestone and others among Romualdi's colleagues favored outright head-on opposition to the Kubitschek government, those who counseled restraint prevailed for a

17. Bodenheimer, "U.S. Labor's Conservative Role."

18. Riordan Roett, *Brazil: Politics in a Patrimonial Society* (Boston: Allyn & Bacon, 1972), p. 132.

19. Radosh, *American Labor and U.S. Foreign Policy*, p. 424.

time. With the establishment of AIFLD and the assumption of power by Goulart, however, the alarmists gained the upper hand.

Following an autumn 1963 meeting in which Adhemar de Barros, governor of São Paulo, informed Romualdi of plans "to mobilize military and police contingents" against Goulart, AIFLD arranged a training session in Washington for "a special all-Brazilian class of thirty-three participants."Upon their return to Brazil, these trained unionists fanned out, some to the major cities and industrial centers and others to the interior.[20]

Their activities thereafter were outlined by AIFLD's Executive Director, William C. Doherty, Jr., in a radio interview in July 1964 with Frank Harden, Tad Szulc, and Harry Conn. Responding to Conn's inquiry as to the results of AIFLD training on Brazilian trade unionists, Doherty said:

> Well, very frankly, within the limits placed upon them by the administration of João Goulart, when they returned to their respective countries [*sic*], they were very active in organizing workers, and helping unions introduce systems of collective bargaining, and modern concepts of labor-management relations. As a matter of fact, some of them were so active that they became intimately involved in some of the clandestine operations of the revolution before it took place on April 1. What happened in Brazil . . . did not just happen—it was planned—and planned months in advance. Many of the trade union leaders—some of whom were actually trained in our institute—were involved in the revolution, and in the overthrow of the Goulart regime.[21]

Doherty did not elaborate on the nature of those clandestine activities, but an article by Eugene N. Methvin published in the October 1966 issue of *Reader's Digest* offered a clue. It revealed that Romullo Martinho, a communications union leader who had been trained at the Front Royal Institute, returned to Brazil and directed seminars concerning "what Red totalitarianism means, how communists infiltrate and control unions, and what must be done to stop them." He also warned key workers of coming trouble and urged them to keep communications going no matter what happened. When the call went out for a general strike to frustrate the coup attempt, the communication workers failed to respond. "The wires kept humming and the army was able to coordinate troop movements that ended the showdown bloodlessly. . . ." According to Methvin, "The new military regime promptly appointed 4 AIFLD graduates to clean out the Red-dominated unions and restore democratic processes."[22]

20. Ibid., ch. 13.
21. Ibid,; Palisi, "CLASC: 1954–1967," p. 466.
22. Methvin, "Labor's New Weapon."

Shortly after the coup, the AFL-CIO sent a group, headed by Inter-American Representative Andrew McClellan, to Brazil. Using Colonel Vernon Walters as an intermediary, they presented to President Castello Branco a set of proposals for a revised labor code. According to Michael Boggs, Assistant Inter-American Representative, the proposals, which called for "democratization" of the code, were accepted by Castello Branco, but vetoed by Finance Minister Roberto Campos.[23]

The CGT was abolished after the coup and some 409 unions, 43 federations, and 4 confederations were taken over by government interventors.[24] By 1966 most of the unions had been purged and returned to "dependable" hands. Article 530 of the revised Labor Code provided that those who had been deprived of their political rights and "those who publicly and ostentatiously, through acts or words, defend the ideological principles of a political party whose registration has been revoked, or of an association or entity of whatever nature whose activities have been considered contrary to the national interest, and whose registration has been cancelled, or whose functioning has been suspended by competent authority" were prohibited from holding office in economic or professional organizations.[25] A decree of September 8, 1967, said that "unions of all kinds ought to be true schools of moral and civic education."[26] Much of the task of imparting this education was allocated to AIFLD.

Evidence that AIFLD's battle against "communism" in the Brazilian labor movement did not subside after the coup is provided by the minutes of the AIFLD Board of Trustees' 1965 Annual Meeting. Romualdi noted that AIFLD was to open a branch center in Recife. The center was to serve as a *campesino* training school and as competition for a similar center already established by the (noncommunist) opposition to the AFL-CIO. It was also reported that in Porto Alegre "new seminar programs are being conducted to reorient workers who had been under Communist domination."[27] (By 1973, AIFLD had established six community centers in the Northeast.)[28]

After more than a year of voicing support for the Brazilian regime and providing rationales for its policies, the AFL-CIO was forced to concede in December 1965 that the "Castello Branco administration

23. Michael Boggs, Assistant Inter-American Representative, AFL-CIO, interview, 9 January 1974, Washington, D.C.

24. Frank, *Latin America*, pp. 195–96.

25. ESG, T139-73, "Legislação Brasileira," Part 2, pp. 19–20.

26. Roett, *Brazil* p. 133.

27. Radosh, *American Labor and U.S Foreign Policy*.

28. Boggs interview.

has recently become an authoritarian regime. It has curtailed civil and political rights and liberties, and the Brazilian labor movement has again been forced back to its original status—an integral part of the state." Nevertheless, on 1 April 1966 William Doherty and Castello Branco appeared on the same platform on the occasion of laying the cornerstone for an AIFLD housing development in São Paulo. And Doherty declared it appropriate that the ceremonies were taking place on the second anniversary of Brazil's "democratic Revolution."[29]

To Brazilian workers this "democratic revolution" has meant frozen wages and a precipitous decline in real income, and to their leaders it has meant, among other things, that under the provisions of "Law 40" they are required to obtain certification of their "good conduct," of "ideology," and of "democratic faith" from the police and from the Division of Political and Social Order (DOPS). To AIFLD Board Chairman and shipping magnate J. Peter Grace, Jr., on the other hand, it has meant decreasing harassment and increasing profits. Listing AIFLD accomplishments for a 1967 article, Grace said, "At the same time the AIFLD trains Latin Americans in techniques of combating Communist infiltration. This training has paid off handsomely in many situations. For instance, AIFLD trainees have driven Communists from port unions which were harassing shipping in Latin America." Along with the "exemplary accomplishments" in several other countries, Grace maintained that these trainees "helped to drive the Communists from strong 'jugular' unions in Brazil. . . ."[30]

Emboldened, perhaps, by previous successes, AIFLD and its affiliate, the International Federation of Petroleum and Chemical Workers (IFPCW), overplayed their hands in 1967. The IFPCW has been cited in numerous reports of the United States press as a recipient, on its own, of CIA funds (the federation's own financial records listed a $30,000 contribution from the Andrew Hamilton Foundation, a CIA front), but its general secretary, Lloyd A. Haskins, conceded in an interview published in 1968 that AIFLD "makes it possible for us to continue in Brazil."[31]

The IFPCW and its hybrid benefactor had been attempting since 1965 to draw the Brazilian petrochemical unions into affiliation with their

29. Radosh, *American Labor and U.S. Foreign Policy.*

30. Palisi, "CLASC: 1954–1967," pp. 319, 460.

31. Ibid., pp. 463–66; Ernest Garvey, "Meddling in Brazil: The CIA Bungles On," *Commonwealth* 37 (9 February 1968): 553–54. Agee claimed that "in the case of the petroleum industry the Agency [CIA] actually set up the ITS [International Trade Secretariat], the International Federation of Petroleum and Chemical Workers [IFPCW], through the U.S. union of petroleum workers, the Oil Workers International Union" (*Inside the Company*, p. 76).

North American counterpart. Despite the proffering of generous loans to favored unions, the U.S. organizations had not been successful in that attempt. They had been given credit, however, for the failure of the country's sixteen petroleum unions to unite in a national federation of petroleum workers.

Lourival Coutinho, leader of Rio de Janeiro's petroleum workers, had long suspected that IFPCW activities were related to efforts of the United States-based petroleum companies to have the military government suppress the state-owned petroleum corporation—PETROBRAS—in order to facilitate the exploitation of oil reserves by private capital. Coutinho had also attempted to call attention to the entanglement among IFPCW, AIFLD, and CIA. In the November 1967 issue of *Petrojornal,* he said of the IFPCW, "It does not operate with autonomy in Brazil. It only executes the programs of AIFLD . . . which for its part receives the imperative influences of not less than 60 large American companies and the vigilance of the . . . CIA."[32]

Coutinho obtained the signatures of 219 members of the Chamber of Deputies on a petition for a congressional investigation of the activities of the IFPCW and other international labor organizations in Brazil. On 27 October 1967 the National Congress authorized the creation of a nine-member investigation team with 10 million new cruzeiros to fund work for 120 days.

In the following December, a São Paulo trade union leader, Egisto Demonicali, uncovered a list of payoffs and other expenditures prepared for IFPCW representative Alberto Ramos, and a note from Ramos to his colleague Alex Nogueira in the São Paulo office. The note read: "I have with me 45,000,000 cruzeiros [U.S. $16,666.67] for you to distribute to the unions for campaigns in accordance with our plans. If you are not available before tomorrow, then arrange to be here on Wednesday, since I will be in Rio conversing with Velasquez about other trips to the United States." The itemized expense sheet attached included:

Bonus to José Abud for his collaboration	$156.25
Special payment for Dr. Jorge M. Filho of Labor Ministry	875.00
Trip for Mr. Glaimbore Guimasães, our informer at Fegundes Street	56.25
Photocopies of books and documents of Petroleum Federation	100.00
Assistance to Guedes and Eufrasio to defeat Luis Furtado of the Suzano Union	140.64

32. Garvey, "Meddling in Brazil."

Bonus to Carlos Feliz Nunez, labor reporter, for
    giving us favorable coverage   312.50
Bonus to Lit. Brandani of the National Investigation
    Service, for help with confidential information   564.48

When accounts of the gathering storm were belatedly picked up by U.S. wire services, the response of AIFLD sponsors and affiliates in the U.S. was predictable. Haskins, IFPCW General Secretary, labeled the charge against his federation as part of a "Communist conspiracy against the democratic trade union movement in Brazil," and a letter from George Meany to Ambassador Vasco Leitão da Cunha, dated 24 January 1968, warned of the serious repercussions that would follow a communist takeover of the Brazilian trade union movement.[33]

In addition to undermining the unity or potential unity of the Brazilian labor movement, AIFLD has had no qualms about attempting to undermine the activities of compatriot organizations that do not share its objectives. A memorandum from Doherty to the staff of AIFLD, dated 18 October 1963, instructed members to "bear in mind the possibility of cooperation with the Peace Corps on our projects in the country to which you are assigned." Although the Peace Corps in general has shunned AIFLD's approaches (and although the legislation creating the Peace Corps contained provisions specifically designed to shield the corps from CIA influence), AIFLD has persisted in its attempts to take advantage of Peace Corps contacts for its own purposes. A letter from Michael M. Richardson, project director for the Peace Corps in Pernambuco, to Arthur B. Lopez of the AIFLD in Recife, dated 28 March 1966, gives an indication of AIFLD's attempts to exploit the Peace Corps and the friction generated thereby:

> Thank you for your lengthy letter and the volunteer placement suggestions. Unfortunately, . . . our methods of Community Development Operation will not permit us to implement those suggestions. We see the Volunteer's close identification with the rural proletariat as absolutely essential. Very frankly, I have not found that AIFLD has a sympathetic image among sugar workers. They feel that AIFLD is "taking over" the rural labor movement. They seem to see it as identified with the present Federal regime, and I am sure you know how they feel about the "revolution." The Peace Corps could not operate successfully in Zona da Mata with this image.[34]

Representatives of the UAW, which does not receive government

33. Ibid.

34. Palisi, "CLASC: 1954–1967," p. 461. In 1974, however, Boggs asserted that a number of Peace Corps Volunteers had worked with AIFLD community centers in the Northeast for several years.

subsidies for its overseas operations and does not share AIFLD's labor/management/government bedfellow orientation, also report some bruising encounters with AIFLD in Brazil. Henry Santiestevan, director of the UAW's Latin American program in 1969–1970, maintains that AIFLD succeeded in splitting the chemical workers' unions, which the UAW representatives were seeking to unite, and that the unions that have fallen under AIFLD sponsorship have the glessings of the Brazilian government.[35]

Despite the furor over the IFPCW's clumsy dealings, AIFLD and several of its affiliated unions continued to operate in Brazil. Documents submitted by AID to the Senate Foreign Relations Committee in 1971 indicated that AIFLD had employed nine U.S. nationals, one third-country national (neither U.S. nor Brazilian), and forty-four Brazilian nationals in 1966; seven U.S. nationals, one third-country national, and thirty-one Brazilian nationals in 1969; and six U.S. nationals, one third-country national, and twenty-two Brazilian nationals in 1971.

Direct AID funding for AIFLD/Brazil amounted to $777,000 for FY 1970 and $468,000 for FY 1971, with $625,000 proposed for FY 1972. In addition, funding through subcontracts to U.S. unions for work in Brazil amounted to $30,400 for FY 1970 and FY 1971, and a total of $45,500 had been proposed for FY 1972. The IFPCW had received $7,200 for its work in Brazil during FY 1970 and FY 1971.[36] AID's contribution to the AIFLD program in fiscal 1974 was about $7 million. The AFL-CIO contributed some $500,000, and U.S. corporations contributed a token amount.[37]

One of AIFLD's major programs in Brazil is the Instituto Cultural du Trabalho—ICT (Cultural Labor Institute), a national training center for workers established in São Paulo in 1963. Its Brazilian director, Hélcio Maghenzani, is a member of AIFLD's board of trustees.[38] AIFLD provides 80 percent of the funding for the Institute, while Brazil's seven major labor federations (all tightly controlled by the government) provide the remainder. Some three hundred students attend the Institute annually, and another eight to nine thousand attend the regional seminars sponsored by the Institute. Lecturers include employers as well as professors and labor leaders.[39]

The ITC's first director, J. V. Freitas Marcondes, anticipated that

35. Henry Santiestevan, interview, 30 October 1972, Washington, D.C.
36. Church Hearings, p. 251.
37. Boggs interview.
38. *AIFLD Report*, June 1972, p. 2.
39. Boggs interview.

through the work of the Institute, Brazilian syndicalism would undergo a profound transformation, cultural and professional as well as ideological.[40] And AFL-CIO Assistant Inter-American Representative Michael Boggs explained that through the Institute and other programs AIFLD serves as a link between the national labor leadership and unions in the outlying areas.

In Washington in late 1973 for an AIFLD training program in communications, Carlos Pontes, a Brazilian "labor" leader (representing the advertising industry), confirmed that the labor movement remained very closely associated with AIFLD at all levels—from local *sindicato* to federation and confederation—and that most labor leaders were trained by AIFLD. Asked if any of the workers resented this relationship with AIFLD, Pontes responded that there are no leftists in the movement any more, as they were all imprisoned. He added that those remaining who held such views would not be likely to admit it, as all labor leaders, himself included, have had to be cleared by DOPS for loyalty to the government. Even though he claimed to be favorably disposed toward the military government and to harbor no resentment toward the United States, Pontes was disillusioned by AIFLD's program. He maintained that he had come in the expectation of a training program devoted exclusively to communications and that he was annoyed by the large amount of time devoted to indoctrination in such topics as political economics, ideology, and Soviet imperialism.[41]

Professor Gibson Luiz Vianna, a lecturer at the ESG in late 1973, lauded the successes of the Brazilian "revolutionary" government in reforming the trade union movement. "The revolutionary movement of 1964," Vianna said, "encountered a labor institution diverted from its goals, lost in a measure of disorder that was well reflected in the country's other sectors of activity. The drastic cleansing measures that were found to be urgent were followed by a phase of persuasion and training of new leaders. Our struggle has been arduous. But through the edifying examples of patriotism, seriousness, and work that the governments of the Revolution have offered in the pursuit of the development of the country, today as never before, the Brazilian trade unionist knows that he, too, is *responsible*."[42]

40. J. V. Freitas Marcondes, "The Evolution of Labor Legislation in Brazil," *Modern Brazil: New Patterns and Development*, ed. John Saunders (Gainesville: University of Florida Press, 1971), ch. 6, p. 152.

41. Carlos Pontes, president of a Brazilian union of advertisers and AIFLD trainee (communications program), interview, 9 November 1973, Washington, D.C.

42. Presidência da República, Estado-Maior das Fôrças Armadas, Escola Superior de Guerra, Departamento de Estudos T183–73, "Sindicalismo no Brasil" (Lecture by Professor Gibson Luiz Vianna, 4 September 1973), no. 167, p. 12.

Addressing graduates of AIFLD's XLII Advanced Course in August 1972, Meany said that the Institute's program for strengthening democracy in the Western Hemisphere was "one of the greatest successes that the trade union movement in this country has ever had.[43] Some U.S. trade union leaders would dispute Meany's contention that AIFLD's programs are among the greatest successes of the movement. But certainly many of the objectives of Meany and his colleagues for the labor movement in Brazil had been met. By 1972, the slogans and policy proposals that had been labeled "communistic" were no longer heard, and the generally quiescent unions did not seem to threaten either the control of the Brazilian government or the interests of U.S. businesses.

It appears that AIFLD made at least a minor contribution to the undermining of the Goulart government, and it has made a perhaps greater contribution since that time to preventing the coalescence of unions in key areas of production. It has also contributed to the facade of labor-management-government harmony that the military regime wished to project. This author doubts, however, that AIFLD in itself can take much of the credit for the 1964 coup or for the condition of the labor movement in Brazil since the coup.

The inability of the labor movement to resist the coup is more readily attributable to its own overconfidence and lack of preparation than to the actions of a handful of U.S.-trained infiltrators. The quiescence of labor since that time would appear to have more to do with the force of arms at the government's command than with the force of alien ideas about the proper role of labor.

43. "Meany Addresses Graduation Luncheon—Calls AIFLD's Programs 'Great Success,' " *The AIFLD Report*, vol. 10, no. 8 (August 1972), p. 1.

[7]

Containing Rural Unrest: The Northeast (Dis)agreement

Excepting such sporadic and isolated conspiracies to revolt as the one instigated by the now legendary Tiradentes in the 1780s, the peasant class until the early 1960s had constituted Brazil's truly silent majority. The rise of populism, the organization of nonelite interest groups (albeit from above), and other developments that expanded the urban political base scarcely touched the rural underclass. The attempts of the central government to expand the paternalistic corporatist system from urban laborers to their rural counterparts were generally abortive. Such an attempt, along with other factors, prompted the military to force the removal of Goulart from his position as labor minister in 1954. The 1943 minimum wage law, which had extended coverage to farm laborers, had rarely been enforced, and in spite of a law of 1944 that sanctioned the formation of rural unions, only five legally recognized rural unions existed in the whole of Brazil in 1961.[1] The "fatalistic" conviction prevalent among the peasantry—that efforts to organize in pursuit of class interest would be dangerous and probably futile—was empirically well-grounded. The illiterate majority of the peasants lacked even the minimum fee for membership in the patrimonial political system—the vote.

By far the greatest concentration of poverty generally, and of rural poverty and powerlessness in particular, was in the Northeast. That area contained 24 percent of the population but accounted for only 11 percent of the national income in 1960.[2] Remaining basically feudal in political and socioeconomic structure and afflicted by periodic

1. Page, *The Revolution That Never Was,* pp. 153–54.

2. Peter Ranis, *Five Latin American Nations: A Comparative Political Study* (New York: Macmillan, 1971), p. 306. The states of the Northeast—Maranhāo, Piauí, Ceará, Rio Grande do Norte, Paraiba, Pernambuco, Alagoas, Sergipe, Bahia, and the small island territory of Fernando de Noronha—account for 18 percent of the national territory.

droughts that resulted in widespread starvation and emigration, the Northeast became the focal point of the efforts of nationalistic politicians to demonstrate their ability to achieve a redistribution of goods and services among both regions and classes, as well as a showcase in which the Alliance for Progress sought to demonstrate the feasibility of bringing about progress without social upheaval. It was also this region that presented the challenge (or the threat, according to one's point of view) of the political awakening of the rural masses. This chapter deals with some of the means employed by the United States in its attempts to confront the perceived threat and to gain control over the direction of development in the Northeast.

After numerous piecemeal and ultimately ineffective efforts by the Brazilian central government to mitigate the disastrous effects of the Northeast droughts, the funding, through a new agency, for a comprehensive approach to the problems of the area cleared Congress in December 1961. The Superintendency for the Development of the Northeast (SUDENE), brainchild of economist Celso Furtado, answered directly to the president and enjoyed administrative autonomy. In addition to its own responsibilities in the planning and execution of development projects, SUDENE was empowered to coordinate programs drawing upon both national and foreign technical assistance to the area.[3]

During World War II, Brazil's Northeast bulge had been of considerable strategic importance to the United States as a location of air bases and as a potential source of critical minerals. But in the postwar period, alleviation of the rural poverty which had been so starkly evident in the Northeast had assumed a lower priority, even within the meager U.S. assistance programs initiated before the launching of the *Alianza*. Dale W. Adams has maintained that rather than offsetting the maldistribution of income and opportunity within and among regions, U.S. agricultural assistance has exacerbated it. Adams concluded, from a study covering the period from 1950 through 1970, that "foreign assistance has had little impact on the rural poverty question. The landless ruralworker and the low income farmer have realized little benefit from twenty years of foreign assistance."[4]

3. Among the books treating in some detail the attempts of the Brazilian government to deal with the problems of the Northeast and the assistance in, or obstruction of, that effort by the United States are Albert O. Hirschman, *Journeys Toward Progress: Studies of Economic Policy-Making in Latin America* (New York: The Twentieth Century Fund, 1963); Stefan H. Robock, *Brazil's Developing Northeast: A Study of Regional Planning and Foreign Aid* (Washington: The Brookings Institution, 1963); and Riordan Roett, *The Politics of Foreign Aid in the Brazilian Northeast* (Nashville, Tenn: Vanderbilt University Press, 1972).

Despite their rhetorical advocacy of land reform, U.S. agencies have actually promoted programs that discouraged redistribution of privately owned land. The major emphasis of AID in Brazil has been on rural credit, expansion of the marketing system for fertilizer, and the training of technicians. Negative interest rates (less than the rate of inflation) in the 1960s appear to have affected income transfers of the equivalent of from $100 to 200 million from the public sector to the recipients of agricultural credit. But only a tiny minority, most of whom have been located in more prosperous southern Brazil, have had access to institutional credit. As in the case of rural credit, almost all the fertilizer made available through agricultural assistance has been consumed by the owners of large landholdings in the commercialized central and southern parts of the country. Even the allocation of technical assistance has been skewed regionally: from 1949 through mid-1960, only 140 of the total of 3,000 Brazilians trained under the Point IV fellowship program came from the Northeast. Less than 5 percent of the total aid effort in agriculture for the 1950–1970 period was directed to that impoverished area.[5]

It is apparent, then, that it was not the perennial misery of the rural masses but a more recent phenomenon that prompted the massive infusion of U.S. assistance in the early 1960s. That phenomenon was the chaotic scramble to organize the rural poor, stimulated by Francisco Julião and the Peasant Leagues. Contrary to prevailing mythology, Julião, a federal deputy (Brazilian Socialist Party) from Pernambuco, did not initiate the movement; rather, he responded to the appeal of an embryonic mutual-benefit association of tenant farmers that the landowner and his political allies were attempting to disband.[6] From that humble beginning in 1955, the Peasant Leagues (Ligas Camponesas) grew to a numerical strength, at the movement's peak in 1961, of about 100,000.[7] An admirer of Castro's Cuba, Julião came to feel that revolution was the only means of effecting desperately needed social and economic reforms.

U.S. policy-makers became convinced that dealing with what they perceived as the "threat of revolt" in the most impoverished region of Latin America's largest and most populous state was the first critical test of the Alliance for Progress. As Joseph A. Page noted, the Alliance "found itself torn between its highly publicized humanitarian, reformist goals and the considerations of U.S. security that were the un-

4. Dale W. Adams, "What Can Underdeveloped Countries Expect from Foreign Aid to Agriculture? Case Study: Brazil, 1950–1970," *Inter-American Economic Affairs* 25 (Summer 1971): 47–63.

5. *Ibid.*

6. Page, *The Revolution That Never Was*, pp. 34–38.

derlying raison d'être of the aid program. The latter prevailed very easily at the outset, as the American involvement sought first to preserve the basic structure of the status quo, and only incidentally to improve conditions in the region in ways that would not weaken the established order."[8] And Riordan Roett, in his study of AID in the Northeast, concluded that the protests of AID personnel who were serious about social and economic objectives were overcome by the arguments of the political staff at the Embassy, who maintained that anything that economic assistance might do to combat "communist" influences in the Northeast must subordinate purely economic development goals.[9]

The overriding security component of the U.S. effort as it evolved had two interrelated purposes. The first was assisting "democratic" (pro-U.S., anti-Goulart) political leaders in defeating leftists or other supporters of the central government. This tactic in the Northeast was an aspect, perhaps the most important one, of the larger strategy, known as the "islands of sanity" policy, for undermining the Goulart government. The second purpose—undermining, containing, repressing, or destroying those organizations that gave aid and comfort to a peasant movement the United States could not control—called for manipulations at the grass-roots level. U.S. strategy on both levels spelled direct confrontation with the agency through which foreign assistance was to be channeled.

After sending a special mission to the Northeast in 1961 to draw up recommendations, the United States entered into the so-called Northeast Agreement with Brazil on 13 April 1962. The United States committed a total of $131 million, of which $760,000 was to be in dollars and the balance in local currency under PL 480. Thirty-three million of this amount was to be earmarked for immediate action, or "impact," projects and $98 million was reserved for long-range development projects.[10] The Brazilian Northeast became the only subnational region in the world to merit its own AID mission.[11]

The large American colony generated by the Northeast Agreement called for considerable administrative support, so the U.S. Consulate in Recife, which had consisted of a single consul and two vice-consuls in

7. Roett, *Politics of Foreign Aid in the Brazilian Northeast*, p. 76.

8. Page, *The Revolution That Never Was*, p. ix.

9. Roett, *Politics of Foreign Aid in the Brazilian Northeast*, p. 76.

10. U.S., House, Committee on Foreign Affairs, Subcommittee on National Security Policy and Scientific Developments, *Report of the Special Study Mission on: I. Military Assistance Training; II. Developmental Television* (hereafter cited as *Special Study Mission*),2d sess.,91st Cong.,7 May 1970, p.22.

11. Page, *The Revolution That Never Was*, p. 126.

1961, began to expand. The rank of the top U.S. diplomatic officer in Recife was upgraded over the next few years from consul to consul general to minister, and the post, at its high point, had ten consular officers. The consular buildup, however, did not relate solely to AID's administrative demands. It also reflected increasing "security" concerns.

The full extent of CIA activities in the area must be largely a matter of speculation, but Page has maintained that the CIA contingent within the Consulate in Recife increased from one in 1960–1961, to two in 1962, to three by 1964. He noted that "Julião's charges that the Paraiban and Pernambucan police sold to the 'FBI' copies of files on local peasant leaders may not have been entirely off the mark." The Consulate maintained dossiers, complete with photographs, on all of the region's political personalities, and the senior CIA official, according to Page, coordinated both intelligence gathering and covert operations, "making good use of Brazilian nationals willing to cooperate."[12]

Fred Morris, U.S. Methodist missionary in Recife from 1964 to 1974, told this author that an acquaintance of his was a member of a group, associated with the Masonic Lodge in Recife, that in 1963–1964 was receiving funds from the CIA. The funds were used to print Marxist literature which was to be distributed after the anticipated coup in such a manner as to confirm the allegations of extensive communist penetration of the region. The group also printed leaflets announcing fictitious rallies of the Peasant Leagues, featuring speeches by Francisco Julião. Thugs would then move into the large crowds, already frustrated by the absence of Julião, and start fights in order to discredit the Peasant Leagues.[13]

12. Ibid., pp. 128, 144–45. Agee's CIA diary indicates that each station maintains a "Subversive Control Watch List" and that data from the lists are passed to agents or collaborators in the local security services.

13. Fred Morris, in conversation, 4 May 1976, Washington, D.C. Morris, who also served as a stringer for *Time* magazine in Brazil, was arrested and imprisoned by officials of the Intelligence section of the Fourth Army in Recife in the fall of 1974, tortured, and ultimately expelled from Brazil.

CIA support for groups engaging in thuggery, terrorism, and sabotage has been noted in several countries. The Senate Select Committee on Intelligence found that the CIA had indirectly funded the right-wing paramilitary group, Patria y Libertad, in Chile in the period between the election of Allende in 1970 and the coup in 1973 (*Covert Action*, pp. 177–78). Agee reported from Quito on 13 May 1962 that he was training a local agent, the head of the Social Christian militant-action squads, including the secret bomb squad, in the use of various incendiary, crowd dispersement, and harassment devices (*Inside the Company*, p. 239). Agee also noted that the Montevideo CIA station had financed right-wing civilian terror organizations in the early 1960s. (Ibid., p. 589).

Whether there was ever a consensus among responsible U.S. officials in Brazil in regard to cooperation with SUDENE remains questionable. Arthur Schlesinger, reporting on his trip to Recife with Food for Peace director George McGovern in February 1961, notes that in the 1950s the U.S. Embassy had regarded Furtado, who became SUDENE's director, "with mistrust as a Marxist, even possibly a communist." Schlesinger had found cause for optimism in the supposition that the alternative of violent revolution symbolized by Julião would strengthen Furtado's hand with the traditional political elite (and possibly with the skeptical "old hands" at State Department).[14] In retrospect, however, it is apparent that a cooperative relationship was foredoomed from the start, as U.S. officialdom and SUDENE were incompatible not only in approach, but also in perception and in purpose. As Roett noted, "Where the U.S. saw ideological subversion, Furtado saw discontent, ignorance, and hunger."[15]

In a post-mortem on the U.S. effort of the early 1960s in the Northeast, a special study mission of the House Foreign Affairs Committee in 1967 asserted that "delays by Brazilian officials caused the emergency impact part of the program to be abandoned, and the U.S. eliminated its time-phased goals."

The special study mission placed the blame for U.S. AID's failure to meet its stated programmatic goals squarely on SUDENE:

> From the beginning, it was apparent that the Brazilian agency responsible for the implementation of the Northeast program, SUDENE, . . . was in basic disagreement with the U.S., both as to the objectives and the implementation of the plan. SUDENE's political orientation in the years before the 1964 revolution was characterized as "leftist nationalist." A large number of its personnel had socialist, nationalist, antiforeign and anti-private enterprise conceptions. In spite of the fact that SUDENE was obstructive, the U.S. regarded itself as obligated to put $131 million into the development of the Northeast and gave the highest priority to getting projects approved and funds obligated.
>
> The study mission saw at first hand some of the failures in programs and projects conceived and carried out under these conditions. Yet to say that on this basis U.S. assistance failed in its objectives is probably incorrect. At the same time that the U.S. poured in these huge sums, Communist agitators were busy in the area. Therefore, it was not in the interest of the United States to permit the recalcitrance of a group of bureaucrats to block U.S. efforts in dealing with the serious problems there.[16]

Speaking in 1970, Arthur Byrnes, Deputy Director of AID/Northeast,

14. Bell, "Brazilian-American Relations."

15. Roett, *Politics of Foreign Aid in the Brazilian Northeast*, p. 91.

16. *Special Study Mission I*, pp. 22–23.

1962–1963, and Director, 1963–1964, recalled, "We were in a very serious political situation; we thought that the Communists were going to run all over the place. That was uppermost in our minds . . . Furtado said that SUDENE only needed capital. They didn't see their problems as clearly as we felt we did."[17]

Celso Furtado, recalling in an interview with the author in 1972 those hectic days of the early 1960s, confirmed the seriousness of the clash between SUDENE and the U.S. government. He maintained that there were already thousands of U.S. functionaries in the Northeast and that the Brazilian Embassy in Washington had told him that the visas of many more North Americans had been processed "in case there was urgent need to send them right away." CIA agents were infiltrating the Peasant Leagues, and public safety assistance was being used to strengthen police all over the area, especially in Pernambuco. "Islands of sanity" aid to the governors of Rio Grande do Norte, Pernambuco, Guanabara, and other states, he claimed, served to divide civilian political leaders and to ensure that they withdrew their support from SUDENE and from the Goulart government.[18]

The ink was hardly dry on the Northeast Agreement before differing interpretations of a key paragraph signaled the gathering storm that was to engulf and debilitate SUDENE. SUDENE understood that its approval was required before the United States could conclude project agreements with state governments or with the federal agencies in the area. The United States maintained that it was free to bypass SUDENE if it chose to do so.[19]

SUDENE's initial support in the Northeast had come from the political left, but Furtado and the president made a serious effort to avoid alienating the traditional elite and to cultivate the cautiously progressive forces of the center. Development could hardly be a politically neutral process, but SUDENE attempted to avoid blatant involvement in local political competition. The United States exercised no such restraint. A memo from an AID official in Rio outlined his interpretations of the U.S. strategy for the Northeast as follows: "It seems to me that each of the nine governors must be made to feel as sharply as possible that he is in competition to demonstrate to the U.S. that he is ready and with better assurance of making good use of our money than any other eight governors."[20] The criteria for determining good use was, of course, political.

17. Bell, "Brazilian-American Relations."
18. Furtado interview.
19. Roett, *Politics of Foreign Aid in the Brazilian Northeast*, pp. 82–83.
20. Page, "The Revolution That Never Was," p. 138.

Although U.S. attempts to influence the outcome of elections in the area through the timely allocations of impact aid were generally unsuccessful, Furtado maintained that the U.S. aid program was instrumental in undermining the regional authority of SUDENE. The case of U.S. assistance to Governor Aluisio Alves of Rio Grande do Norte illustrates this process. Governor Alves was a member of the UDN (generally conservative, though less conservative in some parts of the Northeast than the PSD), which on a national scale opposed Goulart. But Alves' personal orientation was reputedly progressive. Thus both the United States and the Goulart government had considered him a potential ally. Initially Alves had expressed enthusiastic support for SUDENE, but SUDENE's plans did not promise the immediately visible progress that would have been advantageous in terms of Alves' political timetable. Thus, over SUDENE's objections and with considerable fanfare, Alves accepted U.S. AID funding for an ambitious primary education construction project in his state. Under intense pressure from Alves, and still hoping to secure his support in the upcoming plebiscite on restoration of the full powers of the presidency, Goulart finally gave his approval to the project. And SUDENE, undercut by its own administration, had no choice but to acquiesce.

The United States failed to win Alves' unqualified cooperation. By early 1964, Alves had become indignant over the extent of U.S. intervention in the affairs of his state government. The construction project scarcely got off the ground: by April 1965, only forty-five new classrooms had been completed out of the thousand that had been planned. Alves himself hardly profited from his association with the United States and its allies in Brazil. His supposedly brilliant political future was cut short when the military government deprived him of his political rights in 1969.

The United States did not gain long-term or all-purpose allies through such maneuvers, but it deprived SUDENE of anticipated support from the political center and drove it further to the left. The undermining of SUDENE, which had begun as a consequence of that agency's refusal to subjugate its own objectives to U.S. interests, had thus become an end in itself, and the designation of SUDENE as anti-American became a self-fulfilling prophecy.[21]

By the time SUDENE and the U.S. AID mission had established their misalliance, the successes of the Peasant Leagues had inspired or provoked a number of more traditional groups to engage in efforts to orga-

---

21. Roett, *Politics of Foreign Aid in the Brazilian Northeast*, pp. 50–112; Page, *The Revolution That Never Was*, pp. 138–39.

nize rural workers. The most successful of these groups in 1961 and 1962 were the Communist Party and the progressive wing of the Catholic Church. The organization sponsoring the Catholic drive in Pernambuco, the Rural Orientation Service of Pernambuco (SORPE), was led by a group of clergymen among whom Padre Antonio Melo emerged as spokesman, while Padre Crespo served as the principal strategist.

SORPE encouraged the formation of cooperatives as a means of providing legal and other services and in general improving the living standards of the peasants. Its leaders believed that a harmonious solution to the differences between landowners and peasants was feasible and preferable to class conflict. While competing with the more radical Peasant Leagues and communist unions for the allegiance of the workers, SORPE also joined them on some occasions in confronting the landlords and their political allies.

In late 1962 a technician for the Cooperative League of the USA (CLUSA) established close contact with Padre Crespo, and SORPE became the major beneficiary of CLUSA in Brazil. Funds provided through that U.S. "counterpart" organization helped to pay salaries and expenses for SORPE and made it possible for SORPE to provide more services and attract more functionaries and members than would otherwise have been possible. SORPE leaders were apparently unaware that CLUSA was funded in part by foundations that served as CIA conduits and that their young technician (who once advised that "in convincing the peasant that the misery of his condition is unnecessary, one must be careful not to push him to the extreme of revolt against the authorities and vested interests who have held him in his present State") was on the CIA payroll.[22]

After the promulgation in March 1963 of a comprehensive Rural Workers Law, which set forth in detail the rights of rural workers and their unions, the scramble for control of the unionization process became even more intense and complex. Goulart and Arraes injected their

---

22. Page, *The Revolution That Never Was*, pp. 129, 154–55. In its listing of the CIA's foundation-funded covert operations prior to 1967, the U.S. Senate's Select Committee on Intelligence included the following item: "Funding of a legitimate U.S. association of farm organizations. Agency funds were used to host foreign visitors, provide scholarships to an international cooperative training center at a United States university, and to reimburse the organization for various of its activities abroad. A CIA document prepared in 1967 notes that although the organization received some overt government funds from AID, the CIA should continue its covert funding because 'programs funded by AID cannot address themselves to the same political goals toward which Agency operations are targeted . . .'" (*Foreign and Military Intelligence*, p. 183).

own organizers into the fray; students of all manner of leftist persua-
sions, from Trotskyites to Maoists to radical social Christians, com-
peted with priests, communists, and Peasant Leagues, and new leaders
emerged from among the peasantry. Julião's movement, lacking legal
status, lost ground, and in 1962 and 1963 the Catholic groups had the
upper hand. By early 1964, however, more radical elements linked to
Arraes, Goulart, and the Communist Party appeared to be pulling
ahead.

In Pernambuco's gubernatorial campaign of 1962, virtually all
leaders of peasant movements, including Padres Melo and Crespo, had
suspended their competition long enough to unite behind Arraes. But
by late 1963 Padre Melo was openly accepting money from IBAD,
denouncing Arraes, and publicly endorsing ultra right-wing candidates for public office, and Padre Crespo had openly clashed with other
Catholic activists who were willing to collaborate with communists in
pursuit of specific goals.[23] It appears that the United States had
contributed to detaching these leaders from the larger peasant movement. But the more radical groups continued to gain ground in spite of
U.S. efforts to derail the movement.

Under existing electoral laws, the one thing other than organization
that the peasants needed most in order to participate effectively in the
political system was literacy, without which they could not vote. The
various adult education programs that had been launched in the early
1960s, however, attempted to go beyond simple literacy to *concientização*. Paulo Freire, articulator of the concept and creator of the
method for its dissemination, noted that "self-depreciation is a characteristic of the oppressed, which derives from their internalization of the
opinion the oppressors hold of them. So often do they hear that they are
good for nothing and are incapable of learning anything, that they are
sick, lazy, and unproductive—that in the end they become convinced
of their own unfitness."[24] Thus Freire sought to instill in his students
first a realization of their self-worth and then a critical awareness of the
society in which they lived. He wanted to teach them not merely to
read and write, but to think and know and act, as subjects capable of
changing their own environment rather than as objects subject to the
whims of fate. Both supporters and opponents of the Freire method saw
it as a seed of potentially revolutionary change.

Experimentation with Freire's method began in the Northeast under

23. Ibid., pp. 159–66.
24. Coleman McCarthy, "Thinkers and their Thoughts (XXX): Paulo Freire
and Educating the Oppressed," *Washington Post*, 31 July 1972.

the sponsorship of the University of Recife and the state government of Pernambuco under Arraes, but it spread throughout Brazil "like the most contagious of ideas whose time had come." Meanwhile the Movement for Basic Education (MEB), which had been launched in Rio Grande do Norte by the Catholic Church and had become a national program under the governments of Quadros and Goulart, assumed an orientation akin to Freire's *conscientização*. MEB's primer, *To Live Is To Struggle*, invited students to question a social system that left them in abject poverty.

Ironically, U.S. AID sponsored a pilot literacy project in early 1963 in Rio Grande do Norte using the Freire method but discontinued its support in January 1964, as conservatives had begun to claim that "Freire was out to 'Bolshevize' Brazil." One AID official later observed, "It wasn't really a literacy program but rather a means of politicizing people. The goal of the method was to arouse the politically apathetic and get them into an uproar."[25]

With the first wave of arrests in the days and weeks that followed the "revolution" of 1 April 1964, the multifaceted peasant movement that some believed threatened to redistribute political and economic power in the Northeast "collapsed like a house of cards."[26] Throughout the Northeast the new military government found evidence that a communist revolution had been imminent. An electricity generator that had been donated through the efforts of Senator Edward Kennedy after his 1961 visit to the Peasant League stronghold of Galiléia was seen as evidence of a plot to supply power to a radio transmitter that would broadcast subversive messages to the countryside. Ten thousand coveralls found on the premises of a Pernambuco land reform agency constituted proof that Arraes and his supporters were about to issue uniforms to a peasant militia. And an intelligence officer in the Fourth Army Headquarters in Recife maintained that the MEB primer, *To Live Is To Struggle*, was in itself enough to justify the "revolution."[27]

Arrests and purges went far beyond the leadership of the various "leftist nationalist" agencies, parties, or unions, and a member of the CIA-funded group within Recife's Masonic Lodge, Alvaro da Costa Lima, gained early notoriety as a torturer.[28] One SUDENE technician was detained in Recife simply because the FBI had passed on the information that while on an earlier trip to Washington he had visited the

25. Page, *The Revolution That Never Was*, p. 176.
26. Ibid., pp. 174–76.
27. Ibid., pp. 201–14.
28. Morris conversation.

Soviet Embassy. SUDENE was purged and the reconstituted agency adopted a policy of full cooperation with the U.S. AID mission. The new government made it clear that SUDENE did not have the option of balking on projects that had been approved in Washington. The major thrust of the U.S. AID-SUDENE program was the infusion of public investment into infrastructure and the attraction of private investment, domestic and foreign, toward industry. AID's public safety program, which Furtado had finally succeeded in ejecting from Pernambuco shortly before the coup, was reinstituted; and in place of Freire's *concientização* approach to literacy, a program known as the ABC Crusade was initiated. According to Page, this program attempts to train the peasant to accept things as they are and make the best of them.

By 1966 the U.S. AID mission in the Northeast had one-hundred fifty officials. By 1968 AID had expended $249,462,000 in loans to the area, and an additional $40 million had been obligated. Meanwhile, the Peasant Leagues and some of the other more radical peasant unions had been disbanded, and the rural unions that survived, like their urban counterparts, were placed under the control of government interventors. Padre Melo, the only leader the Fourth Army trusted, was given de facto control of the rural labor movement. With the help of the Army and the police he replaced the leadership of virtually all of the rural unions. Although Padre Crespo had clashed with the more radical clergymen in the Federation of Rural Syndicates, the new regime distrusted him and, according to Page, only the intervention of the U.S. AID mission preserved his position as head of SORPE. In December 1964 SORPE signed an agreement with CLUSA, formalizing the continuation of U.S. funding for its operations. When CLUSA's link with the CIA was publicly disclosed in 1967, CLUSA withdrew its financial support, but AIFLD, which had tried unsuccessfully to penetrate the area as early as June 1963, moved in and attempted to assume control, through training courses and "peasant service centers," of the remains of the rural labor movement in Pernambuco.[29]

We have seen that the United States viewed the incipient mobilization of the peasantry in the Northeast as the seed of a Castro-like revolution. Through the apparently coordinated efforts of several agencies, therefore, the U.S. set out to contain the peasant movement and to nurture other leaders and organizations over which it might exercise control. A secondary aim was to promote incremental but demonstrable progress without unsettling the basic socioeconomic structure, thus validating the effectiveness of the Alliance for Progress approach to development.

29. Page, *The Revolution That Never Was*, pp. 212–32.

It appears that the U.S. agencies had not been particularly successful in meeting their top priority goal prior to the coup: the more radical elements of the peasant movement had grown stronger rather than weaker. It might be that in the absence of U.S. efforts to divide and co-opt union leadership and to deprive the unions of their support among political elites, the peasant movement would have presented a united front strong enough to discourage the military conspirators; but such a proposition is subject only to speculation, not to testing. As for its secondary aim of promoting incremental but demonstrable progress for the poverty-stricken of the area, it will be shown in Chapter 15 that the United States was strikingly unsuccessful.

[8]

Redefining Law and Order: The Public Safety Assistance Program

In its quest to prevent or quell civil disorder and to maintain or reestablish the kind of stability it viewed as hospitable to foreign investment in Brazil, as in many other Third World countries, the United States has considered the police forces of those countries as both natural and necessary allies. Thus, the small police assistance program that had been initiated by AID in 1954 was gradually expanded; in the early 1960s, co-optation of and support for domestic police forces, particularly in Vietnam and in Latin America, became an important aspect of the broader policy of fortifying "internal security" forces in client states.

An executive order issued in 1962 led to the creation within AID of an Office of Public Safety. A memorandum issued by the Department of State in 1962 declared that AID "vests the Office of Public Safety with primary responsibility and authority for public safety programs and gives that office a series of powers and responsibilities which will enable it to act rapidly, vigorously, and effectively . . . powers greater than any other office or division of AID."[1]

This chapter elaborates on the rationales set forth in advocacy of the Public Safety Assistance Program and on the nature of the program in general and of the Brazilian program in particular. The actual and potential influences of such a program on the internal balance of political forces in Brazil should become apparent.

Testifying in hearings before the Subcommittee on Inter-American Affairs of the House Foreign Affairs Committee on 18 February 1963, Assistant Secretary of State for Inter-American Affairs Edwin M. Martin

1. Quoted by Holmes Alexander in an undated article reprinted in House Foreign Affairs Committee, *Foreign Assistance Act of 1965*, p. 76.

138

said, "In assessing the internal security situation in Latin America, we found that the civil police forces in many of these countries wanted assistance. . . . Consequently, the public safety program is designed to meet these requests." AID's Special Assistant for Internal Defense Joseph J. Wolf added later, in the same hearings,

> It is important to seek to control Communist efforts at the earliest possible state. . . . The function of police in combatting these activities lies in the fields of identifying and controlling criminal and subversive individuals and groups, and controlling violent manifestations ranging from demonstrations and disorders to riots and lower levels of insurrection. . . . Police forces are the most sensitive point of contact between government and people, close to the focal points of unrest, and more acceptable to the people as a normal regulating force. . . . To these ends, our public safety assistance program offers training, advice, and equipment for police forces of friendly countries which are trying to employ their resources in the struggle against communism.[2]

The importance of the program was further stressed in the Senate Appropriations Committee's Foreign Assistance Hearings in 1965. AID Aministrator David Bell explained that the unique powers granted to the Office of Public Safety enabled it to "act rapidly, vigorously, and effectively" in aiding Latin American governments threatened by popular uprisings. "In order to deal with the dynamics of internal security situations," Bell noted, "the public safety program has developed and utilized methods to deliver to threatened countries, in a matter of days, urgently needed assistance, including equipment, training and technical advice." He conceded that although the assistance is "not given to support dictatorships . . ., we are working in a lot of countries where the governments are controlled by people who have shortcomings." He explained, however, that "the police are a very strongly anti-communist force right now. For that reason it is a very important force to us." Bell concluded his testimony with the observation that "public safety forces have done and can do much to prevent conspiracy and the development of disruptive situations, and to insure an environment of law and order. . . ."[3]

The Inter-American Police Academy was established under the official auspices of AID in 1962 in the Panama Canal Zone. According to Agee, it was actually founded by the CIA's Panama Station and was intended to be "a major counter-insurgency facility similar in many ways to the training programmes for Latin American military officers

2. Frank, "Brazil and Pakistan."

3. Senate Appropriations Committee *Foreign Assistance Appropriations: 1965*, pp. 72–75.

under the military aid programmes.''[4] Byron Engle, Director of AID's
Office of Public Safety (a "retired" CIA officer), explained in the 1963
hearings that "in a total of 455 class hours, 165 are devoted to internal
security subjects and investigative techniques." He maintained that
about a third of the time devoted to internal security would be spent on
Communist Party operations and techniques. Engle assured the committee that this type of assistance was classified as technical rather than
military, but that the officer in charge of the police school in the
Panama Canal Zone was in close contact with the commander-in-chief
of SOUTHCOM, General Andrew O'Meara. "There is close liaison,"
Engle said, "in that General O'Meara knows the work we are doing. He
can give us advice on courses." (Jon Rosenbaum asserts that OPS and
MAP counter-insurgency programs are coordinated in the field as well
as in Washington and the Canal Zone.)[5] Engle went on to explain that
"the delivery of equipment to the police force of a nation is not related
to the student presence at the school. . . . We take into consideration
. . . the whole picture, and if it is found that with all these things
considered there is a security need and that it is in the U.S. interest to
proceed, then we grant equipment to the country."[6]

In 1964 the academy was moved to Washington, D.C. and renamed
the International Police Academy (IPA). By February 1969, some three
thousand students, of whom 60 percent were Latin Americans, had
been graduated from it. The curriculum, as described in 1967 in the
International Police Academy Review, has three major divisions:
Police Management (organization, command and staff relationships,
public relations); Police Operations (criminalistics, communications,
border control, intelligence); and Internal Security (riot control forma-
tions, chemical munitions, terrorist countermeasures).[7]

Training at the academy itself is supplemented by a special program
at the Military Assistance Institute (formerly called the John F. Kennedy Special Warfare Center) at Fort Bragg, North Carolina. The sup-
plemental training deals with "civil-military relationships in
counterinsurgency operations and police support in unconventional
warfare."[8] Courses offered to the foreign police officers at Fort Bragg

4. Agee, *Inside the Company,* p. 262.

5. H. Jon Rosenbaum, with Glenn M. Cooper, *Arms and Security in Latin
America: Recent Developments,* International Affairs Series 101 (Washington,
D.C.: Woodrow Wilson International Center for Scholars, December, 1971).

6. Frank, "Brazil and Pakistan."

7. "Curriculum," *IPA Review* [Washington], January 1967, p. 12.

8. "The IPA Faculty," *IPA Review,* January 1967, p. 11.

include Subversive Insurgent Methodology, Psychological Operations in Support of Internal Defense and Development, and The Role of Intelligence in Internal Defense.[9] IPA trainees also visit the Criminal Investigation Laboratory at Fort Gordon, Georgia, for a course entitled Firearms Identification. The program is actually conducted by the CIA, which has thus far refused to respond to congressional inquiry as to the specifics of course content.[10]

There are more than thirty additional sites across the United States at which foreign police officers are trained under the OPS program. Special programs for foreign trainees include the FBI National Academy Course of Instruction, which is offered to command-level law enforcement officers and stresses investigative techniques and administration, and Police Executive Training, specially arranged orientation tours for executives too busy to attend regular courses. A Program Guide released by OPS in 1971 listed the following courses under the heading of Technical Specialist Training: Questioned Document Examination, conducted at the U.S. Post Office Department's Scientific Identification Laboratory; Police Records Management, at the International Police Services School in Washington, D.C.; Traffic Police Administration, at Northwestern University Traffic Institute, Evanston, Illinois; Special Actions—Riot Control (locale not specified); Police Telecommunications Management; Police Radio Communications; Maritime Law Enforcement, at the U.S. Coast Guard training facilities in Yorktown, Virginia, and New London, Connecticut (participants in this course must have a host country security clearance equivalent to U.S. "Confidential"); Penology and Corrections, at Southern Illinois University; Automotive Repair; and Audio-Visual Communications. One of the many things that these programs have in common with military assistance is the sales promotion function. Training in telecommunications management and radio communications, for example, includes factory visits.[11]

Senator James Abourezk revealed to the press in September 1973 that in addition to these programs, U.S. AID/OPS was indeed operating a

9. Senator James Abourezk, "Amendment to the Foreign Assistance Act," 93d Cong., 2d sess., 21 June 1974, *Congressional Record*, 1974, vol. 120, pp. S1–S4.

10. Thomas Daschle, Staff Assistant to Senator James Abourezk, interview, 9 January 1974, Washington, D.C.

11. Agency for International Development, Office of Public Safety, *Public Safety Training*, Program Guide for internal use, 1971. According to Agee, the International Police Services School is a CIA training facility under commercial cover (*Inside the Company*, p. 612).

"terror school" on the order of that depicted in the movie "State of Seige." AID Assistant Administrator Matthew Harvey conceded in a letter to the senator that since 1969 CIA bomb and booby trap experts have been assisting AID in training foreign police in "the construction, use, and countermeasures against homemade bombs and explosive devices" at the Border Patrol Academy in Los Fresnos, Texas. According to Harvey, the course was developed in response to requests from U.S. embassies for this kind of training.

The first phase of the "Technical Investigations Course," conducted at IPA, includes training in the motivations and objectives of terrorists; police intelligence; surveillance and trailing procedures; explosives and incendiaries; and sabotage. There is also a course entitled Press Release and Press Relations. At the isolated Los Fresnos school, trainees receive practical experience in the fabrication, triggering, and disarming of explosive devices, as well as in investigation.

Documents obtained by Senator Abourezk indicate that most of the 165 policemen who had been trained at the school, including six from Brazil, were from countries under military rule.[12] Senator Abourezk was assured at the time of his 1973 inquiry to AID that the Technical Investigations Course had been terminated, but he reported to the Senate in June 1974 that the course had been "revamped" and had resurfaced in Edgewood, Maryland, as "Prevention and Investigation of Contemporary Violence."[13]

Practical experience provided at the IPA includes the use of a facility known as the Police Operations Control Center. In this center, a map of the mythical city of Rio Bravos has been constructed on a magnetic game board. From the control booth, faculty members posing as field commanders alert the trainees to a communist-inspired riot at the local university, and trainees plan strategies and employ forces much as they would from a real police control center.[14]

IPA spokesmen insist that the training they provide discourages use of so-called "third-degree" tactics in interrogation. If that is the case, however, it appeared to a few persons who were able to inspect the theses of the academy's students that that aspect of the training had not

12. Letter from Matthew J. Harvey, Assistant Administrator for Legislative Affairs, AID, to Senator James Abourezk, 25 September 1973.

13. Abourezk Amendment.

14. Nancy Stein and Mike Klare, "The U.S. 'Public Safety' Program: Police Aid for Tyrants," in *The U.S. Military Apparatus,* prepared by the staff of the North American Congress on Latin America, Berkeley and New York, August 1972, pp. 54–63.

been very persuasive. They found numerous examples of advocacy of the use of force and threats of violence in those papers.[15]

Addressing the cadets at IPA's graduation ceremonies in 1965, General Maxwell Taylor said:

> The outstanding lesson [of the Indochina conflict] is that we should never let another Vietnam-type situation arise again. We were too late in recognizing the extent of the subversive threat. We appreciate now that every young, emerging country must be constantly on the alert, watching for those symptoms which, if allowed to develop unrestrained, may eventually grow into a disastrous situation such as that in South Vietnam. We have learned the need for a strong police force and a strong police intelligence organization to assist in identifying early the symptoms of an incipient subversive situation.[16]

One of the instrumentalities for maintaining old-school ties among alumni of the academy is the *IPA Review*. The *Review*, which began publication (in Spanish as well as English) in 1967, follows the careers of graduates, publishes articles by them, and keeps them up to date on ideas and techniques. The "Director's Message," which introduces each issue, stresses the political nature of the contemporary challenge and threat to policemen. The message for April 1971, for example, warns that:

> Many such infamous deeds are performed by irresponsible criminals operating under the guise of being revolutionaries. Their subversive activities and insurgent objectives, disguised by clever rhetoric, are skillfully laced with the principles of nationalism.[17]

In addition to training programs in the United States and the provision of equipment to foreign police forces, the program also has included "on-the-job" training by U.S. Public Safety Advisers, of whom ninety-one were stationed in Latin America in 1968.[18] Most of these advisers were recruited from the CIA, the FBI, the Special Forces, Military Police, or U.S. state and local law enforcement agencies.[19]

---

15. Jack Anderson, "Questionable Means of Interrogation," *Washington Post*, 3 August. Diane La Voy, who accompanied Anderson's associate, Joe Spear, on his visit to the IPA, confirmed to this author the findings published by Anderson.

16. U.S. Department of State press release, 17 December 1965, cited in Stein and Klare, "The U.S. 'Public Safety' Program," p. 55.

17. *IPA Review* 5 (April 1971).

18. *The Foreign Assistance Program, Annual Report to the Congress: Fiscal Year 1968*, Washington, 1969, p. 51. cited in *Brazil: Who Pulls the Strings* (Chicago: Committee of Returned Volunteers, n.d.)

19. Stein and Klare, "The U.S. 'Public Safety' Program," pp. 56, 60, 63.

Brazil has been the recipient of by far the largest amount of assistance under the Public Safety Assistance Program in Latin America. One of the objectives of the Brazilian government, in entering into agreements with AID in 1959 for assistance under the Public Safety Program, was the establishment of a federal police force. That federal force did not come into being until 1965; however, prior to that time such assistance was channeled to certain state police forces, apparently in accordance with the all-encompassing "islands of sanity" policy. Since 1965 additional states have been included in the agreements, but the trend has been toward an ever-increasing proportion of aid to the new federal force.

The objectives of the program described by AID in a 1961 review were to strengthen Brazilian capacity to maintain law and order, control civil disturbances, and preserve internal security.[20] According to the *Jornal do Brasil* (18 July 1963), Brazilian policeman Peter Costello described the program to São Paulo Governor Adhemar de Barros in more simplistic terms. Costello said he was going to the United States to learn "the latest methods in the field of dispersion of strikes and striking workers . . . employing the method of using dogs against crowds and clubs against its insistent members to modernize the mechanism of repression against agitators in São Paulo."[21]

The number of Brazilian policemen trained in the United States jumped from twenty-six in 1962 to sixty-two in 1963. Forty-three of those sixty-two trainees were from the states of Guanabara, Minas Gerais, and São Paulo, states that had been designated "islands of sanity" and whose governors were key conspirators in the overthrow of Goulart. Although there were four subsequent years in which a greater number of Brazilians were trained in the United States under the program, the number trained from those three states in 1963 was more than twice that of any subsequent year. Of the $10 million in grants expended in Brazil under the OPS program by 1971, the largest annual allocation ($1,159,000) had been for fiscal year 1964, the year in which the coup took place.[22]

The 1965 bilateral agreement concerning the OPS program listed among the functional areas of cooperation: training, communications, criminalistics, records and identification, transportation, administration and management, riot control, urban patrol, reporting procedures,

20. Agency for International Development, Office of Public Safety, *Memorandum on the Public Safety Program in Brazil,* prepared by Johnson F. Monroe for the Subcommittee on Foreign Operations of the House Committee on Government Operations, 30 July 1970.

21. Frank, "Brazil and Pakistan."

22. Church Hearings, pp. 6–7.

industrial security, and public relations. Material provided under the program has included .38-caliber handguns, handcuffs, batons, laboratory equipment, smoke grenades, and other crowd control equipment, including a gas identified as CS. (When mixed with an unspecified "pyrotechnic composition" at the Edgewood Arsenal, this gas was considered so dangerous that Dr. J. S. Foster, the Pentagon's Director of Defense Research and Engineering, included it with nerve gas and mustard gas in asking the National Academy of Sciences to provide a special report on how to dispose of it without major catastrophe.)[23]

A memorandum submitted by AID in 1970 to the Subcommittee on Foreign Operations of the House Committee on Government Operations cited the establishment of the National Police Academy, the Technical Communications Center, the National Institutes of Criminalistics and Identification, and statewide municipal and tactical police networks among the program's accomplishments. The memorandum stated that of the officers trained thus far in the United States, 95 percent had remained with the police, and about one in three had been promoted to higher positions. AID further asserted that "such trained officers actively support in-country training programs and the operation of improvement efforts of the Public Safety Program."[24]

Johnson F. Monroe of the Washington office of the Public Safety Program informed the author in late 1970, however, that the Public Safety Program would be cut back as Brazilians took over direction of the programs currently under way.[25] The Brazilian police were indeed going forward with the expansion of their own programs, modeled after their U.S. counterparts. The Santa Catarina School of Police, for example, was inaugurated on 9 May 1967. Its director, Octacilio Schuler Sobrinho, an IPA graduate, asserted in 1971 that "our objectives and goals for the school program parallel the IPA." Santa Catarina's curriculum reflects the IPA influence, and its operations center (where instruction in the techniques of mob and riot control, civil disturbance, patrol activities, and the like is provided) is a carbon copy of the IPA's, complete with a detailed aerial map of the city. "In this era of social revolution," Schuler declared, "the police should constantly revise and upgrade its technique and operation plans."[26]

23. Arthur Kanegis, "The Hidden Arsenal: You Can't Keep a Deadly Weapon Down," *Washington Monthly* (December 1970): 24–27.

24. AID, *Memorandum on the Public Safety Program*.

25. Johnson F. Monroe, AID, Office of Public Safety, interview, 16 November 1970, Washington, D.C.

26. Octacilio Schuler Sobrinho and José Guilherme de Souza, "Brazil, 'The Making of a Policeman': Santa Catarina School of Police," *IPA Review* 7 (July 1971): 1–4.

The Brazilian police were also showing initiative in the methods of co-optation so effectively employed by U.S. institutions. An article in the *IPA Review*, for example, describes an experimental program of police training for Brazil's unintegrated Indians. Colonel José Ortiga, Commander of the Military Police of the State of Minas Gerais and an IPA graduate, was approached by the Ministry of the Interior and asked if the military police could provide a basic law enforcement training program for selected tribe members. Colonel Ortiga signed an agreement with the Interior Ministry whereby eighty-five members of five tribes from the states of Goiás, Pará, Maranhão, and Minas Gerais were to undergo a three-month training program at the Military Police Academy in Belo Horizonte. The curriculum included: Indian laws; unarmed defense; arrest, search, and seizure; use and care of firearms; crowd control; and civics. As evidence of the success of this training, the article noted that the federally trained guard in one village was able to protect from the wrath of the other villagers and turn over to federal authorities a mestizo who had trespassed on Indian land and murdered a villager.[27]

By 1971, 641 Brazilian police officers had been trained in the United States (trainees remained on the OPS payroll for six months after returning to their own countries). It is interesting to note that in 1969, the year when U.S. economic assistance was suspended for a few months in "cosmetic" protest against the dramatic tightening of the dictatorial noose signified by the dissolution of the Congress in December 1968 and the promulgation of the Fifth Institutional Act, the number of Brazilian policemen brought to the United States for training almost tripled that of the previous year. (The number of Brazilian military trainees in the United States also increased that year and was, in fact, higher than at any other time in the postwar period.)[28] The marked expansion of the training program also coincided with an increase in documented reports of the systematic torture of political prisoners and of the murders of petty criminals, as well as alleged subversives, carried out by the "Death Squads," reportedly composed of off-duty policemen.

Governor Nelson Rockefeller, as President Nixon's special envoy in Brazil and other Latin American countries in 1969, was uninformed, unconvinced, or unconcerned about these reports. Rockefeller recommended that "the training program which brings military and police

27. Olimpio Alves Machado, "Indian Guard Trained in Brazil," *IPA Review* 4 (October 1970): 9, 14.

28. Church Hearings, p. 7.

personnel from the other hemispheric nations to the United States and to training centers in Panama be continued and strengthened." He added:

> The U.S should respond to requests for assistance of the police and security forces of the hemisphere nations by providing them with the essential tools to do their jobs. Accordingly, the United States should meet reasonable requests from other hemispheric nations for trucks, jeeps, helicopters, and like equipment to provide mobility and logistical support for these forces; for radios, and other command control equipment for proper communications among the forces; and for small arms for security forces.[29]

An OPS press release in early 1970 indicated that the office continued to take a broad view of what police operations should encompass. It noted that most countries possess a unified "civil security service," which "in addition to regular police include paramilitary units" which "have as their primary mission maintaining internal security." Thus, Public Safety programs "are focused in general on developing within the civil security forces a balance of (1) a capability for regular police operations, with (2) an investigative capability for detecting and identifying criminal and/or subversive individuals and organizations and neutralizing their activities, and with (3) a capability for controlling militant activities ranging from demonstrations, disorders, or riots through small-scale guerrilla operations."[30]

A total of 210 U.S. Public Safety Advisers served in Brazil from 1959 through 1970, at an average annual rate of twenty per year between 1961 and 1970.[31] One of those who served in Brazil in the late 1960s was Dan Mitrione. His death in 1970 at the hands of Uruguay's bold urban guerrilla organization, the Tupamaros, brought upon the OPS program some unwelcome publicity. A committee of the Uruguayan Senate had found some months before Mitrione's death that torture was being systematically practiced on political prisoners, and Alejandro Otero, former chief of the Uruguayan Police Service of Investigation and Information, confirmed in an interview (published by the *Jornal do Brasil*) what the Tupamaros had charged—that Mitrione, who had been

29. Nelson A. Rockefeller, *The Rockefeller Report on the Americas: The Official Report of a Presidential Mission for the Western Hemisphere* (Chicago: Quadrangle Books, 1969), pp. 63–64.

30. "AID Assistance to Civil Security Forces," Office of Public Safety press release, 11 February 1970, cited in Committee of Returned Volunteers, *Brazil: Who Pulls the Strings*, p. 31.

31. Church Hearings, p. 11.

serving in Uruguay for the previous two years, had used torture in his work.[32]

According to Agee, Otero was an agent of the CIA station in Montevideo and had been trained in early 1966 at the CIA's International Police Services School in Washington, D.C. The CIA had been largely responsible for the establishment and expansion of the Public Safety Assistance program in Uruguay and had one of its officers, Bill Cantrell, there under Public Safety cover. Agee's disillusionment with his own role as a CIA officer was intensified when he heard screams from the torture rooms located next to a CIA listening post in police headquarters. The victim was a person whose name Agee had given to Otero for "preventive detention."[33]

Senator Abourezk has received some two dozen letters from both U.S. citizens and foreign nationals who alleged to have witnessed instruction in methods of torture and in death squad tactics by U.S. Public Safety Advisers.[34] Father Louis Colonnese, director of the U.S. Catholic Conference's Division for Latin America, noted that, in Brazil, Mitrione had worked with the police in Belo Horizonte, where instruction in torture techniques has involved live classroom demonstrations using political prisoners as guinea pigs. Colonnese insisted that it must be determined "whether Mitrione was paid with tax money by an agency of the U.S. government to teach and perform torture under the euphemistic guise of promoting internal security."[35]

By the time of the May 1971 Senate Foreign Relations Committee hearings, chaired by Senator Frank Church, on U.S. Policies and Programs in Brazil, and perhaps to some extent because of them, the number of U.S. Public Safety Advisers in Brazil had been scaled down to four. Two of the four had served previously as Public Safety Advisers in South Vietnam, where tens of thousands of civilians were tortured and murdered under the OPS- (and CIA-) funded Operation Phoenix. It might be assumed that such duty in Vietnam would have been a bru-

32. *Brazil: Order and Progress* (Cambridge, Mass.: Action Latin America, May 1971), p. 2.

33. Agee, *Inside the Company*, pp. 429, 445–46, 461–65, 478. Agee left the Montevideo station in 1966, before Mitrione arrived. Julius Mader's *Who's Who in the CIA*, published in West Berlin in 1968, lists Mitrione as a CIA officer. The author, however, is unable to assess the reliablity of this source. For more information on Mitrione and the Public Safety Assistance Program, see a forthcoming book by A. J. Langguth, to be published by Pantheon Books.

34. Daschle interview.

35. "Death of a Policeman: Unanswered Questions about a Tragedy," *Commonweal*, 18 September 1970.

talizing experience, but recent studies of the U.S. prison system suggest that the process of brutalization might have less exotic roots. For perspective it might be recalled that in response to the exposure by Representative William Anderson of the "tiger cages" in South Vietnam's Conson Island prisons, AID's spokesman reassured the American people that conditions there were no worse than in some U.S. prisons. Likewise, in 1971, a Brazilian translator for AID, visiting her son who had been paralyzed by torture, was told by a Brazilian officer guarding him, "Do you think that the police in other countries don't beat their prisoners? Even in the U.S.A. it goes on, because it was with them that we learned how to do it."[36] And General Vernon Walters, in discounting the reports of systematic torture in Brazil, told this author in 1976 that if he went around visiting U.S. prisons, he could give me "a splendid dossier on torture in the United States."[37]

Anthony Russo of the Rand Corporation, indicted with Daniel Ellsberg in the celebrated Pentagon Papers case, stated in an interview, "I have finally understood why we torture people in Vietnam—because we torture people *here*. The American advisors to the people who run the prisons in Vietnam are retired wardens, retired policemen, retired highway patrolmen, people who work in the so-called law-and-order field here in the United States." Russo went on to explain:

> I knew a man who worked for USAID public safety who had been a warden here in the United States. I used to try to talk to him and try to get some reason out of him concerning the prisons, the condition of prisons in Vietnam. He would always come back to his experience with prisons in the United States. . . . He was trying to get across to me that convicts are scum. He said, "We go to all this trouble to keep them in prison when we should take them out in a ship and drop them out at sea, just throw them overboard. They're worthless human beings. There's no reason to keep them alive. They're no good to anybody."[38]

Whether as a consequence of their own prejudices against dissenters and their contempt for prisoners or as a consequence of their extraordinarily well-guarded ignorance, spokesmen of the Public Safety Assistance Program have shown little concern for the most basic human rights, much less for civil and political rights. At the Church Hearings in 1971, OPS appeared to be suffering from a severe case of myopia. Under questioning from committee members, Theodore D.

36. Jack Anderson, "U.S. Is Accused in Brazilian Torture," *Washington Post*, 1 February 1971.

37. Walters interview.

38. Studs Terkel, "Servents of the State: A Conversation with Daniel Ellsberg," *Harper's Magazine* 244 (February 1972): 56–59.

Brown, AID's Chief Public Safety Adviser in Brazil, maintained initially that, as far as he knew, Brazil's state governors were chosen by general popular election, and he ultimately conceded that he was not qualified to answer. After acknowledging that the police did not work under any particular political or judicial restraints, he backtracked to say that they operate within the law. Asked if the people had elected the government, he responded, "Yes sir, they legislate laws." Asked if the president had been elected by the people, however, he responded, "Not by vote."

Mr. Brown insisted that the control and direction of the police were carried out independently of the armed forces and that OPS had experienced no difficulties in working with a government under military control. In fact, he noted that "the Director General of the Federal Police, even though he is a regular military officer, has been most anxious that we work with and assist in improving the capabilities of the Federal police. . . ." Asked to summarize the important provisions of Institutional Act No. 5, Brown responded, "The most important one is, that which affected our own operations, had to do with the reorganization of the military police and the placing, better coordinated training activities and in many ways improved the operations of the State police or the military police which are the State police. Aside from that insofar as our program is concerned, the police work is concerned, it was not a great difference."

Mr. Brown claimed to have little or no information concerning such infamous Brazilian instruments of surveillance, repression, and torture as the National Intelligence Service (SNI), Operation Bandeirantes, Operation Birdcage, and the Internal Defense Operation Centers (CODI). Questioned as to whether or not he believed the reports of torture, he responded, "I do not believe it is my right, sir, to judge the Brazilian people or the police." But he ultimately conceded that "within any organization there is always the possibility that there might be isolated cases of unnecessary use of force." Of the death squads, Brown acknowledged that "it is alleged that they are a group of irresponsible police that has taken the law into their own hands, so to speak, and felt that it was their duty to take direct action and not bother about recourse to the courts."

Senator Church asked, "In light of the many reports that we hear of torture in Brazil, do you think you have been successful in inculcating humane methods in restraint?" Mr. Brown: "Yes sir; I do, Senator." Senator Church: "You do. You think our program has been successful in Brazil in achieving its objectives?" Mr. Brown: "Yes, sir." Senator Church: "You really believe that?" Mr. Brown: "Yes, sir."

Mr. Brown assured the committee that the impact of the AID/PSO program had been felt throughout the Brazilian police system, composed of 271,000 men:

> Let me say that the 641 trained are only those trained in the United States. Since the inception of our program in 1959 we have had advisors in the country assisting in their training programs and their academy programs and in establishing academies, and that impact has been immense. In addition, the 641 returned and are utilized in training throughout the country, and through the multiplier effect they have been able to reach a great number of their brother officers.

Mr. Brown asserted, however, that by 1971 U.S. assistance had become concentrated in "specific institutional Federal Police elements." "U.S. advisors," he maintained,

> worked directly with the director of the [National Police] academy, division chiefs, course coordinators, and individual instructors to determine training needs, develop curriculum and courses, teaching aids and provide textual and other source materials for the preparation of lesson plans, pamphlets, class handouts, et cetera. Translation of source material and training aids in the English language, which could be used in a course, is done by USAID/PSO staff.
>
> Personal contacts between public safety advisors and senior state police officials are also utilized as a means to discuss and evaluate training needs within state police organizations. U.S. advisors also participate in the establishment of prerequisites for National Police Academy courses and selection of students.

Responding to questions concerning the academy, Mr. Brown denied that U.S. advisers had anything to do with courses on censorship and on tactical units of security and investigation, but he acknowledged that "we assist in planning and forming the curricula for the overall academy operation."

Mr. Brown testified that to the Brazilian National Institute of Criminalistics, "USAID/PSO has furnished scientific instruments, photographic equipment and texts, US training of institute criminalistics and advisory technical assistance." To the National Institute of Identification, "USAID/PSO has provided automated card files, mechanical data processing equipment, fingerprint magnifiers and smaller items of equipment and intensive advisory assistance at the time the Institute was being created and organized. Some US training has been provided." Mr. Brown noted that "the Institute can, upon request of a police agency, provide past criminal record or make a mechanical search of their files for a suspect, type of crime, modus operandi, and personal characteristics of the suspect."

For the telecommunications service of the Federal Police, Mr. Brown said, "USAID/PSO has provided technical assistance in the planning and design of the national network and in establishment and preparation of training courses in the telecommunications field." He added that limited U.S. training had also been provided to this service, as well as equipment in the form of transmitters, receivers, portable transceivers, laboratory repair equipment and tools, and demonstration and training aids.

Mr. Brown saw the U.S. contribution to the capabilities of the Brazilian police system as particularly important in the areas of organization and management and in bringing about "modern techniques in the handling of people, whether it be crowd control or whether it be investigations." He noted that communications equipment provided by AID "has been used extensively, and this is, has been an important factor in improving their capability to better control crowds. The vehicles that have been furnished, the increased mobility, has been helpful to them." In addition to communications and mobility, he listed surveillance training as an important aspect of the assistance provided for dealing with such matters as kidnappings.

Having stated that "the image of the police has improved in recent years" and that "generally they are respected," Mr. Brown was somewhat at a loss to explain why the AID/PSO program was designed in part to improve the image of the police, through public relations films and the like. He maintained, however, that even in the short time he had been there—since 1967—there had been improvement in the "image as a civil, as opposed to military organization. . . . The fact that military officers are assigned to head the various organizations is really aside from that."

Responding to Mr. Brown's assertion that he would feel safer on the streets of Rio than on those of Washington, D.C., Senator Church asked, "If that is the case, then how is it that we are so well qualified to instruct the Brazilians on adequate police protection methods?" Mr. Brown insisted that "the police of Brazil have come a long way in the past ten years in changing from a military concept of rule to a civil police concept." He added, "We have had and have now communications equipment that is second to none in the world, and by introducing, demonstrating, the value of communications, I think it has been most helpful to them." He conceded, however, that "they are approaching right now very fast a full capacity indeed to train their own people."[39]

OPS reported to the Senate Appropriations Committee that its pro-

39. Church Hearings, pp. 3–51.

gram in Brazil amounted to $5.1 million in fiscal 1972 and $3.5 million in fiscal 1973. The proposed budget for fiscal 1974, tucked away under the category of education, was $3.9 million. Hearings on Foreign Assistance and Related Programs Appropriations for Fiscal Year 1974 before the Senate Committee on Appropriations included the following exchange relating to educational grants to Brazil:

> Senator Inouye. Do the figures we have been talking about include funds for public safety programs?
> Mr. Birnbaum. Yes: that is correct.
> Senator Inouye. If you look at page 15 of our report, the direction of this committee in the matter of reporting, it says, and I quote, "Obligations or expenditures under the public safety program should be excluded from its presentation," because it is difficult for many of us to consider training officers how to use mace and riot control as being education in the real sense.[40]

Senator Abourezk's amendment to the Foreign Assistance Act of 1961 eliminated U.S. Public Safety Advisers for fiscal 1974 except in the area of narcotics control. (If experience is any guide, that "area" may be expected to prove elastic.) But the training of foreign police officers in the United States and the provision of financial and material "supporting" assistance to foreign police forces continued to be funded.

The Abourezk amendment, effective in fiscal 1975, virtually nullified the executive order that had created the Office of Public Safety. As introduced, the amendment "prohibiting police training" provided that:

> None of the funds made available to carry out this or any other law, and none of the local currencies accruing under this or any other law, shall provide any financial support for police, prisons or other internal security forces of any foreign government or any program of internal intelligence or surveillance on behalf of any foreign government within the United States or abroad.[41]

As a consequence of CIA lobbying, however, the "any other law" clauses were deleted before final passage of the foreign aid bill in December 1974. In a letter to Senator J. William Fulbright, the Foreign Relations Committee Chairman, William E. Colby, Director of the CIA, had argued:

> The amendment would appear to restrict activities now undertaken by the CIA under the National Security Act of 1947 for the purpose of obtain-

40. 93rd Cong., 1st sess., pp. 710, 821.

41. Abourezk Amendment.

ing foreign intelligence information from cooperative foreign security and intelligence services, some of which are within national police forces. In addition, in many areas of the world the protection of U.S. personnel, installations and security interests depends heavily on the effectiveness and support of foreign internal security services, as does effective action to counter terrorist activities and narcotics traffic. An essential ingredient of many CIA relationships with foreign security and intelligence is some limited and specialized training and other support, as well as the exchange of information and advice. If the agency were restricted in these activities, our ability to perform our assigned intelligence mission would be severely curtailed.[42]

In addition to the CIA loophole, the amendment specifies inapplicability to assistance rendered under the authority of the Drug Enforcement Administration or the FBI and under any contract entered into prior to the enactment of that section.[43]

Although the precise nature of the relationship between the Public Safety Assistance Program and the CIA is not clarified in Agee's CIA diary, the promotion of the program by the CIA and its usefulness to the agency—as a cover for officers, a means of recruiting agents, and a support for station operations and objectives—is manifest throughout the book. Nevertheless, CIA liaison with foreign police and other intelligence forces did not begin with, and cannot be expected to end with, the Public Safety Assistance program.

The Senate Select Committee on Intelligence noted that the CIA, throughout its history, had entered into liaison agreements—both for intelligence exchange and for operational support—with the intelligence services of foreign powers, and that such agreements had not been systematically reviewed by the U.S. Congress. The Committee recommended that the CIA be prohibited by statute from causing, fund-

---

42. Letter from CIA Director William E. Colby to Senate Foreign Relations Committee Chairman J. William Fulbright, 31 July 1974.

43. Vaughn Young, freelance writer currently working on a book on "Interpol," informed this author in a conversation on 27 February 1975 that the DEA sometimes serves as a front for the CIA. He said also that the DEA and the FBI are among several U.S. agencies which make use of the intelligence network maintained by Interpol, a private organization with member branches, generally headed by the leadership of national police forces, in 120 countries. In addition to annual dues of $118,000 (paid by the United States through its official representative, the Treasury Department), the United States in 1974 made a special contribution to Interpol, through AID, of $135,000 for the establishment of a narcotics intelligence network. Brazil had also made generous contributions to Interpol.

ing, or encouraging liaison services to engage in actions which are forbidden to the CIA.[44]

In general, the fortification of a country's police forces strengthens the government that happens to be in power. We have seen, however, that that need not be the case. While the government of Goulart was in power in Brazil, the United States used the program to strengthen the police forces of those states whose governors were conspiring to depose Goulart. It was only after the Brazilian military had seized power that the U.S. program was directed toward enhancing the capabilities of the central government.

The potentialities of such a program for the external manipulation of the internal balance of political forces, however, go beyond the short-term selective use of the police to facilitate a coup or to tilt the balance in favor of a particular group or faction. The ideological content of the training program may be expected to have the long-term effect of imbuing the police with the attitude that they are engaged in a civil war and that those of their own compatriots who advocate redistribution of wealth and power are the enemy.

Disregarding those individuals who are by nature sadistic, policemen are more likely to engage in torture and other dehumanizing tactics if they view their prisoners as war time enemies. Furthermore, regardless of whether the charges of direct U.S. complicity in torture are confirmed, it is suggested here that those who derive their expertise in and orientation toward law enforcement from experience in the U.S. system may be ill prepared for inculcating respect for human rights.

44. *Foreign and Military Intelligence*, p. 459. The Committee noted in a separate report (*Covert Action*, pp. 185 and 187) that in the period between the election of Allende in 1970 and the military coup in 1973, the Santiago CIA station "collected operational intelligence necessary in the event of a coup," including arrest lists. After the coup, CIA officials claimed that the agency's support for the junta's security and intelligence forces was designed to assist in controlling subversion from abroad, but they acknowledged that this support could be adaptable to the control of internal subversion as well.

Part III:

Transnational
Institutional Interests
and the Interaction
of Military Elites

Introduction

We have seen in the preceding section that various programs and initiatives undertaken by U.S. civilian agencies, as well as by U.S. corporate entities in collaboration with the government, were designed to weaken power holders and contenders who were viewed as unsympathetic toward the United States, to strengthen political and business elites who were viewed as potential allies, and, in laying the groundwork for the 1964 coup, to generate an atmosphere of chaos and fear. This section will deal with the manner in which U.S. military programs contributed to the technical capabilities of the Brazilian military as well as to the officer corps' role orientation and collective self-image of "governing elite."

In the early 1960s it was suggested by Victor Alba, among others, that Latin American militarism was destined soon to wither away, as the military had no useful function, and as there was an emergent generation of U.S.-trained, technocratically oriented "laboratory" officers.[1] A very different view was presented in 1971 to Joseph Novitski of the *New York Times* by a Brazilian "leftist," who said, "Whatever happens in Brazil, Argentina, Paraguay, Bolivia, and Peru, the United States must accept partial responsibility: The missions taught the military how to think politically."[2]

The history of the role of the military in the political process of most Latin American countries indicates that these military establishments hardly needed instruction from the Colossus of the North in how to think politically. It is obvious, however, that Alba's assumption was equally inaccurate.

1. Victor Alba, "The Stages of Militarism in Latin America," in *The Role of the Military in Underdeveloped Countries*, ed. John J. Johnson, (Princeton: Princeton University Press, 1962), pp. 165–84.

2. Joseph Novitski, "Latin Lands Turning to Europe for Arms," *New York Times*, 4 May 1971, pp. 1, 7.

It appears that for a highly significant portion of Brazil's military elite, the U.S. military has indeed served as a value-orienting "reference group." But when, whether, and with what level of priority the United States has actually sought to discourage military seizures of power are questions that deserve more careful consideration, along with the question of whether the U.S. military can be regarded as a reliable repository of what have generally been assumed to be the prevailing social and political values of the U.S. citizenry.

Some of the mythology surrounding the relationship between U.S. policy (military policy and programs in particular) and the behavior of Latin American military establishments can be laid to rest by examining the nature of the relationship between U.S. and Brazilian military elites in light of the institutional characteristics and self-interests of the military. These relationships suggest that the military—at least in the Western Hemisphere—might be regarded as a transnational subculture, rather than as a repository of national values.[3]

Many high-ranking officials of the U.S. defense establishment have expressed the opinion that the most valuable aspect of the military assistance program for Latin America is the training of Latin officers. One of the supposed dividends that has always been presented in advocacy or justification of the training programs is the indoctrination of the Latin officers in democratic ideas and values that results from their exposure to U.S. military institutions and contacts with U.S. advisors. On 9 April 1962, Defense Secretary McNamara told a Senate committee:

> Probably the greatest return on our military assistance investment dollar comes from the training of selected officers and key specialists at our military schools and training centers in the United States and overseas. . . . I need not dwell upon the value of having in positions of leadership men who have firsthand knowledge of how Americans do things and how they think. . . . Each of these men will receive an exposure to democracy at work.[4]

3. At the House Foreign Affairs Committee Hearings on Military Assistance Training in 1970, an "expert" witness, Dr. Ernest W. Lefever of The Brookings Institution, was asked by Representative L. H. Fountain if he had found any evidence that "the broad effect of the program has been to establish a kind of military culture that cuts across national lines" (pp. 34–35). Lefever's answer was affirmative. This tendency has in some cases dampened xenophobic nationalism; however, military establishments and military regimes have not hesitated to brandish the flag when external pressures threatened to circumscribe their own freedom of action or when they have felt the need of popular support.

4. Raymond Estep, "United States Military Aid to Latin America," manuscript (Maxwell Air Force Base, Alabama, Documentary Research Division, Aerospace Studies Institute, Air University, September 1966), p. 55.

Between 1960 and 1969, eighteen regimes in Latin America, of which eleven had held office constitutionally, were overthrown by the military. By 1969, more than two-thirds of the people of Latin America were living under military dictatorships.[5] It might be expected that in a profit-conscious society such a "return" on the investment would be considered less than impressive, but General Robert W. Porter, Commander-in-Chief of the U.S. Southern Command, nerve center of U.S. military activity in Latin America, stated in 1968 that "dollar for dollar, U.S. training assistance pays the greatest dividend of any of our military assistance programs in Latin America."[6]

The allegation that exposure to United States officers and institutions will generate democratic attitudes within Latin military establishments rests upon a number of assumptions that will be made explicit and reexamined in the following chapters. Among these are: that the value-orienting ambient of the U.S. military officer corps is a democratic system; that the predominant direction of influence through such contacts is from U.S. civilian policy-makers to U.S. officers to Latin officers; that the world-view held and proselytized by U.S. officers is consistent with the advocacy of civilian supremacy and democratic government generally (as set forth, for example, in the U.S. and in most Latin American Constitutions) and for Latin America in particular; that U.S. military policies and programs are conducive to the establishment and protection of democratic systems; and that overall U.S. objectives in the hemisphere, as interpreted by those who make and/or implement military policy, dictate the promotion of democratic self-government in the Latin American states.

5. U.S., Senate, Committee on Foreign Relations, Subcommittee on Western Hemisphere Affairs, *United States Military Policies and Programs in Latin America,* Hearings, 91st Cong., 1st sess., 24 June and 8 July 1969, pp. 68–69. By mid-1976, only seven of the twenty-one Latin American countries were under civilian rule, and of those only four had a generally accepted claim to a significant measure of democratic procedure.

6. General Robert W. Porter, "Look South to Latin America," *Military Review* 48 (June 1968): 82–90.

[9]

The "Special Relationship" Between U.S. and Brazilian Military Elites

In Senate Hearings in 1971, Major General George S. Beatty, chairman of the U.S. delegation to the Joint Brazil-U.S. Military Commission, and subsequently director of the Inter-American Defense College, asserted that

> Brazil's Armed Forces have been largely U.S. oriented since World War II. This orientation is the result of close professional collaboration between United States and Brazilian Armed Forces over the years. Brazil has adopted U.S. military doctrine, tactics, and techniques and has, until recently, almost exclusively sought U.S. equipment and logistic support.[1]

This chapter traces some of the means through which the Brazilian military came to depend largely on U.S. equipment, to adopt U.S. tactics and techniques, and to internalize and adapt U.S. military doctrines to its own institutional needs.

The Expansion of U.S. Military Programs in Brazil

The beginnings of a "special relationship" between U.S. and Brazilian military elites can be traced back to 1922, when a U.S. Naval Mission, the first in South America, was established in Brazil.[2] U.S. Army and Army and Navy Air Force missions followed in the late 1930s.[3] A number of Brazilian officers had been trained in Germany prior to World War I, however, and a French army mission diffused its concepts of military professionalism among the Brazilian officer corps

1. Church Hearings, p. 56.
2. King interview.
3. Church Hearings, p. 51.

162

from 1919 until its departure in 1940.[4] So it was not until World War II that the United States acquired a near-monopoly over the training and equipping of the Brazilian armed forces.

The personnel of the U.S. missions already in Brazil served as the U.S. representation on the Joint Brazilian-United States Military Commission (JBUSMC), which coordinated the military activities of the two countries during the war. Collaboration was extensive. The United States sent ships, planes, ground equipment, and tens of thousands of troops to protect the Brazilian bulge and made use of Brazilian air bases, ports, and other facilities, especially for transporting supplies to North Africa. The Brazilian Navy cooperated in patrolling the South Atlantic, and the Brazilian Army and Air Force provided some twenty thousand to thirty thousand troops for a Brazilian expeditionary force in the Italian campaign.[5] The Brazilian armed forces emerged from World War II completely re-equipped and re-outfitted by the U.S. Army. Their new equipment even included U.S. Army-issued clothing. Some Brazilians complained in the postwar years that the only Brazilian thing in the Independence Day parades was the flag.[6]

In 1947 and 1948 the U.S. sold ground equipment for an entire infantry division, other light equipment, and over one hundred combat aircraft to Brazil, at approximately 10 percent of procurement cost, as surplus disposals.[7] And in 1949, at the urging of Brazilian officers who had fought alongside the United States in Italy, the U.S. military assisted in the establishment of the Brazilian Superior War College (Escola Superior de Guerra—ESG). The school was modeled after the U.S. National War College, and a U.S. advisory mission remained at the ESG until 1960, when the U.S. contingent was reduced to a single liaison officer. That officer, who has full faculty privileges, offers advice on curricula and provides the school with U.S. training manuals, military journals, and other materials.[8]

Agreement was reached in 1952 between the U.S. and Brazilian military establishments for the inclusion of Brazil in the U.S. Mutual

4. Nunn, "Military Professionalism and Professional Militarism." For diplomatic correspondence relating to the mission agreements and wartime cooperation, see National Archives State Decimal File, 1940–44, from 832.20/129 to 832.20/572.

5. Church Hearings, p. 52.

6. Baker, Ross R. *A Study of Military Status and Status Deprivation in Three Latin American Armies* (Washington, D.C.: Center for Research in Social Systems, October 1967).

7. Kaplan, "U.S. Military Aid to Brazil," p. 42.

8. Stepan, *The Military in Politics*, p. 129.

Defense Assistance program. The Vargas government delayed its entry into force until 1953, but excess stock grants for the program's first year alone, fiscal 1953, amounted to U.S. $52.8 million.[9] The wartime JBUSMC had continued to function as the agency for military collaboration between the two countries, and in 1954 it was given permanent status and registered with the United Nations as an international agency. (The only other Latin American country that maintains such a joint commission with the United States is Mexico, which has not participated in the bilateral military assistance program.) At the same time, the Joint Brazil-United States Defense Commission was created as the Washington counterpart to the JBUSMC. The former is headed by a Brazilian, the latter by a North American.

Military assistance and sales and all other aspects of military cooperation, with the exception of attaché matters, are channeled through these two agencies. The U.S. Military Group (milgroup), a centralized command structure established in the early 1960s to incorporate the missions of the three services and the Military Assistance Advisory Groups in most countries receiving bilateral assistance, is formally known in Brazil as the U.S. delegation to the JBUSMC. The joint commission in Washington is an ad hoc body composed of three American delegates detailed from the Joint Chiefs of Staff (JCS) and the three Brazilian military attachés. Attaché posts at the Brazilian Embassy are generally a reward for services performed or preparation for higher office. Médici was an attaché and a member of that commission just prior to being selected for the presidency in 1969, as was General Orlando Geisel before becoming Minister of War.[10]

The commission network links the military establishments of the two countries more closely than would the milgroup arrangement, as it provides a more direct communication link. The U.S. delegation to the JBUSMC, which shares office space with the Brazilian delegation, may communicate with the JCS either through the U.S. Southern Command (SOUTHCOM) in Panama or directly through its counterpart commission in Washington. The delegation's activities and communications theoretically take place under the guidance of the chief of the diplomatic mission, but in practice that is not necessarily the case.[11]

The JBUSMC agreement provides that the functions of the U.S. dele-

9. Kaplan, "U.S. Military Aid to Brazil."

10. Major General Richard J. Seitz (JBUSMC member, September 1954–July 1957; Commander, October 1968–July 1970; Commander of Fort Bragg since July 1973), interview, 4 June 1973, Washington, D.C.

11. King interview.

gations shall include maintaining "constant liaison, by personal conferences and visits, with appropriate Brazilian governmental departments and agencies, i.e., Ministry of Finance, Chief of Police, Director of Traffic, Post Office Department, Ministry of Foreign Affairs, Inspector of Customs, Post Director and the Vehicle Registration Bureau, in order to facilitate JBUSMC interests within those agencies." Among the U.S. Defense Department's stated objectives for the twin commissions was to "facilitate preparation of joint military planning between the two governments." And a letter of 2 July 1970 from Assistant Secretary of State Charles Meyer to Senator William Fulbright explained that the U.S. military mission in Brazil "helps the host government assess the threat to the nation's security and counsels on the strategy and tactics for dealing with the threat."[12] In 1958, this delegation or milgroup consisted of 102 persons. The size of the group grew steadily until 1968, when it peaked at about 200. By 1971 the authorized size of the group had been reduced to 60.[13]

U.S. grants and credits to Brazil under the military assistance program amounted to $93.3 million for the period from 1951 through 1955, $97.4 million from 1956 through 1960, $113.5 million from 1961 through 1965, and $107.8 million from 1966 through 1970. About two-thirds of the total for the entire period was in the form of grants.[14] (Most economic assistance, by contrast, has been in the form of loans.) Much of this grant assistance has been for the training of 6,858 Brazilians in the United States and the Panama Canal Zone between 1950 and 1970.[15]

In addition to the service attachés and the JBUSMC, U.S. military representation in Brazil in 1971 included members of the Inter-American Geodetic Survey, the Naval Communications Technical Group (NAVCOMTECH), the Defense Research Office Latin America, and a liaison detachment from the Military Airlift Command. The survey team works with Brazilian counterparts in producing geographic, cartographic, and geophysical information and topographic maps on Brazil. In exchange for its assistance, the United States receives copies of the maps produced.

12. See Church Hearings, pp. 84–90.

13. Ibid., p. 147; Ellender Report, p. 336.

14. Kaplan, "U.S. Military Aid to Brazil," p. 4. In general, figures on military assistance should be regarded with some skepticism. Congressional and other investigators have noted that actual spending on military assistance tends to be much higher than any particular set of figures released to the public.

15. Church Hearings, p. 85.

The NAVCOMTECH Group originated as a compromise measure to preserve the use of a U.S.-owned and -operated radio installed in Rio de Janeiro during World War II. Rather than vacating the facility after the war, the U.S. navy reached an agreement with the Brazilian Navy whereby the NAVCOMTECH Group "is to provide technical training and operational assistance to the Brazilian Navy in order to make possible the communications assistance of the Brazilian Naval Communications System to the U.S. Navy and other U.S. Governmental Agencies."[16] At Senate hearings in 1971, Major General George S. Beatty, Chairman of the U.S. Delegation to the JBUSMC, testified that without the facility, the U.S. Navy would be unable to communicate with some of its vessels in the South Atlantic, but he conceded that the Brazilian government could close down the operation any time it chose to.

The Defense Research Office, established in 1962, served as a "contact point for South American scientists and research agencies for receiving and evaluating research proposals pertinent to R&D missions of the U.S." The MAC liaison "facilitates the arrival, maintenance, loading, and dispatch" of the one MAC flight each week, which, General Beatty explained, brings "both people and things."[17]

John Duncan Powell has pointed out a number of ways in which a seemingly small (relative to the country's GNP or national resources) amount of material assistance to a military establishment can be highly significant in terms of institutional autonomy and sheer physical power vis-à-vis contending political groups.[18] But historically, in most Latin American countries, including Brazil, the military itself has reflected the political cleavages of the larger national society. Thus, both critics and defenders of the program generally agree that training, with its potentialities for political indoctrination and the development of personal ties, has been the most consequential aspect of U.S. military assistance to Latin America.

Training and Political Indoctrination

Even before the heyday of counterinsurgency, U.S. institutions engaged in the training of Latin American military officials proceeded on the assumption that Latin America's primary contributions to the defense of the "free world" were to be the maintenance of internal

16. Ibid., p. 96.

17. Ibid., pp. 91–100.

18. John Duncan Powell, "Military Assistance and Militarism in Latin America, Part I, "*The Western Political Quarterly* 18 (June 1965): 382–92.

order and the prevention of subversive activities. Much of the doctrinal and practical content that was to be incorporated into training for this geographically confined but functionally expanded military role represented a refinement of the techniques employed by the U.S. Marines in Central America and the Caribbean in the first three decades of the twentieth century and of the methods devised to isolate or repress potential enemies in the Western Hemisphere during World War II.

A precedent had been established for formal instruction in unconventional warfare as early as 1924–1925, when Lieutenant Colonel W. P. Upshur, who had fought guerrillas (*cacos*) in Haiti, initiated a lecture series at the Quantico, Virginia, Field Officers School on the conduct of "small wars," a term applied in those years to the pacification of "less-developed" peoples by major powers. By 1932 the course had been expanded and was directed by Major Harold H. Utley, who had commanded Marine forces in Eastern Nicaragua.[19]

The "lessons" of Marine engagements in Latin America, along with examinations of operations ranging from the French conquest of Indochina to the Battle of Little Big Horn, are set forth in the Marine Corps Small Wars Manual, published in 1940.[20] For the protection of the interests of the United States and the property of U.S. citizens in countries threatened by revolution, the Manual offered precise instructions for gathering intelligence, running a military government, patrolling waterways and jungles, bombing and strafing of villages, attacking houses and a variety of other specific operations. The occupying forces were reminded to consider the reaction of the American public, as anti-interventionist "propaganda" could normally be expected from Congress and the press. The Manual anticipated that no declaration of war would be sought, that such small wars would be fought solely under executive authority. Further, it noted that such wars are "conducted often with precarious responsibility, and doubtful authority, under indeterminate orders lacking specific instructions," and that the force commander might have to deduce his mission "from the general intent of higher authority, or even from the foreign policy of the United States."

The process of intervening in a revolutionary or pre-revolutionary country was divided into five phases (which incidentally bear a striking resemblance to the sequence of events in the U.S. intervention in

19. Ronald Schaffer, "The 1940 Small Wars Manual and the 'Lessons of History,' " *Military Affairs* 36 (April 1972): 46–51.

20. Ibid.

the Dominican Republic in 1965). After the marines had "dribbled in" in numbers strong enough to achieve their objective, the second phase, occupation of principal cities and economically vital areas, placing garrisons in fortified posts and sending out small patrols, would be undertaken. While extending their control over the host country, the Marines were to establish a "constabulary" or native army. Constabulary units were to take charge of "civil affairs" projects, such as flood and earthquake relief, in order to gain the confidence of "law abiding" natives, and in the third phase they would begin to assume some responsibility for policing their country.

In the third phase, however, the Marines would assume control, direct or indirect depending on the circumstances, of local executive agencies, and Marines would retain major responsibility for anti-guerrilla activities until "lawless elements" were subdued. Thereafter, preparations would begin for "free and fair" elections (quotation marks in Manual). There were to be two electoral agencies, a National Board of Elections, staffed by natives, and an American Electoral Mission, which was to exercise actual control. In the fifth phase natives would assume control of domestic affairs and the Marines would depart, leaving perhaps a legation behind.

The Manual is laced with contradictions. It admonished the Marines to be nonpartisan, while making it clear that they would be intervening for partisan reasons—to keep revolutionaries out of power, to protect the property of U.S. citizens, and to remove or pressure local governments as U.S. interests (as they interpret them) dictate. The political "neutrality" of the constabulary was to be assured by screening of candidates by the Marines with the assistance of local officials, as well as by good pay and proper discipline. When possible, this "nonpartisan" constabulary was to replace the Marines in guarding the polls to give "the impression" that elections were conducted under native control, although it was also suggested that patrols of warplanes be sent over outlying areas to give voters "tangible evidence . . . that they are receiving protection in the exercise of their civil rights."

The Manual cautioned the Marines against acting superior to the natives, but it emphasized their civilizing mission. Enlisted men were to be indoctrinated prior to landing in the "racial characteristics" of the target country, including whether those characteristics inclined the natives to be corrupt, excitable, superstitious, vacillating, or susceptible to propaganda. They were instructed, also, that if the country had a high illiteracy rate, its inhabitants would tend to be childlike.

The intervention was described as "friendly assistance," but it was conceded that the majority would see the intervention as an unfriendly act, to be opposed in the interest of self-preservation, and that all natives were therefore to be viewed as "potential enemies." It was also conceded that in the process of defeating the insurgents, who would probably be indistinguishable from and aided by ordinary citizens, the lives and property of friendly or neutral natives would be endangered as well.

Finally, the Marines were instructed to deal with the political, social, and economic problems that give rise to revolutionary feelings. Yet they were encouraged to cooperate with local governments whose tyrannical acts, the Manual stated, might have led to the insurgency. It was also recommended that the Marines go along with class distinctions, and it was understood, of course, that they would be there to protect U.S. holdings that were a part of an economic status quo benefiting foreigners at natives' expense.

The small wars that had provided the insights for the Manual had been fought almost exclusively against poorly organized and poorly equipped native forces. The authors of the Manual felt that anti-revolutionary interventions would continue indefinitely, but that they would become increasingly difficult.[21]

Civil Affairs as a regular component of military training, initially of U.S. officers, but later of foreign officers and enlisted men as well, was an outgrowth of World War II. The experience of the U.S. armed forces in governing civilian populations, both foreign and domestic, dated back to the War with Mexico and the Civil War, but it was not until martial law was declared in Hawaii, in the wake of Pearl Harbor, and the West Coast Japanese and other supposed enemy aliens were interned that the issue of specialized training in "politico-military," or civil, affairs assumed urgency.

An order of 2 April 1942 by the Secretary of War established a school "to be known as The School of Military Government" at the University of Virginia and the first course, with fifty officers in attendance, opened on 11 May 1942.[22] The issue, however, of whether governing civilians, friendly or enemy, was a job for the military, had not been resolved. The press had dealt disdainfully with the new School for Military Government, and a number of civilian departments and agencies either had mandates to engage in foreign administration or could claim such authority by extension of their domestic domains.

Following a stormy cabinet meeting on 29 October 1942, President

21. Ibid.

22. Earl F. Ziemke, "Civil Affairs Reaches Thirty," *Military Affairs* 36 (December 1972): 130–33.

Roosevelt informed Secretary of War Stimson that he regarded governing civilian territory as "predominantly a civilian task." However, after
a year's inconclusive effort to bring civilian agencies into play, the
President conceded to Stimson that "it is apparent that if prompt
results are to be obtained, the Army will have to assume the initial
burden." The School of Military Government graduated its last class at
Charlottesville in February 1946, but it reopened in March at Carlisle
Barracks, Pennsylvania, and since then, as the Army Civil Affairs
School at Fort Gordon, Georgia, and Fort Bragg, North Carolina, it has
maintained a continuous existence. From its inception, this school has
sought to impart area expertise as well as training in the techniques
of government. An uneasy coexistence between the terms "military
government" and "civil affairs" was finally resolved when it was decided that "civil affairs" was military government conducted in one's
own or friendly territory, and "military government" was civil affairs
conducted in enemy territory.[23]

This training in "unconventional warfare" and the conduct of "small
wars" was to assume increased importance for the hemisphere when,
as "counterinsurgency" training, it was extended in the early 1960s
through the military assistance program to the Latin American military
establishments. The insurgents or potential insurgents these Latin
Americans were being trained to deal with as the enemy were their
own compatriots. And the governments they were being trained to
operate, through "civic action" and "civil affairs" programs, were their
own.

More than 140 military installations in the continental United States
(CONUS) were accomodating foreign military trainees in the mid-
1960s. Furthermore, the Panama Canal Zone, in addition to serving as
the Headquarters for the U.S. Southern Command, had become a special center for training Latin American military personnel in the U.S.
armed forces version of the "political science" of the cold war and the
internal security techniques required for winning it. More than 200,000
Latin American officers and men have been trained in the United
States, and an additional 30,000 men in the Canal Zone, since World
War II. General Robert Wood, Military Assistance Director, claimed in
1965 that "nearly all of Latin America's commissioned and noncommissioned officers have been trained either in the States or in
Panama."[24]

All U.S. training programs for foreign military personnel (including

---

23. Ibid.
24. Wolpin, *Military Aid and Counterrevolution* pp. 69–73.

the programs of the infantry school at Fort Benning, Georgia, and the artillery school at Fort Sill, Oklahoma, where large numbers of Latin Americans are trained, and the Defense Language Institute English Language School, Lackland Air Force Base, that equips incoming officers for further training) include a certain amount of political indoctrination. But the CONUS courses and programs most sensitive to shifts in political strategy and those apparently considered by the U.S. armed forces most important for the training of Latin American officers have included: The Special Forces Officer course, Psychological Operations, and Civil-Military Operations (formerly the Civil Affairs School of Fort Gordon, Georgia), consolidated in the early 1970s at the Institute for Military Assistance, Fort Bragg, North Carolina; the Senior Foreign Officers Intelligence Course at Fort Huachuca, Arizona; and the U.S. Army Command and General Staff College at Fort Leavenworth, Kansas.[25]

Foreign officers also attend the academies, war colleges, and command and general staff colleges of each of the U.S. service branches and enroll in correspondence courses offered by the U.S. National War College and the Industrial College of the Armed Forces. These correspondence courses have been incorporated into the curricula of the military staff or war colleges of a number of Latin American countries, including Brazil.[26] Most of the U.S. schools that train foreign officers have intensive follow-up programs to maintain contact with graduates. These include the free distribution of the school's journals and other materials, often in the host country language, the formation of alumni clubs, and the inclusion of graduates in social affairs sponsored by U.S. military groups abroad.

The upbeat mood of these schools in the early 1960s is suggested by an article in the *Air University Quarterly Review*, Summer 1963. It begins: "The Air Force recognizes the increasing tempo of technological advances, the significant economic, political, and social developments having international implications and the expanding mission of the military. The related urgent requirement for every officer to continue his education throughout his career is increasingly evident."[27]

25. Cecilia Lyles, Training Division, Department of the Army, interview, 4 October 1972, Washington, D.C. (Army insists that there is no central record of which schools have been attended by trainees of a particular country.)

26. Wolpin, *Military Aid and Counterrevolution*, p. 68.

27. Colonel John P. Lisack, U.S.A.F., "Air Force Review: Identification and Use of Educational Qualifications in the New Personnel Management System," *Air University Quarterly Review* 14 (Summer 1963): 85–89.

The school generally considered most important in cementing relations with upwardly mobile foreign officers is the U.S. Army Command and General Staff College (CGSC). Although the school has accepted foreign officers since 1893, most of the influx of "allied," and particularly Latin American, officers has taken place since World War II. The Latin American officers selected for training at Fort Leavenworth fall into two categories—the "political comer" and the "political exile."

According to Colonel D. Forest Ballou, former director of the strategic studies program, the school became particularly concerned around 1960 and 1961 with the need for a greater understanding by the military of communism, the cold war, and international relations generally, and attention was focused on questions like, "Why is it that politics is important to the military?" At about the same time, a massive increase in overseas assignments for military advisors drew attention to the Third World and to counterinsurgency doctrine and tactics. By the early 1970s, in response to the "Nixon Doctrine," even greater emphasis was being placed on the maintenance of internal security in the Third World.[28]

The curriculum of the CGSC, offered to U.S. and foreign students alike, includes: strategic studies (utilizing, for example, the World Politics Simulator); security assistance, including internal security, counterinsurgency, nation-building, and military assistance (security assistance training has been described as "largely political science, with heavy use of case studies"); operations, including civil disturbance and offensive and retrograde (retreat) operations; employment of weapons, including nuclear, chemical, and biological; intelligence; decision-making and management; and civil affairs.[29] Ballou said that the courses most often selected as electives by foreign officers are in the categories of strategic studies and security assistance. As in most other U.S. schools, foreign officers are encouraged to contribute to classroom presentations when the topic under discussion involves their countries. In 1973 there were six allied officers on the faculty. The only Latin American among them was a Brazilian, who was contributing, in particular, to instruction in security assistance.[30]

Manuals produced for the CGSC are translated and distributed to schools in the Canal Zone and throughout Latin America. The school's

28. Colonel D. Forest Ballou, III, Director of Course 5: Strategy, Command and General Staff School, Fort Leavenworth, Kansas, 1970–1973, interview, 22 June 1973, Washington, D.C.

29. Lesson plans, assignments, class notes, and manuals, U.S. Army Command and General Staff College, 1969–1972.

30. Ballou interview.

journal, *Military Review,* also has very broad circulation among allied military establishments. A Portuguese language edition has been published in Brazil since 1952 and one or more Brazilians have served on its editorial staff for at least a decade. An article published in the journal in 1964 explained that the CGSC was attempting to show students how

> U.S. strategy combines in proper proportion all elements of national power—political, economic, psychological, and military. . . . It has been in response to the Army's growing worldwide responsibilities that the college has increased its instruction dealing with strategic matters. The curriculum could not ignore that the search for victory in the cold war struggles has placed additional responsibilities on the military man at all echelons.[31]

CGSC graduates had by no means shirked their "additional responsibilities." In 1973 the school boasted that among its graduates were about ninty heads-of-state, cabinet ministers, and chiefs-of-staff; a "Hall of Fame" was being compiled to commemorate their achievements.[32] General Ernesto Geisel, who assumed the presidency of Brazil in 1974, is an alumnus of the CGSC.[33]

The training complex in the Panama Canal Zone includes the School of the Americas (Army) at Fort Gulick, the Inter-American Air Force Academy at Albrook Air Force Base, the smaller Inter-American Geodetic Survey School at Fort Clayton, operated jointly by the three service branches, and the U.S. Army Jungle Warfare School at Fort Sherman. The School of the Americas was officially opened in 1949 and by 1956 it was offering courses exclusively in Spanish and Portuguese. The school counts so many political leaders among its alumni that it is known throughout Latin America as the "escuela de golpes" (coup d'état school).[34] From the beginning, the U.S. interpretation of the Latin American role in the cold war served as the framework for instruction, but in the wake of the Cuban Revolution renewed emphasis was placed on internal security and riot control.

General Andrew O'Meara, Commander-in-Chief of the Southern Command, affirmed in 1962 that the traditional political influence goals of the training would be strengthened by assigning *highest* priority to anti-Communism. By 1967 close to 70 percent of the school's

31. Wolpin, *Military Aid and Counterrevolution,* pp. 75–91.

32. Interviews with Ballou and Lyles.

33. Rollie E. Poppino, "Brazil After a Decade of Revolution," *Current History* 66 (January 1974): 1–5, 35–38.

34. John M. Goshko, "Latins Blame the United States for Military Coups—AID is Suspect," *Washington Post,* 5 February 1968.

course hours were allocated to internal security instructions, and in the 1969 catalog even the supposedly technical courses sounded more like political science. The course entitled Radio Operator (E–23), for example, was described as follows:

"Irregular Warfare," encompasses the "causes and backgrounds of insurgent movements, nature of the communist threat in Latin America; the military, political and community development programs that should be instituted by the government to control insurgent movements at any stage of development. Forty students, 14 weeks, for enlistees who pass the Morse Code Aptitude Test."

And the course entitled Basic Medical Technician (E–30) was described as:

"Intelligence and Security," includes "Nature of the Communist world insurgency threat; countering the insurgency threat." Forty students, 20 weeks, for noncoms with an elementary school education."

Descriptive training pamphlets on communism emphasized that a major goal of communist insurgents in Third World countries is isolating those countries from the United States. Thus, communist elements seek to take advantage of nationalistic sentiments among the populace. One Special Forces training exercise at Fort Gulick involves the organization of a guerrilla force to restore a deposed "pro-Western government."[35]

Regular courses for Latin American officers were initiated at Albrook Air Force Base in 1943. In addition to training in technical skills such as aircraft maintenance, Albrook's program has expanded, since the early sixties, to include nation-building and civic action, special air operations in counterinsurgency, jungle and water survival, and the use of napalm.[36] The Jungle Warfare School at Fort Sherman, in operation since 1952, served as a model for the Brazilians, who, with U.S. equipment and technical assistance, established their own jungle warfare school in Manaus in the mid-1960s. (A U.S. military attaché stationed in Brazil in the late 1960s maintained that the Brazilian military had concluded that the training offered in the Canal Zone was not rigorous enough.) The Brazilian school now accepts trainees from other Latin American countries as well as from the United States.[37]

In addition to those trained in the continental United States and the Canal Zone, an indeterminate number of Latin American military

35. Wolpin, *Military Aid and Counterrevolution*, pp. 75–91.

36. Ibid.; Barber and Ronning, *International Security and Military Power*, pp. 161–64.

37. Colonel Milton Callero, Army Attaché, Brasilia, 1968–1970, interviews, 31 October 1972 and 21 February, 1973, Washington, D.C.

personnel have been trained in their own countries by U.S. Mobile Training Teams. The program began with the activation in 1963 of the Army's Third Civil Affairs Detachment from Fort Clayton in the Canal Zone.[38] Mobile Training Teams were also provided by the Special Air Warfare Center, Eglin Air Force Base, Florida; the 800-man U.S. Eighth Special Forces Group (Green Berets) from Fort Gulick; and the 605th Air Commando Squadron from Howard Air Force Base in the Canal Zone. The Air Force Special Operations Force (SOF), secretly established in 1961, has carried out extensive training in Latin America and in the early 1970s maintained air commando units at Eglin Air Force Base as well as in the Canal Zone. Not to be outdone, the Navy SEABEES maintain their own mobile Technical Assistant Teams in both the Atlantic and the Pacific.[39]

One aspect of this in-country training is suggested by Sidney Lens' account of an event in 1963:

> One day . . . watchmen at the San Francisco hydroelectric plant in Brazil were overpowered and handcuffed by armed men who then proceeded to cut telephone wires and to occupy the facilities. In the morning it was discovered that these were parachutists, trained by the U.S. in fighting internal aggression, who were staging a mock attack.[40]

(As it turned out, such tactics did not have to be used when the military seized control of the government the following year.)

From 1964 through 1972, the U.S. Army sent 27 mobile training teams to Brazil, the Air Force, 28; and the Navy, 12.[41] A U.S. officer stationed in Brazil in the late 1960s said that among other missions, these teams assisted in fashioning or reorienting civic action projects in such a way as to serve counterinsurgency goals; he cited, for example, developing the capability of identifying and keeping tabs on persons not native to an area.[42]

---

38. Ed Ossim, a U.S. Army Reserve officer assigned to a civil affairs unit in the Washington, D.C., area, said that training for his unit included an exercise in taking over Prince George's County, Md. (Conversation, April 1973, Washington, D.C.)

39. Wolpin, *Military Aid and Counterrevolution*, p. 74; Barber and Ronning, *Internal Security and Military Power*, pp. 157–67; Donald Robinson, "America's Air Guerrillas—Will They Stop Future Vietnams?" *Parade*, 31 January 1971, pp. 6–7. According to Agee, the Special Forces Group in the Canal Zone also maintains special interrogation teams which are dispatched to Latin America (*Inside the Company*, p. 301).

40. Sidney Lens, "Failures in Latin America," *The Progressive* 31 (January 1967): 29–33.

41. Lyles interview.

42. Schuler interviews.

Other U.S.-subsidized programs for training and coordination of defense strategy in the hemisphere include the Inter-American Defense College at Fort McNair, regular joint maneuvers conducted in Latin America and its coastal waters, and the annual Inter-American Army Conference, initiated in 1960, which draws together the highest officers of the hemisphere armies.[43] The directorship of the Inter-American Defense College is permanently held by the United States, but the U.S. provides only 25 to 30 percent of the faculty, the other faculty slots being filled by Latin Americans. One of the Brazilians teaching there in the late 1960s, Colonel Araujo, was the author of the Brazilian army's basic manual on insurgency in Brazil; it has reportedly served as a bible for officers involved in intelligence operations.[44]

The Nurturing of the Sorbonne Group

While top priority in inter-American military cooperation was placed on the protection of the hemisphere from external aggression, local military units receiving U.S. grant aid were limited in number: as late as 1960 they constituted no more than one-sixth of the total personnel of the national armed forces in any Latin American country. The shift in priorities to internal security and civic action resulted in a change from the provision of complete support for a fraction of the country's armed forces to the provision of at least a modicum of support to virtually all of the country's military personnel.[45]

Until the early 1960s the preponderant influence of the U.S. military was largely concentrated in a single clique or faction within the Brazilian military. It was the faction that, as the Brazilian Expeditionary Force (BEF), had fought alongside the U.S. Army Fourth Corps in Italy. The primary objectives of the U.S. armed forces in involving the BEF in the Italian campaign were reportedly the establishment of close ties with the Brazilian military elite and the exposure of that group to the modus operandi of the U.S. military so that it could go back and build up a "first class" military organization in Brazil.[46]

43. Tom Compere, ed., *The Army Blue Book, 1961–Vol. I* (New York: Military Publishing Institute, 1960), p. 282.

44. King interview.

45. Harold A. Hovey, *United States Military Assistance: A Study of Policies and Practices* (New York: Praeger, 1965), p. 63.

46. This information was reported to Fred Morris, U.S. missionary and journalist in Brazil, by a U.S. Air Force Major with dual U.S./Brazilian citizenship who acted as a liaison between the U.S. Air Force in Italy and the air force contingent of the BEF (Morris conversation).

The BEF, under U.S. tutelage, established and staffed Brazil's Superior War College (ESG). A book on the BEF written by its commander, Marshal J. B. Mascarenhas de Moraes, suggests something of the imitation of, admiration for, and sense of camaraderie and identity with the U.S. military developed by that group. Mascarenhas noted that "with the adoption of U.S. organization . . . and with war material until then unknown to the Brazilian military, it was natural, not to say logical, to incorporate into our professional teaching heritage regulations and processes of instruction very different from those which we had been used to employing in exercises in times of peace." The new regulations adopted "in copying the American system" included even those relating to discipline and punishment of troops, and the translation of U.S. manuals was undertaken while the war was in progress. Moraes noted finally that the performance of the BEF had been considered "magnificent" by U.S. military leaders and that upon their return to Rio de Janeiro, "parading through the principal arteries of the metropolitan center, the first EID (Expeditionary Infantry Division) gave the first public presentation of a division modeled along U.S. lines."[47]

Impressed with the military might of the United States and with the dynamism of the capitalistic economic system, the faction found the germination of ideas such as nonalignment, economic nationalism, and socialism in postwar Brazil an ominous development. Such ideas were by no means unrepresented in the Brazilian military in the early 1950s, and economic nationalism remained particularly strong. A dozen general officers of the armed forces, for example, were members of the Centro de Estudos e Defesa de Petroleo e da Economia Nacional, which supported the creation of PETROBRAS. General Euclides Zenobia da Costa, a leader of the BEF, found this development to be a manifestation of communist infiltration in the military.

The Military Club in Rio de Janeiro has long been considered the weathervane of political trends in the military, the place where factional debates and intrigues are sheltered from public disclosure. In 1950 the nationalist slate, pro-Vargas and pro-PETROBRAS, won the elections in the Military Club, but in 1952 the anti-communist "Cruzada Democrática" won. For some time the fortunes of the major military factions and their civilian allies oscillated. The anti-communist faction, disturbed by what it considered "ultranationalism," drove Vargas to suicide in 1954, but its attempts to prevent

47. Marshal J. B. Mascarenhas de Moraes, *The Brazilian Expeditionary Force, by its Commander*, translated from 2d ed., rev. and enl. (Washington, D.C.: Government Printing Office, 1966), pp. 10–12, 202–29.

the inauguration of Kubitschek in 1955 and the accession to the vacated presidency by Goulart in 1961 aborted due to the opposition of other military groups.[48] As late as 1962, a pro-Goulart general was narrowly defeated in the elections of the Military Club, but a number of trends favoring the ascension of the anti-communist faction, by then known (because of its association with the ESG) as the Sorbonne group, were converging. In particular, while the slavish attachment of the Sorbonne group to the United States and to capitalism was not shared by the majority, the sense of threat to the military institution was, and the generalized acceptance of internal warfare as the mission of the military meant that the "enemy" could only be the potential civilian allies of the more nationalistic officers.

Alfred Stepan found that of the variables distinguishing the core group of conspirators against Goulart and backers of the Castello Branco government from the other active-duty line generals in 1964, the most salient were participation in the BEF; membership on the permanent staff of the ESG; attendance at foreign, mostly U.S., schools; graduation as number one in the class at one of the three major army schools, and membership in the technically most advanced branch of the army.[49]

We have seen that in the period since World War II the U.S. military had displaced European military establishments as the major source of both material assistance and training for the Brazilian armed forces. In fact, the organizational links between the U.S. and Brazilian Armed Forces were so direct and comprehensive that officers of both countries spoke of their military alliance as a "special relationship." Through its many training programs for Latin American officers, the U.S. military had exposed Brazilian officers to its own concepts of the expanding role of the military in international politics and of the challenges and threats to the military in Latin America.

There has indeed emerged in Brazil a generation of U.S.-trained, technocratically oriented officers, among whom one faction in particular had come to look upon the U.S. armed forces as the reference group by which it could measure its own achievement and to which it could look for approval. It was that faction, the so-called Sorbonne Group, that spearheaded the coup of 1964. The following chapters focus in greater detail on the argument that the support of, association with, and training by the U.S. military reinforced the anti-democratic biases of the Brazilian military elite.

48. Baker, *Study of Military Status*, p. 25.
49. Stepan, *The Military in Politics*, pp. 44–45, 185–86, 236–52.

[10]

The Institutional Ambient of the Military

It has been noted that Defense Secretary McNamara argued in 1962 that training by the U.S. military would expose Latin American officers to "democracy at work." One of the most fundamental questions suggested by McNamara's means-ends juxtaposition is whether or not the military is an appropriate institution for the teaching and exhibition of democracy. It was assumed in his statement that the experience of the U.S. officer corps was that of living and participating in, thus presumably understanding and valuing, a democratic system. While the U.S. political tradition may be democratic (and that, of course, is a matter of degree), the immediate political environment of these officers is that of the military establishment, and the military is the antithesis of a democratic institution. It is argued in this chapter that as a consequence of the nature of the institution and of the mentality that it spawns, the exposure of Brazilian officers to the U.S. military establishment would be more likely to reinforce authoritarian biases than to engender democratic ones.

In the view of one disillusioned officer, Lieutenant Colonel Edward L. King, whose twenty years in the service included experience in Latin America, Europe, Korea, Vietnam, and on the staff of the Joint Chiefs of Staff,

> The Army structure is permeated by fear. Only lip service is paid to the concepts of justice, equality, and constitutionally guaranteed freedom for members. . . . Any deviation from the rules, any basic criticism of the system is swiftly and ruthlessly punished.

Furthermore, King perceived among U.S. officers a growing sense of being in an adversary relationship to those "outside" the Army system:

> Those on the outside are frequently viewed as the enemy by those in the Army. In the minds of many officers there is an incontrovertible con-

179

viction that theirs is the ultimate patriotism. Consequently, they are able
to rationalize all their acts as patriotic, no matter how self-serving. It is
easy for these ultimate patriots, well intentioned as they may be, to act in
a repressive or vindictive manner toward people who do not agree with
their definition of patriotism and what they believe best for the country.[1]

Brazilian journalist Oliveiros S. Ferreira, analyzing the philosoph-
ical and institutional bases of the political behavior of the so-called
Sorbonne group in Brazil, saw nothing of the flamboyant *caudillismo*
that, at least from the U.S. point of view, has stereotyped Latin
American militarism. Rather, he largely attributed the political orientation of Castello Branco and his colleagues to the "bureaucratic ethos,"
an institutional phenomenon characteristic of military establishments
generally. What distinguishes this relationship among persons and
groups, according to Ferreira, is that it makes little difference to the one
who gives orders whether they are obeyed because they are believed to
be beneficient, or because disciplinary sanction is feared.[2]

While the bureaucratic ethos is not exclusive to the military, it is
intensified within the military, especially at the professional level, because institutional directives govern the overall life of the individual,
not merely his conduct during the workday. Furthermore, gains and
losses are reckoned not in terms solely of material things, but in terms
of human life. It is a rarely questioned axiom that the life of the individual may hinge on obedience, and that it is ultimately dependent
upon the success of the institution. The ease with which this orientation to the stakes of competition can be transferred to the political arena
was indicated by General Alexander Haig in commenting upon how
much at home he felt in his new job as chief of staff to President Nixon.
"Politics and soldiering are very, very close. . . . It's a field where a

1. Edward L. King, *The Death of the Army: A Pre-Mortem* (New York: Saturday Review Press, 1972), p. 76. Similarly, the CIA has been able to rationalize
unthinkable acts in the name of patriotism. The Senate Intelligence Committee
reported that in 1954 a special committee on covert activities had advised the
president that the U.S. might have to adopt tactics "more ruthless than [those]
employed by the enemy." It elaborated "we are facing an implacable enemy
whose avowed objective is world domination . . . There are no rules in such a
game. Hitherto acceptable norms of human conduct do not apply." In 1960,
when the CIA was considering the assassination of Patrice Lumumba, a
particular agent was recommended because "he can rationalize all actions"
(*Alleged Assassination Plots*, pp. 258–59).

2. Oliveiros S. Ferreira, "La geopolitica y el ejercito brasileno," *Aportes*
[Paris] 12 (April 1969): 112–32.

man lays everthing on the line to win or lose. When one doesn't win, the results are fatal, in the case of the military, quite fatal."[3]

While the Brazilian military has become an increasingly middle-class, rather than upper-class, institution since World War II, recruitment from the lower class has significantly decreased during the same period. Along with class homogeneity, institutional characteristics have apparently been rendered even more salient by a high degree of nepotism. The files of the Brazilian Army Academy (Academia Militar das Agulhas Negras) reveal that sons of career military men represented 21.2 percent of cadets entering in 1941–1943 and 34.9 percent in 1962–1966. By 1966 they represented more than 40 percent.

Sons of career military men could attend the high school academies tuition-free, whereas offspring of civilians had to pay and could only attend if there were extra places. In 1939 61.6 percent of the cadets entering the military academy had attended civilian high schools, but by the 1962–1966 period that figure had dropped to 7.6 percent. Up to 90 percent of the contemporary generation of army officers entered the military academic system at about the age of twelve. Stepan found that sons of military officers were overrepresented among the general officers plotting to overthrow Goulart in 1964, and concluded that increasing self-recruitment, coupled with the intensification of the military educational programs, were undoubtedly factors in the growing corporate consciousness of the military and their loosening of links with civilians in the period leading up to and after their seizure of power in 1964.[4]

After a spurt of optimism in the early 1960s that the integration of the middle and, to a lesser extent, the lower classes into the Latin American military establishments would mitigate anti-democratic tendencies, many scholars have concluded that institutional characteristics tend to outweigh such factors in determining the behavior of the military. Eric Nordlinger, for example, has maintained that military values and corporate interests attach overriding importance to a kind of stability characterized by strict observance of hierarchical authority and a supposedly apolitical calm.[5] And Miles Wolpin noted that these

3. Nick Thimmesch, "Chief of Staff," *Washington Post, Potomac,* 25 November 1973, pp. 12–15.

4. Stepan, *The Military in Politics,* pp. 31–42, 167–68.

5. Eric A. Nordlinger, "Soldiers in Mufti: The Impact of Military Rule upon Economic and Social Change in the Non-Western States," *American Political Science Review* 64 (December 1970): 1131–48.

values engender antipathetic dispositions to political demonstrations, strikes, and the uncertainties associated with redistributive political conflict.[6]

Others have suggested that political debate and open competition for popular support are seen by the military as intrusions in a decision-making process that should be characterized by unity and consensus. This theme finds expression in the "Message of the Revolutionary Junta to the Argentine People," released to the press at the time of the overthrow of civilian president Arturo Illia in 1966. It condemned the "fallacy of a formal and sterile legality," which in the name of liberty and electoral freedom had fostered a "vote-seeking system" that divided the country and mocked true democracy. The announcement concluded with an exhortation to unity.[7] In a similar vein, President Médici, in a speech to the nation on the ninth anniversary of the Brazilian "Revolution," boasted, "Uniformity in thought and action is the principal reason for the speed and efficiency with which our country is being modernized and the bonds of solidarity between Brazilians are being forced."[8] And the Chilean Ambassador to the United States in March 1974, in response to a question about elections, said that the trouble with politicians is that they make politics instead of governing, that they just set one group against another. And he asserted, "At this moment we have no time for politics; we have to rebuild the country."[9]

Likewise, the concept of good government espoused by the ESG calls not for the resolution of discord, but for the elimination of it. "National Security," an ESG lecturer explained in 1973, "is the complete functionalism of essential matters, to which the Human Collectivity, directly or indirectly, lays claim, preserved for it through its respective State. Functionalism implies the elimination of dangers, antagonisms, and pressures that confront the nation." He defined Internal Security as "the social-political-economic-juridical-cultural state that results from the normal functioning of the essential matters in the ambit of the national community. . . . Functional normality . . . means the removal of antagonisms, pressures, and opposition of appreciable form." And punishable antagonism, he explained, in the words of a former permanent staff member of the school, is "an attitude of willful dispute of the National Objectives" (as set forth, presumably, by the ESG). Such

6. Wolpin, *Military Aid and Counterrevolution*, p. 13.

7. Corbett, *The Latin American Military as a Socio-Political Force*, p. 112.

8. Poppino, "Brazil After a Decade of Revolutions."

9. Chilean Ambassador Walter Heitmann, Panel Discussion, American University, Washington, D.C., 29 March 1974.

an attitude is not to be confused, he said, with simple democratic opposition.[10]

As the security of the nation is presumed to be dependent upon the efficiency of the military, national security is seen first of all in terms of the security of the military as an institution. *At least* as it applies to Latin America, U.S. military officers appear to be in overwhelming agreement with this point of view.[11] Lieutenant General Alva R. Fitch, Deputy Director of the Defense Intelligence Agency, appearing before the Subcommittee on Inter-American Affairs of the House Committee on Foreign Affairs on 25 February 1965, maintained that "during the long interim period before those goals (solution of economic and social problems and evolution of stable democracy) can be attained . . . the security forces of individual countries will remain the major obstacle to Communist seizures of power."[12]

Captain Raymond J. Toner, Chief of the Naval Mission and Naval Advisor to the Ecuadorean Ministry of Defense, and Commander of the U.S. Naval Station in San Juan during both the Cuban quarantine and the Dominican intervention, asserted in 1968 that "of all the instruments of power, the military still remains the most powerful and possesses the greatest capability to maintain stability against pressures from within and without."[13] But SOUTHCOM Commander, General Porter, warned that "one main Communist objective is to discredit and eventually destroy the Latin American armed forces. To this end, a persistent Communist tactic is to belittle the Latin American military man."[14] From Porter's perspective, then, criticism of the military is likely to be a manifestation of the communist conspiracy and a threat to the national security.

In his report on the official investigation of communism and corrup-

10. ESG, T139-73, Part 2, pp. 8, 29–33.

11. In fact, the applicability appears to be far more general. In response, for example, to a civil suit filed against the U.S. Army by American civilians residing in Berlin, on the grounds that they had illegally been placed under surveillance, Army attorneys argued, "An incidental chilling effect [on an individual's constitutional rights] must be tolerated when it flows from an investigation directed to avert a clear and present danger of illegal activities directed against the security of the U.S. forces" (Timothy S. Robinson, "Berlin Surveillance Defended by Army," *Washington Post*, 12 June 1974).

12. U.S., Congress, House Committee on Foreign Affairs, Subcommittee on Inter-American Affairs, *Communism in Latin America*, Hearings, 89th Cong., 1st sess., 16 and 25 February, 2, 10, 16, and 30 March 1965, p. 9.

13. Captain Raymond J. Toner, "The Latin American Military" *U.S. Naval Institute Proceedings* 94 (November 1968): 65–73.

14. Porter, "Look South," p. 82.

tion in the Goulart Administration, conducted after the coup, Colonel Ferdinando de Carvalho charged the "communists" with multiple sins against the Armed Forces: undermining of hierarchy and discipline; inadequate promotions and deficient remuneration; "characterization of a supposed militarism with totalitarian and retrograde traits"; and "weakening of the military spirit by employing the Armed Forces in missions of secondary importance and ones which, in general, were incompatible with the characteristics and equipment of military organizations."[15] (Ironically, it is not at all unlikely that the last item in this series referred to certain aspects of "civic action.")

Likewise, students at the ESG in 1973 were being admonished to be on guard against criticism of the military. They were warned that even a developed state that allowed itself to become excessively penetrated by pacifism, liberalism, or anti-militarism would find itself unprepared to meet external or internal challenges.[16]

Ferreira argued that the manner in which the Brazilian political parties were reorganized by the Castello Branco regime reflects the "bureaucratic-military vision" of the political process—not as an adjustment of conflict, but rather as an exercise in unity and order.[17] U.S. Lieutenant Colonel Lyle E. Stockton, who in 1967 analyzed the "revolutionary" military government of Brazil, apparently shared this orientation to the political process; and, perhaps because his own immediate environment in U.S. society was that of the military, he saw the U.S political process as such an exercise. Stockton wrote:

> The author views the Acts and decrees [First and Second Institutional Acts and presidential decrees] . . . as an effort to emulate the political system of the United States. It was, in all probability, the most expeditious and easy way to do it. The fact that President Branco retained the congress and forced the country into a two-party political system refutes those who cry dictatorship. . . . He has been arbitrary, but how else could he affix political responsibilities with party loyalty and discipline. . . . The new constitution gives the president very strong and broad powers, but he does not necessarily have to use them. The author views these powers as a necessary reserve force whereby the president can foster the growth of a strong, two-party political system operating a sound representative government on a sound fiscal basis.[18]

15. Carvalho, "Revolutionary War in Brazil."

16. Presidência da República, Estado-Maior das Forças Armadas, Escola Superior de Guerra, Departamento de Estudos, T139-73, "Legislação Brasileira e Segurança Nacional," lecture by Professor Mario Pessoa, 18 July 1973, no. 206, p. 6.

17. Ferreira, "La geopolítica y el ejército brasileño," p. 117.

18. Lieutenant Colonel Lyle E. Stockton, "An Analysis of the Brazilian Revolution of 1964: The Role of the Military and the Probable Impact of Continued

Colonel Milton Callero, U.S. Army Attaché in Brasilia from 1968 through 1970, has maintained that Brazilian officers trained in the United States are particularly impressed by the material progress and *order* there.[19] At House Foreign Affairs Committee hearings in 1970, Representative Vernon Thompson was told by Assistant Secretary of Defense for International Security Affairs G. Warren Nutter that trainees were being effectively exposed to the democratic process. Thompson inquired as to how they were receiving such exposure at military camps and bases. Secretary Nutter replied, "We have a program of orientation tours . . . through which we achieve the kind of exposure *that we want them to have* [italics added] to the way the American system works."[20]

Some 85 percent of the Brazilians trained in the United States have been beneficiaries of these orientation tours. At first glance the tours would appear to be ordinary junketeering, relatively harmless except as another drain on hard-pressed U.S. taxpayers. But a perusal of more than a thousand items on the itineraries of thirteen tours for graduates of the ESG, the Army and Air Force Command and General Staff Colleges, and the Naval War College suggests that what is being exposed is hardly democracy at work, but rather the power and opulence of the U.S military. The country is portrayed as a military picnic to which the multinational corporations have been invited. Aside from straight entertainment excursions of the Disneyland variety, almost all items refer to visits to military installations and factories or social events hosted by the U.S. military or U.S. corporations or businessmen's associations. Not a single legislative or deliberative body was included, and about the only places where the trainees might have observed open expression of political dissent were a couple of nonmilitary universities.[21]

Secretary Nutter added that an informational program provided trainees with important information on the nature of governmental institutions, political parties, and so on in the United States. Some recent guides for trainees have mentioned anti-war protests in the United States, linking them to communism, but, for the most part, the system described is a consensual one in which, for example, there are no fundamental differences between the two parties. And the "loyal opposi-

Military Control of the Political Structure and the Economy of U.S. Defense," Manuscript, M-32983-U, Professional Study no. 3518, Maxwell Air Force Base, Alabama, Air War College, 1967, pp. 52–54.

  19. Callero interview, 21 February 1973.
  20. House Foreign Affairs Committee, *Military Assistance Training*, p. 137.
  21. Church Hearings, pp. 101–36.

tion" provided by the two-party system in the United States is contrasted with the "ideological" parties of underdeveloped countries, which make a competitive party system undesirable.[22]

As for the exposure of trainees in the Canal Zone, Alfred Stepan pointed out in the above-mentioned 1970 hearings that "the atmosphere and life style of U.S. citizens within the Canal Zone, and especially the sense of their different social and economic status vis-à-vis Panamanians, leaves one with an overall impression of U.S. colonialism."[23]

Callero mentioned technical know-how as one of the main things Brazilian officers hope to gain through U.S. training and association with their U.S. counterparts.[24] Brady Tyson saw this fixation on technological advancement as an important factor distinguishing the modern variety of militarism in Latin America, and in Brazil in particular, from earlier ones. Tyson viewed the regimes of the "militechnocrats" as manifestations less of a distinctive ideology than of a distinctive mentality, which assumes that there are managerial and technological solutions to political and social problems.[25] Whether or not this "mentality" was to some extent acquired through association with the U.S. military, it certainly appears to be shared by the U.S. officers who have been closely associated with their Brazilian counterparts.

General Robert Seitz, chairman of the U.S. Delegation to the JBUSMC in the late 1960s, told the author that he was not entirely convinced that a communist takeover was imminent in 1964, but he felt that the coup was necessary anyway for the purpose of stemming corruption and inflation. He saw in the Brazilian political system, from the end of World War II until 1964, a pattern of progressive deterioration. The situation was "chaotic" from 1945 until the election of Kubitschek. His rule turned out to be "nothing but corruption." Quadros' "hare-brained ideas, like decorating Cubans, when they were being sanctioned elsewhere, made a military coup inevitable," and the rebellion of non-commissioned officers indicated that Goulart was "bent on taking over the military."

Seitz could hardly contain his enthusiasm for what the "revolu-

22. Wolpin, *Military Aid and Counterrevolution*, pp. 59–64.

23. House Foreign Affairs Committee, *Military Assistance Training*, p. 129.

24. Callero interview, 21 February 1973.

25. Brady Tyson, "The Emerging Role of the Military as National Modernizers and Managers in Latin America: The Cases of Brazil and Peru," *Latin American Prospects for the 1970s. What Kinds of Revolutions?*, ed. David H. Pollock and Arch R. M. Ritter (New York: Praeger, 1973), ch. 8.

tionary" government had accomplished. He attributed its success in part to the fact that "the military is immune to political pressures and political favoritism" and that with military backing policy-makers are not subject to pressures from political constituencies. He doubted that the "economic miracle" and "social advances" could have been achieved by a civilian government, as the political pressures would have been too great. The eradication of the *favelas* around Rio de Janeiro would have been difficult, for example, because the *favela*-dwellers had to be relocated in their new inland housing by force.

Seitz said that even though there is greater efficiency in dictatorship, he hoped that the government would be turned over to a civilian in 1974. He said that by that time a decade would have passed since the coup and that ample time would have been allowed "for the military to have gotten the government on the right course." Seitz wondered, however, whether by that time civilians would have come along who could "control the system."[26]

While this mentality is particularly pronounced in modern military establishments, it is by no means confined to them. Celso Furtado has said that it was shared by the industrialists who attended the ESG, and Ferreira, observing in 1966 that the conduct of civic business was being viewed by the Brazilian government as a military operation in which men are mere pawns, predicted, "It will make little difference whether those who govern us tomorrow are military or civilian as a professional condition; the fact is that it will be a military and bureaucratic mentality that guides the Brazilian process from now on."[27]

We have seen that U.S. military training programs that have purported to offer exposure to "democracy at work" have more often exposed participants to the power and opulence of the U.S. military (rather than stressing its submission to civilian authority) and to a military bureaucratic view of politics as an orderly consensual process in which there is little room for genuine debate and competition. The projection of the decision-making norm that guides a single institution as the norm that should guide national societies has been encouraged by the view that national security resides within that institution. It has also been encouraged, as we shall see in the next chapter, by the Cold War world-view.

26. Seitz interview.

27. Oliveiros S. Ferreira, *O Fim do poder civil* São Paulo: Editôra Convivio, 1966), pp. 8, 18–19.

[11]

Implications of the Cold War World-View

The assumption that democratic values would be imparted through training and other contacts with U.S. officers presupposed that those officers advocated civilian supremacy generally and for Latin America in particular and that the political indoctrination in the training program reflected that bias. The content of that political indoctrination, however, derived overwhelmingly from the Cold War world-view. This chapter will deal with some of the ways in which the Cold War world-view encouraged Brazilian officers to view their own role as encompassing the control and direction of all aspects of national life.

Lieutenant General Alva R. Fitch reported to the House Committee on Foreign Affairs in 1965:

> From the United States point of view, the military forces of Latin America are ideologically well-equipped for their crucial role. Throughout the area, the officer corps are anti-Communist, anti-Castro, and friendly toward the United States.[1]

Anti-communism in itself hardly constitutes an ideology. Implanted as an absolute rather than a relative value, however, it does have far-reaching implications. When Talleyrand stated that war was too important a matter to be left to the generals, the assumption was that military affairs were an extension of political affairs, that war-making and war-makers were to be governed by the larger political process. With the Cold War world-view that order is reversed. The political

---

1. House Foreign Affairs Committee, *Communism in Latin America*, p. 9.

process itself, at both the national and international levels, becomes an instrument in a perpetual global war and is too important to be left to civilians.[2]

As was true of the United States military, the assumption by the military in Brazil that it had a role to play in internal security evolved in the nineteenth century out of attempts to subdue or eliminate the indigenous population. Skirmishes with the *caboclos* at Canudos in the 1890s, according to Frederick Nunn, "at once vindicated [the Brazilian army's] existence and made [it] look pitiful," as it was ill-prepared for such tasks. The Brazilian military had also had early and extensive experiences with projects such as road-building, which later were to be categorized as civic action. Futhermore, German training of Brazilian officers prior to World War I and French training in the period between the wars had instilled some of the concepts of military professionalism that remained pronounced in the 1960s.

As early as 1913, a military journal edited by Germanophile officers proclaimed that the army was "the only truly organized force in the midst of an amorphous mass of ferment" and "a decisive factor of political change or social stability." In the interwar years the highly politicized French army imparted to the Brazilian officer corps some of the experience it had gained in colonial administration.[3] But it was ultimately the U.S. military, with its Cold War world-view, that provided the Brazilians with the rationale or legitimation for reviving and refining internal security doctrine and using it as a weapon against political opponents; for expanding the concept of civic action from road-building to "nation-building"; for assuming the permanent role of a professional political elite; and for implanting a colonial regime on their own turf.

In its condemnation of torture in Brazil in 1970, the International Commission of Jurists pointed out that "since the second military coup of 1968 the Brazilian government has adopted the policy of subversive war. Brazilian officers have learned such methods from American experts and theoreticians whom they meet in great numbers either in their own military schools in Brazil or during regular training courses

---

2. At least as it relates to the U.S. approach to Latin America, it appears that the civilian role in the political process has been linguistically obliterated. Appearing before the 1969 Senate hearings on U.S. military policies and programs in Latin America, Charles A. Meyer, Assistant Secretary of State for Inter-American Affairs, spoke of U.S. social, economic, and "politico-military" efforts in Latin America.

3. Nunn, "Military Professionalism and Professional Militarism."

in the Panama Canal Zone."[4] And Manfred Kossok saw the praetorian function characteristic of Latin American armed forces—the primacy of internal over external or defense functions, which attains its most extreme form with the de facto fusion of the state, military, and police powers—as having been determined since 1961–1962 by an orientation toward the "anti-subversive preventive war."[5]

Although the French had extensive experience in counterinsurgency in the 1950s and 1960s, their experience was transmitted to Latin America through the intermediary of the U.S. military. The most significant contribution of European advisors to Latin American military doctrine was the transplantation of balance of power theories and strategies, including emphasis on the protection of borders and the avoidance of permanent alliances. U.S. training after World War II stressed the necessity of a permanent alliance in the face of a permanent war, and, as General Robert Seitz remarked in 1973 in an interview with the author, it provided the impetus in the early 1950s for a focus on nation-building (bringing "civilization" to remote areas).[6] More importantly, however, as Colonel D. Forest Ballou explains it, the U.S. military tried to focus the attention of Brazilian officers on "external enemies." (That is, the Brazilians were being told to view their own compatriots who differed with them politically as the external enemies.) "Even though we're talking about counterinsurgency, the focus is external. We try to tell them, your real worry is not the guys next door, [neighboring countries] but insurgents."[7] Furtado said that by the early 1960s Brazilian military schools, libraries, and clubs were saturated with U.S. military journals and technical papers projecting internal security doctrine and that this doctrine was thoroughly absorbed by Brazilian officers.[8]

A 1962 article in the official *U.S. Army Information Digest* proclaimed that counterinsurgency includes all military, political, economic, and socio-psychological activities directed toward preventing and suppressing resistance groups. . . . Civil affairs, intelligence, psychological warfare, engineer, medical, signal, transportation, and other Army units can be used to enhance the stature of local military

---

4. Church Hearings, p. 151.

5. Manfred Kossok, "The Armed Forces in Latin America: Potential for Change in Political and Social Functions," *Journal of Interamerican Studies and World Affairs* 14 (November 1972); 375–98.

6. Seitz interview.

7. Ballou interview.

8. Furtado interview.

forces by training them to undertake civic action or "nation-building" tasks.[9]

A revision of the U.S. Army's basic doctrinal manual, published the same year, had much in common with the Marine Corps Small Wars Manual of 1940. The Army manual noted that "stability and law and order are essential to the success of Cold War efforts" and urged maximum use of indigenous forces and personnel to achieve these ends; but it also observed that U.S. land forces in overseas areas are a real and visible deterrent. In situations short of war, it envisaged any or all of the following goals: (1) encouragement of a weak and faltering government; (2) stabilization of a restless area; (3) deterrence or actual thwarting of aggression; (4) reinforcement of a threatened area; (5) checking or countering aggressive moves by some hostile power; (6) maintenance or restoration of order. And it asserted that the U.S. armed forces must support both military and nonmilitary programs of the United States and its allies.[10]

As the decade of the 1960s wore on, the humiliation of the U.S. military in Vietnam appeared to enhance rather than discredit these doctrines. A training manual on Internal Defense in use at Fort Leavenworth, among other places, in the early 1970s opens with this admonition:

> Defining war as an extension of politics is virtually unquestioned in the modern age. Inverting the relationship to conclude that politics is also an extension of conflict could be considered as an even more accurate definition of the ideological struggles as executed in the contemporary world arena. Since the mid-1960s, the relative parity of destruction potential held by the super-powers has encouraged war by proxy, most commonly assuming the form of insurgencies fought in the lesser developed areas of the world. This form of struggle is waged with a totality never before experienced in human history—a totality that encompasses all elements of population and all aspects of life to include the thinking as well as the activities of society.[11]

A 1968 manual entitled *Psychological Operations, U.S. Army Doctrine* explains that U.S. Army stability operations include tactical, intelligence, psychological, civil affairs, advisory assistance, and popu-

---

9. Brigadier General William B. Rosson, "Accent on Cold War Capabilities," *Army Information Digest* 17 (May 1962): 2–9.

10. Office of the Deputy Chief of Staff for Military Operations, Department of the Army, "Doctrinal Guidance for the Future," *Army Information Digest* 17 (June 1962): 44–49.

11. U.S. Army Command and General Staff College, *Internal Defense* (Reference Book), USACGSC RB 31-100, vol. I, Fort Leavenworth, Kans., 1 August 1971, p. -i-.

lace and resources control. Psychological operations are designed to gain, preserve, and strengthen civilian support for the host government and its stability operations, as well as to establish and maintain a "suitable image" of the U.S. elements supporting the host country. Meanwhile, they seek to create dissension, dissatisfaction, and defection among insurgent forces. Unconventional Warfare operations are even more ambitious: they seek to "influence ideological, religious, psychological, political, economic and social factors which promote intense, emotional partisanship."[12]

It is not surprising, then, considering what was being presented as within the scope of military responsibility, that General Seitz found that the officers exposed to U.S. training have "a chance to establish more challenging goals," and to "develop broader perspectives."[13] Colonel Edward King, representative of the Joint Chiefs of Staff on the Joint Brazil-U.S. Defense Commission, also saw among the U.S. trained officers a new wave of "intellectualism," inspired in part by the large number of U.S. officers seeking advanced degrees, and manifest in an expansion of the definition of the military role to include many aspects of the art of governing.[14]

General Seitz claimed in 1973 that the entire military educational system in Brazil was a "mirror" of that of the United States. Major General J. Bina Machado, Vice-Chief of Staff of the Brazilian Army in 1970 and a former commandant of the Army Command and General Staff School (ECEME), describes the transformation of that school as a consequence of the increased exposure of Brazilian officers to their U.S. counterparts:

> From the experience of the Brazilian Expeditionary Force in Italy during World War II, it became apparent that the influx of new ideas and equipment necessitated a revision of the instruction and organization of the ECEME. Thus began the period of influence of U.S. military ideas.
>
> Today, the study of the military doctrine of various countries, especially that of the United States, continues. The school is constantly striving to adapt the experience of others to the conditions peculiar to Brazil. The fight against Communist revolutionary activities and subversion has provided invaluable experience in that particular field.[15]

12. *Psychological Operations, U.S. Army Doctrine*, Department of the Army Field Manual, FM 33-1 (Washington: Headquarters, Department of the Army, June 1968), pp. 6–4, 7–11.

13. Seitz interview.

14. King interview.

15. Major General J. Bina Machado, Brazilian Army, "Brazilian Staff Officers," *Military Review* 50 (April 1970): 75–81.

Within the highly developed educational complex of the Brazilian armed forces, the ESG remains the most prestigious school and the one most self-consciously engaged in the recruitment and preparation of a ruling elite. By 1969 all generals on active duty had passed through the school; and the professional officers had taken upon themselves the task of "professionalizing" select elements of the civilian sector, particularly the industrialists.[16] About half of the school's graduates were civilians.

The rationale for the creation of the school, as expressed in a 1949 document, was that national security was a function of the general power of the nation and that the armed forces, as the institution responsible for national security, were obligated to intervene in order to develop the general power of the nation.[17] A lecturer at the ESG in 1956 declared, "We live in a climate of world-wide war that will decide the destiny of Western civilization," and he added that periods of war "demand a centralized and hierarchic structure." At least five years before the "Revolution," very specific plans for the restructuring of the political system were being discussed at the ESG.

In 1963 the ESG was describing its mission as that of preparing its students to "perform executive and advisory functions especially in those organs responsible for the formulation, development, planning, and execution of the policies of national security," and the school's academic divisions suggested the scope of their concept of national security. The divisions encompassed political affairs, psychological-social affairs, economic affairs, military affairs, logistical and mobilizational affairs, intelligence and counterintelligence, and doctrine and coordination.[18]

In a press conference on 14 May 1964, President Castello Branco said that although the ESG was not the driving force behind the "Revolution," the school had had an "extraordinary influence" on those who had participated in it and had formed the revolutionary government. In particular, he said, all who passed through the school became convinced that practical solutions to national problems should be completely divorced from partisan interests. Furthermore, he said, they had

16. Frances M. Foland, "Whither Brazil." *Inter-American Economic Affairs* 24 (Winter 1970): 43–68.

17. Augusto Fragoso, "A Escola Superior de Guerra," *Problemas Brasileiros* [São Paulo] 8 (December 1970): 19–34.

18. Alfred Stepan, "The New Professionalism of Internal Warfare and Military Role Expansion," *Authoritarian Brazil: Origins, Policies, and Future*, ed. Alfred Stepan (New Haven: Yale University Press, 1973), pp. 54–55.

learned to work as a team, and they had "a global perspective" and a broad understanding of the problems of national security.[19]

General Augusto Fragoso, Director of the ESG in 1970, described the mission and the major contribution of the school as the "formation of the national elite—through methodically preparing, year after year, military officers and civilians of the highest intellectual and moral rank, for the functions of planning and directing the national security . . . in the sense in which we have always understood it, involving directly or indirectly all the activities of the nation." Fragoso maintained that the masses lack a "critical sense of time and space" and that "the national elites—the authentic elites of the global society—must not and cannot escape the mission of directing the political community."[20]

The identity of the "external" internal enemy so threatening as to require the military to expand the area of its domestic concerns was suggested by General William Westmoreland, U.S. Army Chief of Staff. Addressing the Eighth Conference of the American Armies in Rio de Janeiro in September 1968, he warned:

> One only needs to read his newspaper to know that the communists have used insurgent warfare throughout the world with varying degrees of success. I feel that the prospects of repeated Vietnams around the world present a very real danger to the security of every freedom-loving people. . . the propaganda describing each insurgency will picture what they term as an "oppressed" people rising to overthrow the alleged oppressor. . . . The world has many dissatisfied people whom the communists can exploit in their quest for destruction of free society.[21]

Frances Foland said of the Sorbonne group that "their Cold-War psychology and U.S. orientation conjured up a communist behind every plea for reform; and a positivist trait confirmed their belief that only they as technocrats, immune to the vagaries of civilian politics, could discipline the economy and the populace so as to achieve the essential economic development."[22] Frederick Nunn observed that "subject to United States military influence on anti-communism the professional army officer became hostile to any sort of populism."[23] Celso Furtado pointed out that the Brazilian military's close association

19. Humberto de Alencar Castello Branco, *Entrevistas, 1964–1965* (Rio de Janeiro: Secretaria de Imprensa, 1965).

20. Fragoso, "A ESG," pp. 19–27.

21. Gary MacEoin, *Revolution Next Door: Latin America in the 1970s* (New York: Holt, Rinehart and Winston, 1971), pp. 133–34.

22. Foland, pp. 48–49.

23. Nunn, "Military Professionalism and Professional Militarism," pp. 29–54.

and "identification" with U.S. officers enhanced its sense of the importance of its own role and contributed to its alienation from liberal and populist civilian political leaders, and Thomas Skidmore maintained that the pervasive anti-communism at the ESG fostered contempt for all civilian politicians.[24]

The perception or attitude of being engaged in internal warfare continued to grow and intensify (and thereby to become to some extent a self-fulfilling prophecy) among the Brazilian ruling circles (as well as among their U.S. military advisors). After 1964, those compatriot civilians, and even dissident military officers, who had been viewed in previous decades as political opponents became cast in the dehumanized image of an alien military enemy. By the late 1960s this image had been projected upon virtually anyone whose ideological conformity was subject to question.

In 1969 a Brazilian intelligence officer confided to *Newsweek's* Rio station chief, Peter Kramer:

> In our view there are two basic things to remember when considering the question of torture. The first is that we are at war—a war of subversion—and that these people are the enemy. If they get to power, it won't be torture and a prison term for us, but death from bullets in the back. The other thing is that a person with an ideology doesn't give information as a gift.[25]

In 1971, General Humberto de Souza Mello, Commander of the Second Army, stationed in São Paulo, warned that "the threat of Latin American subversion will have deep and grave repercussions for all America and Brazil, with its geographic position and style of life, will be the main target of the Communist attack." He added that "the Communist Monster is taking advantage of the inexperienced youth to spread anarchy and to subvert the moral tradition, character, and religious patterns."[26] General Breno Borges Fortes, Commander of the Army General Staff, told his new generals in April 1973, "The most tragic error we could make, at the present moment, would be to conclude that the problem of communism had been overcome. It exists and is always present, whatever the level of the development reached by the country."[27]

24. Furtado interview; Skidmore, *Politics in Brazil, 1930–1964*, pp. 331–32.

25. *Newsweek*, 8 December 1969, pp. 67–68; reprinted in Committee of Returned Volunteers, *Brazil: Who Pulls the Strings*, p. 28.

26. "General Warns of Subversion," *The Times of the Americas* [Miami] 10 March 1971.

27. Presidência da República, Estado-Maior das Forças Armadas, Escola Superior de Guerra, Departamento de Estudos, T196-73, "O Exército Brasileiro," lecture by Gen. Div. Dilermando Gomes Monteiro, 18 September 1973, no. 208, p. 25.

Anti-communism, of course, is a negative, the opposite of which can only be "anything but." Many of the U.S. officers have dealt with this by simply assuming, or at least asserting, that the opposite is democracy. This assumption is often bolstered by an inability or unwillingness to distinguish between rhetoric or trappings and substance. Captain Toner, for example, asserted in 1968 that "all the Latin American countries except Cuba are democracies under a republican form of government."[28]

Others have maintained that the danger of communist takeovers in virtually all of the Latin American countries is so great and the eventuality of another communist victory in the hemisphere so unthinkable that the only kind of "democracy" that can be tolerated is that imposed and controlled from above, preferably by the military. Major Douglas L. Weers wrote in 1967, "With one communist country in *our* [italics added] hemisphere, can we afford to allow even a possibility of another one?" Of the Brazilian "revolution" he said:

> Castello Branco has been determined to "redemocratize" Brazil, but according to his own plans. He has ruled primarily by decrees and regulations. . . . The constitution and methods used are not "democratic" in our sense of the word, but they are effective and were necessary in order to stop the trend toward communism and disaster which the Goulart regime was following.[29]

Lieutenant Commander Dayton R. Hahne, also writing in 1967, asserted:

> It is generally accepted that Brazil was at the brink of total chaos and was ripe for a Communist coup. It was subsequently discovered that a Communist coup had been planned for a month later.

Hahne therefore concluded,

> The Brazilian military desires a strong, capable constitutional and democratic government, but if the civilian politicians cannot provide this type government, the Brazilian armed forces will take action which they deem appropriate to achieve their desires.[30]

In a lecture at the U.S. Naval War College in 1967, Lyman B. Kirk-

---

28. Toner, "The Latin American Military," p. 66.

29. Major Douglas L. Weers, "Brazil: Target for Communism," unpublished paper, M-35562-7-U, Thesis no. 2780–67, Maxwell Air Force Base, Alabama, Air Command and Staff College, June 1967, p. 46.

30. Lieutenant Commander Dayton R. Hahne, "The Brazilian Military Establishment in Government: An Analysis," manuscript, M-35562-7-U, Thesis no. 0960-67, Maxwell Air Force Base, Alabama, Air Command and Staff College, June 1967, pp. 31, ii.

patrick, former CIA executive, said that "the Communists are a powerful and potentially dangerous force in nearly all of Latin America"[31]
And in 1968, Captain Toner wrote:

> Communist-directed sources of internal disorder are reaching into the
> unions, the universities, and the teeming slums that surround all of the
> major Latin American cities. For the foreseeable future there will
> probably be no decrease in Communist-inspired "Wars of Liberation,"
> with concomitant guerrilla warfare, requiring continued counterinsur-
> gency operations by the Latin American military.

Toner further stated,

> *As is the case with all other military forces* [italics added], the Latin
> American military today performs two major roles . . . the Exterior Role
> is the traditional role of the military as a balance of forces to protect the
> nation from aggression or a threat to its vital interests. Its Interior Role is
> the performance of those duties which may significantly affect the orga-
> nization and functioning of the administration of the government and na-
> tional economy.[32]

In defense of the military assistance programs, Assistant Secretary of
Defense G. Warren Nutter pointed out at the 1969 Senate hearings that
the instance of "illegal and unscheduled changes of heads of state" was
decreasing over the long term. In the period from 1930 to 1939 there
were 35; from 1940 to 1949, 28; from 1950 to 1959, 29; and from 1960 to
1969, only 18.[33] What he failed to note, however, was that the majority
of the "unscheduled changes" in the 1950s were in the direction of deposing dictators. Needler listed only three of the Latin American
governments in 1961 as dictatorships.[34] The direction of "irregu-
larities" in the 1960s and early 1970s was predominantly the reverse—
that is, the demise of civilian constitutional regimes. By mid-1976 there
were only four Latin American governments that were not generally
regarded as dictatorships.

Furthermore, it might have been expected that the toleration of elitist
authoritarian governments and the prevalence of palace coups as the
means of presidential succession would have been reduced as political
infrastructure became more complex and as the ranks of the politically

31. Lyman B. Kirkpatrick, "Cold War Operations: The Politics of Communist
Confrontation. Part VIII—Communism in Latin America," *Naval War College
Review* 20 (June 1968): 3–10.

32. Toner, "The Latin American Military," p. 66.

33. Senate Foreign Relations Committee, *U.S. Military Policies and Programs in Latin America*, p. 68.

34. Needler, "Political Development and Military Intervention in Latin
America," p. 248.

articulate were swelled. The rise and maintenance of authoritarian rule has increasingly called for all-encompassing justification and for ever greater sophistication in organization, strategy, weaponry, and technology. The traditional role of the military establishments in most Latin American countries suggests that their predilection to maintain at least a veto power over civilian authorities and their policies owes little or nothing to the prodding of their U.S. counterparts. However, the Cold War world-view so assiduously marketed by the United States has provided not only the justification that the authoritarian rulers present to their own people, but also the justification presented to the U.S. taxpayer for his provision of material, technical, and political support for the modernization of the mechanisms of repression.[35]

Argentine writer Rogelio García Lupo saw the anti-communism of the Brazilian generals as a tactic to tip the continental balance of power in Brazil's favor. He noted the "flexibility of the pro-Nazi Brazilian generals of the Thirties, who sent troops to Naples to fight for the Allies in the Forties, became leftists in the Fifties, and are today the champions of anti-communism. This versatility," García Lupo says, "is only a tactical one: the gyrations of the Brazilian generals are not based on ideology or conviction. Their strategy rests on so unromantic a foundation as geo-politics." This observation appears in an article he wrote in 1965:

> General Golbery Couto e Silva, Chief of Military Intelligence in Rio de Janeiro, is now circulating mimeographed copies of a position paper among the officers in the War College. Its thesis is quite simple: the U.S. will put all of South America under the tutelage of Brazil, in the same way that Great Britain handed domination of the hemisphere over to the U.S. in the nineteenth century. There is only one condition—that Brazil take on the role of Washington's leading satellite, in return for some rewards.[36]

We have seen that the Cold War world-view, toward which foreign officers exposed to U.S. military programs were being proselytized, encouraged those officers to view their own countrymen who advocated

---

35. In some cases the provision of the justification for use by authoritarian rulers has been quite literal and immediate. The Senate Intelligence Committee reported that in the fall of 1971 the CIA station in Santiago proposed to "provide information—some of it fabricated by the CIA—which would convince senior Chilean Army Officers that the Carabineros' investigations unit, with the approval of Allende, was acting in concert with Cuban intelligence (DGI) to gather intelligence prejudicial to the Army High Command (*Covert Action*, pp. 184–85).

36. Rogelio García Lupo, "Brazil and the United States: the Privileged Satellite," *Atlas* 10 (November 1965): 286–87.

redistribution as agents or dupes of an external military enemy. The war against that enemy was portrayed as total, global, and permanent. It followed that the military establishment was under obligation to maintain control over all aspects of national life in order to maintain national security.

It is not suggested that those Brazilian officers who have governed their country for the past decade were lacking in self-motivation or were unwilling converts to the Cold War world-view. On the contrary, it appears that they grasped it enthusiastically and proceeded to refine it to meet their precise needs. It is suggested, however, that this world-view, and the fact that it was being marketed by the world's greatest military power, providing them the justification and legitimation required for pursuing their own sweeping ambitions. Some of the implications of this world-view for the policies and operations of the U.S. military are elaborated in the next chapter.

[12]

Policy and Operations

The Cold War world-view that has provided the ideological framework for U.S. military operations since World War II has influenced the relations of the U.S. military elite with U.S. civilian policy-makers as well as with foreign military regimes. In this chapter we examine some of the ways in which the U.S. military has expanded its own role in the making, interpretation, and implementation of foreign policy and some of the consequences of relatively unfettered U.S. military operations and influence in Brazil. We examine in particular the political implications inherent in the focus on counterinsurgency and civic action as proper and necessary roles for the military elites. Finally, we will note the enhanced potential for counterrevolutionary violence in the hemisphere that lies in transnational military cooperation and U.S. contingency planning.

Two of the questions that need to be dealt with are: who are the effective policy-makers and what are their objectives, or the national objectives as they see them? While the questions are far too large for the scope of this study, it might at least be suggested that an adequate answer is not likely to be found in the Constitution and laws of the United States, nor on any bureaucratic organization chart.

The U.S. Congress has, of course, been involved in making policy toward Latin America, and the thrust of congressional involvement in the last several years has been toward placing restrictions on military assistance, but the distance from Capitol Hill to the Pentagon to Command Headquarters in Panama to the individual countries is very great, especially as it is apparent that many within the military hierarchy view limiting legislation as unwarranted interposition in their affairs.

Senator Wayne Morse pointed out, in 1968 hearings on amendments to the OAS Charter, that the executive branch had gone so far as to "get around the restrictions this committee has put on military aid in the annual foreign aid legislation by increasing our loans of military equipment to Latin America under the guise that the weapons are obsolete."[1]

In the 1969 hearings on military programs, Senator William Fulbright said:

> This committee . . . tried its best to reduce these arms sales programs by putting restrictions upon credit. . . . I thought we had succeeded in the action taken in the Congress, but the ingenuity of our bureaucracy is something to behold. It is almost impossible for a legislature to keep up with it.

And Senator Frank Church, in the same hearings, added:

> Against the combined opposition of the State Department, the Pentagon, and most often the White House, it [elimination of military assistance] is not easy to accomplish. . . . Two years ago we finally ended the revolving fund on arms sales, and attempted to reduce the size and scope of the military assistance program, but other methods have been found. It is like a hydraheaded monster.[2]

The attitude of the military toward legislative limitations was indicated in a 1968 speech by General Robert W. Porter, who said:

> I am therefore concerned that the sharp cuts in MAP made by Congress will force governments to divert monies to defense that otherwise would have gone for economic and social programs. . . . I explain these Latin American facts of life to members of Congress whenever I have the opportunity. But it is definitely upwater swimming when so many misconceptions about the area are so generally and sometimes so *mischievously* [italics added] disseminated.[3]

Ralph Dungan, former special assistant to President Kennedy, expressed the belief that the current U.S. preoccupation with counterinsurgency represents an "incomplete evolution of an intention on the part of the Kennedy Administration to eventually disengage from significant military activity in Latin America." He maintained that the military assistance effort was refocused on counterinsurgency and civic action in an attempt to get away from tanks, planes, and ships. "This weaning away from major armaments," Dungan says, "was

1. U.S. Congress, Senate Committee on Foreign Relations, *Amendments to the OAS Charter*, 90th Cong., 2d sess., 6 February 1968, p. 18.

2. Senate Foreign Relations Committee, *U.S. Military Policies and Programs in Latin America*, 37–39.

3. General Robert W. Porter, "Latin America: The Military Assistance Program," *Vital Speeches of the Day* (1 July 1968), pp. 573–76.

partly a reflection of Washington's perception of the security problem as it existed at the time, but partly a conviction that we ought to encourage a concentration on the development problem as the root cause of instability." He saw the basic defect of this tactic in the U.S. military's perception of stability as an end in itself.[4]

A number of scholars have noted that a certain amount of social upheaval is probably inevitable and possibly essential to the resolution of the grievances of marginal social sectors and to their entry into the political system as participants rather than subjects. Albert Hirschman, for example, said:

> To paraphrase Marx, decentralized, unrequited violence is frequently found in the role of indispensable midwife to reform. To advocate reforms in Latin America without tolerating, accepting, and sometimes even welcoming and promoting the only kinds of pressures which have proven to be effective in getting reforms is to risk being accused of hypocrisy and deception.[5]

The view prevalent within the U.S. military, however, and apparently among U.S. civilian policy-makers as well, has been that any manifestation of unrest is threatening to "progress." An *Air University Review* article of September–October 1973 is illustrative of the scope of the responsibility assumed by the military. "The new concept of counterinsurgency is therefore much broader than merely the defeat of overt communist guerrilla uprisings. The *prevention* of Communist insurgency and the attainment of stability through progress are the goals of U.S. policies."[6]

It has frequently been observed in congressional testimony that the control supposedly exercised by the ambassador over all members of the country team exists only on paper. Nor can higher echelons at the State Department necessarily expect to have the last word on policy matters of interest to the Pentagon. Jack Hood Vaughn related one of his encounters as follows:

> I confess that my unsuccessful efforts at reasoning with Pentagon brass on Canal Zone issues have caused me considerable frustration and disillusionment over the years. My last failure occurred one very hot afternoon in 1966, when as Assistant Secretary of State, I was visiting the American embassy in Panama. My innocuous objective was to convince

4. Senate Foreign Relations Committee *U.S. Military Policies and Programs in Latin America*, p. 5.

5. Hirschman, *Journeys Toward Progress*, p. 260.

6. Lieutenant Commander Robert J. Miller and Lieutenant Commander James A. Cochran, U.S. Navy, "Counterinsurgency in Perspective," *Air University Review* 14 (September–October 1963): 64–73.

the general in charge of the Southern Command that it was hardly in the U.S. interest to continue teaching napalm bombing to Latin American pilots. I pointed out that the first time a Latin pilot dropped napalm on his own people—napalm he had been trained to mix and launch at a Canal Zone training course—the U.S. would be in a totally indefensible position, not just with God and Bill Fulbright, but with the world as well. I made not a dent.[7]

General Eugene LeBailey revealed his attitude on the matter to a Georgetown University audience in 1971 when he said that the major obstacle to harmonious relations between the United States and the Latin American countries was the persistent effort of Congress to interject itself into the conduct of military relations. He cited in particular the hearings on relations with Brazil scheduled by the Subcommittee on The American Republics of the Senate Foreign Relations Committee.[8]

Ralph Dungan has maintained that operations are in fact the tail wagging the dog of foreign policy; that is, operations generate policies that must be implemented through the continuation or expansion of those operations. Joseph Novitski, in April 1971, quoted a Colombian officer as conceding that "military assistance created some of its own needs."[9]

On 5 May 1971 President Nixon announced that he was exercising his authority to waive the $75 million annual ceiling set by Congress in 1967 on arms aid to Latin America, alleging that the waiver was important to the security interests of the United States. (Representative Dante B. Fascell, Chairman of the Subcommittee on Inter-American Affairs of the House Foreign Affairs Committee, suggested that the announcement was made at the end of the fiscal year in order to avoid congressional review.) The value of U.S. military assistance and sales to Brazil increased sharply thereafter, according to AID, from $800,000 in fiscal 1970, to $12,100,000 in 1971, to $20,800,000 in 1972.[10]

7. Jack Hood Vaughn, "A Latin American Vietnam?" *The Washington Monthly* 5 (October 1973): 30–34.

8. Lieutenant General Eugene B. LeBailey, Guest Lecturer, Lecture Series on the Military in Latin America, Georgetown University, Washington, D.C., 4 March 1971.

9. Novitski, "Latin Lands Turning to Europe."

10. Agency for International Development, *U.S. Overseas Loans and Grants and Assistance from International Organizations: Obligations and Loan Authorizations, July 1, 1945–June 30, 1972* (Washington, D.C., Government Printing Office, May 1973). Figures cited by Simon G. Hanson ["Kissinger on the Chilean Coup." *Inter-American Economic Affairs* 27, no. 3 (1973): 61–85] are even higher: from $3,330,000 in FY 1970 to $34,540,000 in FY 1972 to $42,008,000 in FY 1973.

Attempting to justify the waiver, a "senior official" of the Nixon administration said, "There is no point in having United States military training missions in the hemisphere if there is less and less American equipment to train with."[11] One of the original arguments for the training missions was that they were needed to teach the Latin Americans how to use U.S. equipment. Now it is being argued that the equipment is needed because the training missions are there. Some unnamed Nixon administration officials conceded that one of the purposes of the waiver of the congressional ceiling on arms aid in 1971 was to open Latin American markets to U.S. arms manufacturers.[12] Under Defense Department regulations, U.S. military advisors are in fact mandated to cooperate with private industry in promoting the sales of American arms abroad.[13]

Under the authorization of Public Law 87-195, Section 505 (b), (4 September 1961), the Latin American military assistance program, for the first time, stressed internal security and civic action. The training, further elaborated in 1963, was to concentrate on riot control, counterguerrilla operations and tactics, intelligence, public information, psychological warfare, and counterinsurgency.[14]

Senator Morse introduced an amendment to the Foreign Assistance Act of 1963 providing that:

> Internal security requirements shall not, unless the President determines otherwise and promptly reports such determination to the Senate Committee on Foreign Relations and to the Speaker of the House of Representatives, be the basis for military assistance programs for American Republics.

Although the amendment was still in effect, about half of the Latin American military assistance program was earmarked for internal security purposes in 1964.[15] The option of presidential waiver, incorporated into most foreign assistance legislation since 1956, has served to nullify most congressional prohibitions.

The broad political and socioeconomic scope encompassed in the reorientation toward internal security and civic action constitutes what Alfred Stepan has designated "the new professionalism," a

11. Benjamin Welles, "Nixon Moving to Meet Latin Pleas for More Arms Aid," *New York Times*, 19 May 1971, p. 2.

12. Ibid.

13. Michael Klare, "U.S. Arms Sales to the Third World: Arm Now, Pay Later," *The U.S. Military Apparatus*, pp. 64–71.

14. Estep, "U.S. Military Aid to Latin America," pp. 33–35.

15. Michael J. Francis, "Military Aid to Latin America in the U.S. Congress," *Journal of Inter-American Studies* 6 (July 1964): 389–404.

phenomenon which he sees developing within the United States as well as the Latin American military establishments.[16] George C. Lodge has pointed out that there was no reason to believe that a "professional" and well-trained Latin American military would participate less in domestic politics. "Our (U.S.) experience," Lodge said, "is exactly the reverse."[17]

José Nun noted that "by definition, programs of counterinsurgency erase the limits between the spheres of military and political competence." He maintained that "since the adversary cannot be clearly recognized his identification depends on the military operations themselves." Thus, Nun held, political intervention becomes a justifiable "professional" role for the military.[18]

This justification is found in the "Principles of Counterinsurgency" as outlined by a U.S. Army official, Slavko N. Bjelajac. The author noted that "in counterinsurgency, military strategy and tactics cannot be dissociated from political and social measures, for the enemy seeks to impair not only the military potential of a government but also its administrative machinery, political support, and oral sanction." He said, "There can be only one commander-in-chief at the head of a wholly unified counterinsurgency command structure." And he suggested that "in some cases—for example, where there is lack of capable and honest civilian officials—it may be necessary to integrate a country's civil administration into its military structure."[19]

A contributor to the *Military Review* in 1970 described subversive war as consisting largely of "the impact which agents of Communist subversion can develop at all levels of human activity—political, economic, intellectual, psychological, and military." As there is no apparent limit to what may be defined as subversive activity, neither is there any apparent limit to the methods for, or priority assigned to, countering it. The article explained that before the guerrilla structure could be destroyed, the intelligence services must infiltrate the guerrilla organization. "By working among the subversives in their own environment, the task of suppression will be simplified.[20] In *The CIA and*

16. Alfred Stepan, Lecture at American University, Washington, D.C., 15 May 1971.

17. Senate Foreign Relations Committee, *U.S. Military Policies and Programs in Latin America*, p. 23.

18. Nun, *Latin America*, p. 54.

19. Slavko N. Bjelajac, "Principles of Counterinsurgency," *Orbis* 8 (Fall 1964): 655–69.

20. Enrique Martinez Codo, "Continental Defense and Counterinsurgency," *Military Review*, 50 (April 1970): 71–74.

the Cult of Intelligence, former CIA official Victor Marchetti revealed that in 1969 the CIA had successfully infiltrated the Brazilian guerrilla organization headed by Carlos Marighella. The agency had advance information that an airline hijacking was to take place; but it failed to issue a warning and abort the hijacking because to do so would have exposed its infiltrators, and it placed a higher priority on trapping Marighella.[21]

The civic action program, although it did not constitute the major effort in terms of funds appropriated, was given a big propaganda buildup in the early 1960s in order to indicate the commitment of the military (U.S. and Latin American) to development. But *A Guide to Military Civic Action,* compiled in 1969 by the 30th Civil Affairs Group, revealed the inherent contradictions involved in presenting a liberal rationale for an essentially conservative program.[22] Without denying the value of irrigation ditches, roads, rural schools, and the like, one might ask if the military is the proper institution to undertake this role. Edward Glick, researcher for the Systems Development Corporation, noted in 1964 that the military effort in teaching youngsters was the second largest civic action operation in Latin America, and General Seitz confirmed that the Brazilian military was operating grade schools in areas that were being opened up and developed. He saw lack of education as a serious problem for Brazil "because people can't operate complex machines, such as computers, if they can't read the instructions."[23]

Not only are military functionaries thereby denying such jobs to civilians, but they are placing themselves in a position to mold the political values of future generations. If the same activities were being carried out by the Church or by a political party, for example, the political implications would be obvious. Indeed, the implications were quite obvious to the Brazilian military itself in the early 1960s when basic education—under the Paulo Freire and similar methods—was being offered by groups with a very different view of the nature and function of education.

Davis B. Bobrow has contended that the governments best suited to the realization of the "ideal" of civic action are those already best

21. Victor Marchetti and John D. Marks, *The CIA and the Cult of Intelligence* (New York: Alfred A. Knopf, 1974), pp. 250–51.

22. Ronald Schaffer, "Review of *A Guide to Military Civic Action,* by the 30th Civil Affairs Group, Major David K. Halstead," *Military Affairs* 34 (April 1970): 64.

23. Edward Glick, "The Non-Military Use of the Latin American Military," manuscript, no. SP-1439, Systems Development Corporation, Santa Monica, Calif., 18 July 1964, p. 9, and Seitz interview.

qualified to meet popular aspirations. Civic action, even of the "ideal" type, Bobrow insisted, weakens civilian authority as it increases the ability of the military to behave autonomously and as it establishes the military as an intermediary between civilian leaders and local constituencies. He noted, however, that the probability that the military will accept the grubby tasks of village-level modernization and refrain from demands for significant authority in development programs declines with acquisition of complex mechanical and administrative skills. Furthermore, if a standard of combat excellence predominates, military personnel tend to reject civic action as irrelevant to their mission or even as a deliberate attempt by civilian officials or U.S. advisors to demean the indigenous armed forces.[24]

In fact, the small-scale development tasks apparently envisioned by Kennedy Administration civilians tended to be rejected both by U.S. military advisors and Brazilian officers. General Edson do Figueiredo, a former aid to Castello Branco in the Italian campaign who was sent to Washington immediately after the 1964 coup to cement relations, complained to Colonel Edward King, "We're not Boy Scouts." King maintained that regardless of the intent of civilian policy-makers, the basic purpose of civic action, both for U.S. officers and foreign ones, was counterinsurgency.[25]

The upgrading of the military's "image" through involvement in civic action or "Nation-building" has been a major U.S. objective. Defense Secretary McNamara told the House Foreign Affairs Committee on 8 June 1961:

> Civic action must be compatible with the military missions of these forces; this is not a covert use of the military channel for economic purposes. But where the mission is, wholly or in large part, one of internal security, we know . . . that armed forces will do a better job if they are identified with civic progress.[26]

While the military in most Latin American countries has apparently failed to enhance its image with the local populations, (applications for enrollment in Brazil's military academies, for example, have dropped precipitously), the institution's extensive training and involvement in traditionally civilian matters appears to have enhanced its self-image.[27]

24. Davis B. Bobrow, "The Civic Role of the Military: Some Critical Hypotheses," *Western Political Quarterly* 19 (March 1966): 101–11.

25. King interview.

26. Estep, "U.S. Military Aid to Latin America," pp. 66–67.

27. Samuel Huntington conceded this point in a question-and-answer session following his lecture at American University, Washington, D.C., 15 May 1971.

One dissident retired U.S. general, Bonner Fellers, reported to the House Foreign Affairs Committee that when U.S.-trained Latin American officers return home,

> . . .their governments appear inadequate, sluggish, and antiquated. They find U.S. dollar handouts have bred corruption in high places. They form a clique separate and apart from others. Convinced that they could run their country far better than their present chief-of-state, they plot his overthrow. With weapons and training which we have provided, they have the means to take over the government by force. Thus, our military assistance programs are creating potential military dictatorships.[28]

Each of the U.S. officers whom this author interviewed stressed the development of self-confidence as a major contribution of U.S. military training to the Brazilian officer corps. In this connection, Stepan has observed that the willingness of the Brazilian military to return the country to civilian rule following previous coups could be attributed in part to its own sense of inadequacy for the task.

The conspirators who toppled the constitutional government in 1964, however, were convinced that the military was the only institution capable of running the government. This point of view has apparently been shared by U.S. officers. Of Brazil in 1964, Lieutenant Commander Hahne, for example, said:

> The first order of business for Branco [sic] was to oust or restrict those individuals who proved the greatest threat or impedence [sic] to his energetic and idealistic program. . . . A Supreme Command of the Revolution was formed and it asked Congress to take some necessary but extraordinary measures. When Congress hesitated, the Command promulgated the first "Institutional Act."[29]

In a paper that "examines the tools the military leaders found compelled to use against a lethargic congress and a wholly corrupted and communist-infiltrated political system," Lieutenant Colonel Stockton expressed his opinion of those leaders as follows:

> The Act of Institution actually reduced the congress to a rubber stamp of the President. Brazil was extremely fortunate to have a far-sighted man of General Branco's [sic] caliber wielding this type of power. Political scientists will argue as to whether this type of power was necessary, but the fact remains that a powerful force was necessary to reform the Brazilian houses of Congress.

---

28. Captain David Zook, Jr., U.S.A.F., "United States Military Assistance to Latin America," *Air University Review* 14 (September–October 1963): 82–85.

29. Hahne, "Brazilian Military Establishment in Government," pp. 31–32.

> The military in Brazil represents a well organized and efficient bureaucracy. They are probably the best educated and most unified of all the forces in operation in Brazil. Because of their training and discipline, they probably surpass their civilian counterparts in many administrative skills. This talent is being utilized to great advantage by the government in the present revolutionary stabilization and reform period.[30]

Likewise, U.S. Army Colonel Milton Callero has maintained that the Brazilian military was the only group qualified to develop the country. He said that the only alternatives open to civilian government in 1964 were rule by the oligarchy and rule by the left, either of which would have inhibited development. Colonel Edward King noted that in many cases Brazilian officers, through U.S. training, did indeed become more highly skilled in technical and managerial matters than their civilian counterparts. Thus, having contributed to this imbalance in the first place, U.S. military spokesmen, in congressional testimony, have persistently justified support for military governments and argued for increases in military assistance because of the role of the Latin American military as "educators and managers in all walks of life."[31] The House Special Study Mission reported in 1970 that proponents of MAP training pointed to "the effective communications of anti-insurgency dogma in several threatened countries and increased levels of efficiency and professionalism in armed forces which have been aided" as evidence of the program's success.[32]

General Porter has written that, in addition to improving the image of the armed forces, "civic action has contributed to internal security by denying safe havens to insurgent groups in remote areas, and by improving the intelligence collecting capabilities of the internal security forces."[33] The fourteen observation posts installed during the Castello Branco regime, manned by U.S. technicians and equipped with scanning devices, no doubt enhanced Brazilian intelligence gathering capabilities, but as the sense of being under seige escalated, new measures appeared to be required.[34] Thus, in 1968, with the strong encouragement of U.S. military advisors, the Brazilian government initiated "Operation Presence," whereby military units were spread more evenly across the entire national territory and especially into areas deemed to be potential targets for insurgents. The military hoped

30. Stockton, "Analysis of the Brazilian Revolution," pp. 44, 57.
31. Ibid.
32. House *Foreign Affairs Committee, Special Study Mission*, p. 29.
33. Porter, "Look South," p. 88.
34. On the observation posts, see Lens, "Brazil's Police State," pp. 31–34.

to be able not only to suppress existing revolutionary activity, but also, by its mere presence, to discourage potential insurgency.[35]

Examining political change in Latin America, George C. Lodge, has said, "There is good reason to doubt that the truly *macho* . . . Latin American soldier who has learned to fight with the latest U.S. weapons in U.S. Army and Special Forces training programs will be satisfied with only good works. It is quite probable that he will respond much more enthusiastically to fighting guerrillas and revolutionaries wherever they may be." So, Lodge argued, this shield against insurgency "presumably will seek and expect insurgents against which to exercise itself."[36]

Who these "insurgents" are likely to be, says Lodge, will vary from country to country and from rural to urban areas. In rural Honduras, he found that an "insurgent" was anyone a landowner identified as troublesome. This particularly included rural union organizers, and peasants generally feared reprisal from military authorities for attending *campesino* meetings.[37]

Herbert Klein has observed in a study of Bolivian politics that "we train Bolivian special forces to fight insurgents, but they use their training to massacre mine workers or put down student disorders."[38]

Writing on the U.S. military assistance program, General Porter warned:

> Communism has made impressive and dangerous penetration in many fields, notably among youth and in educational, informational media and trade union spheres. It is relentlessly waging warfare against established societies in Latin America as well as in our own country. Their battleground is across the whole spectrum of national life and activity. . . . Communism is engaged in protracted conflict. Violence is but one string of its bow. Its strategists have increasingly emphasized that power can be

---

35. Stepan, *The Military in Politics*, p. 27.

36. George C. Lodge, *Engines of Change: United States Interests and Revolution in Latin America* (New York: Alfred A. Knopf, 1969), pp. 181–83. If this observation can be assumed to apply to an institutional, rather than an exclusively Latin American, phenomenon, it is reinforced by the statement of a Ceylonese major quoted in Lee Lescaze, "Ceylon's Youth Insurrection," *Washington Post*, 9 May 1971. The major said that the insurrection was not unwelcome. "We have never had the opportunity to fight a real war in this country," he said. "All these years we have been firing at dummies; now we are being put to use."

37. Ibid.

38. John M. Goshko, "Latin Arms Boomerang," *Washington Post*, 4 February 1968. Reprinted in Senate Relations Committee, *Amendments to the OAS Charter*, pp. 7–11.

won and influence gained through political, economic, and psychological warfare.[39]

If insurgents, then, are to be found across the whole spectrum of national life and working "within the system," how are they to be identified? Perhaps they may be tagged through the opinions they express. Lieutenant Colonel Stockton noted that in Brazil in early 1964, "subversives took keen advantage of a free press."[40] And Major Weers explained that "the efforts of the Communists have been to portray the United States as a money-grubbing country, and not as a democratic symbol." Weers said that the communists who had infiltrated the labor movement and other phases of Brazilian life "supported Goulart against the military and against the United States."[41]

Stepan noted that the Sorbonne group considered any criticism of the United States to be subversive. Likewise, a contributor to the Brazilian *Revista do Clube Militar* in 1973, having noted that more than ever before we are seeing the development of "two moral poles: that of Good and that of Evil," asserted that the criminal intent of the National Student Union (UNE) was made obvious, in particular, by the intensification of its campaign against the hemispheric policies and prestige of the United States.[42] It would probably be impossible to ascertain whether the views held by Brazilian and U.S. officers as to the identity of the insurgents in Brazil and the measures that should be taken to counter them originated with the Brazilians or with their North American counterparts, but it is apparent that the views of the two military establishments have generally been compatible.

In his 1968 speech, General Porter said: "In order to facilitate the coordinated employment of internal security forces within and among Latin American countries, we are also endeavoring to foster interservice and regional cooperation by assisting in the organization of integrated command and control centers; the establishment of common operating procedures; and the conduct of joint and combined training exercises.[43]

The idea of expanded military cooperation within Latin America has had considerable appeal among some like-minded military rulers. Exalting the accords between the military establishments of Argentina

39. Porter, "Latin America," p. 574.

40. Stockton, "Analysis of the Brazilian Revolution," p. 10.

41. Weers, "Brazil: Target for Communism," p. 48.

42. J. Camarinha Nascimento, "Conflitos Contestatorios," *Revista do Clube Militar* [Rio de Janeiro] 48 (November-December 1973): 35.

43. Porter, "Look South," p. 86.

and Brazil in 1965, General Juan Carlos Ongania of Argentina referred to a "Military America" which has "not only a mechanical, but a mental system of communications."[44] The 1964 coup in Brazil and the 1966 coup in Argentina clearly alleviated some of the anxieties of President Stroessner of Paraguay. A 1969 report of the Paraguayan Ministry of the Interior acclaimed the cooperation and reciprocity that existed between the security forces of Paraguay and their counterparts in Brazil and Argentina.[45] Colonel Roberto Cubas of the Paraguayan Army informed the author that the military intelligence services of the three countries meet regularly to coordinate their plans and activities, and that Stroessner's secret police, unpopularly known as Pyragües (Guaraní for people with hairy feet), are allowed to move about freely in Brazil and Argentina to apprehend or conduct surveillance on Paraguayan exiles.[46]

The attempt (following the Dominican "crisis" of 1965) to expand inter-American military cooperation even more through the establishment of a permanent inter-American peacekeeping force had a chilly reception in most of the Latin American countries. It was conceived by some U.S. officials as an extension of the counterinsurgency program. Foreign Service Officer Raymond J. Barrett, for example, expressed the opinion that it would be desirable to adapt each U.S. Military Assistance Program to help equip and develop each country's unit, which would be maintained in a high state of readiness. Barrett suggested that "the orientation of the armed forces of the American nations toward the internal security functions of peacekeeping would help them in countering *potential* [italics added] or actual subversion in their own countries."[47]

The permanent inter-American peace-keeping force died aborning, but there remained sufficient "show of force" in the hemisphere at the disposal of the U.S. military and its counterrevolutionary allies to inhibit the squeamish "potential" revolutionary. In case the "deterrent" should fail and the U.S. military should feel compelled to intervene in

44. García Lupo, "Brazil and the U.S."

45. República del Paraguay, Sub-secretaría de Informaciones y Cultura de la Presidencia de la República, Mensaje del Excelentísimo Señor Presidente de la República y Commandante en Jefe de las FF.AA. de la Nación General de Ejército Don Alfredo Stroessner al Congreso Nacional, Asuncion, 1 April 1969, p. 27.

46. Coronel Roberto Cubas, Paraguayan Army, interview, 14 April 1971, Washington, D.C.

47. Raymond J. Barrett, "Inter-American Peace Force," *Military Review* 47 (May 1967): 85–91.

order to quell insurgency, there would be a number of U.S. military units in a state of "readiness" to handle any contingency. In fact, Admiral LaRocque noted that the long-term Joint Strategic Objectives Plan calls for the structuring of offensive strategic forces for contingencies in the Third World. He added that the United States is the only country in the world that has the entire globe divided up into commands and that there are contingency plans for "the evacuation of U.S. citizens" from every country.[48] (Kenneth Boulding has observed that technological and organizational advances have made it possible for decision-makers to make and implement with maximum speed and efficiency decisions that should not have been made in the first place.)

U.S. Army and Air Force spokesmen for the Joint Strike Command (since renamed Readiness Command) admonished in 1962, "We will have to prepare a plan ready for any possible mission the Joint Chiefs might assign to us." And they asserted, "The U.S. Strike Command provides this country with a highly mobile, hard-hitting military team of any size required—a highly trained professional force capable of reacting with selective military power to any threat which faces this nation anywhere on the globe."[49] U.S.A.F. General Joe W. Kelly said in 1963 that the Cuban missile crisis had demonstrated the value of the Military Air Transport Services (MATS) worldwide command and control system and "demonstrated again that in any emergency situation MATS is often the first to 'go.' " Kelly noted that "like the scores of other contingency plans that the Joint Chiefs of Staff require for possible major military actions in any part of the world, the Caribbean area plans were maintained under constant review to keep them current." As another example of the usefulness and efficiency of MATS, he cited an incident in November 1962: MATS had been called upon to come to the rescue of the Creole Petroleum Company (Standard Oil of New Jersey) in Venezuela, which "had become the victim of Communist sabotage." "Responsiveness to any degree of emergency," he added, "can exist only to the extent that MATS, as a full-time active-duty member of the defense team, is D-day ready every day. . . . For MATS, in effect, the only operational difference between war and peace is one of degree, not of kind."[50]

48. LaRocque interview.

49. "U.S. Strike Command; for Swift, Tactical Reactions in Every Known Environment" (Interviews with General Paul Adams, USA, and Lieutenant General Bruce Holloway, USAF), *Army Information Digest* 17 (May 1962): 18–25.

50. General Joe W. Kelly, U.S.A.F., "MATS Looks at the Cuban Crisis," *Air University Review* 14 (September-October 1963): 2–20.

The scope of contingency planning is suggested by a U.S. Air Force Research Project for which a team at Harvard University was bidding in 1963–1964. As part of an in-depth study of Latin America, Joseph Page was asked to be the "field man" in northeast Brazil "to determine how various sectors of the local populace would react to an invasion and occupation by foreign troops."[51] Admiral LaRocque observed that contingency plans provide the rationale for building up and readying forces, and Colonel King added that the pressure in the intelligence community to resort to "worst possible case" analysis heightens the probability that those forces will be used.

General Porter has warned that "Latin America threatens to become another Vietnam unless the United States helps armed forces there provide a shield against insurgency while the governments build a stable society."[52] The implications of that statement go beyond the proposition that insurgency might reach such proportions that local authorities could not repress it to the suggestion that in such an eventuality U.S. forces would be obligated to step in. Likewise, a Spanish language training manual used at the Fort Bragg complex in the 1960s advised foreign trainees to accept modest numbers of foreign military and civilian counterinsurgency advisors in order to avoid the introduction of large foreign armies which would make the indigenous regime appear to be a "puppet" government, and a 1967 field manual stated that when a host country army is unable to contain insurgent forces, U.S. Army units might be sent in.[53] The threats or reassurances contained in such statements are lost neither on authorities nor on "dissidents."

A lecturer at the ESG in 1973 said that "the United States considers that to adopt the principle of nonintervention would be to give the advantage to the Soviet bloc."[54] And Archbishop Dom Helder Câmara has warned: "If there should appear in any part of the world, but above all in Latin America, an outbreak of violence, they can be certain that, im-

---

51. Page, *The Revolution That Never Was*, p. 258. A similar project that resulted in strained relations between the United States and Chile was criticized by Irving L. Horowitz in *The Rise and Fall of Project Camelot: Studies in the Relationship between Social Science and Practical Politics* (Cambridge: The M.I.T. Press, 1967).

52. Lodge, "Engines of Change," p. 181.

53. Wolpin, *Military Aid and Counterrevolution*, p. 88.

54. Presidência da República, Estado-Maior das Fôrças Armadas, Escola Superior de Guerra, Departamento de Estudos, T138-73, "O Direito Internacional e as Leis de Guerra," lecture by Dr. Celso D. de Albuquerque Mello, 19 July 1973, no. 171, p. 18.

mediately, the great powers will arrive—even without a declaration of war—and we will have a new Vietnam."[55]

It has been argued that the U.S. military, imbued with its own concept of global mission, has been inclined to interpret legislation and executive intent and to conduct its own operations as it sees fit. Thus, whatever civilian policy-makers might have viewed as the objectives of counterinsurgency and civic action programs, these programs have been conducted in Brazil, among other countries, in such a way as to expand the political role and enhance the political power of the military. At the same time, the promotion of higher education in management and technology for foreign military officers has provided them with the self-confidence required for a governing elite. Finally, it may be assumed that their self-confidence and disinclination to compromise with civilians is further bulwarked by the belief that their control over their own national societies is underwritten by the readiness of the U.S. military to intervene on their behalf at a moment's notice.

55. Dom Helder Câmara, "Is Violence the Only Option," *Models of Political Change in Latin America*, ed. Paul E. Sigmund (New York: Praeger, 1970), pp. 146–48.

[13]

Institutional Interests and Defense Strategy

Secretary of Defense McNamara's 1962 proposition that a policy of promoting democratic attitudes among the Latin officer corps should be implemented by putting Latin American officers into extensive contact with their U.S. counterparts presupposed that the predominant direction of influence would be from U.S. civilian policy-makers and U.S. officers to the Latin American officers. Senator Frank Church has concluded that the reverse is more commonly the case. During the 1969 hearings on U.S. Military Policies and Programs in Latin America before the Subcommittee on Western Hemisphere Affairs of the Senate Foreign Relations Committee, Church suggested that "our own personnel are being influenced by Latin American viewpoints, rather than vice versa." He said that he had been disturbed by "the extent to which American military officers located in these countries come to espouse and to parrot the viewpoints of the local military people."[1]

Certainly the exertion of influence is not unidirectional. The U.S. officers function, in effect, as liaisons between the U.S. civilian policy-makers and the Latin American military establishments. On balance, then, do the U.S. officers serve U.S. civilian policy-makers when and if the latter advocate democratic government, or do they serve the Latin American military establishments as lobbyists for political backing and for the instruments of power?

This author is not convinced that the predominant direction of influence can be empirically established, but a more significant factor to be considered is that of individual and institutional self-interest. From

1. Senate Foreign Relations Committee, *U.S. Military Policies and Programs in Latin America*, p. 82.

216

that perspective, it is argued in this chapter that the interests of the U.S. and Latin American officers are complementary or similar, if not identical.

That the U.S. military establishment has an interest in expanding its own operations is self-evident. The competition among the services and, more recently, the many varieties of "special" forces and operations, has only intensified that institutional imperative. General W. B. Palmer wrote of the military assistance program in 1962: "Well, good heavens, we all consider it important to have a base of influence in every country we can, and if a little equipment, a few aircraft, and some invitations to our service schools make this possible, what earthly objection can there be?"[2] Colonel Edward King has written that it was in the limited-war role in the underdeveloped countries that the Army saw its brightest prospects. To justify involvement in places where "aggression against freedom" did not reach the level of a bushfire war, he argues, the counterinsurgency dimension was added. King maintains that from what he read, saw, heard, and participated in on the staff of the Joint Chiefs in the late 1960s, the Joint Chiefs' policy was "to use U.S. military power as the answer to every worldwide problem. . . . They acted like executives charged with expanding the base of a business."[3]

This enthusiasm for the expansion of the "duties" of the services and their special groups through new instruments and rationales is particularly manifest in military journals of the early and mid-1960s, before the Vietnam War became a raging national controversy. The following article titles are exemplary:

"Accent on Cold War Capabilities" (*Army Information Digest*, May 1962);
"Counterinsurgency is Your Business" (*Army Information Digest*, July 1962);
"Win Friends—Defeat Communism" (*Instructors Journal*, July 1964);
"Civic Action Helps Counter the Guerrilla Threat" (*Army Information Digest*, June 1962).

Appearing before Senate hearings on the Mutual Security Act of 1958, Secretary of Defense Neil H. McElroy reported that the U.S. missions, by the terms of their agreements, were responsible to the host government to which they were assigned, and that in this capacity the missions constituted an integral part of the advisory and training eche-

2. General W. B. Palmer, "Military Assistance Program: A Progress Report," *Army Information Digest* 17 (April 1962): 40–46.
3. King, *The Death of the Army*, pp. 31, 64.

lons of the host country. He maintained that in fulfilling their role they advised on every aspect of the respective military programs and were most influential in advising on the acquisition of new materiel and on the varied aspects of training.

Of the 584 military personnel assigned to missions in nineteen Latin American countries in 1958, 436 were accredited to and received compensation, ranging from $240 to $4,500 annually, from the governments to which they were assigned. The apparent conflict of interest involved in this arrangement aroused congressional criticism and the practice was halted by legislation on 1 April 1959.[4]

Nevertheless, the House Foreign Affairs Committee Special Study Mission to Latin America reported in 1970 that transportation to and from Brazil for U.S. Navy officers and enlisted men and their dependents, along with household goods and automobiles, was still provided by the Brazilian government under the terms of the 1922 agreement. Members of the mission were also granted free entry for articles for personal and family use, and the mission chief was provided with an automobile and a driver. All U.S. Navy officers assigned to the mission were considered senior to Brazilian officers of the same rank. The Brazilian government continued to fulfill these half-century old conditions "on the grounds that the U.S. Naval Mission is an adjunct of the Brazilian Navy." Similar provisions bind the U.S. Army and Air Force missions to the Brazilian military establishment.[5]

An obvious aspect of the interest of foreign officers in training and other relations with the U.S. military has been pointed out by Colonel D. Forest Ballou: "Assistance can only come from one or two places. If you know how it works, you're better off. If you were a Brazilian officer, how could you plan any action without knowing how the U.S. does things?" Ballou also observed that "the sharpest Third World guys are going where the action is," that is, to military rather than civilian careers and to U.S. rather than European schools.[6]

Some military insiders have observed that, in general, U.S. officers assigned to milgroups in Latin America were those whose careers had peaked. These officers naturally preferred the status and the plush offices and residences and other luxuries abroad to obscurity in a Pentagon cubbyhole or a Stateside base. In order to justify their assignments and enhance their positions, they had to continue to perceive a "security threat." Likewise, foreign officers, in order to acquire more

4. Estep, "U.S. Military Aid to Latin America," pp. 46–47.
5. House *Foreign Affairs Committee, Special Study Mission I*, pp. 4–5.
6. Ballou interview.

weapons or support in overcoming immediate challenges to their power or perquisites, also exaggerate the "security threat."

A Brazilian described as having been "a high aide to the Foreign Minister" prior to the 1964 coup told New York Times reporter Joseph Novitski of a call he had received from the Minister of War. "He asked me whether we were trying to abolish his ministry. He said that the United States military mission had told him it might be very difficult to get aid and supplies for the next year unless Brazil supported the United States."[7] In fact, there was a decrease of over $9 million in deliveries to Brazil in 1963.[8] A discontinuation of military aid would obviously have been a blow to the U.S. missions as well as to the Brazilian military.

That Latin American military establishments have little to gain and much to lose through the democratization of their own countries is readily apparent. Numerous studies indicate that the percentage of national budgets allocated to defense tend to be up to twice as high in countries under military rule (see Appendix, Table 4); and such studies only reveal the tip of the iceberg of the perquisites accruing to a ruling elite. That the U.S. military stands to gain through the militarization of countries over which the United States exercises hegemony is equally obvious. At the very least, this militarization affords all the tangible and intangible bonuses to U.S. officers of greater camaraderie with the ruling circles and greater prestige than State Department personnel enjoy. These bonuses include a larger role in U.S. policy-making, as a result of more direct lines of communication with the centers of power and therefore supposedly more "reliable" information, and greater leverage in influencing host-country policies. They also include all the pettier perquisites that accompany proximity to those in power. These are amply demonstrated by the fact that in the late 1960s the entertainment allowance of the military missions in Brazil was running about $17,900 annually, approximately three times that allotted to the ambassador.[9] (Military entertainment allowances for Latin America in fiscal 1970 actually exceeded the total for the rest of the world.)[10] And

---

7. Novitski, "Latin Lands Turning to Europe." The Senate Intelligence Committee reported that in its attempt to provoke a coup against the government of Salvador Allende in Chile in 1970, the United States threatened to cut off military aid if the military refused to act, and promised support in the aftermath of a coup (*Covert Action*, p. 184).

8. Hovey, *U.S. Military Assistance*, p. 244.

9. Goshko, "Latins Blame U.S. for Military Coups."

10. Wolpin, *Military Aid and Counterrevolution*, p. 115.

military rulers can be expected to heap honors on their military counterparts from benefactor countries. General Porter, for example, who maintains that our training programs are reaping such dividends, has twice been decorated by Brazil's military government.[11] It also means a potent rationale for the continuation or expansion of U.S. military programs in the area. Colonel Milton Callero, Army Attaché in Brasilia in the late 1960s, said, "The people who more and more are calling the shots in Latin America are the military," and he added that military-to-military rapport is a fact, an indispensable channel of communication, and a link that Foreign Service officers could not fill.[12]

U.S. military officers have long been honorary members of the Brazilian Clube Militar. The House Special Study Mission noted in 1970:

> U.S. military personnel report being welcome at all activities of the Brazilian Armed Forces. Their advice is often solicited on military problems, and, at times, through personal contacts, individual U.S. representatives have been able to exert beneficial influence on authorities.[13]

On the question of camaraderie and prestige, Colonel Ballou maintained that informal relationships and the "old school tie" of the Fort Leavenworth experience is probably more important than the training itself. He added that it is possible for the U.S. military to influence the course of events in allied countries through such contacts, especially if U.S. officers have friends in power. "We have ways of doing these things—overt and covert."[14]

Many Brazilians are convinced that Colonel (later promoted to Brigadier General) Vernon D. Walters had a great deal to do with prodding his close friend Castello Branco into leading the 1964 coup.[15] Celso Furtado maintained that U.S. military personnel provided a net-

11. Senate Foreign Relations Committee, *U.S. Military Policies and Programs in Latin America*, p. 75.

12. Callero interview.

13. House *Foreign Affairs Committee, Special Study Mission*, p. 8.

14. Ballou interview. According to Wolpin, a former CIA Deputy Director explicitly designated foreign officers who may conspire to overthrow existing governments as a CIA target elite, so it stands to reason that Military Advisory Assistance Groups and attaché positions constitute for the agency an important cover (*Military Aid and Counterrevolution*, p. 105). It probably matters little to the oppressed, however, whether the uniformed foreigners advising their rulers are CIA or straight military.

15. Similarly, according to Goshko, politically knowledgeable Bolivians, including ousted civilian President Victor Paz Estenssoro, are convinced that U.S. Air Force Attaché Colonel Ed Fox, a flying instructor and drinking companion of General René Barrientos Ortuño, was behind the coup that catapulted Barrientos into the presidency ("Latins Blame U.S. for Military Coups").

work of communication whereby Brazilian officers could be drawn into the conspiracy without openly committing themselves and overplaying their hands prematurely. Walters, Furtado said, was the focal point of this communications network.[16] Colonel Edward King noted that the assessment of an impending communist takeover permeating communication channels from Brazil to the Joint Chiefs of Staff and back again represented for the U.S. officers, as for Brazilian ones, an inextricable mix of conviction and self-interest: "it would have been career suicide for any U.S. officer involved to express disagreement."[17]

It has been noted that on several occasions in the early 1960s the State Department and the Pentagon appeared to be pulling in opposite directions in the supposedly bilateral relations between the United States and various Latin American countries. In particular, on the occasions of the coups d'état in Peru in 1962, the Dominican Republic and Honduras in 1963, and Bolivia in 1964, U.S. Embassy civilians appeared to be backing the sitting civilian governments while representatives of the military were encouraging the coup-makers. Both advocates and opponents of the 1964 coup in Brazil see the period before and after that event as one in which U.S. policy—military and civilian— was exceptionally well coordinated. However, the portrayal of U.S.-Brazilian relations in the late 1960s that emerges from interviews with three well-positioned U.S. officers—Lieutenant Colonel Edward King, Joint Chiefs of Staff delegate to the Joint Brazilian-U.S. Defense Commission in Washington; Colonel Milton Callero, Army Attaché in Brasilia; and Major General R. J. Seitz, Commander of the U.S. delegation to the JBUSMC, headquartered in Rio de Janeiro—is one of an alliance between the Brazilian government and the U.S. military against the U.S. Ambassador and Embassy civilians and some Brazilian civilian politicians.

Colonel King maintained that, largely as a consequence of the communication channel linking the JBUSMC directly with the Joint Chiefs of Staff Plans and Policy Division, the real policy-making and execution power of the military was much greater than that of the State Department. The military, King said, needs not, and generally does not, channel its communications through the Embassy, and there is no way for State Department to get information the military doesn't want it to have. Furthermore, the Joint Chiefs only tell their civilian superiors at the Department of Defense what they wish to.

Colonel Callero said that whereas U.S. civilian diplomats were in a

16. Furtado interview.
17. King interview.

sense caught off guard or confounded by the 1968 consolidating coup, one who occupied his position (with formal and, more importantly, informal contacts with military decision-makers) would have seen it as the direction in which the military could be expected to move. (In fact, Callero had been told of the plans for the closing of congress by some close friends who were aides to President Costa e Silva.) He said that "anyone in the position of guarding the security of the country would have had to be concerned about what might have happened had all the various groups [plotting to overthrow the government] coalesced."

The Brazilian military (and consequently the U.S. military), Callero said, had information that the Brazilian Congress didn't have about the real activities, connections, and schemes of Brazilian student leaders and others. (He added that the same is true in the United States, "where the military and the CIA, for example, have information on individuals that members of Congress couldn't be trusted with.") Many of these student leaders who pretended to be concerned about conditions in the university cafeteria, Callero maintained, were actually part of a large-scale national and international network, supported by the Soviet Union, among other countries, aimed at wars of national liberation. Whether or not members of Congress were involved, there were a lot of "innocent and stupid" ones. He added that a lot of people were tortured because the shadow of suspicion spread. "It's best to get such movements under control before they get out of hand," he said.

General Seitz said that the security threat to Brazil grew after the 1964 coup and had reached very serious proportions by 1967. "This was one of the things that precipitated the takeover in 1968." He maintained that groups bent on overthrowing the government were organized nationally as well as internationally and were receiving support from Cuba and probably the Soviet Union and China as well. The conspiratorial network, he said, included the left wing of the Catholic Church (although these Catholics may not have been aware of the real nature of the alliance), and Congressman Moreira Alves, if not a leader, was at least a spokesman of the conspirators. "All of [Brazil's] embassies throughout the world were infiltrated by these people; that's why they were getting such a bad press."

Meanwhile, according to General Seitz, from sometime in 1967 on, and especially after December 1968, the U.S. Embassy was "anti-government." Ambassador Tuthill was having "clandestine meetings with the opposition" (specifically, with Lacerda) and became a "de facto persona non grata." President Costa e Silva allegedly called him in and confronted him with information about those meetings. "That was Tuthill's last audience" while he was in the country. Thus, Seitz says, the embassy ceased to be able to function normally vis-à-vis the government and found it hard to collect information.

The Embassy apparently found it hard also to collect information from the U.S. military. Seitz said that the milgroup is the best source of intelligence, but that his predecessor had left the country early because "he could not tolerate Tuthill." (It was evident that Seitz did not find him easy to tolerate either.) And he added that Defense Attaché Colonel Arthur Moura was probably the best informed person politically in the country at the time, but that Tuthill couldn't get much information from him because the two "did not see eye to eye." When communications between the Embassy and the Brazilian government broke down, ties between the two military establishments helped to keep things going. This was possible in part, Seitz said, because of the "inherently close relationship" that developed through sharing offices with the Brazilian military hierarchy.

Colonel Callero confirmed that competition between the State Department and the military was intense, and that the military was the usual channel for the transmission of "delicate" information: as a consequence of common institutional bonds it was more comfortable for one military man to talk with another. He said for example, that the Brazilian government's formulated but unannounced policy on the two hundred-mile limit for territorial waters was first outlined to him informally; he passed it on to the Embassy. And Seitz added that although the Embassy was supposed to be in charge of military sales, the Brazilians didn't expect cooperation from the civilians, so they asked him to intercede for them.

At the aforementioned 1969 hearings before the Senate Foreign Relations Committee, G. Warren Nutter, Assistant Secretary of Defense for International Security Affairs, asserted that among the benefits accruing to the United States from the military assistance groups was the fact that "they provide advice to our ambassadors as well as to the host countries." Questioned by Senator Church as to the nature of this advice, Nutter responded with the circuitous explanation that a major purpose in the milgroups' presence was to keep the ambassador advised as to what they were doing there. The inference, stripped of bureaucratic doubletalk, was that the military assistance groups were there to fashion, sustain, and extend their own programs in perpetuity.[18]

Some perspective on the nature and direction of influence in the

18. Senate Foreign Relations Committee, *U.S. Military Policies and Programs in Latin America*, pp. 63, 78–79.

three-step linkage of U.S. civilian policy-makers—U.S. officers—Brazilian officers can be gained by examining the advice that has been offered to U.S. policy-makers by the U.S. officers. It appears that in general, rather than urging democracy and submission to civilian leadership on their Brazilian counterparts, the officers have urged U.S. policy-makers to accept or support military control of government.

General Robert J. Wood, Director of Military Assistance, argued in Senate Appropriations Hearings in 1965 in favor of continued military assistance to Brazil on the grounds that there existed a "vacuum in the civilian political structure so far as running the country is concerned, and the only force for stability and orderliness is the military."[19] U.S. Navy Captain Raymond J. Toner explained in a 1968 article in the *U.S. Naval Institute Proceedings* that when the Latin American military performs its "Super Mission Role" (the example Toner gave was the overthrow of Argentina's civilian president Arturo Illia in 1966), it is "reacting within the social and political body of its state, not as a foreign and separate entity upon it." He continued, "The aspects of the Spanish-Moorish-Jewish-Indian cultures will continue to influence Latin Americans. Their concepts of 'democracy' will differ from 'democracy' as we of North America conceive it. We, then, must outgrow our own provincialism and adjust to a world-ranging viewpoint consistent with our responsibilities as a world power."[20] And Lieutenant Colonel Stockton advised that the United States, in its relations with Brazil, "should soft pedal criticism and demands for a true democratic government of the one man, one vote concept we have here. The overriding priority of our policy toward Brazil and all South America should be to foster stable governments that are Western-oriented."[21]

Likewise, in 1970, the Special Study Mission found U.S. officers in Brazil to be undisturbed about supporting an authoritarian government:

> U.S. military personnel to whom we spoke uniformly reported their relationships with their Brazilian counterparts to be warm and cordial. Milgroup personnel see Brazilian officers as one of the best educated and informed social groups in the country and, more than any other group, dedicated to national rather than regional or personal interests. Rather than dwell on the authoritarian aspects of the regime, they emphasize assertions by the Brazilian armed forces that they believe in, and support, representative democracy as an ideal and would return government to ci-

19. Wolpin, *Military Aid and Counterrevolution*, p. 50.
20. Toner, "The Latin American Military," p. 73.
21. Stockton, "Analysis of the Brazilian Revolution," p. 56.

vilian control if this could be done without sacrifice to security and development. This withdrawal from the political arena is not seen as occurring in the near future. For that reason, they emphasize the continued importance of the military assistance training program as a means of exerting U.S. influence and retaining the current pro-U.S. attitude of the Brazilian Armed Forces. Possible disadvantages to U.S. interests in being so closely identified with an authoritarian regime are not seen as particularly important.[22]

The milgroup's lack of embarrassment about this identification with authoritarianism is apparent in their policy of cohabitation of headquarters. General Beatty confirmed in 1971 Senate hearings that the joint headquarters of the U.S. and Brazilian delegations to the JBUSMC in Rio de Janeiro was located in the Palacio Monroe, formerly the home of the Federal Senate. The headquarters of each of the U.S. service missions is located in the ministry building of its Brazilian counterpart. The NAVCOMTECH Group likewise is located in the Navy Ministry. Beatty was questioned in the hearings about an Associated Press story regarding torture facilities on the floor of the Brazilian Navy Ministry where the Naval Mission and the NAVCOMTECH group are located. One American assigned to the floor reported having heard screams and groans over a two-year period, and other U.S. personnel reported having seen Brazilians being dragged to and from the room by Brazilian naval agents. The AP account related that Admiral Hill had ordered his personnel not to discuss the subject. Asked if Hill had given such an order, Beatty replied that he had "invoked a Navy regulation, which requires that if there are things out of line in any organization these facts be made known to persons in the chain of command. . . . And that is the same time they all said, 'I didn't know about it and I didn't talk to anybody about it.' "[23]

The Special Study Mission reported that milgroup personnel claimed that they exerted a restraining influence on the purchase of unnecessary military equipment "since their advice is reputedly sought and valued by the Brazilians," but they were reportedly "sympathetic to the Brazilians' feelings about U.S. attempts to limit the country's arms purchases."[24]

General Beatty explained in the 1971 hearings that exchanges of advice and opinions concerning the kinds of U.S. training that would be beneficial to the Brazilians evolved out of day-to-day contacts, but that the usual procedure was for the Brazilians to request a certain kind of

22. House Foreign Affairs Committee, *Special Study Mission I*, p. 5.
23. Church Hearings, p. 93.
24. House Foreign Affairs Committee, *Special Study Mission I*, p. 5.

training and for the missions to make arrangements for it to be provided. He affirmed that what the Brazilians did with the training they had received was quite outside his area of concern.

American Republics Subcommittee Counsel Pat Holt noted in the hearings that topics from outlines submitted by the Defense Department of courses offered to Brazilians included "censorship, checkpoint systems, chemical and biological operations, briefings on the CIA, civic action and civil affairs, clandestine operations, cryptography, defoliation, dissent in the United States, electronic intelligence, electronic warfare and countermeasures, the use of informants, insurgency intelligence, counterintelligence, subversion, counter-subversion, espionage, counterespionage, interrogation of prisoners and suspects, handling mass rallies and meetings, nuclear weapons effects, intelligence photography, polygraphs, population and resources control, psychological operations, raids and searches, riots, special warfare, surveillance, terror, and undercover operations." Asked if the military assistance program ever turned down requests on the grounds that the training the Brazilians were seeking was inappropriate, Beatty replied, "Happily we have never had to."[25]

General Beatty asserted that the U.S. Armed Forces advisors, who "have been closely associated with the host military at all levels of Brazilian Armed Forces professional training and education, . . . maintained strictly apolitical attitudes."[26] On a visit to Brazil in 1971, Richard Barnet, had some exposure to these "apolitical attitudes." He reported that one high-ranking U.S. military officer with whom he spoke expressed complete satisfaction with the Brazilian regime and suggested that perhaps we were getting to a point in the United States at which some similar strong measures might be necessary. "These people understand that sometimes you have to sacrifice a little liberty for the country."[27]

If it were to be assumed that the military assistance program in general, and the training programs in particular, had actually been designed to encourage military submission to civilian authority and to foster democratic attitudes, it would have to be conceded that the means have been monumentally ill-suited to the ends. It has been pointed out, however, that the policy-making process is at best frag-

25. Church Hearings, pp. 88–91. Pat Holt observed in an interview with the author that the subcommittee had caught a couple of Brazilians in courses classified "Secret." Defense Department regulations restrict foreign trainees to courses classified "Confidential."

26. Church Hearings, p. 56.

27. Barnet, "Letter from Rio," pp. 16–21.

mented and that the more significant policy decisions or interpretations are often those at the operational level.

It has been argued that the national and transnational institutional self-interests of the military, reinforced by the bureaucratic ethos and the Cold War world-view, weigh heavily on the outcome of interactions between the U.S. military establishment and its Brazilian counterpart. Military programs as their own raison d'être, however, do not make for imposing rhetoric. Institutional objectives must be viewed and presented as consistent with national objectives. What, then, are the long-term national objectives underlying military policy in the hemisphere?

In 1951 an Administration spokesman outlined four objectives which military assistance was designed to promote:

> One is to secure the sources of strategic materials, such as the petroleum fields of Venezuela, the tin mines of Bolivia, and the copper mines of Chile; secondly to keep open the lines of access to those strategic materials; third, to have the armed forces of those countries in readiness to keep the strategic areas defensible from small air and submarine raids from abroad; and fourth, to reduce the call upon our own Armed Forces for the defense of those areas.[28]

The enemy at that time, in accordance with the Rio Treaty and the Washington Consultation of 1951, was assumed to be extra-continental, and the statement had the ring of conventional military alliance strategy. The enemy, however, was not a nation, nor even a group of nations, but an ideology. This perception was made explicit when Secretary of Defense Robert McNamara testified before the Foreign Relations Committee in 1961. Of the "single-threat" area, which included all of the Latin American states, McNamara asserted:

> Our objective here is to provide the means for local military establishments, with the support and cooperation of local populations, to guard against external covert intrusion and internal subversion designed to create *dissidence* [italics added] and insurrection.[29]

If dissidence (defined by Webster's New Collegiate Dictionary as "disagreement"), presumably with the Cold War world-view, or with U.S. policies, or with governments and military establishments supported by the United States, is assumed to be inspired by communism, and if communism is identified as the enemy in a total and perpetual global war, it is easy to understand the apocalyptic view of and the inquisitional approach to developments in Latin America and elsewhere.

28. Estep, "U.S. Military Aid to Latin America," p. 58.
29. Ibid., p. 59.

Such an apocalyptic view is expressed in geopolitical terms in Lieutenant Colonel Stockton's analysis of the Brazilian Revolution of 1964:

> Brazil was carried to the brink of Communism but did not take the tum-
> ble, thanks to the military. Had the military not acted, and just in the nick
> of time, the United States would have awakened on the morning of 2 May
> 1964 with Brazil under Communist control. That development could
> have converted Brazil into a China of the Western Hemisphere, present-
> ing the United States with problems of national security dwarfing those
> of Cuba. Brazil has a contiguous border with every South American
> country except Chile and Ecuador. She could have exported revolu-
> tionaries almost at will. It would have been only a matter of time before
> all South American countries exploded in People's Wars of National
> Liberation. All of the continent would have gone behind the iron and
> bamboo curtains, unless the United States intervened militarily. . . .[30]

The objective of securing sources of strategic materials also has far-
reaching economic implications. One means of securing such sources
is to own them. Or is it that they must be secured because U.S. companies already own them? Pointing out that U.S. investments in Latin
America totaled more than $12 billion, General Porter admonished a
New York audience in 1968 to "consider the small amount of U.S.
public funds that have gone for military assistance and for AID public
safety projects as a very modest premium on an insurance policy protecting our vast private investment in an area of tremendous trade and
strategic value to our country."[31]

Just as the pseudo-religious themes of the divine right of monarchs
and the white man's burden provided justification in the past for the
exploits of powerful nations and groups, the Cold War has thrown the
cloak of legitimacy over the exploits of contemporary military establishments and those other sectors of the national populations whose
interests are similar or complementary. However, as the superpowers
move toward detente and as their behavior in both external and
domestic affairs shows increasing similarity, the Cold War clichés become ever more transparent.

In regard to its military relations with Latin America, the United
States has been caught in the bind of having to continue to claim, in the
face of the amassed evidence to the contrary, that its military programs
promote democracy, or to maintain that the "Communist threat" is so

---

30. Stockton, "Analysis of the Brazilian Revolution," p. 54.

31. Porter, "Latin America," p. 576. Several U.S. officers who have worked
with Brazilian and other Latin American officers maintain that those trained in
the United States or otherwise extensively exposed to the U.S. military tend to
value the "free enterprise" system and to welcome U.S investment in their
countries.

overwhelming as to require support for repressive dictatorships, or to come up with some new justification. The Nixon administration appeared to be somewhat at a loss in this semantic game. At the 1969 Senate hearings on U.S. Military Policies and Programs in Latin America, Assistant Secretary Meyer walked into the trap of admitting that counterinsurgency programs were needed to prevent the subversion of "inadequate and inequitable economic and social structures." He then had to retreat and argue that the programs should be continued because "military relationships between the United States and Latin America have been long-standing."[32]

Military strategists, however, are long on ingenuity. The House Special Study Mission reported in 1970 that "according to the prevailing view at SOUTHCOM, Latin American military men play a major role in national political life, whether or not the U.S. approves, and their views have direct effects on the potential for attaining U.S. objectives in each country. Hence, the SOUTHCOM commander and his staff claim they are in a position to exert maximum constructive influence on Latin American armed forces not only in military matters, but in support of political, social, and economic modernization." The Mission added that according to SOUTHCOM's general staff, "the U.S. military presence in the Canal Zone serves as a credible deterrent to adventurism by radical elements who would be more active in the hemisphere if SOUTHCOM did not exist."[33]

To Colonel Ballou, detente with the major communist powers produces no dilemma at all. He welcomes it, he has said, because it "will allow us to focus on the real problem areas. Our action is in the Third World nations. We've already lost our shirts in one war of National Liberation."[34] The lead article in the twenty-fifth anniversary issue of the Spanish and Portuguese editions of the U.S. Command and General Staff College's *Military Review* asserted that with the easing of pressures in Southeast Asia, the United States should be able to devote greater attention to the improvement of the inter-American defense forces, as "the forces of anarchy, terror and subversion have selected Latin America as a prime target in the 1970s."[35]

Colonel King asserted that the "professional killers and organization men" in the U.S. military see Latin America as the war theater of the fu-

---

32. Senate Foreign Relations Committe, pp. 59–68.

33. House Foreign Affairs Committee, *Special Study Mission I*, pp. 21–22.

34. Ballou interview.

35. Anthony Harrigan, "Inter-American Defense in the Seventies," *Military Review* 50 (April 1970): 3–10.

ture. To illustrate the point, he quoted Colonel David H. Hackworth, who had served five volunteer tours in Vietnam and collected two promotions and "a sackful of medals," as having said, "Well, now I'm going to study Latin American affairs. That's where its going next, because the bastards think they can win it all now. Yessir, Latin America COMUSMACL [Combined U.S. Military Advisory Command Latin America]. I guess I just like war."[36]

Irving Horowitz sees in the present situation

> . . . the breakdown of neo-colonialism and its replacement with imperial politics of more classic vintage. The present turn to counterinsurgency as a style of politics marks a return to military solutions to economic problems, rather than economic solutions to military problems. . . . What has taken place in increasing degrees is the external or foreign management of internal conflicts in Latin America.[37]

It has been argued that the geographical expansion of its base of operations is viewed by the U.S. military establishment as an institutional imperative, an imperative made even more salient by competition among the services. And we have seen that just as the assumption of governmental power is in the collective and individual interest of the Brazilian military elite, the control of the Brazilian government by the Brazilian military is likewise in the collective and individual interest of U.S. military officers who make and/or implement policy toward Brazil. It is not surprising, then, that those U.S. officers applauded both the coup of 1964 and the supercoup of 1968.

It appears that the combination of the material interests of the U.S. business community in Latin America and the institutional interests of the U.S. military in the area is so powerful that, even in the face of detente (the virtual elimination of the original rationale for the internal security focus), U.S. military penetration and political reinforcement of local military elites will increase rather than wither if the U.S. military has its way.

36. King, *The Death of the Army*, p. 222.

37. Irving L. Horowitz, "The Military Elites," *Elites in Latin America*, ed. Seymour M. Lipset and Aldo Solari (New York: Oxford University Press, 1967).

Part IV:

Security for Whom?

Introduction

We have seen in previous chapters that in the early 1960s many U.S. policy-makers felt that Brazilian national security—and, by extension, hemispheric security and U.S. national security—were threatened by social unrest and political mobilization in Brazil. In this view, the coup of 1964 and the institutionalization of military rule were seen as victories for security.

It has been noted that "security" is a flexible concept. If it is to be viewed as "survival," it is a rather far-fetched argument that the security of the United States was threatened by developments in Brazil in the early 1960s. If security is to be viewed as "freedom from fear," then it must be asked, "whose fear of what?" For the U.S. businessman with overseas investments, the answer is generally obvious: freedom from fear of nationalization or of unacceptable limits on his ability to earn a profit. But what of the Brazilian worker who owns nothing? Has he no security interests?

In the chapters that follow we attempt to strip away the rhetorical clothing of the security issue and focus upon the balance sheet, as it affects real people and institutions here and now rather than hypothetical future wars. That is, we will examine some of the gains and losses flowing in part from the U.S. taxpayers' investment in a "secure" Brazil.

[14]

Beneficiaries and Victims of the Penetrative Process

Since the beginnings of World War II, Brazil has received more U.S. assistance, both military and economic, than any other Latin American country. That would not be true, of course, on a per capita basis, but since aid is not extended directly to 100 million individuals, per capita calculations merely obfuscate the impact of such aid on internal power balances and consequent allocations of values. In any poor or dependent country the circle of those whose power positions are directly enhanced by aid to central governments, military establishments, or individuals and groups selected as beneficiaries by the donor country is relatively small. This assistance, and particularly the massive transfer of public capital that has taken place since 1964, has consistently been justified by its architects and advocates in terms of the overriding considerations of security. It is reasonable, then, to ask just whose security has been and is being served. Exact figures as to who is getting what vary considerably, but the trends indicated, regardless of source, are consistent.

A report of the Government Operations Committee of the U.S. House of Representatives in 1968 was highly critical of AID operations in Brazil, citing specifically failures in housing, education, and agrarian reform, vagueness in regard to priorities, a reluctance to audit, and AID funding of the importation of luxury items.[1] Nevertheless, AID proposals for fiscal year 1971 included $155 million in development loans and $12.7 million in technical assistance for Brazil, far more in each

1. U.S., Congress, House, Committee on Government Operations, *U.S. AID Operations in Latin America under the Alliance for Progress: Thirty-Sixth Report*, no. 1849, 90th Cong., 2d sess., 5 August 1968.

category than for any other Latin American country. In technical assistance (which includes the Public Safety Program), for example, the nearest competitor was Guatemala, for which $3.65 million was proposed.[2] The amount proposed in development loans for Brazil constituted almost one-third of the amount proposed for all Latin America, including regional programs.[3]

The Payoff for Foreign Investors

In the 1971 hearings on U.S. Policies and Programs in Brazil, Senator Church expressed the opinion that U.S. programs in Brazil had not been particularly effective in accomplishing any of their stated aims, except in providing a favorable climate for U.S. investment.[4] In that area, however, they had been extremely successful. By the end of 1972, U.S. private investment in Brazil amounted to about $2.4 billion.[5] U.S. corporations generally expect their profits from overseas ventures to be at least twice as great as profits from domestic ventures, and in Brazil they apparently have not been disappointed. U.S. investment in Brazil increased by 71 percent, $680 million, over the decade of the 1960s. Most of this increase (91 percent) was financed by reinvested earnings rather than new investments. Meanwhile, profits remitted to the U.S. increased from five million dollars in 1964 to 75 million dollars in 1968, and the average return on all U.S. investment ranged from a low of 5.7 percent in 1963 to a high of 10.7 percent in 1968.[6]

Actual earnings cannot be calculated with much precision, as the companies involved naturally report such things in the manner most advantageous to them, and there are countless gimmicks for overestimating costs and underestimating profits. Investment capital is not always registered, and companies organized as "limitados" (limited liability corporations), as much of the Hanna Mining Company's equity is, are not required in Brazil to publish profits. Furthermore, many entities actually owned wholly or predominantly by Americans are registered elsewhere. The Brascan conglomerate, for example, the largest foreign corporation in Brazil, is registered as Canadian, but 35 percent of its shares—more than those owned in any other single country—are held

2. AID, *U.S. Foreign Aid and the Alliance for Progress.*

3. U.S., Congress, House, Committee on Appropriations, *Foreign Assistance and Related Programs Appropriation Bill, 1971,* Report no. 91–1134, 91st Cong., 2d sess., 1 June 1970.

4. Griffin, "Senator Church Assails . . .," *Washington Post,* 25 July 1971.

5. Rowe interview.

6. Church Hearings, p. 215.

in the United States. And an Amazonian estate the size of Holland, owned by U.S. shipping billionaire Daniel Ludwig, is listed as Liberian.

It appears, however, from the 1969 study by the Fundacão Getúlio Vargas, that those U.S. companies with investments of more than $5 million tended to show profits much higher than the Commerce Department's averages for the decade. Exxon, for example, with a registered equity of $95 million, reported a profit of 15.7 percent that year. Johnson and Johnson reported 16 percent; General Motors and RCA, 20 percent; Squibb, 20.5 percent; Anderson Clayton, 21 percent; Union Carbide, 21.8 percent; General Electric, 22.6 percent; Goodyear and Atlantic Richfield, 23 percent; Texaco, 28 percent; and Xerox, 64 percent.[7]

For the decade of the 1960s profits repatriated to the United States exceeded new capital invested by close to $100 million. Direct new investment from 1965 through 1967 was much lower than in 1961 and the outflow of earnings and dividends for that period exceeded all new foreign investment by about $140 million. To that outflow must be added payments for technical assistance, patents, royalties, and the like, which amounted to $170 million in 1967 alone, and interest and amortization payments which amounted to an outflow of $500 million in 1968. Tied loans meant higher prices for imported goods and some $110 million in 1967 to foreign companies for freight and insurance. In addition to these drains, the Central Bank estimates that $300 million left Brazil in 1966 and 1967 through illegal remittances.[8] By the end of 1972 Brazil's foreign debt stood at $7 to $10 billion, and the country had become the World Bank's biggest borrower.[9]

Far more wealth apparently left Brazil in the late 1960s than entered it. One analyst concluded, for example, that about 70 percent of the income generated by exports went in various ways to the service of foreign capital. The economic dynamism—money changing hands—recorded in the "miraculous" GNP growth rates (7 to 9 percent in the late 1960s, rising to 10 to 11 percent in the early 1970s) is a reflection of the acceleration of the denationalization of Brazilian industry.[10] By 1970, according to the Rio de Janeiro daily newspaper, *Jornal do Brasil*, in the private sector, foreign enterprise controlled 72 percent of capital

7. Rowe interview.

8. Galeano, "De-Nationalization of Brazilian Industry," pp. 11–30.

9. Dan Griffin, "The Boom in Brazil: An Awful Lot of Everything," *Washington Post*, 27 May 1973. By early 1974 the foreign debt was up to about $13 billion.

10. Galeano, "De-Nationalization of Brazilian Industry."

goods, 78 percent of durable consumer goods, and 52 percent of nondurable consumer goods. Data released by the Brazilian government was cited by Schilling to show that foreign capital controlled 70.2 percent of the country's 679 largest businesses.[11]

Prospects for the foreign companies in the 1970s looked even better. The Central Bank registered $2 billion in foreign investments in 1970, of which $867 million was registered by U.S. investors.[12] A survey conducted by *Business Latin America* of fifty-two leading publicly traded companies, thirty-five of which have some foreign ownership, showed that in fiscal year 1971 profits soared 64 percent over the previous year and return on net worth averaged 16 percent. This average aggregate return on investment, the highest ever recorded in a *Business Latin America* survey, came during a year when these companies increased their net worth by an average of 28 percent.

Profits in the automobile industry, 100 percent foreign-owned, increased by 128 percent. General Motors profits, for example, increased 96.9 percent to a 31.5 percent return on investment. In tire production, also 100 percent foreign-owned, the increase was an even more dramatic 300 percent for an average return of 30 percent. Firestone increased its profits by 608.8 percent to a return of 49.7 percent, and Goodyear had a 113.9 percent increase to a 37.2 percent return.[13]

We have seen that these prosperous companies have shown their gratitude for advantageous policies in the past or their hopes for a continuation of such advantageous policies by hiring retired Brazilian military officers. When these same multinational corporations have hired retired U.S. officers it has generally been explained in terms of defense contracts, but in many cases it might just as easily be seen as a recognition of the contacts, and thus influence on economic policy, which these officers exercise with the governing elites in much of the Third World.

The volume of U.S. investment in Brazil has continued to grow, reaching about $3.5 billion by early 1976.[14] The proportion of Brazilian industry controlled by U.S. investors has dropped relative to both the

11. MacEoin, *Revolution Next Door*, pp. 105, 189; Schilling, "Brazil: The Rebellion of the Downtrodden."

12. Joseph Novitski, "Brazil's Neighbors Watch Warily as the Sleeping Giant Stirs," *New York Times*, 21 March 1971, p. A–2.

13. "Profitability in Brazil Looms High as Companies Continue to Cash in on Boom," *Business Latin America*, 7 December 1972, pp. 385–86.

14. Information given by State Department representative at the Seminar on Brazil, organized by the Bureau of Inter-American Affairs of the U.S. Department of State. Washington, D.C., 19–20 January 1976.

shares controlled by multinational corporations based elsewhere and the portion controlled by the Brazilian government. Thus, Brazil's dependency has been to some extent diversified and the government has enhanced its ability to regulate the activities of foreign investors. Nevertheless, approximately one-half of the country's industry remains under foreign control. The three industries—transportation, chemicals, and machinery—most strongly dominated by U.S. investors account for more than two-thirds of sales in manufacturing. Multinational corporations have continued to expand their holdings at the expense of independent Brazilian entrepreneurs, and the trend toward oligopolistic control of markets has accelerated.[15]

The high cost of imported oil caused an economic setback in 1974–1975, and the issue of denationalization continued to be a live one. Representatives of sixty-five foreign and multinational firms who met in Brasilia in June 1975 complained about all constraints on their freedom of action and expressed "strong corporate dislike" of the policy of political decompression. In October 1975 President Geisel announced that PETROBRAS would enter into contracts with foreign oil companies for the exploration and development of offshore oilfields. It was reported in May 1976 that Brazil's Minister of Mining and Energy, Shigeaki Ueki, said, "My dream is to see Petrobras shares quoted on the New York stock exchange." And there were published rumors of pressure to sell the large state-controlled companies to foreign groups as a means of paying the foreign debt.[16]

Former congressman Marcio Moreira Alves remarks upon the humiliation suffered, even by those fortunate enough to be consumers, from foreign domination of the economy:

> Everything we consume in our daily lives betrays a foreign presence. We are bandaged at birth by Johnson & Johnson. We survive on Nestle or Gloria Milk. We dress in synthetic clothes produced by French, British, or American firms. Our teeth are kept clean by Colgate toothpaste and Tek brushes. We wash with Lever Brothers' and Palmolive soaps, shave with Williams and Gillette. Resting in the sun we drink Coca-Cola—and now even the largest producer of *cachaca*, the white rum national drink, is owned by Coca-Cola. We ride Otis elevators, drive Volkswagens and Fords and ship our goods on Mercedes-Benz trucks fueled by Esso and

15. U.S., Congress, Senate, Committee on Foreign Relations, Subcommittee on Multinational Corporations, *The Multinational Corporations in Brazil and Mexico: Structural Sources of Economic and Non-Economic Power*, a report by Richard S. Newfarmer and Willard S. Müller, 94th Cong., 1st sess., August 1975, pp. 95–145.

16. Robert M. Levine, "Brazil: The Aftermath of 'Decompression,' " *Current History* 70 (February 1976): 53–56, 81; *Latin America* [London], 28 May 1976.

Shell, our rubber is Pirelli, we talk with Ericsson telephones, communicate through Siemens telex, type on Olivetti machines and receive IBM-processed bills. We eat out of American and Canadian made cans packed by Armour, Swift, and Wilson. The Beatles' beat comes out of Phillips radios, and we dance to RCA records. Our General Electric TV sets are connected to ITT satellites. We can rely on old Bayer for aspirin, or, if trouble develops, on Squibb for antibiotics. From the comfortable Goodyear mattresses of our American hospital beds we can look through Saint-Gobain windows on gardens tended by Japanese lawnmowers. If we die (say, from lung cancer puffed from British or American cigarettes) we may finally have a chance of entering into our 94 percent share of the economy—graveyards are owned by the Santa Casas de Misericórdia, an old Brazilian institution. But the family must pay the electricity bills to Canadian Light and Power—with money manufactured by Thomas de la Rue or by the American Bank Note Company.[17]

The Plight of Brazilians

President Médici commented in 1970, "The economy is doing fine, but the people aren't."[18] Statistics from virtually all sources tended to bear him out. They reveal that the income of the majority had dropped relatively and that that of an indeterminate but substantial proportion of the population had dropped absolutely as well. The Brazilian government's own compilations, as cited by fourteen bishops and archbishops of the Northeast, show that the top one percent of the population increased its share of the national income from 12 to 17 percent between 1960 and 1970, while the share of the 50 million Brazilians at the lower end of the scale dropped from 17.6 to 13.7 percent.[19] Calculations by various scholars demonstrate this great disparity in income distribution: the poorest 80 percent received only about 27.5 percent of the national income in 1970, compared to 35 percent in 1960, while the richest five percent increased its share from 44 to 50 percent;[20] every decile of the population except the top one experienced a relative loss of income during that period;[21] and the 45 million at the bottom of the heap had the same total income at the end of the decade as 900,000 at the top.[22] The Gini coefficient of inequality in Brazil's income distribution rose from a modest .488 in 1960 to .574,

17. Marcio Moreira Alves, *A Grain of Mustard Seed: The Awakening of the Brazilian Revolution* (New York: Doubleday, 1973), pp. 164–65.

18. Griffin, "The Boom in Brazil."

19. Leonard Greenwood, "Brazil Bishops Rap 'Economic Miracle,'" *Washington Post*, 27 May 1973.

20. Burns, "Brazil: The Imitative Society," pp. 17–20.

21. Albert Fishlow, "Brazil's Economic Miracle," *The World Today* 29 (November 1973): 474–94.

22. Furtado, cited in Galeano, "De-Nationalization of Brazilian Industry."

the highest ever recorded at the national level in Latin America, in 1970.[23]

Nor was the federal tax system, modernized with the assistance of the U.S. Internal Revenue Service, designed to reverse this trend. Receipts from income taxes decreased from 30 percent to 26 percent of total federal tax receipts between 1961 and 1969.[24] In 1971 the more regressive indirect taxes provided 63.2 percent of central government revenues.[25]

Furthermore, regional imbalance, exacerbated by government policies, is such that some have envisioned a future Brazil resembling a little Japan surrounded by a vast India. Regional redistribution of wealth was one of the avowed purposes of the military government's value-added tax. The claim was, however, that the redistribution would be from the richer to the poorer states; the effect has been the reverse. In 1973 São Paulo, which produces 35 percent of the GNP, collected 47 percent of the nation's total value-added tax for its own use, while northeastern states such as Ceara, which have to "import" manufactured goods from São Paulo, ran into severe deficit on the tax.[26]

The government's own cost-of-living estimates indicate that the percentage of total income spent on food for the country as a whole rose from 40.3 to 41.2 between 1964 and 1970, while the per capita consumption of meat dropped from 41 kilos in 1961 to 39 kilos in 1967.[27] A nutrition study of a sample group of rural workers in the Northeast revealed that they were consuming fewer calories in 1968 than in 1962.[28] The Northeast Bishops reported that three-fourths of the five million homes in that area had no light, water, or sewage systems. They also noted that almost one child in five is stillborn and that half of the babies born in the Northeast die before the age of five.[29] For the country as a whole, it is estimated that 43 percent of the deaths of children under four years of age are from malnutrition.[30]

Although the economic boom had exaggerated the already enormous "developmental" gap (or structure of internal colonialism) between the

23. Philippe C. Schmitter, "The 'Portugalization' of Brazil?" in Stepan, ed. *Authoritarian Brazil*, ch. 6.

24. Church Hearings, p. 238.

25. Schmitter, "The 'Portugalization' of Brazil?"

26. "Brazil: Unto Him That Hath, Much Shall Be Given," *Latin America* 8 (1 March 1974): 71.

27. Schmitter, "The 'Portugalization' of Brazil?"

28. Page, *The Revolution That Never Was*, p. 230.

29. Greenwood, "Brazil Bishops."

30. *Latin America*, 14 April 1972.

center South and the rest of the country, the majority of the citizens in the booming cities have not fared so well either. In São Paulo, for example, infant mortality has continued to rise, reaching 80 deaths per 1,000 live births in 1972. Almost one-half of the people of São Paulo live in substandard housing; 35 percent lack running water and 60 percent lack sewage systems. Per capita monthly income for about half of the Paulistas is $35 or less. Meanwhile, the booming cities have seen a massive increase in such status symbols as pollution and street crime. The incidence of robberies and assaults in São Paulo more than tripled between 1968 and 1971.[31]

Public health care, always sorely inadequate, has seriously deteriorated in recent years. Even though it is estimated that half of the population is infected with tuberculosis, and the mortality rate from that disease is the highest in the hemisphere, government expenditure on public health fell by 30 percent in real terms between 1967 and 1971.[32] The proportion of the federal budget allocated to the Ministry of Health declined from 4.29 percent in 1966 to 0.99 percent in 1974, leaving the ministry ill-equipped to combat the epidemic of meningitis that reportedly infected some twenty-seven thousand persons and took about three thousand lives in 1974.[33]

The military government has claimed great progress in housing construction, but priority has been given to middle-class housing. As for housing for the very poor, the government points with pride to the fact that, with U.S. assistance, it has virtually eradicated the unsightly *favelas* that used to dot the hills overlooking Rio de Janeiro. Transferring the *favelados* from their make-shift communities to the new complexes, Vila Aliança and Vila Kennedy, built some 30 miles inland from Rio de Janeiro with AID funds, proved to be no easy matter. Community leaders were incarcerated prior to the transfer, and many others had to be handcuffed for the move to their new homes. General Seitz, former commander of the U.S. delegation to the JBUSMC, attributed this reaction to the long hours and costs of commuting and to the general inertia of the poor in developing countries, but there are other possibilities.[34] This author visited some of the *favelas* in 1964 and thought at the time that, in spite of the general deprivation in which these Brazilians lived, they had something money couldn't buy, one of

31. Brady Tyson, "Brazil: Nine Years of Military Tutelage," *Worldview* 16 (July 1973): 29–34.

32. *Latin America*, 14 April 1972.

33. Fred B. Morris, "The Human Dimension of the Brazilian Economic Miracle," manuscript, February 1975, Washington, D.C.

34. Seitz interview.

the most fabulous views in the world—the sweep of the harbor of Rio de Janeiro. That view is now being enjoyed by the occupants of luxury hotels and high-rise apartment buildings.

The area in which social progress under the military regime has been most "demonstrable" has been education. Reported increases in school enrollment have indeed been impressive, especially at the level of higher education, where enrollment has increased by 460 percent since 1964.[35] However, as a consequence of administrative and curriculum changes, the depletion of the country's best creative and scholarly minds through job dismissals, imprisonment and exile, and the generally stifling repression of free expression, it appears that what is being billed as education is more akin to a combination of indoctrination and technical and managerial training, stripped of overt debate on socioeconomic and political issues.

U.S. assistance earmarked for education in Brazil had amounted to $187.1 million between 1965 and 1972. The General Accounting Office, in a Report to Congress dated 30 July 1973, recommended that such aid be discontinued, on the grounds that "U.S. education assistance has directly and indirectly supported Brazil's education development objectives, which are not designed to improve inequities in Brazil's education system." The report went on to state that the decisions of both AID and the Brazilian government represented "an education policy based solely on economic considerations and not on a more equitable distribution of education opportunities within a developing nation."[36]

As for the creative arts, even the most subtle suggestion of social criticism in a folk song has on occasion landed its composers and performers in jail. The São Paulo bicentennial of the arts, prestigious throughout the world in the early 1960s, has become a nonevent, and a critic of Brazilian literature noted that while the quantity of publications in the late 1960s was impressive, the quality of these works was the most disappointing he had seen in his twenty years of experience in that field.[37] Meanwhile, E. Bradford Burns has noted that the intellectual sterility of the work by Brazilians available to Brazilians has enabled foreign culture to dominate.[38] More than 70 percent of all Bra-

---

35. Tyson, "Brazil: Nine Years of Military Tutelage."

36. Morris, "The Human Dimension."

37. Ralph E. Dimmick and Benjamin M. Woodbridge, Jr., "Brazilian Literature," *Handbook of Latin American Studies: Humanities 34*, ed. Donald E. J. Steward (Gainesville: University of Florida Press, 1972), pp. 535–52.

38. Burns, "Brazil: The Imitative Society."

zilian television programs, for example, in the early 1970s, were reruns of U.S. programs, dubbed in Portuguese.[39]

The group that has suffered the greatest loss of status and income since 1964 has been urban labor. While strikes have been defined as political crimes, subject to the death penalty, the real minimum salary by 1970 had dropped by 30 to 38 percent below that of 1960.[40] And the 1970 census showed that more than 60 percent of the population earned less than the minimum wage. A survey conducted in São Paulo indicated that the worker earning the minimum wage had to work more than twice as long in 1974 as in 1966 to purchase the same staple commodities.[41]

Capital intensive industry has done little to expand employment, and in many cases new technology has eliminated jobs. A survey of four of the technically most advanced (and foreign-penetrated) sectors indicated that while productivity increased by 128.5 percent between 1955 and 1966, wages paid to workers increased by only 6.1 percent in real value in that period.[42] Between 1940 and 1970 the percentage of men over the age of fourteen who were employed had dropped from 50.8 to 44.8. In Recife, with a population of 1,100,000, 20 percent of the labor force was listed as unemployed in 1971 and another 35 percent was listed as underemployed.[43]

Furthermore, the fact that economic growth is being promoted through the expansion of exports rather than through expansion of the internal market has led many to believe that the poor have simply been written off. Celso Furtado, among others, has maintained that income concentration is being promoted deliberately, in order to benefit the producers (largely the multinational corporations) and consumers (upper and middle classes) of durable consumers' goods, and to accelerate the GNP growth rate.[44]

Jean Marc von der Weid, former president of the UNE, said that one of the most discouraging things he discovered in conversation with workers and peasants who shared prison cells with him was the "individualization of deprivation."[45] Massive propaganda had convinced

39. Morris, "The Human Dimension."

40. Tyson, "Brazil: Nine Years of Military Tutelage." Some estimates are even more alarming. Schmitter suggests that worker purchasing power in the major industrial centers declined by 64 percent between 1958 and 1970.

41. Morris, "The Human Dimension."

42. Galeano, "De-Nationalization of Brazilian Industry."

43. Morris, "The Human Dimension."

44. Ibid.

45. Von der Weid interview.

these Brazilians that the country was enjoying great prosperity and that they were isolated in their poverty.

Testifying in Senate Hearings in 1971, William A. Ellis, director of the U.S. AID mission in Brazil, accredited the "improvement" in the economy in part to the flexibility and creativity afforded to the government's U.S.-trained economists.[46] He subsequently noted that the Finance Minister could now do by decree things that had previously had to go through Congress. The Congress, as then constituted, however, proved to be no problem. In 1971 it approved 100 percent of the bills introduced by the executive branch.[47]

By the early 1970s, the civilian political process had been reduced to a cynical charade. The two official parties were being referred to in private as the parties of "sim" and "sim senhor" ("yes" and "yes, Sir"). The government had been fastidious in its attempt to maintain a facade of constitutional government without allowing a critic to slip through its sieve. The new electoral code required that candidates be approved by both an electoral tribunal and the government's intelligence apparatus. Furthermore, Institutional Act No. 5, still in effect, gave the president the "right" to suspend the political rights of any citizen, to decree a congressional recess, and to cancel any electoral terms of office at any level—federal, state, or municipal—of government. Direct elections for president, state governors, and mayors of state capitals and dozens of cities along the border with neighboring states had been abolished in favor of indirect election or appointment. In fact, most major cities had been declared zones of national security in which no elections of any kind were allowed.

Meanwhile, the majority of the "electorate" has clearly indicated that it recognizes the process for what it is. Voting remained compulsory for literates and those who refused to participate were subject to severe penalties. Therefore, in the elections of 15 November 1972 voter turnout was higher than it had ever been before, but blank or nullified ballots outnumbered legitimate ones.[48] This produced some interesting electoral results. For example, in the city of São Sebastião de Lagoa de Roca, in Paraiba, an ARENA candidate ran without opposition and "lost"; that is, there were more blank or nullified ballots than votes for the sole candidate. In various cities a significant number of votes were cast for "Sujismundo," a government-created cartoon character push-

46. Church Hearings, p. 172.

47. *Veja*, 25 October 1972, cited in *Brazilian Information Bulletin*, no. 9 (January 1973), p. 14.

48. Schmitter lecture.

ing a nationwide cleanliness campaign, for a reputed international Mafia figure who had been arrested in Brazil, and for "onca" (wildcat), a term widely used in colloquial speech as a symbol of arrogance and falsity. And in Salvador, in the state of Bahia, a wildcat named Peteleca, which had just escaped from the local zoo, polled more than five thousand votes, beating the candidates of both government and "opposition" parties. Peteleca's fate was not unlike that of previous popular choices—eight days after it won the election, it was captured and killed by the state police.[49]

Ambassador William M. Rountree testified in the Senate hearings of 1971 that the official count of those deprived of their political rights since 1964 was 1,200. While reporting that the Brazilian government only admitted to holding 500 political prisoners, who were common criminals anyway, he conceded that unofficial estimates ranged around 12,000. Some 2,000 Brazilians were said to be living in political exile.[50] Estimates on the number of political arrests since 1964 range from some 20,000 to more than 35,000, and estimates of death squad assassinations range from 200 or 300 to some 2,000. Brady Tyson wrote that it is estimated that some 2,000 prisoners have been physically abused and that between 40 and 120 have been beaten or tortured to death.[51] Furthermore, an indeterminant number of "leftists" have been officially reported killed by their own comrades, or in crossfire, or while trying to escape. And many more seem to have simply disappeared without a trace.

In 1974, Amnesty International published the names of 1,081 individuals whose ordeal of torture had been thoroughly documented, and another list of 210 persons whose imprisonment, torture, and disappearance or death at the hands of the Brazilian security forces had occurred since 1971 only. Fred Morris, a U.S. Methodist missionary and stringer for *Time* magazine, spent seventeen days in the torture chambers of the Fourth Army in Recife in 1974 and later reported that he personally knew of some thirty-five persons who had undergone torture in Recife in the past four years, none of whose names appeared on

49. *Miami Herald*, 18 November 1972; *Los Angeles Times*, 18 November 1972; *San Francisco Chronicle*, 25 November 1972; cited in *Brazilian Information Bulletin*, no. 9 (January 1973), p. 14.

50. Burns, "Brazil: The Imitative Society"; *Brazil Herald* [Rio de Janeiro and São Paulo], 19 April 1970, reported that Senator Edward Kennedy had estimated that there were some 1,800 such exiles.

51. Tyson, "Brazil: Nine Years of Military Tutelage." See also "Killing of 9 Criminals Laid to Brazil's 'Death Squad.' " *New York Times*, 28 November 1973.

the Amnesty International list of 1,081.[52] (Morris also said that three of his torturers, who referred to him as a "prisoner of war," told him that they had undergone military training in the United States.)

The numbers involved, by any estimate, seem small compared to the carnage in Chile since the coup of September 1973, but most observers of contemporary Brazil have come to the chilling conclusion that the selective use of torture (not only of "suspects" but of their relatives and friends as well) as a means of squelching dissent by implanting generalized terror, is highly effective. Aside from political office-holders and civil servants, repression has fallen most heavily on students and teachers, members of the clergy, labor leaders, writers, artists, scientists, lawyers, and other professionals. Most of the victims of torture have reportedly been in their twenties, but no age, sex, profession or class has been excluded. First-hand evidence indicates that victims have included children tortured in the presence of their mothers, women in late pregnancy, and elderly priests, nuns, and professors. And lawyers who have had the temerity to represent political prisoners have often found themselves subjected to the same abuses.

By the early 1970s the repression had given rise to a new generation of victims. In 1972, a 17-year-old political prisoner who had been par-ticipating in a hunger strike at the Tiradentes Prison in São Paulo was reportedly transferred to Belo Horizonte's Operação Bandeirantes and imprisoned in the same torture chamber where he had watched his father die at the hands of the torturers a year earlier.[53]

A young Brazilian, who preferred not to be named, told this author in 1975 that it was not until he had been politically sensitized through association with a small clandestine group at his university and had narrowly escaped arrest that his parents told him they had been active supporters of the Goulart government and opponents of the military regime in the 1960s. For his own protection and theirs, they had kept that information from him.

The military establishment as a whole has profited greatly from the generalized power of the institution, from the lucrative positions in government and private enterprise formerly held by civilians, and from a defense allocation that more than tripled in constant dollars between 1963 and 1973.[54] The three armed services received 19 percent of the

52. Morris, "The Human Dimension."

53. *Brazilian Information Bulletin*, no. 8 (October 1972), p. 1.

54. U.S. Arms Control and Disarmament Agency, *World Military Expendi-tures and Arms Trade, 1963–1973* (Washington: Government Printing Office, 1975), p. 23.

national budget in 1972, while the social welfare agencies, including health, education, pensions, and "land reform," received only 16 percent.[55] But the advantages accruing to the military have not included freedom of expression. The heavy surveillance experienced by many civilian sectors since the coup has recently moved into the military itself. Twenty percent of the field officers had been removed from their posts for ideological deviation by 1973, and in 1975 eleven army officers were arrested for "studying literature from the Portuguese Armed Forces Movement."[56]

Hemispheric Insecurity in the Seventies

And what of the security interests of the United States? Responding to the testimony of U.S. AID mission director William Ellis at the 1971 hearings, Senator Church said, "So we have pumped in $2 billion since 1964 to protect a favorable climate of investment that amounts to about $1.6 billion."[57] Senator Church found it hard to understand how the exportation of U.S. public and private capital—and thus to some extent the jobs of U.S. workers—and the further enrichment of the big corporations served the interests of the U.S. taxpayers. As for considerations of global military and political strategies, the military government, for its own reasons, can be counted upon to continue to take a hard line against insurgency anywhere in the hemisphere; but on matters such as territorial waters or the nonproliferation of nuclear weapons the United States retains little leverage. Having identified itself so intimately with a repressive regime, the U.S. government is virtually bound to continue to support it, as any popular government that might replace it would almost surely be vehemently anti-American.

By the mid-1970s, Brazil's posture of militant anti-communism had been largely confined to internal affairs and to relations with neighboring states. Its relations with most countries beyond the Western Hemisphere were conditioned primarily by the pragmatic considerations of attracting foreign capital, expanding exports, and securing external sources of energy. And the country was defying both superpowers in its insistence on developing its own nuclear power capabilities. Consciously striving for major power status, Brazil opposed any international accord that tended to freeze the contemporary global configuration of power.

55. "Brazil's New Budget," *Business Latin America*, 7 September 1972, pp. 283–84.

56. Stepan, "New Professionalism," p. 64; Levine, "Brazil: The Aftermath of 'Decompression.' "

57. Church Hearings, p. 165.

When the United States and the Soviet Union, at the Geneva disarmament conference in October 1969, reached agreement on a draft treaty barring nuclear weapons from the ocean floor, Brazil was the most outspoken critic. Planning Minister João Paulo dos Reis Velloso, addressing the Superior War College in 1970, stressed Brazil's determination not to permit the developed nations to transform themselves into a closed club "on the pretext of pollution and disarmament." And a senior diplomat and former foreign minister, speaking at the Brazilian Embassy in Washington, D.C., in 1972, accused the superpowers of attempting to "institutionalize the inequality between nations." The Military Engineering Institute announced in early 1974 that its nuclear reactor would become operational before the end of the year. It was estimated at that time that by 1980 Brazil would have the capability to build and arm intermediate-range ballistic missiles.[58] In 1975 Brazil's nuclear power agency, NUCLEBRAS, entered into a $4.5 billion agreement with a West German firm for the construction of eight nuclear reactors. The agreement, which carried few of the controls urged by the United States, includes the provision of the technology and facilities for the production of plutonium, necessary for the production of nuclear weapons.[59]

The informal triangular alliance of the South Atlantic (Brazil, Portugal, and the Union of South Africa) which had been an important feature of geopolitical strategy in the early years of military rule, had been rendered obsolete by the energy crisis of 1973 and by the overthrow of Portugal's half-century-old authoritarian regime in April 1974. Brazil adopted the Arab stance on the recovery of occupied territories from Israel, condemned "Zionism" at the U.N., and began to expand diplomatic and commercial ties rapidly with Middle Eastern and African states. It also established diplomatic and commercial relations with the People's Republic of China. And, during the Angolan civil war of 1975–1976, Brazil recognized the ultimately successful Popular Movement for the Liberation of Angola (MPLA) while the United States was supporting MPLA's armed adversaries.

Brazil's bilateral relations with the Latin American states generally

58. Norman A. Bailey and Ronald M. Schneider, "Brazil's Foreign Policy: A Case Study in Upward Mobility," *Inter-American Economic Affairs* 27 (Spring 1974): 3–25; see also Roger W. Fontaine, "The Emergence of Brazil's Foreign Policy" (manuscript prepared for the American Enterprise Institute, Washington, D.C., 1974).

59. Riordan Roett, "Brazil Ascendant: International Relations and Geopolitics in the Late 20th Century," *Journal of International Affairs* 29 (Fall 1975): 139–54.

paralleled those of the United States in both means and objectives. By 1974 Brazil had extended loans, tied to the purchase of Brazilian products, to most of the Latin American countries. It had also extended technical assistance in various forms and had engaged in joint ventures with most of its neighbors for the development of transportation and communication networks and hydroelectric power facilities. Exports to the other Latin American states were growing at the rate of U.S. $50 million annually, and Brazilian capital was being invested in neighboring states to secure a steady flow of the raw materials needed for its booming industries.[60]

Brazil was obtaining oil and gas from Bolivia, and the two countries were cooperating in the exploitation of Bolivia's enormous Mutun iron ore deposits. BRASPETRO, the external arm of PETROBRAS, had reached agreement with Venezuela's state oil monopoly for joint exploration and exploitation of abandoned fields and offshore drilling, and with Tenneco's Colombian subsidiary for joint exploration and the construction of a refinery. Brazil had also arranged to join Colombia in the development of the latter's coal deposits. With Paraguay, Brazil was building a U.S. $3 billion hydroelectric power facility which will be South America's largest, and talks were underway with Ecuador for the joint exploitation of Ecuadorean oil.[61]

The military government, commanding by far the largest and best-equipped armed forces in Latin America, had cultivated close ties with the military establishments in neighboring countries. It had cooperated with them in campaigns against insurgent movements assumed to be transnational and had extended military assistance in the forms of both equipment and training.

The development of the Amazon Basin, particularly of the Trans-amazon and peripheral highway systems, is an important aspect of Brazil's geopolitical strategy for the continent. The nation's policy-makers have long feared population spillover from neighboring countries, and, more recently, the military government has seen the vast undeveloped basin as a potential haven for national or transnational guerrilla groups. In 1973 Colonel Camara Sena, superintendent of the Amazon development agency, warned of the danger of "moral pollution" arising from the "chaotic conditions" of neighboring countries.[62]

In recent years population spillover has actually been in the opposite

60. Bailey and Schneider, "Brazil's Foreign Policy"; and *Washington Post*, 31 March 1974.

61. Ibid., and U.S. *Joint Publications Research Service*, 26 March 1974.

62. U.S., *Joint Publications Research Service*, 10 December 1973.

direction, and that, plus the increasing frequency of military maneuvers in border areas, has caused unease among all neighbors. Brazilian settlers have been overflowing the country's borders and purchasing large tracts of land, especially in Uruguay, Paraguay, and
Bolivia. It is estimated, for example, that Brazilians own 30 percent of
the land in four border provinces of Uruguay, that there are more Brazilians than Bolivians living in the Bolivian department of Pando, and
that some forty thousand Brazilian families have settled on the
Paraguayan side of the Parana River. In February 1976, Brazilian
deputy Pedro Lauro, proposed the annexation of Paraguay to Brazil.

The Venezuelan government had decided to move some three thousand settlers into its Amazon region to counteract exploitation by
foreigners. Several members of the Venezuelan Congress have alleged
that Brazil is attempting to establish a "continental hegemony," and in
January 1974 the Caracas evening paper, *El Mundo*, claimed to have
discovered a secret Brazilian plan to invade neighboring countries if
any of their governments go communist.[63]

Although the concept of "ideological frontiers," to which Brazil's
military leaders have made frequent reference since 1964, has had little
practical application beyond the Western Hemisphere, it has been
highly significant in Brazil's relations with its neighbors. The government has taken the position that leftist governments or movements
anywhere in the continent constitute a potential threat to national security. It has considered the maintenance of friendly governments in
the buffer states of the River Plate Basin essential, and it was particularly alarmed by the radicalism of the government of Juan José Torres in
Bolivia in 1970–1971 and by the strength of the leftist Frente Amplio
(Broad Front) that emerged in Uruguay about the same time. Although
Chile does not border on Brazil, the government of Salvador Allende
was also seen as threatening to Brazilian security, as it had offered
asylum to political refugees from other Latin American states. Brazilian complicity was alleged in the military coups d'état in Bolivia in
1971, Uruguay in 1972, and Chile in 1973. Brazil extended immediate
recognition and emergency assistance to the new military regimes;
their presidents were the only heads of state in attendance at the
inauguration of President Geisel in March 1974.[64]

By the mid-1970s it was clear that the regime the United States had
nurtured was by no means an all-purpose ally. Nor was the ruling elite

63. Bailey and Schneider, "Brazil's Foreign Policy"; see also *Washington
Post*, 31 March 1974; and *Latin America*, 25 January and 22 March 1974, and 7
May 1976.

64. *Washington Post*, 21 March 1971, and 6 January 1974.

highly susceptible to U.S. pressures to assume positions that were not in keeping with its own ambitions.

Thus far, Brazilian hegemony over its South American neighbors appears to have been exercised with the full support of the United States. And Secretary of State Henry Kissinger reinforced that general perception in 1976 when he publicly pledged to consult with Brazil on foreign policy initiatives contemplated by the United States.[65] It is at least conceivable, however, that at some point in the not too distant future, Brazil's hegemonic role might be seen as competitive with or contrary to the interests of the United States. And if a future president of the United States should decide that he (or she) were serious about urging respect for human rights and economic justice in Brazil (as elsewhere in Latin America), there is no reason to believe that the president would have the unqualified support of even the foreign policy arms of his own government, much less the U.S. overseas business community, in attempting to exert influence in that direction.

The term "security" at its most extravagant reaches must surely relate to an individual or collective state of mind. That being the case, evidence in the form of defense expenditures, arms peddling, and the like suggests that the United States continues to be among the least secure countries in the world. In an inadvertent "admission against interest" in his 1971 State of the World Message, President Nixon warned that "the difficulties facing U.S. policy [in Latin America] will grow rather than diminish as the decade unfolds."[66]

As for the ruling clique in Brazil, continued waves of political arrests indicate that it still does not feel secure. In August 1972, *O Estado de São Paulo*, in a marked departure from the caution generally displayed by all of the information media, questioned why the frequency of arbitrary arrests should be even greater at that time than at the height of the incidence of political kidnappings and other such revolutionary acts.

By 1976, the hopes that had been aroused by President Geisel's promises of political "decompression" and by the electoral victory of the MDB in the November 1974 congressional elections had been

65. Brazilian political scientist Fernando Henrique Cardoso has suggested that this mutual consultation pledge was prompted by Kissinger's pique that Brazil had been formulating some of its policies without consulting the United States or over U.S. opposition. But this author is inclined to take Kissinger's pledge at face value. After all, he needs to consult with someone about U.S. foreign policy and there are obviously few in the U.S. with whom he cares to consult!

66. Richard Nixon, *A Report to the Congress: U.S. Foreign Policy for the 1970s: Building for Peace*, 25 February 1971.

soundly dashed. Waves of arrests through the last half of 1975 had been provoked in particular by the military command's fears of internal subversion on the Portuguese model and by actual or anticipated criticism of economic policies. The death, apparently by torture, of noted professor and journalist Vladimir Herzog, one of at least two hundred persons arrested in São Paulo during the week of 15 October, unleashed the largest spontaneous protest demonstration the country had seen since the "revolution."[67] This, in turn, provoked the closing of universities, the removal of elected officials, and exhortations to armed forces' unity.

At the level of the unavoidable minimum definition of security—survival—it appears that the individual U.S. citizen in Latin America is less secure than ever. The rioting provoked by the Rockefeller tour, the kidnapping of Elbrick, and the killing of Dan Mitrione are among the cases in point. And those U.S. citizens who are not likely targets for insurgents are suspect to the U.S.-backed military governments. Professor Joe Page, for example, was arrested in Recife shortly after the 1964 coup. The cases of three U.S. scholars, two priests, two freelance photographers, and one girl with dual citizenship, all of whom had been arrested by Brazilian authorities since 1968 and in some cases "treated roughly," were discussed in the Senate hearings in 1971. It is alleged by a former Peace Corps evaluator (and denied by the State Department) that a Volunteer was arrested in the late 1960s and charged with subversive activities. (Fortunately for the Volunteer, who had just recently arrived, his Portuguese was so poor that interrogation proved exasperating to the police, and he was released and allowed to leave the country.)[68] Many additional cases appeared in the press in the early 1970s, including the arrest in 1973 on charges of subversion of the Brazilian wife of a member of the U.S. AID mission and the torture of Fred Morris in 1974.[69]

As for the Brazilians, one U.S. journalist in Brazil was told that "the poor are dying of hunger, and the rich are dying of rage."[70] The individual, assuming that he can provide for his physical needs, is secure only so long as he is not suspected of being unsympathetic to the military regime or of having unsympathetic friends or relatives.

67. Levine, "Brazil: The Aftermath of 'Decompression.' "

68. Jack Cobb, Executive Secretary of the Latin American Studies Association and former Evaluation Officer for the Peace Corps Interview, 20 November 1970, Washington, D.C.

69. *Washington Post,* 3 April 1973.

70. José Yglesias, "Report from Rio de Janeiro: What the Left is Saying," *New York Times Magazine,* 7 December 1969, pp. 52–53, 162–79.

[15]

Conclusion

Uruguayan journalist Eduardo Galeano charged that Brazil's 1964 coup was the product of a conspiracy financed by the United States—the inevitable result of a dependent country challenging the influence of an imperialist power.

> It is at once logical and absurd that the only Latin American government which tried to bring into practice the principles contained in the Charter of Punta de Este—which gave birth to the Alliance for Progress—should fall, destroyed precisely as a victim of a conspiracy which the United States financed. As it unmasks the hypocrisy of the Alliance for Progress, the fall of Goulart confirms an old conviction of the left wing: no dependent country, situated in imperialism's sphere of influence, can set out to create a policy of industrialization and national development; inevitably the necessary structural changes will be considered challenges to the stability of the imperialist power and to the security of the native ruling oligarchy.[1]

Whether *O Golpe Começou en Washington* (*The Coup Began in Washington*), as one Brazilian book title proclaims, may never be known, and, in fact, may not be knowable, as a convergence of interests has many sources and many beginnings and the variables cannot be isolated in order to determine which constituted the necessary and sufficient causes.[2]

We have no incontestable proof, on the order of a public admission by the top-ranking officials, that the United States government adopted a policy of "destabilizing" the constitutional government of Brazil and contributing to its demise in 1964. It is to be hoped that future

1. Galeano, "Ambivalence of Goulart," pp. 201–5.
2. Edmar Morel, *O Golpe Começou en Washington* (Rio de Janeiro: Editôra Civilização Brasileira, 1965).

congressional investigations and scholarly research will produce a more detailed and systematic account of the nature and consequences of U.S. influence in Brazil in the 1960s, as well as of the extent to which the pattern of penetration described in this case study has been replicated in Chile and elsewhere in the hemisphere.

We have seen, however, that Brazil's residence in the United States sphere of influence generated the high level of dependency and the associational links that led important groups of Brazilians to see their own interests as disassociated from or contrary to the interests of the majority of their countrymen, or to define the national interest in terms outlined by the United States rather than by the national community, as imperfectly expressed by the electorate.

We have seen that U.S. officials had been concerned in 1961 that Quadros might be vulnerable to communist influence, and that when Goulart assumed the presidency the mood among virtually all U.S. officials, civilian and military, involved in analyzing Brazilian politics and in making policy toward Brazil at the time turned to panic. In the absence of incontestable proof, this author nevertheless finds the weight of the evidence persuasive that the United States anticipated the coup of 1964, encouraged it, intervened covertly, and was prepared to intervene overtly with arms and even troops had it appeared that the conspirators faced defeat. Evidence cited in support of this argument has included numerous allegations, from sources with widely varying interests, that Brazilian business groups, state governors, and military conspirators had been promised or led to believe that if they declared a state of rebellion and ran into trouble they could count on the United States for assistance. We have also noted various indications of close contact and of shared interests and fears among U.S. officials and the Brazilian conspirators. And we have the acknowledgment of a few U.S. officials that their agencies or clients participated or contemplated participation in that supposedly domestic conflict.

Although it has not been possible to verify the accuracy of each allegation, the general pattern of support for the conspirators seems clear. Furthermore, it is not necessary to confirm direct United States complicity in the coup itself in order to conclude that U.S. actions contributed to the success of the conspirators, because we have seen that the United States had been engaged in a long-term effort to weaken the leftist-nationalist or populist movement and to strengthen the opponents of that movement.

Johan Galtung observed in "A Structural Theory of Imperialism" that "only imperfect imperialism needs direct violence."[3] The process

3. Galtung, "A Structural Theory of Imperialism," pp. 81–117.

whereby the elite of the poor countries is lured or coerced into a state of dependency upon—and ultimately, in many cases, a convergence of interests and values with—the elite of a hegemonic power is an ongoing one.[4] If the system is in good working order, the hegemonic power should be able to meet a perceived threat to its interests through more or less covert assistance to already dependent local elite groups. Armed occupation by the hegemonic power indicates a breakdown in the penetrative process.

The denationalization of key elite groups in Brazil had been well under way since World War II. Through the infusion of funds—economic and military assistance and private investment—and the concomitant briefcase brigades, U.S. links with various important sectors of the society, particularly with the armed forces and the industrialists, had been expanded and intensified. It has been argued that in the early 1960s there was an accelerated effort, cloaked in the euphemisms of the Alliance for Progress, to strengthen these "linkage" groups, to alienate them from the attitudinal trend of the majority of the national community (as expressed in elections), and to use them, along with other devices such as the external credit squeeze, to hasten the demise of a constitutional government.

As U.S. investment already amounted to more than a billion dollars by 1961, businessmen linked to the multinational corporate structure were natural allies. We have seen that some of these businessmen formed an organization called the Institute for Research and Social Studies (IPES) to agitate, and later to conspire, against the government of Goulart. IPES was one of the groups that reportedly met with Ambassador Lincoln Gordon and came away confident of U.S. help, if needed. A more shadowy organization known as the Brazilian Institute for Democratic Action (IBAD), by its own admission, pumped the equivalent of some $12 million into the 1962 congressional and gubernatorial elections. IBAD was outlawed in 1963 after a Brazilian congressional investigating commission uncovered circumstantial evidence that its funding came from foreign sources. And, more recently, a former CIA agent has confirmed that IBAD was a CIA "political-action" operation.

These organizations flooded the communications media with scare propaganda; but an even more serious threat to the integrity of the media was the fact that most of the companies that could afford to advertise were U.S.-owned and all of the major advertising agencies were.

4. Some critics of foreign assistance have defined it as a means whereby the poor of the rich countries contribute to the rich of the poor countries. It might be added that it is also yet another means whereby the poor of the rich countries further enrich their own economic elite.

Periodicals that took a pro-labor or nationalistic stance were thus denied advertising and driven out of business.

We have seen that U.S. officialdom was particularly panicked by peasant unrest in the Northeast. In 1962, the U.S. and Brazilian governments signed the Northeast Agreement, involving a commitment of $131 million. Several observers concluded that the program's two interrelated purposes were to defeat leftist candidates and to suppress or co-opt the peasant movement. AID was supposed to work through the Superintendency for the Northeast, but SUDENE objected to AID's strategy. Undermining SUDENE then became one of the purposes of the program.

The penetration of labor was to be accomplished through the American Institute for Free Labor Development—a bedfellow arrangement of labor, management, and government (AID and CIA) established in 1961. It has been noted that in the fall of 1963 AIFLD's executive director met with the governor of São Paulo and was briefed on plans for the coup. AIFLD then arranged a training session in Washington for a special all-Brazilian group. After the coup an AIFLD official boasted in a radio interview that AIFLD trainees had been involved in the conspiracy.

By mid-1963 the U.S. effort to undermine Goulart had been formalized in the so-called "islands of sanity" policy. Under this policy, aid to the central government was suspended, while more than $100 million was committed to state governors who were pro-U.S. and anti-Goulart. The public safety assistance program was apparently geared at that time to the "islands of sanity" policy, because most of the policemen trained in 1963 were from the states of Minas Gerais, Guanabara, and São Paulo, whose governors were central figures in the conspiracy. And the largest sum ever expended on the program in Brazil was expended in 1964.

Nevertheless, the momentum of the leftist-nationalist direction of development was such that it appears that these countervailing forces might have been isolated and contended with—save one. Short of violent revolution, a hypertrophied (at least in terms of role and self-image), alienated military establishment cannot simply be cut off from the national community by the civilian leaders. Its link with the community is broken only when it assumes control of the government and cuts the civilians out.

We have seen that the Sorbonne faction, which spearheaded the coup, was the faction that had been cultivated by the United States ever since World War II. A high proportion of its members fought alongside U.S. troops in the Italian campaign; these officers staffed the Superior

War College (ESG), which the U.S. military had helped to establish and operate; and they had been trained in the United States. The Cold War world-view to which they were exposed had made them contemptuous of politicians and suspicious of those who advocated social reform. And extensive training in systems analysis, managerial skills, and the like had convinced them that they were the only group capable of governing.

It has been noted that in the face of the Brazilian "crisis" of 1964, there was an extraordinary degree of coordination among agents of United States government and business. But what was the fruit of all these efforts? Certainly a number of the country's most important civilian politicians, in particular those state governors favored by the "islands of sanity" policy, had joined the conspiracy against Goulart, but United States efforts to tilt the political balance through electoral economics had yielded a mixed bag. Miguel Arraes was elected governor of Pernambuco despite the efforts of the United States to defeat him. Despite the propaganda and campaign-funding provided by IBAD, IPES, and related organizations, the PTB gained strength in the elections of 1962 and the congress restored full presidential powers to Goulart in 1963. AIFLD boasted of having drawn a number of labor leaders into the conspiracy against Goulart, but it is doubtful that AIFLD can take much credit for the ineffectiveness of the labor movement as a whole at the time of the coup. AID and other United States agencies in the Northeast had succeeded in undermining SUDENE, but despite all their efforts the peasant movement had not been contained or deradicalized.

We do not know whether such a coup would have occurred and whether the military regime would have become so firmly entrenched if the United States position in 1964 had been neutral or opposed to the conspiracy. It has been shown that the civilian political structure was poorly equipped to cope with economic stress and with interclass conflict. Certainly there were individuals and groups whose inclinations and self-interests would have favored the toppling of Goulart regardless of United States policy in that particular instance. But would they have been so strong or so bold without United States support? It is apparent that contenders on both sides anticipated civil war. Would those on the right, clearly outnumbered in the overall clash of interests, have been willing to risk armed confrontation without the expectation of United States backing? Celso Furtado, for one, doubts it, and so does this author.

Colonel Vernon Walters, defense attaché in Brazil at that time (subsequently deputy director of the CIA), had served as liaison between

U.S. and Brazilian troops in Italy and had developed a close friendship with Castello Branco and others in the Sorbonne group. Furtado maintains that Walters served as a focal point of communication among military conspirators who were hesitant at first to commit themselves and that the assurance of U.S. backing was important in strengthening their resolve.

We have seen that the long-term linkages and short-term tactics of the United States in the civilian sector contributed to the disaggregation of the state and the polarization of the national community that facilitated the overthrow of the Goulart government. But efforts to shift the political balance in the civilian sector had only frustrated the reformist policies of the government, the leftward trend of the electorate, and the mobilization of the lower classes; they had not reversed them. So the most crucial target of U.S. influence was the military. To paraphrase Nelson Werneck Sôdre, while the background accompaniment was certainly useful, the orchestra, in the final analysis, was reduced to a single instrument.

We do not know that the Brazilian military's conception of its political role would not have expanded or that the mental image of political opponents would not have been transformed into the dehumanized "enemy" image without United States influence. But we do know that the massive weight of U.S. influence was on the side of those developments.

As James Kurth expressed it, the United States really "chose to pull the trigger."

> The role of the United States military aid program in Latin American politics is like the role of one soldier out of the several who form a firing squad. A soldier in the firing squad who shoots a civilian may defend himself with the argument that the victim would have been shot by the other soldiers anyway, or that his own bullet was not the first to hit the mark. And it is true that the important point about the civilian is that he would still be dead. But the important point about the soldier—and about the United States policymaker—is that he chose to pull the trigger.[5]

While denying any role in the coup itself, the United States did not deny that the massive dollar transfusion in the years following it were intended to strengthen the "revolutionary" government, and U.S. spokesmen have effusively praised Brazil's "economic miracle" and its stability. The country has indeed exhibited political stability, but it is a stability imposed through terror.

A number of Brazilians who have been subjected to torture have claimed that their torturers were trained by the United States, that

5. Kurth, "U.S. Foreign Policy and Latin American Military Rule," p. 314.

Americans were present at their interrogations, or that United States equipment was used. The United States military and AID's Public Safety Division, of course, have denied any involvement in this messy business. But whether or nor any of the inspiration for or methods of torture can be traced to United States sources, the issue pales to insignificance beside the contributions that these agencies acknowledge and, in fact, boast of. Torture is one of the oldest techniques of political repression known to man; no country really needs the help of the United States to institute it. But the provision of the most advanced technology in transportation, communication, and identification, of the latest equipment for crowd control, and of managerial expertise is another matter. Brazil could hardly have established the network of political surveillance it now commands without United States assistance. It is discomforting that in reporting to the Senate in 1971 that the provision of United States public safety advisors to Brazil was to be terminated, Ambassador Rountree said that this discontinuance was possible because "the purposes of the program have been largely accomplished."[6]

There can be little doubt that continuing United States assitance, whether bilateral or channeled through the supposedly multilateral agencies, strengthens the immediate oppressors of the Brazilian people. But it would be naive to assume that a cutoff of this assistance would undo the damage that has been done, that it could open the floodgates of liberation from militarism and exploitation. The infusion of funds does not reduce the interaction process to simple bribery, nor, for that matter, to complex bribery. Bribery implies transactions with precise objectives in a limited time-frame, and while some of the linkages in this case have probably been of that nature, a great many more have been of long standing and are more subtle and more pervasive. These should be of greater concern to the individuals and groups of the so-called Third World who strive to turn the tide of the co-optation and exploitation of their peoples by the forces spawned in the overdeveloped world.

Every empire has had its Herodean class; but the spread of the "modernization" process and the general shrinkage of the world have led, in the space of a few decades, to an unprecedented diffusion of the values of the most highly industrialized Western states and the absorption or near-suffocation of less aggressive cultures. If the denationalization process with which we are dealing reflected merely a grasping for status and personal gain, it would be bad enough, but the malignancy

---

6. Church Hearings, p. 282.

goes much deeper. Marx granted that the upper classes, in their determination to preserve a system from which they benefited, were not driven merely by greed; rather, their actions flowed from the projection of their own value systems as universals.

So it appears that Uruguayan writer José Enrique Rodó was right all along. It was not the conquest of Latin America's material resources by the Colossus of the North that he warned his countrymen against at the turn of the twentieth century, but the conquest of its soul by materialism. "I see no good," Rodó said, "in denaturalizing the character of a people—its personal genius—to impose on it identity with a foreign model. . . . Those without rank or fortune ineffectually imitate only the foibles of the mighty."[7]

And little wonder, because it has been precisely the foibles rather than the virtues—the sleaziest side of the national character of the United States—that have governed relations with Latin America and that have increasingly been fed into the larger international system. And increasingly the American people have reaped at home what they have sown abroad. In the troubled year of 1973, Senator Hubert Humphrey said:

> There is a familiar maxim—that power corrupts and absolute power corrupts absolutely. This admonition applies to both nations and individuals. With Watergate we have seen officials of our government commit criminal acts that strongly resemble the practices and methods directed against foreign governments and other peoples. Counterespionage, coverups, infiltration, wire-tapping, political surveillance, all done in the name of national security in faraway places, have come home to haunt us. The spirit and the purpose of domestic policy is said to condition our foreign policy. The reverse is also true.[8]

Watergate is but a boomerang.

If this process of denationalization cannot be reversed, perhaps, as Dom Helder Câmara says, the hope for the underdeveloped world lies in the transformation of the developed world. Ironically, the legions of intellectual elites driven from their own countries to the United States by repressive regimes supported by the United States might just help to speed the process of *conscientização* in the metropolis. Meanwhile, back in Brazil, to borrow the language of E. Bradford Burns:

7. José Enrique Rodó, "Democracy and Cultural Aristocracy," from *Ariel*; reprinted in Harold E. Davis, *Latin American Social Thought* (Washington, D.C.: The University Press, 1961), pp. 318–19.

8. Senator Hubert H. Humphrey, "The Threat to the Presidency," *Washington Post*, 6 May 1973.

Atop a high hill dominating the quiet waters of Botafogo Bay in Rio de Janeiro stands a giant Coca-Cola sign. Blinking rhythmically in the evening air, it casts its bright reflection across the waters to taunt the Brazilians, reminding them that so much of their present culture is being imported, that so much of their genius is being suppressed, that so much of their originality is being discarded. Throughout 1972, as the celebrations marking Brazil's "independence" continue, the bands blare martial music, flags flutter, patriotic oratory resounds and the Coca-Cola sign flashes its silent mockery through the long Brazilian night.[9]

9. Burns, "Brazil: The Imitative Society."

Appendix

The first two tables in this appendix indicate the parsimonious dispersal of foreign assistance to Brazil by the United States Government and the international lending agencies during the ill-fated constitutional government of Goulart and the generous proffer of such assistance, beginning in 1964, to bolster the military regime. The third table shows the considerable increase in U.S. private investment and in profits repatriated after 1964, and the fourth indicates the high rate of increase in defense expenditures in Brazil and in other Latin American countries that experienced military takeovers in the 1960s.

TABLE 1

Assistance to Brazil from International Organizations, 1953–1973

(Millions of Dollars)

	1953–1961	1962	1963	1964	1965	1966	1967
IBRD	149.5	—	—	—	76.8	49.0	100.6
IFC	9.9	—	—	—	—	10.7	10.7
IDB	11.2	25.6	18.6	21.8	80.4	87.2	125.7
UNDP	7.2	1.4	3.2	2.1	1.0	4.4	4.6
Other UN	0.9	0.6	1.3	2.0	1.7	1.1	0.4
TOTAL	178.7	27.6	23.1	25.9	159.9	152.4	242.0

	1968	1969	1970	1971	1972	1973	TOTAL
IBRD	61.9	74.9	205.0	160.4	437.0	133.7	1,566.3
IFC	—	9.4	8.2	10.9	27.6	47.4	134.8
IDB	76.6	99.8	160.6	119.9	210.1	180.2	1,217.7
UNDP	3.3	5.0	2.9	6.3	4.9	6.4	52.7
Other UN	0.5	0.6	0.7	1.4	2.3	0.9	24.5
TOTAL	142.3	189.7	377.4	298.9	681.9	368.6	2,986.0

Source: Agency for International Development, Statistics and Reports Division, Office of Financial Management.
U.S. Overseas Loans and Grants and Assistance from International Organizations: Obligations and Loan Authorizations, July 1, 1945–June 30, 1973, May 1974

IBRD—International Bank for Reconstruction and Development (World Bank)
IFC—International Finance Corporation
IDB—Inter-American Development Bank
UNDP—United Nations Development Program

TABLE 2

U.S. Assistance to Brazil, 1945–1973
(U.S. Fiscal Years - Millions of Dollars)

PROGRAM	U.S. OVERSEAS LOANS AND GRANTS - OBLIGATIONS AND LOAN AUTHORIZATIONS: POST-WAR RELIEF PERIOD 1946–1948	MARSHALL PLAN PERIOD 1949–1952	MUTUAL SECURITY ACT PERIOD 1953–1961	FOREIGN ASSISTANCE ACT PERIOD: 1962–1965	1966	1967	1968	1969	1970	1971	1972	1973	TOTAL FAA PERIOD 1962–1973	TOTAL LOANS AND GRANTS 1946–1973	REPAY-MENTS AND INTEREST 1946–1973	TOTAL LESS REPAY-MENTS AND INTEREST
I. ECONOMIC ASSISTANCE[a]—TOTAL	19.9	5.4	314.2	954.5	329.0	240.0	280.7	29.2	154.0	117.6	21.0	53.8	2,179.8	2,414.9	201.2	2,213.7
Loans	16.3	-	180.5	727.9	258.4	199.0	243.7	3.1	95.0	90.8	2.1	33.3	1,653.3	1,759.6	201.2	1,558.4
Grants	3.6	5.4	133.7	226.7	70.6	41.0	37.0	26.1	59.0	26.8	18.9	20.5	526.6	655.4	-	655.4
a. A.I.D. and Predecessor Agencies	-	2.6	50.3	586.0	243.7	214.9	193.8	12.4	88.0	79.4	12.1	40.6	1,470.9	1,419.4	68.9	1,350.5
Loans	-	-	0.5	523.0	229.3	199.0	180.9	*	75.0	67.5	2.1[b]	33.2	1,310.0	1,220.0	68.9	1,151.1
Grants	-	2.6	49.8	63.0	14.4	15.9	12.9	12.4	13.0	11.9	10.0	7.4	160.9	199.4	–	199.4
(Security Supporting Assistance)	(-)	(-)	(-)	(75.5)	(-)	(-)	(-)	(-)	(-)	(-)	(-)	(-)	(75.5)	(75.5)		
b. Food for Peace (PL 480)	-	-	241.4	295.9	79.1	21.6	82.9	10.2	62.4	35.1	5.7	9.6	602.5	843.9	58.3	785.6
Title I - Total	-	-	220.0	191.4	29.1	-	62.7	-	19.9	23.3	-	-	326.4	546.4	58.3	488.1
Repayable in U.S. Dollars - Loans	-	-	-	-	29.1	-	62.7	-	19.9	23.3	-	-	135.0	135.0	39.1	95.9
Payable in Foreign Currency - Planned for Country Use	-	-	220.0	191.4	-	-	-	-	-	-	-	-	191.4	411.4	19.2	392.2
(Total Sales Agreements, incl. U.S. Uses)	(-)	(-)	(262.8)	(240.6)	(-)	(-)	(-)	(-)	(-)	(-)	(-)	(-)	(240.6)	(503.4)	(-)	(503.4)
Title II - Total	-	-	21.4	104.5	50.0	21.6	20.2	10.2	42.5	11.8	5.7	9.6	276.1	297.5	-	297.5
Emergency Relief, Econ. Development, & World Food	-	-	-	37.9	33.5	9.3	9.7	2.4	35.0	3.8	-	4.9	136.5	136.5	-	136.5
Voluntary Relief Agencies	-	-	21.4	66.6	16.5	12.3	10.5	7.8	7.5	8.0	5.7	4.7	139.6	161.0	-	161.0
c. Other Economic Assistance	19.9	2.8	22.5	72.6	6.2	3.5	4.0	6.6	3.6	3.1	3.2	3.6	106.4	151.6	74.0	77.6
Peace Corps	-	-	-	11.1	6.2	3.5	3.9	3.5	3.5	3.1	2.9	2.6	40.3	40.3	-	40.3
Other[c]	19.9	2.8	22.5	61.5	-	-	0.1	3.1	0.1	-	0.3	1.0	66.1	111.3	74.0	37.3
II. MILITARY ASSISTANCE—TOTAL	-	-	170.6	108.4	30.6	32.6	36.1	0.8	0.8	12.1	20.8	17.7	259.9	430.2	58.4	371.8
Credits or Loans	-	-	-	23.4	11.6	18.4	18.5	-	-	9.4	20.0	15.0	116.3	116.4	58.4	58.0
Grants	-	-	170.6	84.9	19.0	14.2	17.6	0.8	0.8	2.7	0.8	2.7	143.5	313.8	-	313.8
a. MAP Grants	-	-	121.2	64.9	17.3	12.2	2.6	0.8	0.8	0.8	0.8	0.8	101.0	222.0	-	222.0
b. Credit Sales under FMS	-	-	-	23.4	11.6	18.4	18.5	-	-	9.4	20.0	15.0	116.3	116.4	58.4	58.0
c. Military Assistance Service-funded (MASF) Grants	-	-	-	-	-	-	-	-	-	-	-	-	-	-	-	-
d. Transfers from Excess Stocks	-	-	22.6	2.9	1.7	0.5	0.1	-	-	-	-	-	5.2	27.7	-	27.7
e. Other Grants	-	-	26.8	17.1	-	1.5	14.9	-	-	1.9	-	1.9	37.3	64.1	-	64.1

III. TOTAL ECONOMIC AND MILITARY ASSISTANCE																
Loans	16.3	-	180.5	751.3	270.0	217.4	262.2	3.1	95.0	100.2	22.1	48.3	1,769.6	1,876.0	259.6	1,616.4
Grants	3.6	5.4	304.3	311.7	89.6	55.2	54.6	26.9	59.8	29.5	19.7	23.2	670.2	969.2	-	969.2
(Total)	19.9	5.4	484.8	1,062.9	359.6	272.6	316.8	30.0	154.8	129.7	41.8	71.5	2,439.7	2,845.1	259.6	2,585.5
Other U.S. Government Loans and Grants...	54.0	104.5	996.8	6.0	16.9	30.0	66.6	27.9	63.2	75.0	301.3	145.7	732.6	1,882.5	1,522.5	360.0
a. Export-Import Bank Loans ...	54.0	104.5	996.8[d]	6.0[d]	16.9	30.0	50.8	27.9	63.2	75.0	299.8	142.3	711.9	1,861.8	1,504.5	357.3
b. All Other[e] ...							15.8				1.5	3.4	20.7	20.7	18.0	2.7

*Less than $50,000.

[a]Official Development Assistance (ODA) - Official concessional aid for development purposes.
[b]Capitalized interest on prior year loans.
[c]Includes $22.5 million Surplus Property Credits and $16.4 million Defense Mobilization Development.
[d]Excludes refunding of $292.2 million in FY 1961; $85.6 million in FY 1964; and $6.6 million in FY 1965.
[e]Includes $4.8 million in OPIC direct loans.

Source: Agency for International Development, *U.S. Overseas Loans and Grants and Assistance from International Organizations; Obligations and Loan Authorizations, July 1, 1945–June 30, 1973*, May 1974.

TABLE 3
U.S. Private Investments in Brazil, 1960–1969
(Millions of dollars, year end)

	Extractive Industries	Manufacturing	Transportation and Utilities	Trade	Other	Total	Repatriated Profits	Reinvested Earnings
1960	86	515	200	130	23	953	45	39
1961*	106	543	198	127	26	1,006	35	39
1962*	105	611	195	136	41	1,084	24	63
1963	90	664	193	148	38	1,132	13	57
1964	93	668	41	153	41	997	5	59
1965	108	723	37	162	45	1,074	19	84
1966	127	846	38	183	53	1,247	33	85
1967	147	893	32	195	61	1,327	66	39
1968	164	1,022	27	197	75	1,484	75	73
1969	199	1,112	25	188	108	1,633	66	83

*Revised total only; revision by industries not available.
Source: Ronald A. Krieger, Brazil: An Economic Survey by First National City Bank, March 1971.

TABLE 4
Selected Trends in Latin American Central Government Expenditures: 1961–1971

Region and Country	Average Annual Rate of Change: 1961–1971		
	Total Expenditures	Capital Expenditures	Defense Expenditures
TOTALS			
18 L.A. Countries	4.3	5.8	5.3
5 C.A. Countries*	8.7	12.7	5.0
Argentina	0.9	4.5	-1.4
Bolivia	9.7	15.9	3.2
Brazil	2.1	4.0	10.8
Chile	9.8	14.8	4.0
Colombia	5.1	6.4	4.8
Costa Rica	11.4	15.4	N.A.
Dominican Republic	4.0	9.2	-3.7
Ecuador	5.4	1.6	4.3
El Salvador	7.5	15.3	6.9
Guatemala	7.0	7.8	6.0
Honduras	8.1	11.6	2.4
Mexico	6.9	5.7	5.9
Nicaragua	9.6	12.9	3.7
Panama	8.3	14.5	13.0
Paraguay	10.6	14.5	7.6
Peru	6.6	12.6	9.5
Uruguay	0.3	2.3	6.6
Venezuela	4.4	2.0	5.7

*Costa Rica, El Salvador, Guatemala, Honduras, Nicaragua.

Source: *Summary Economic and Social Indicators, 18 Latin American Countries: 1960–71*. Office of Development Programs, Bureau for Latin America, AID, June 1972.

Note: Data are based on constant 1970 prices.

Selected Bibliography

Books

Agee, Philip. *Inside the Company: CIA Diary*. London: Penguin Books, 1975.

Aguilar, Alonso. *Pan-Americanism from Monroe to the Present: A View from the Other Side*. Translated by A. Zatz. New York: Monthly Review Press, 1968.

Arraes, Miguel. *Brazil: The People and the Power*. Harmondsworth, Mx.: Penguin Books, 1972.

Astiz, Carlos A., ed. *Latin American International Politics: Ambitions, Capabilities and the National Interests of Mexico, Brazil and Argentina*. Notre Dame Ind.: University of Notre Dame Press, 1969.

Baer, Werner. *The Development of the Brazilian Steel Industry*. Nashville, Tenn.: Vanderbilt University Press, 1969.

————. *Industrialization and Economic Development in Brazil*. Homewood, Ill.: Richard D. Irwin, 1965.

Baker, Ross K. *A Study of Military Status and Status Deprivation in Three Latin American Armies*. Washington: Center for Research in Social Systems, October 1967.

Baklanoff, Eric N., ed. *New Perspectives in Brazil*. Nashville, Tenn.: Vanderbilt University Press, 1966.

Bandeira, Moniz. *Presença dos Estados Unidos no Brasil*. Rio de Janeiro: Editôra Civilização Brasileira, 1973.

Barber, Willard F. and C. Neale Ronning. *Internal Security and Military Power: Counterinsurgency and Civic Action in Latin America*. Columbus: Ohio State University Press, 1966.

Barnet, Richard J. and Ronald E. Müller. *Global Reach: The Power of the Multinational Corporation*. New York: Simon and Schuster, 1974.

Beaulac, Willard L. *A Diplomat Looks at Aid to Latin America*. Carbondale and Edwardsville: Southern Illinois University Press, 1970.

Black, Joseph E. and Kenneth W. Thompson, eds. *Foreign Policies in a World of Change*. New York: Harper & Row, 1963.

Botelho, Caio Lossio. *Brasil: A Europa dos tropicos*. Rio de Janeiro: Grafica Record Editôra, 1967.

Burns, E. Bradford. *Nationalism in Brazil: A Historical Survey*. New York: Frederick A. Praeger, 1968.

————. *The Unwritten Alliance: Rio Branco and Brazilian-American Relations*. New York: Columbia University Press, 1966.

Carneiro, Glaução. *História das Revoluções Brasileiras*. Rio de Janeiro: Edições Cruzeiro, August 1965.

Colonnese, Louis M., ed. *Human Rights and the Liberation of Man in the Americas*. Notre Dame, Ind.: University of Notre Dame Press, 1970.

Corbett, Charles D. *The Latin American Military as a Socio-Political Force: Case Studies of Bolivia and Argentina*. Coral Gables, Fla.: University of Miami Press, 1972.

Connell-Smith, Gordon. *The Inter-American System*. London: Oxford University Press, 1966.

Couloumbis, Theodore A. *Greek Political Reaction to American and NATO Influences*. New Haven: Yale University Press, 1966.

Daugherty, Charles, James Rowe, and Ronald Schneider, eds. *Brazil Election Factbook No. 2*. Washington: Institute for the Comparative Study of Political Systems, September 1965.

Davis, Harold E. *Latin American Social Thought*. Washington: The University Press, 1961.

Deutsch, Karl W. *The Analysis of International Relations*. Foundations of Modern Political Science Series. Englewood Cliffs, N.J.: Prentice-Hall, 1968.

Dines, Alberto, et al. *Os Idos de março e a queda em abril*. Rio de Janeiro: José Alvaro, Editor, 1964.

Dreier, John C. *The Organization of American States and the Hemisphere Crisis*. New York: Harper & Row, 1962.

Dulles, John W. F. *Unrest in Brazil: Political Military Crises 1955–1964*. Austin: University of Texas Press, 1970.

Dutra, Eloy. *IBAD, Sigla da Corrupção*. Rio de Janeiro: Editôra Civilização Brasileira, 1963.

Edelmann, Alexander T. *Latin American Government and Politics.* Rev. ed. Dorsey Series in Political Science. Homewood, Ill.: The Dorsey Press, 1969.

Fagen, Richard R. and Wayne A. Cornelius, Jr., eds. *Political Power in Latin America: Seven Confrontations.* Englewood Cliffs, N.J.: Prentice-Hall, 1970.

Farrell, Barry R., ed. *Approaches to Comparative and International Politics.* Evanston, Ill.: Northwestern University Press, 1966.

Ferreira, Oliveiros S. *O Fim do poder civil.* São Paulo: Editôra Convivio, 1966.

Frank, Andre Gunder. *Capitalism and Underdevelopment in Latin America; Historical Studies of Chile and Brazil.* New York: Monthly Review Press, 1967.

————. *Latin America: Underdevelopment or Revolution.* New York: Monthly Review Press, 1969.

Frank, Lewis A. *The Arms Trade in International Relations.* Praeger Special Studies in International Politics and Public Affairs. New York: Frederick A. Praeger, 1969.

Galbraith, John Kenneth. *Economics and the Public Purpose.* London: Andre Deutsch, 1974.

Gil, Federico. *Latin American–U.S. Relations.* New York: Harcourt Brace Jovanovich, 1971.

Golbery do Couto e Silva, General. *Geopolítica do Brasil.* Rio de Janeiro: Livraria José Olympio Editôra, 1967.

Goldhamer, Herbert. *The Foreign Powers in Latin America.* Princeton: Princeton University Press, 1972.

Gordon, Lincoln. *A New Deal for Latin America.* Cambridge: Harvard University Press, 1963.

Gordon, Lincoln and Engelbert Grommers. *United States Manufacturing Investment in Brazil: the Impact of Brazilian Government Policies, 1946–1960.* Boston: Harvard University Press, 1962.

Graham, Richard. *Britain and the Onset of Modernization in Brazil, 1850–1914.* Cambridge: Cambridge University Press, 1968.

————, ed. *A Century of Brazilian History Since 1865.* New York: Alfred A. Knopf, 1969.

Green, David. *The Containment of Latin America: A History of the Myths and Realities of the Good Neighbor Policy.* Chicago: Triangle Books, 1971.

Hahner, June E. *Civil-Military Relations in Brazil, 1889–1898.* Columbia: University of South Carolina Press, 1969.

Hamilton, J., Albert Rees and Harry G. Johnson, eds. *Landmarks in Political Economy*. Chicago: University of Chicago Press, 1962.

Hayter, Teresa. *Aid as Imperialism*. Baltimore: Penguin Books, 1971.

Helder Câmara, Dom. *Revolution Through Peace*. New York: Harper & Row, 1971.

Hill, Lawrence F. *Diplomatic Relations Between the United States and Brazil*. Durham, N.C.: Duke University Press, 1932.

Hirschman, Albert O. *Journeys Toward Progress: Studies of Economic Policy-Making in Latin America*. New York: The Twentieth Century Fund, 1963.

Horowitz, Irving Louis, ed. *Masses in Latin America*. New York: Oxford University Press, 1970.

————. *Revolution in Brazil: Politics and Society in a Developing Nation*. New York: E. P. Dutton & Co., 1964.

————. *The Rise and Fall of Project Camelot; Studies in the Relationship between Social Science and Practical Politics*. Cambridge: The M.I.T. Press, 1967.

Horowitz, Irving Louis, Josué de Castro, and John Gerassi, eds. *Latin American Radicalism: A Documentary Report on Left and Nationalist Movements*. New York: Random House, Vintage Books, 1968.

Hovey, Harold A. *United States Military Assistance: A Study of Policies and Practices*. New York: Frederick A. Praeger, 1965.

Huntington, Samuel P. *Political Order in Changing Societies*. New Haven: Yale University Press, 1968.

Ianni, Octavio. *Crisis in Brazil*. Translated by Phyllis B. Eveleth. New York: Columbia University Press, 1970.

Jaguaribe, Helio, *Economic and Political Development: A Theoretical Approach and a Brazilian Case Study*. Cambridge: Harvard University Press, 1968.

Johnson, John J. *The Military and Society in Latin America*. Stanford, Calif.: Stanford University Press, 1964.

————, ed. *The Role of the Military in Underdeveloped Countries*. Princeton: Princeton University Press, 1962.

Julião, Francisco. *Que são as Ligas Camponesas*. Cuadernos do Povo Brasileiro. Rio de Janeiro: Editôra Civilização Brasileira, 1962.

Jurema, Abelardo. *Sexta-Feira, 13; as últimos dias do govêrno João Goulart*. 3d ed. Rio de Janeiro: Edições o Cruzeiro, October 1964.

King, Edward L. *The Death of the Army: A Pre-Mortem*. New York: Saturday Review Press, 1972.

Lacerda, Carlos, *Brasil entre a verdade e a mentira.* Rio de Janeiro: Bloch Editôres, 1965.

————. *O poder das idéias.* 5th ed. Rio de Janeiro: Distribuidora Record, 1964.

Levinson, Jerome and Juan de Onis. *The Alliance that Lost its Way: A Critical Report on the Alliance for Progress.* A Twentieth Century Fund Study. Chicago: Quadrangle Books, 1970.

Lieuwen, Edwin. *Generals Versus Presidents: Neo-Militarism In Latin America.* New York: Frederick A. Praeger, 1964.

Lipset, Seymour Martin and Aldo Solari, eds. *Elites in Latin America.* New York: Oxford University Press, 1967.

Lodge, George C. *Engines of Change: United States Interests and Revolution in Latin America.* Introduction by Samuel P. Huntington. New York: Alfred A. Knopf, 1969.

MacEoin, Gary. *Revolution Next Door: Latin America in the 1970s.* New York: Holt, Rinehart and Winston, 1971.

Macridis, Roy C., ed. *Foreign Policy in World Politics.* 2d ed. Englewood Cliffs, N.J.: Prentice-Hall, 1962.

Malloy, James M. and Richard S. Thorn, eds. *Beyond the Revolution: Bolivia Since 1952.* Pittsburgh: University of Pittsburgh Press, 1971.

Marchetti, Victor, and John D. Marks. *The CIA and the Cult of Intelligence.* New York: Alfred A. Knopf, 1974.

Marighella, Carlos. *For the Liberation of Brazil.* Translated by John Butt and Rosemary Sheed. Introduction by Richard Gott. Baltimore: Penguin Books, 1971.

Martz, John D., ed. *The Dynamics of Change in Latin American Politics.* 2d ed. Englewood Cliffs, N.J.: Prentice-Hall, 1971.

Mason, Bruce B., ed. *The Political-Military Defense of Latin America.* Tempe: Arizona State University, Bureau of Governmental Research, 1963.

McAlister, Lyle N., et al. *The Military in Latin American Socio-Political Evolution: Four Case Studies.* Washington: Center for Research in Social Systems, 1970.

McCann, Frank D., Jr. *The Brazilian-American Alliance, 1937–1945.* Princeton: Princeton University Press, 1973.

McMillan, Claude. *International Enterprise in a Developing Economy: A Study of U.S. Business in Brazil.* MSU Business Studies, no. 10. Ann Arbor: Michigan State University Press, 1964.

Meira Penna, José Oswaldo de. *Política Externa, Sequrança e Desenvolvimento.* Rio de Janeiro: Livraria Agir Editôra, 1967.

Melo, Father Antônio. *The Coming Revolution in Brazil.* Translated and with Introduction by Robert Menzel. New York: Exposition Press, 1970.

Mills, C. Wright. *The Power Elite.* New York: Oxford University Press, 1956.

Momsen, Richard P., Jr. *Brazil: A Giant Stirs.* Princeton: D. Van Nostrand, 1968.

Moniz, Edmundo. *O Golpe de Abril.* Rio de Janeiro: Editôra Civilização Brasileira, 1965.

Moreira Alves, Marcio. *A Grain of Mustard Seed: The Awakening of the Brazilian Revolution.* Garden City, N.J.: Doubleday, Anchor Press, 1973.

Morel, Edmar. *O Golpe Começou en Washington.* Rio de Janeiro: Editôra Civilização Brasileira, 1965.

Munro, Dana G. *The United States and the Caribbean Republics, 1921–1933.* Princeton: Princeton University Press, 1974.

Mourão Filho, General Olympio. *Reforma para o Brasil.* Imagem do Brasil, 8. Rio de Janeiro: Editôra Saga, 1969.

Needler, Martin C., ed. *Political Systems of Latin America.* Princeton: D. Van Nostrand, 1964.

———. *The United States and the Latin American Revolution.* Boston: Allyn & Bacon, 1972.

Nun, José. *Latin America: The Hegemonic Crisis and the Military Coup.* Politics of Modernization Series, No. 7. Berkeley: University of California Press, 1969.

Núñez, Carlos. *Brasil: satélite y gendarme.* Montevideo: Aportes, 1969.

Oliveira, Franklin de. *Revolución y Contrarevolución en el Brasil.* Introduction by Luis V. Sommi. Buenos Aires: Ediciones Iguazú, 1965.

Page, Joseph A. *The Revolution that Never Was: Northeast Brazil, 1955–1964.* New York: Grossman, 1972.

Petras, James, ed. *Latin America: From Dependence to Revolution.* New York: John Wiley & Sons, 1973.

Pollock, David H., and Arch R. M. Ritter, eds. *Latin American Prospects for the 1970s: What Kinds of Revolutions?* New York: Frederick A. Praeger, 1973.

Quartim, João. *Dictatorship and Armed Struggle in Brazil.* Translated by David Fernbach. New York: Monthly Review Press, 1971.

Rabelo, Genival. *O Capital Estrangeiro na Imprensa Brasileira.* Rio de Janeiro: Editôra Civilização Brasileira, 1966.

———. *Ocupação da Amazonia.* Rio de Janeiro: Empresa Jornalística PN, 1968.

Radosh, Ronald. *American Labor and United States Foreign Policy: The Cold War in the Unions from Gompers to Lovestone.* New York: Random House, 1970.

Raine, Philip. *Brazil: Awakening Giant.* Washington: Public Affairs Press, 1974.

Ranis, Peter. *Five Latin American Nations: A Comparative Political Study.* New York: Macmillan, 1971.

Reidy, Joseph W. *Strategy for the Americas.* A Foreign Policy Research Institute Book. New York: McGraw-Hill, 1966.

Robock, Stefan H. *Brazil's Developing Northeast: A Study of Regional Planning and Foreign Aid.* Washington: The Brookings Institution, 1963.

Rockefeller, Nelson A. *The Rockefeller Report on the Americas: The Official Report of a United States Presidential Mission for the Western Hemisphere. New York Times* Edition with an introduction by Tad Szulc. Chicago: Quadrangle Books, 1969.

Rodrigues, José Honôrio. *Conciliação e Reforma no Brasil: un disafio histórica-político.* Rio de Janeiro: Editôra Civilização Brasileira, 1965.

Roett, Riordan, ed. *Brazil in the Sixties.* Nashville, Tenn.: Vanderbilt University Press, 1972.

———. *Brazil: Politics in a Patrimonial Society.* Boston: Allyn & Bacon, 1972.

———. *The Politics of Foreign Aid in the Brazilian Northeast.* Nashville, Vanderbilt University Press, 1972.

Rojas, Robinson. *Estados Unidos en Brasil.* Santiago, Chile: Prensa Latinoamericana, 1965.

Rosenau, James N., ed. *International Politics and Foreign Policy: A Reader in Research and Theory.* New York: The Free Press, 1969.

———, ed. *Linkage Politics: Essays on the Convergence of National and International Systems.* New York: The Free Press, 1969.

Rosenbaum, H. Jon and William G. Tyler, eds. *Contemporary Brazil: Issues in Economic and Political Development.* New York: Frederick A. Praeger, 1972.

Said, Abdul A., ed. *Protagonists of Change: Subcultures in Development and Revolution.* Englewood Cliffs, N.J.: Prentice-Hall, 1971.

San Tiago Dantas, Francisco Clementino de. *Política Externa Independente.* Rio de Janeiro: Editôra Civilização Brasileira, 1962.

Saunders, John, ed. *Modern Brazil: New Patterns and Development.* Gainesville: University of Florida Press, 1971.

Scantimburgo, João de. *A Crise de Republica Presidencial do Marechal Deodoro au Marechal Castelo Branco.* São Paulo: Livraria Pioneira Editôra, 1969.

Schmitter, Philippe C., ed. *Military Rule in Latin America: Function, Consequences and Perspectives.* Beverly Hills, Calif.: Sage Publications, 1973.

————. *Interest Conflict and Political Change in Brazil.* Stanford, Calif.: Stanford University Press, 1971.

Schneider, Ronald, ed. *Brazil: Election Factbook No. 2, Supplement.* Washington, D.C.: Institute for the Comparative Study of Political Systems, November 1966.

————. *The Political System of Brazil.* New York: Columbia University Press, 1973.

Scott, Andrew M. *The Revolution in Statecraft: Informal Penetration.* New York: Random House, 1965.

Sigmund, Paul E., ed. *Models of Political Change in Latin America.* New York: Frederick A. Praeger, 1970.

Skidmore, Thomas E. *Politics in Brazil, 1930–1964: An Experiment in Democracy.* New York: Oxford University Press, 1967.

Smith, T. Lynn and Alexander Marchant. *Brazil: Portrait of Half a Continent.* Westport, Conn.: Greenwood Press, 1951.

Snow, Peter G., ed. *Government and Politics in Latin America: A Reader.* New York: Holt, Rinehart and Winston, 1967.

Sôdre, Nelson Werneck. *Introdução a revolução brasileira.* 3d ed. Rio de Janeiro: Editôra Civilização Brasileira, 1967.

Solaún, Maurício and Michael A. Quinn. *Sinners and Heretics: The Politics of Military Intervention in Latin America.* Urbana: University of Illinois Press, 1973.

Souza, Amaury de. *Annotated Bibliography of the Brazilian Political Movement of 1964.* Latin American Research Program. Bibliography Series Report, No. 2 (1294). Riverside, Calif.: University of California, 1966.

Souza Junior, Antonio de. *O Brasil e a Terceira Guerra Mundial.* Rio de Janeiro: Biblioteca do Exército, 1959.

Staff of the North American Congress on Latin America. *The U.S. Military Apparatus.* Berkeley and New York: NACLA, August 1972.

Stepan, Alfred. *Authoritarian Brazil: Origins, Policies, and Future.* New Haven: Yale University Press, 1973.

————. *The Military in Politics: Changing Patterns in Brazil.* Princeton: Princeton University Press, 1971.

Steward, Donald E. J., ed. *Handbook of Latin American Studies: Humanities 34.* Gainesville: University of Florida Press, 1972.

Tomasek, Robert D., ed. *Latin American Politics: 24 Studies of the Contemporary Scene.* Garden City, N.Y.: Doubleday, 1966.

Turner, Louis, *Multinational Companies and the Third World.* New York: Hill & Wang, 1973.

Varas, Florencia and José Manuel Vergara. *Operación Chile: la Caída de Allende relatado minuto a minuto.* Barcelona: Editorial Pomaire, 1973.

Véliz, Claudio, ed. *Latin America and the Caribbean: A Handbook.* New York: Frederick A. Praeger, 1968.

————, ed. *Obstacles to Change in Latin America.* New York: Oxford University Press, 1965.

Wells, Alan. *Picture Tube Imperialism? The Impact of Television on Latin America.* Maryknoll, N.Y.: Orbis Books, 1972.

Wolpin, Miles. *Military Aid and Counterrevolution in the Third World.* Lexington, Mass.: D. C. Heath & Co., 1972.

Worcester, Donald E. *Brazil: From Colony to World Power.* New York: Charles Scribner's Sons, 1973.

Young, Jordan M., ed. *Brazil, 1954–64: End of a Civilian Cycle.* New York: Facts on File, Inc., 1972.

————. *The Brazilian Revolution of 1930 and the Aftermath.* New Brunswick, N.J.: Rutgers University Press, 1967.

Periodicals

Adams, Dale W. "Aid Agencies and Land Reform in Latin America." *Land Economics* 46 (November 1970): 423–34.

———. "What Can Underdeveloped Countries Expect From Foreign Aid to Agriculture? Case Study: Brazil, 1950–1970." *Inter-American Economic Affairs* 25, no. 1 (1971): 47–63.

"Amazonia: A Geo-Political Triangle." *Latin America* [London] 5, no. 22 (1971): 175.

Baer, W. and M. H. Simonsen. "American Capital and Brazilian Nationalism." *Yale Review* 53 (December 1963): 192–98.

Bailey, Norman A. and Ronald M. Schneider. "Brazil's Foreign Policy: A Case Study in Upward Mobility." *Inter-American Economic Affairs* 27, no. 4 (1974): 3–25.

Baines, John M. "U.S. Military Assistance to Latin America: An Assessment." *Journal of Interamerican Studies and World Affairs* 14 (1972): 469–87.

Barnet, Richard. "Letter from Rio: Fairly Cruel But Sensible Policies." *Harper's Magazine*, September 1972, pp. 16–22.

Bauer, Major Charles F. "USARCARIB's Biggest Little School." *Army Information Digest* 17, no. 10 (1962): 24–28.

Bechtos, Ramona. Series of articles on Brazil's advertising agencies. *Advertising Age* 44 (February and March 1973).

Binning, William C. "The Nixon Foreign Aid Policy for Latin America." *Inter-American Economic Affairs* 25, no. 1 (1971): 31–36.

Bjelajac, Slavko N. "Principles of Counterinsurgency." *Orbis* 8 (1964): 655–69.

Blum, E. "Time-Life Caper, Brazil's Yankee Network: Infiltration of Communications Media." *Nation*, 29 May 1967, pp. 678–81.

Blume, Norman. "Pressure Groups and Decision-Making in Brazil." *Studies in Comparative International Development* 3, no. 11 (1967–68): 205–23.

Bobrow, Davis B. "The Civic Role of the Military: Some Critical Hypotheses." *The Western Political Quarterly* 19 (1966): 101–11.

Bode, Kenneth A. "An Aspect of United States Policy in Latin America: The Latin American Diplomats' View." *Political Science Quarterly* 85 (1970): 471–91.

Bodenheimer, Suzanne. "U.S. Labor's Conservative Role in Latin America." *The Progressive* 31, no. 11 (1967): 26–30.

Bogart, Major General Theodore F. "The United States Army Caribbean Command and Operation Friendship." *Army Information Digest* 17, no. 10 (1962): 22–23.

"Booming Brazil Finds a Key to Growth." Business Week, 13 March 1971, pp. 90–93.

"Brazil: The Escola Superior de Guerra." Bolsa Review [London] 5, no. 49, (1971): 2–7.

Burns, E. Bradford. "Brazil's Foreign Policy: Traditionalism vs. Nationalism." Orbis 13 (1969): 643–44.

———. "Brazil: The Imitative Society." The Nation 215 (1972): 17–20.

———. "Tradition and Variation in Brazilian Foreign Policy." Journal of Inter-American Studies 9 (April 1967); 195–212.

Castello Branco, Humberto de Alencar. "Speech Commemorating the Twentieth Anniversary of the Instituto Rio Branco (Rio de Janeiro, 31 July, 1964)." Discursos, 1964, pp. 107–17.

Cochrane, James D. "U.S. Policy Towards Recognition of Governments and Promotion of Democracy in Latin America Since 1963." Journal of American Studies [London] 4, no. 2 (1972): 275–91.

Cox, Harvey G. Christianity and Crisis 30, no. 7 (1970): 1.

Drury, Bruce. "Civil-Military Relations and Military Rule: Brazil Since 1964." Journal of Political and Military Sociology 2 (1974): 191–203.

Easterbrook, Major General Ernest F. "Realism in Counterinsurgency Training." Army Information Digest 17, no. 10 (1962); 12–21.

Editorial Staff, Editôra Civilização Brasileira, S.A. "Uma política alienada de desenvolvimento económico para a America Latina: Breve nota sobre a Aliança para o Progresso." Política Externa Independente (tremestrial) 1 (1965): 119–26.

Ferreira, Oliveiros S. "La geopolítica y el ejército brasileño." Aportes [Paris] 12 (1969): 112–32.

Fishlow, Albert. "Brazil's Economic Miracle." The World Today [London] 29 (1973): 474–94.

Fitch, Major General Alva R. "I and S: The Army's Newest Basic Branch." Army Information Digest, 17, no. 8 (1962): 2–8.

Foland, Frances. "Whither Brazil?" Inter-American Economic Affairs 24 no. 3 (1970), 43–68.

Forman, Shepard. "Disunity and Discontent: A Study of Peasant Political Discontent in Brazil." Journal of Latin American Studies [London] 3, no. 1 (1971): 3–24.

Fragoso, Augusto. "A Escola Superior de Guerra." Problemas Brasileiros [São Paulo] 8, no. 88 (1970): 19–34.

Francis, Michael J. "Military Aid to Latin America in the U.S. Congress." *Journal of Inter-American Studies,* 6 (1964): 389–404.

Galeano, Eduardo. "The De-Nationalization of Brazilian Industry." *Monthly Review* 21, no. 7 (1969): 11–30.

Galtung, Johan. "A Structural Theory of Imperialism." *Journal of Peace Research* 8, no. 2 (1972): 81–117.

García Lupo, Rogélio. "Brazil and the U.S.: The Privileged Satellite." *Atlas* 10 (November 1965): pp. 286–87.

García-Zamor, Jean-Claude. "Regionalism and Political Stability in Brazil." *Revista Interamericana* [University of Puerto Rico] 3, no. 2 (1973): 143–58.

Garvey, Ernest. "Meddling in Brazil: The CIA Bungles On." *Commonweal* 37 (1968): 553–54.

Gordon, Lincoln. "Brazil's Future World Role." *Orbis* 16 (1972): 621–31.

———. "Relações dos Estados Unidos com a America Latina, Especialmento o Brasil." *Revista Brasileira de Política Internacional* [Rio de Janeiro], September 1961, pp. 13–30.

———. "U.S. and Brazil: Partners in Progress." *Department of State Bulletin* 54, 18 April 1966, pp. 620–24.

Hall, Clarence W. "The Country that Saved Itself." *Reader's Digest,* 1964, 133–58.

Hanreider, Wolfram F. "Compatibility and Consensus: A Proposal for the Conceptual Linkage of External and Internal Dimensions of Foreign Policy." *The American Political Science Review* 61 (1967): 971–82.

Hanson, Simon G. "The Alliance for Progress: The Sixth Year." *Inter-American Economic Affairs* 22, no. 3 (1968): 1–95.

———. "Kissinger on the Chilean Coup." *Inter-American Economic Affairs* 27, no. 3 (1973): 61–85.

Hersh, Seymour. "Censored Matter on Book on CIA." *New York Times,* 11 September 1974.

Hilton, Stanley. "Military Influence on Brazilian Economic Policy, 1930–1940." *Hispanic American Historical Review* 53, no. 1 (1973): 71–94.

Huberman, Leo and Paul M. Sweezy. "Brasil, Latinoamerica y los Estados Unidos." *Monthly Review* 1, no. 1 (1964): 3–27.

Hyman, Elizabeth H. "Soldiers in Politics: New Insights on Latin American Armed Forces." *Political Science Quarterly* 87 (1972): 401–18.

Jablonsky, Major General Harvey J. "Counterinsurgency is Your Business." *Army Information Digest* 17, no. 7 (1962): 46–51.

Kanegis, Arthur. "The Hidden Arsenal: You Can't Keep a Deadly Weapon Down." *The Washington Monthly* 2, no. 10 (1970): 24–27.

Kaplan, Stephen S. and Norman C. Bonsor. "Did United States Aid Really Help Brazilian Development? A Perspective of a Quarter-Century." *Inter-American Economic Affairs* 27, no. 3 (1973): 25–46.

Kossok, Manfred. "The Armed Forces in Latin America: Potential for Changes in Political and Social Functions." *Journal of Interamerican Studies and World Affairs* 14 (1972): 375–98.

Lang, Kurt. "Trends in Military Occupational Structure and Their Political Implications." *Journal of Political and Military Sociology* 1, no. 1 (1973): 1–18.

Lansdale, Brigadier General Edward G., USAF. "Civic Action Helps Counter the Guerrilla Threat." *Army Information Digest* 17, no. 6 (1962): 50–54.

Lens, Sidney. "Brazil's Police State." *The Progressive* 30, no. 12 (1966): 31–35.

———. "Failures in Latin America." *The Progressive* 31, no. 1 (1967): 29–33.

———. "Labor and the CIA." *The Progressive* 31, no. 4 (1967): 25–28.

Levine, Robert M. "Brazil at the Crossroads." *Current History* 64, no. 378 (1973): 53–56, 86.

———. "Brazil: The Aftermath of 'Decompression.' " *Current History* 70, no. 413 (1976): 53–56, 81.

Lieuwen, Edwin. "Neo-Militarism in Latin America: The Kennedy Administration's Inadequate Response." *Inter-American Economic Affairs* 16 (Spring 1973): 11–19.

MacBride, Sean, ed. "Latin America: A Crisis for Democracy." *Review of the International Commission of Jurists*, December 1969, pp. 15–18.

McNamara, Robert S. "Government Documents: Assessment of the Latin American Situation (January 1968) as it Bears on Military Policy." *Inter-American Economic Affairs* 21, no. 4 (1968): 89–92.

Meira Penna, José Oswaldo de. "Brazilian Relations with Eastern Europe." *Studies on the Soviet Union* (new series) 3, no. 2 (1968): 81–90.

Methvin, Eugene H. "Labor's New Weapon for Democracy." *Reader's Digest*, 45th year, October 1966, pp. 21–28.

Michalski, Jan. "Brazilian Bizarrerios." *Censorship* 2, no. 3 (1966): 25–29.

Military Review 50, no. 4 (1970). 25th anniversary issue of publication in Spanish and Portuguese.

Modelski, George, ed. "Multinational Corporations and World Order." *International Studies Quarterly* 16, no. 4 (1972). Whole issue.

Murphy, Charles J. V. "The King Ranch South of the Border." *Fortune* 80, no. 1 (1969), 132–44.

Myhr, Robert O. "The University Student Tradition in Brazil." *Journal of Inter-American Studies and World Affairs* 12 (1970): 126–40.

Needler, Martin C. "The Latin American Military: Predatory Reactionaries or Modernizing Patriots?" *Journal of Inter-American Studies* 11 (1969): 237–44.

———. "Military Motivations in the Seizure of Power." *Latin American Research Review* 10, no. 3 (1975): 63–79.

———. "Political Development and Military Intervention in Latin America." *The American Political Science Review* 60, no. 3 (1966): 616–26.

Nordlinger, Eric A. "Soldiers in Mufti: The Impact of Military Rule upon Economic and Social Change in the Non-Western States." *American Political Science Review* 64 (1970): 1131–48.

Nunn, Frederick M. "Military Professionalism and Professional Militarism in Brazil, 1870–1970: Historical Perspectives and Political Implications." *Journal of Latin American Studies* [London] 4, no. 1 (1972): 29–54.

O'Shaughnessy, Hugh. "A Chance to Make Amends." *The Financial Times* (Brazil: Financial Times Survey) [London], 13 November 1972, p. 1.

"Our Foreign Policy Serves Our Economic Development." Translation of Special Supplement of *O Globo* [Rio de Janeiro], 15 March 1967, p. 20.

Poppino, Rollie E. "Brazil: Second Phase of the Revolution." *Current History* 56, no. 329 (1969): 7–12, 52–53.

———. "Brazil After a Decade of Revolution." *Current History* 66, no. 389 (1974): 1–5, 35–38.

Porter, General Robert W. "Latin America: The Military Assistance Program." *Vital Speeches of the Day* 34 (1968): 573–76.

Powell, John Duncan. "Military Assistance and Militarism in Latin America." *The Western Political Quarterly* 18 (1965): Part I, 382–92.

"Prices Down, Arrests Up: News You Won't Find in Brazil's Newspapers." *The New Republic*, 2 August 1969. (Reprinted in the *Congressional Record*, 8 August 1969, S9441-2.)

"El Programa del Nuevo Gobierno." *The Economist para América Latina*, 29 October 1969, pp. 10–11.

Robinson, Donald. "America's Air Guerrillas: Will They Stop Future Vietnams?" *The Washington Post, Parade*, 31 January 1971, pp. 6–7.

Roett, Riordan. "Brazil Ascendant: International Relations and Geopolitics in the Late 20th Century." *Journal of International Affairs* 29, no. 2 (1975): 139–54.

Rosenbaum, H. Jon. "Brazil Among the Nations." *International Journal* [Toronto], 24 (1969): 529–44.

―――. "Brazil's Foreign Policy: Developmentalism and Beyond." *Orbis* 16 (1972): 58–84.

Rowe, James W. "A Note on Brazil." *East Coast South America Series*, American Universities Field Staff Reports 13, no. 5 (1967).

―――. "The 'Revolution' and the 'System': Notes on Brazilian Politics, Part II: The 'System'—Full Flower and Crisis." *East Coast South America Series*, American Universities Field Staff Reports 12, no. 4 (1966).

Ruff, First Lieutenant Doyle C. "Win Friends: Defeat Communism." *Instructors Journal* 2, no. 1 (1964): 25–34.

Russett, Bruce and Alfred Stepan. "New Jobs for the Brass: The Military in Public Affairs." *The Nation* 215 (1972): 655–57.

Schaffer, Ronald. "Review of *A Guide to Military Civic Action* by 30th Civil Affairs Group, Major David K. Holstead." *Military Affairs* 34, no. 2 (1970): 64.

―――. "The 1940 Small Wars Manual and the 'Lessons of History.' " *Military Affairs* 36, no. 2 (1972): 46–51.

Siekman, Philip. "When Executives Turned Revolutionaries, A Story Hitherto Untold: How São Paulo Businessmen Conspired to Overthrow Brazil's Communist-infested Government." *Fortune* 70, no. 3 (1964): 147–49, 210–21.

Slover, Colonel Robert H. "Action Through Civic Action." *Army Information Digest* 17, no. 10 (1972): 7–11.

Smith, Peter Seaborn. "Bolivian Oil and Brazilian Economic Nationalism." *Journal of Inter-American Studies and World Affairs* 13 (1971): 166–81.

"Talk with a Terrorist: Isolate the Cities." *Newsweek*, 8 December 1969, pp. 66–68.

Terkel, Studs. "Servants of the State: A Conversation with Daniel Ellsberg." *Harper's Magazine*, February 1972, pp. 56–59.

Thimmesch, Nick. "Chief of Staff." *Washington Post, Potomac*, 25 November 1973, pp. 12–15.

Tuthill, John Wills. "Economic and Political Aspects of Development in Brazil—and U.S. Aid." *Journal of Inter-American Studies* 11 (1969): 186–208.

Tyson, Brady. "Brazil: Nine Years of Military Tutelage." *Worldview* 16, no. 7 (1973): 29–34.

———. "Encounter in Recife." *The Christian Century* 86 (1970): 720–22.

———. "O sistema interamericano depois de Santo Domingo." *Política Externa Independente* 1, no. 3 (1966): 83–95.

Ultima Hora [Santiago, Chile], 24 July 1964, p. 1.

U.S. Agency for International Development. "Public Safety Assistance Programs in Latin America." *Inter-American Economic Affairs* 26, no. 3 (1972): 92–96.

Vaughn, Jack Hood. "A Latin American Vietnam." *The Washington Monthly* 5, no. 8 (1973): 30–34.

Wedge, Bryant. "The Case Study of Student Political Violence: Brazil, 1964, and the Dominican Republic, 1965." *World Politics*, 21 (1969): 183–206.

Windle, Charles and T. R. Vallance. "Optimizing Military Assistance Training." *World Politics* 15 (1962): 91–107.

Yglesias, José. "Report from Rio de Janeiro: What the Left is Saying." *New York Times Magazine*, 7 December 1969, pp. 52–53, 162–79.

Ziemke, Earl F. "Civil Affairs Reaches Thirty." *Military Affairs* 36, no. 4 (1972): 130–33.

Various issues of the following periodicals and news services (1960–1974) have been used in the preparation of this study:

The *AIFLD* Report
Air University Quarterly
Air University Review
Army Information Digest
Brazil Herald [Rio de Janeiro]
Brazilian Information Bulletin
Business Latin America
Business Week
Christian Science Monitor
Commonweal
The Economist para America Latina [London]
O Estado de São Paulo
International Police Academy Review
Jornal do Brasil [Rio de Janeiro]
Latin America [London]
Le Monde [Paris]
Manchester Guardian
Marcha [Montevideo]
Military Review
NACLA Newsletter
NACLA's Latin America and Empire Report
Naval War College Review
New York Times
Quarterly Economic Review [London]
Review of the International Commission of Jurists [Geneva]
The Times of the Americas
U.S. Congressional Record
U.S. Foreign Broadcast Information Service
U.S. Joint Publications Research Service
U.S. Naval Institute Proceedings
Washington Post
Washington Star-News

U.S. Government Publications

The Army Blue Book, 1961. Vol. 1. Edited by Tom Compere. New York: Military Publishing Institute, 1960.
Broadcasting Stations of the World. 25th ed., Part I and Part II. Washington, D.C. Foreign Broadcast Information Service, 1 July 1972.

Heare, Gertrude E. *Trends in Latin American Military Expenditures, 1940–1970.* Department of State, Inter-American Series, no. 99. Washington, D.C.: Government Printing Office, 1971.

Mascarenhas de Moraes, Marshal J. B. *The Brazilian Expeditionary Force, by its Commander.* Translated from 2d ed., revised and enlarged. Washington, D.C.: Government Printing Office, 1966.

U.S. Arms Control and Disarmament Agency. *World Military Expenditures and Arms Trade, 1963–1973.* Washington, D.C.: Government Printing Office, 1975.

U.S. Central Intelligence Agency. *National Intelligence Handbook.* Washington, D.C.: Government Printing Office, January 1976.

U.S. Comptroller General. *Review of Administration of United States Assistance for Capital Development Projects in Brazil.* Report to the Congress, no. B–133283. 16 May 1968.

U.S. Congress. House. Committee on Appropriations. *Foreign Assistance and Related Programs Appropriation Bill, 1971.* Report no. 91–1134. 91st Congress, 2d session. 1 June 1970.

————. Committee on Armed Services. Special Subcommittee on National Defense Posture. *Review of U.S. Military Commitments Abroad: Phase III—Rio and ANZUS Pacts.* 90th Congress, 2d session. 31 December 1968.

————. Committee on Foreign Affairs. *Foreign Assistance Act of 1965.* Hearings. 89th Congress, 1st session. 1964–65.

————. *Foreign Assistance Act of 1969.* House Report no. 91–611. 6 November 1969.

————. Subcommittee on Inter-American Affairs. *Communism in Latin America.* Hearings. 89th Congress, 1st session. 16 and 25 February, 2, 10, 16, and 30 March 1965.

————. Subcommittee on National Security Policy and Scientific Developments. *Report of the Special Study Mission on I. Military Assistance Training and II. Developmental Television.* 91st Congress, 2d session. 7 May 1970.

————. Subcommittee on National Security Policy and Scientific Developments. *Military Assistance Training.* Hearings. 91st Congress, 2d session. 6, 7, and 8 October, 8 and 15 December 1970.

————. Committee on Government Operations. *U.S. AID Operations in Latin America under the Alliance for Progress: Thirty-Sixth Report.* Report no. 1849. 90th Congress, 2d session. 5 August 1968.

U.S. Congress. Senate. Committee on Appropriations. *Foreign Assistance and Related Appropriations for 1965.* Hearings on H.R. 11812. 88th Congress, 2d session. 1964.

——————. *Foreign Assistance and Related Programs Appropriations, Fiscal Year 1974.* Hearings. 93rd Congress, 1st session. 1973.

——————. *Special Report on Latin America: United States Activities in Mexico, Panama, Peru, Chile, Argentina, Brazil, and Venezuela.* 1962.

——————. Committee on Appropriations. *Review of United States Government Operations in Latin America.* Report by Senator Allen J. Ellender. Senate Document no. 18. 90th Congress, 1st session. 1966.

——————. Committee on Foreign Relations. *Amendments to the OAS Charter.* Hearings, 90th Congress, 2d session. 6 February 1968.

——————. *Brazil and United States Policies.* Report by Senator Michael Mansfield. 87th Congress, 2d session. February 1962.

——————. Subcommittee on American Republics Affairs. *Survey of the Alliance for Progress: Insurgency in Latin America.* Washington, D.C.: Government Printing Office, 1968.

——————. Subcommittee on American Republics Affairs. *Survey of the Alliance for Progress: The Political Aspects.* Washington, D.C.: Government Printing Office, 1967.

——————. Subcommittee on Multinational Corporations. *The Multinational Corporations in Brazil and Mexico: Structural Sources of Economic and Non-Economic Power.* Report by Richard S. Newfarmer and Willard S. Muller. 94th Congress, 1st session. August 1975.

——————. Subcommittee on Western Hemisphere Affairs. *United States Military Policies and Programs in Latin America.* Hearings. 91st Congress, 1st session. 24 June and 8 July 1969.

——————. Subcommittee on Western Hemisphere Affairs. *United States Policies and Programs in Brazil.* Hearings. 92d Congress, 1st session, 4, 5, and 11 May 1971.

——————. Select Committee to Study Governmental Operations with Respect to Intelligence Activities. *Alleged Assassination Plots Involving Foreign Leaders.* Report no. 94-465. 94th Congress, 1st session. 20 November 1975.

——————. Volume 6. *Federal Bureau of Investigation.* Hearings. 94th Congress, 1st session. 18 and 19 November, 2, 3, 9, 10, and 11 December 1975.

——————. Volume 7. *Covert Action.* Hearings. 94th Congress, 1st session. 4 and 5 December 1975.

——————. Final Report, Book I. *Foreign and Military Intelligence.* 94th Congress, 2d session. 26 April 1976.

——————. Final Report, Book II. *Intelligence Activities and the Rights of Americans.* 94th Congress, 2d session. 26 April 1976.

U.S. Department of the Army. Army Command and General Staff College. *Internal Defense.* Vol. I. RB 31-100. Fort Leavenworth, Kans., August 1971.

——————. *Strategy and Strategic Studies Handbook.* RB 100-1. Fort Leavenworth, Kans., August 1971.

——. Headquarters. *Civil Affairs Operation.* Field Manual 41-10. October 1969.

——. Headquarters. *Combat Service Support.* Field Manual 100-10. October 1968.

——. Headquarters. *Military Publications.* DA PAM 310-4. June 1971.

——. Headquarters. *Operations of Army Forces in the Field.* Field Manual 100-5. September 1968.

——. Headquarters. *Psychological Operations: Techniques and Procedures.* Field Manual 33-5. October 1966.

——. Headquarters. *Psychological Operations: U.S. Army Doctrine.* Field Manual 33-1. June 1968.

U.S. Department of Commerce. Commerce Committee for the Alliance for Progress. *Proposals to Improve the Flow of U.S. Private Investment to Latin America.* Washington, D.C., 1963.

U.S. Department of Defense. Office of the Assistant Secretary, Internal Security Affairs. *Military Assistance and Foreign Military Sales Facts.* Washington, D.C.: Government Printing Office, March 1970.

U.S. Department of State. Agency for International Development. Bureau for Latin America. *A Review of Alliance for Progress Goals.* Report submitted to House Committee on Government Operations. March 1969.

——————. Office of Public Safety. *Memorandum on the Public Safety Program in Brazil.* Prepared by Johnson F. Monroe for the Subcommittee on Foreign Operations of the House Committee on Government Operations. 30 July 1970.

——————. *Public Safety Training.* Program Guide for internal use. 1971.

────────. *U.S. Economic Assistance Programs Administered by the Agency for International Development and Predecessor Agencies, April 3, 1948–June 30, 1969.* 15 May 1970.

────. Bureau of Public Affairs. Historical Office. *Foreign Relations of the United States, 1947. The American Republics.* Vol. VIII. Washington, D.C.: Government Printing Office, 1972.

────────. Office of Media Services. *Arms Sales to Latin America.* News Release. July 1973.

────────. Office of Media Services. "The Realities of the Western Hemisphere." *Current Foreign Policy.* Washington, D.C.: Government Printing Office, July 1973.

────────. Office of Media Services. Public Inquiries Division. *Historical Chronology: U.S. Policy Toward Governments of Brazil, 1821–Present.* Washington, D.C., August 1973.

────. Foreign Service Economic-Commercial Staff. *Economic Trends of Brazil and their Implications for the United States.* Rio de Janeiro: U.S. Embassy, December 1967.

U.S. Department of the Treasury. *Foreign Credits by the United States Govenment.* Washington, D.C., 31 December 1972.

U.S. Executive Branch. *U.S. Foreign Assistance in the 1970s: A New Approach.* Report prepared for the President by the Task Force on International Development. 4 March 1970.

────. *U.S. Foreign Policy for the 1970s: Building for Peace.* President's Report to the Congress. 25 February 1971.

United States Information Agency. *Country Data: Brazil.* Washington, D.C., 1 November 1973.

U.S. Library of Congress. Congressional Research Service, Foreign Affairs Division. *The United States and the Multilateral Development Banks.* Report prepared for the House Committee on Foreign Affairs. 93rd Congress, 2d session. March 1974.

"Visit of President Médici of the Federative Republic of Brazil," *Weekly Compilation of Presidential Documents.* Vol. 7, no. 50, 13 December 1971, pp. 1625–26.

Weil, Thomas E., Jan Knippers Black, Howard I. Blutstein, Kathryn Therese Johnston, and David S. McMorris. *Area Handbook for Brazil.* 3d ed. DA PAM 550–20. Washington, D.C.: Government Printing Office, 1975.

Brazilian Government Publications

Brazilian Army Public Relations Center. *Sentinels of the Amazon.* Honor of the National Chamber of Industry to the Brazilian Army. Graficos Bloch, n.d.

Camarinha Nascimento, Professor J. "Conflictos Contestatorios," *Revista do Clube Militar* [Rio de Janeiro] 48, no. 202 (1973): 35.

Castello Branco, Humberto de Alencar. *Entrevistas, 1964–1965.* Rio de Janeiro: Secretaría de Imprensa, 1965.

Estado-Maior da Armada. *Alguns Estudos sôbre a Guerra Revolucionária.* Rio de Janeiro: 1958.

Gibson Barboza, Mario, Minister of Foreign Relations of Brazil. *Brazil's Foreign Policy for the 1970s* (Speech delivered at the Superior War College, Rio de Janeiro, 17 July 1970.) Brasilia: Departamento de Imprensa Nacional, 1970.

Presidência da República. *Metas e Bases para a Ação de Govêrno.* Rio de Janeiro: Serviço Gráfico da Fundação IBGE, 1970.

Presidência da República. Estado-Maior das Fôrças Armadas. Escola Superior de Guerra. Departamento de Estudos. T102–73. "A ONU e os Interesses do Brasil no Campo do Desenvolvimento." Lecture by Sec. Alvaro Gurgel de Alencar Neto. No. 178.

――――. T112-73. "Relações do Brasil com a Europa Ocidental." Lecture by Eng. José Luiz de Almeida Bello, 2 August 1973. No. 172.

――――. T115-73. "O Brasil e o Extremo Oriente." Lecture by Carlos Antonio Bettencourt Bueno. 6 June 1973. No. 175.

――――. T118-73. "Conjuntura dos Países da Bacia Amazónica." Lecture by Conselheiro Joaquim Iguacio Amazonas Macdowell, No. 181.

――――. T130-73. "Conjuntura Política Nacional e o Poder Executivo." Lecture by Prof. Manoel Gonçalves Gerreira Filho. 8 August 1973. No. 169.

――――. T132-73. "Conjuntura Política Nacional e o Poder Judiciário." Lecture by Ministro Carlos Medeiros da Silva. 8 August 1973. No. 210.

――――. T138-73. "O Direito Internacional e as Leis de Guerra." Lecture by Dr. Celso D. de Albuquerque Mello, 19 July 1973. No. 171.

――――. T139-73. "Legislação Brasileira e Segurança Nacional. Lecture by Prof. Mário Pessoa, 18 July 1973. No. 206.

―――. T139-73, part 2. "Legislação Brasileira e Segurança Nacional" Presented by a panel consisting of Desembargador Antonio de Arruda, do Corpo Permanento; Ministro Carlos Coqueijo Porreão da Costa, do Corpo de Estagiários e dos Assessores de Ministério das Communicações; Dr. Vicente Greco Filho e Dr. Gaspar Luiz Vianna, 18 July 1973. No. 206.

―――. T150-73. "O Planejamento e a Coordenação do Desenvolvimento Brasileiro." Lecture by Ministro João Paulo dos Reis Veloso. No. 187.

―――. T151-73. "O Plano Nacional de Desenvolvimento 72/74 e o Sistema Brasileiro de Planejamento." Lecture by Henrique Flanzer, Secretário-Geral do Ministério do Planejamento e Coordenação Geral. No. 168.

―――. T155-73. "Minerais Estratégicos e Críticos." Lecture by Dr. Ronaldo Moreira da Rocha. 16 July 1973. No. 185.

―――. T162-73. "A Política Nacional de Comunicações." Lecture by Ministro Higino Caetano Corsetti, 19 July 1973. No. 191.

―――. T176-73. "Desenvolvimento Regional e Integração Nacional; Papel do Ministério de Interior." Lecture by Ministro José Costa Cavalcanti. 3 August 1973, No. 186.

―――. T183-73. "Sindicalismo no Brasil." Lecture by Professor Gibson Luiz Vianna, 4 September 1973. No. 167.

―――. T184-73. "A População Economicamente Ativa do Brasil." Lecture by Joaquim Faria Goes Filho, Director do Centro de Estudos e Treinamento de Recurços Humanos (CETRHU), Fundação Getúlio Vargas, No. 194.

―――. T187-73. "Problemática da Juventude Brasileira." Lecture by Prof. José Leime Lopes. 6 September 1973. No. 190.

Pamphlets, Lectures, Correspondence, and Unpublished Papers

Baklanoff, Eric N. "U.S. Investments and Alternative Strategies in Latin America; Studies of Cuba, Chile, and Brazil." Prepared for Workshop B on Multinational Corporations and States. Convention of the International Studies Association, 18 March 1972. (Department of State Foreign Affairs Research Series 15554-p.)

Binning, William Charles. "The Role of the Export-Import Bank in Inter-American Affairs." Ph.D. dissertation, University of Notre Dame, 1970.

Black, Edie and Fred Goff. "The Hanna Industrial Complex." New York: North American Congress on Latin America, 1969.

Blong, Clair Karl. "External Penetration and Foreign Policy Behavior." Ph.D. dissertation draft. University of Maryland, 1975.

Brazil: Order and Progress. Cambridge, Mass.: Action Latin America, May 1971.

Busey, James L. "Brazil's Reputation for Political Stability." Madison: University of Wisconsin, December 1965. (Department of State Foreign Affairs Research Series 2859.)

Carvalho, Colonel Ferdinando de, Representative of the Brazilian Army to the Inter-American Defense Board. Lecture. American University, Washington, D.C., 10 December 1969.

Cochrane, James D. "Changes During the Past Decade in U.S. Policy Toward the Military and Military Regimes in Latin America." Prepared for the annual conference of the Midwest Association for Latin American Studies. University of Nebraska, 1–3 October 1970. (Department of State Foreign Affairs Research Series 12248.)

Colby, William E., Director of the Central Intelligence Agency. Letter to Senate Foreign Relations Committee chairman J. William Fulbright. 31 July 1974.

Committee of Returned Volunteers. *Brazil: Who Pulls the Strings?* Chicago, n.d.

Estep, Raymond. "The Military in Brazilian Politics, 1821–1970." Maxwell Air Force Base, Air University, Aerospace Studies Institute, Documentary Research Division, 1971. (Department of State Foreign Affairs Research Series 13929.)

———. "United States Military Aid to Latin America." Maxwell Air Force Base, Air University, Aerospace Studies Institute, Documentary Research Division. September 1966.

Fontaine, Roger W. "The Emergence of Brazil's Foreign Policy." Washington: The American Enterprise Institute, 1974.

Frank, Andre Gunder. "Brazil and Pakistan: A Comparison of American Aid." Santiago: University of Chile, n.d.

———. Letter to the author. 6 March 1973.

Glick, Edward. "The Non-Military Use of the Latin American Military." Santa Monica, Calif.: Systems Development Corporation. 18 July 1964. SP–1439.

Greenfield, Sidney. "Power, Politics and Patronage: A Model of National Integration," Unpublished manuscript. Milwaukee: University of Wisconsin, 1971.

Hahne, Lieutenant Commander Dayton R. "The Brazilian Military Establishment in Government: An Analysis." Maxwell Air Force Base, Air Command and Staff College, June 1967. M-35562-7-U. Thesis No. 0960-67.

Harvey, Matthew J., Assistant Administrator for Legislative Affairs, Agency for International Development. Letter to Senator James Abourezk, 25 September 1973.

Heitmann, Walter, Chilean Ambassador to the United States. Panel Discussion. American University, Washington, D.C., 29 March 1974.

Herrera, Felipe, President of the Inter-American Development Bank. Lecture. American University, Washington, D.C., 9 November 1970.

Huntington, Samuel. Lecture. American University, Washington, D.C., 15 May 1971.

International Activities of U.S. Banks, with Cross-Index by Countries. New York: American Banker, 1972.

Kaplan, Stephen S. "U.S. Military Aid to Brazil and the Dominican Republic: Its Nature, Objectives, and Impact." Department of State Foreign Affairs Research Series 16217. September 1972.

Kossok, Manfred. "Potentialities and Limitations of the Change of the Political and Social Function of the Armed Forces in the Developing Countries; The Case of Latin America." Presented at the meeting of the Seventh World Congress of Sociology, Varna, Bulgaria, September 1970. Department of State Foreign Affairs Research Series 13872.

Krieger, Ronald A. *Brazil.* New York: First National City Bank, March 1971.

Kurth, James R. "Multinational Corporations as New Actors in International Politics." Prepared for delivery at the 1973 conference of the International Studies Association, Washington, D.C., 16–17 November 1973.

Landis, Fred. "Psychological Warfare and Media Operations in Chile, 1970–1973." Ph.D. dissertation. University of Illinois at Urbana, October 1975.

LeBailey, Lieutenant General Eugene B., Director of the Inter-American Defense Board. Lecture. Seminar on the Military in Latin America. Georgetown University, Washington, D.C., 4 March 1971.

Ministries in Higher Education, West Coast Region. "Press Censorship in Brazil Intensified in Connection with Rockefeller's Visit." Mimeographed, n.d.

Morris, Fred B. "The Human Dimension of the Brazilian Economic Miracle." Manuscript. Washington, D.C., February 1975.

National Archives State Decimal File. *Brazil: 1940–44,* from 832.20/129 to 832.20/572.

Palisi, Joseph John. "The Latin American Confederation of Christian Trade Unions (CLASC), 1954–1967." Ph.D. Dissertation, American University, Washington, D.C., 1968.

Perry, Captain Lowell E., U.S. Navy. "The Emergence of Brazil as a Major Power." Presented at the 15th Session of the Senior Seminar in Foreign Policy, U.S. Department of State, 1972–73. Department of State Foreign Affairs Research Series 17644-S.

Petras, James F. and Morris H. Morley. "U.S.-Chilean Relations and the Overthrow of the Allende Government: A Study of U.S. Relations with Chile, Brazil, and Peru." Department of Sociology, State University of New York at Binghamton, August 1974.

República del Paraguay. Sub-secretaría de Informaciones y Cultura de la Presidencia de la República. Mensaje del Excelentisimo Señor Presidente de la República y Comandante en Jefe de las FF.AA de la Nación General de Ejército Don Alfredo Stroessner al Congreso Nacional. Asunción, 1 April 1969.

Rocha, Wilson. *Brazil 70: an Answer to Many Questions.* São Paulo: The American Chamber of Commerce for Brazil, July 1970.

Rogers, William W. "The Agony of National Development in Brazil." Ithaca, N.Y., October 1970.

Ronfeldt, D. F. and Luigi R. Einaudi. *Internal Security and Military Assistance to Latin America in the 1970s.* Santa Monica, Calif.: The Rand Corporation, December 1971. R-924-ISA.

Rosenbaum, H. Jon, with Glenn M. Cooper. *Arms and Security in Latin America: Recent Developments.* International Affairs Series 101. Washington, D.C.: Woodrow Wilson International Center for Scholars, 1971.

Siegel, Gilbert B. "Diffusion and Centralization of Power in Brazil; a Sample of Consequences for Development Administration." Austin: University of Texas, Institute of Latin American Studies, Latin American Development Administration Committee, 1970.

Sklar, Barry. "The Foreign Policy of Brazil, 1964–1968." Washington: American University, January 1970.

Stepan, Alfred. Lecture. American University, Washington, D.C., 15 May 1971.

Stockton, Lieutenant Colonel Lyle E. "An Analysis of the Brazilian Revolution of 1964: The Role of the Military and the Probable Impact of Continued Military Control of the Political Structure and the Economy on U.S. Defense." Maxwell Air Force Base, Air War College, 1967. M-32983-U. Professional Study No. 3518.

Storrs, Keith Larry. "Brazil's Independent Foreign Policy, 1961–1964: Background, Tenets, Linkage to Domestic Politics, and Aftermath." Ph.D. dissertation, Cornell University, January 1973. Latin American Studies Program Dissertation Series, no. 44.

Tyson, Brady. "The Foreign Policy of Brazil," Chapter 11 in Harold E. Davis and Larman C. Wilson, eds., Latin American Foreign Policies. Washington: American University, 1974.

U.N. Economic Commission for Latin America. *Estudio Económico de America Latina, 1969, Tercer Parte*. Estudios Especiales. New York: United Nations, 1970.

U.S. Army Command and General Staff College. Lesson Plans, Assignments, Class Notes, and Manuals for 1969–72.

Wall, James T. "American Intervention in Nicaragua, 1848–1861." Ph.D. dissertation. University of Tennessee, Knoxville, August 1974.

Weers, Major Douglas L. "Brazil: Target for Communism." Maxwell Air Force Base, Air Command and Staff College, June 1967. M-35562-7-U. Thesis No. 2780-67.

Yanqui Dollar: The Contribution of U.S. Private Investment to Underdevelopment in Latin America. New York: North American Congress on Latin America, 1971.

Interviews

Ballou, Colonel D. Forest, III, Director of Course 5: Strategy, U.S. Army Command and General Staff School, Fort Leavenworth, Kansas, 1970–73. Washington, D.C., 22 June 1973.

Berger, Ethel, Brazilian employee of the United States Information Agency. Copenhagen, 25 April 1973.

Boggs, Michael, Assistant Inter-American Representative, AFL–CIO. Washington, D.C., 9 January 1974.

Bond, Niles, U.S. Foreign Service Officer in Brazil 1959–1968. Chargé d'Affaires July–October 1961; Consul General, São Paulo, 1964–1968. Washington, D.C., 17 May 1976.

Callero, Colonel Milton, U.S. Army Attaché, Brasilia, 1968–1970. Washington, D.C., 31, October 1972, and 21 February 1973.

Cobb, Jack, Executive Secretary of the Latin American Studies Association and former Evaluation Officer for the Peace Corps. Washington, D.C., 20 November 1970.

Correia Pacheco, Armando, Director of the Division of Philosophy and Letters, Department of Cultural Affairs, Pan American Union. Washington, D.C., 21 January 1970.

Cubas, Coronel Roberto, Paraguayan Army. Washington, D.C., 14 April 1971.

Daschle, Thomas, Staff Assistant to Senator James Abourezk. Washington, D.C., 9 January 1974.

Furtado, Celso, Brazilian Economist and former Director of the Superintendency for the Development of the Northeast. Washington, D.C., 18 December 1972.

Gordon, Lincoln, U.S. Ambassador to Brazil, 1961–1966, and Assistant Secretary of State for Inter-American Affairs, 1966–1967. Washington, D.C., 12 March 1975.

Holt, Pat, Chief Counsel, U.S. Senate Foreign Relations Committee. Washington, D.C., 2 February 1973.

Kelly, William, Bureau of Intelligence and Research, Department of State. Washington, D.C., 28 October 1969.

King, Lieutenant Colonel Edward L., Representative of the Joint Chiefs of Staff to the Joint Brazil-United States Defense Commission and the Inter-American Defense Board, 1966–1969. Washington, D.C., 10 January 1973.

Lanphier, Vernard, Bureau of Intelligence and Research, Department of State. Washington, D.C., 16 November 1970.

LaRocque, Admiral Eugene, Assistant Chief of Naval Operations for Strategic Plans, 1967–1968, Director of Pan American Affairs, Navy, 1968–1969, and Director of the Inter-American Defense College, 1969–1972. Washington, D.C., 5 April 1973.

Levinson, Jerome, chief loan officer for AID in Brazil in 1964, Staff Director, U.S. Senate Foreign Relations Committee, Subcommittee on Multinational Corporations. Washington, D.C., 13 March 1975.

Lieuwen, Edwin. University of New Mexico. Albuquerque, N.M., 19 July 1976.

Lyles, Cecila, Training Division, Department of the Army. Washington, D.C., 4 October 1972.

Michalski, Jan, Drama Critic for the *Jornal do Brasil*. Washington, D.C., 21 January 1970.

Monroe, Johnson F., Office of Public Safety, Agency for International Development. Washington, D.C., 16 November 1970.

Moreira Alves, Marcio, Brazilian journalist and former member of the Chamber of Deputies. Washington, D.C., 10 March 1972.

Morris, Fred, U.S. Methodist Missionary in Brazil, 1964–1974, and stringer for *Time* magazine in Recife. Washington, D.C., 4 May 1976.

Ouro-Preto, Affonso Celso de, Political Officer, Brazilian Embassy. Washington, D.C., 7 November 1969.

Pontes, Carlos, President of a Brazilian union in the advertising industry and AIFLD trainee in communications. Washington, D.C., 9 November 1973.

Rowe, James, formerly of the American Universities Field Staff in Brazil. Washington, D.C., 27 February 1974.

Santiestevan, Henry, former Latin American Field Representative, United Auto Workers. Washington, D.C., 30 October 1972.

Schmitter, Philippe C., University of Chicago. Washington, D.C., 23 February 1973.

Schuler, Lieutenant Colonel Robert, U.S. Army Attaché in Brazil, April 1964–1967. Washington, D.C., 30 November 1970, and 4 October 1972.

Seitz, Major General Richard J., Joint Brazil-United States Military Commission member, September 1954–July 1957, Commander, October 1968–July 1970; Commander of Fort Bragg, N.C., since July 1973. Washington, D.C., 4 June 1973.

Von der Weid, Jean Marc, former President of the Brazilian National Student Union (UNE). Washington, D.C., 23 February 1973.

Walters, Vernon A., U.S. Defense Attaché in Brazil 1961–1967; Deputy Director of the CIA, 1972–1976. Washington, 21 May 1976.

Young, Vaughn, freelance writer. Washington, D.C., 27 February 1975.

Several other persons, both U.S. and Brazilian citizens, who contributed information will not be named, as their positions might be jeopardized.

Index